Essays in Jewish Thought

NAHUM N. GLATZER

ESSAYS IN
JEWISH THOUGHT

THE UNIVERSITY OF ALABAMA PRESS • UNIVERSITY, ALABAMA

Library of Congress Cataloging in Publication Data

Glatzer, Nahum Norbert, 1903–
   Essays in Jewish thought.

   (Judaic studies series ; no. 8)
   Includes bibliographical references and index.
   1. Judaism—History—Addresses, essays, lectures.
2. Zunz, Leopold, 1794–1886. 3. Buber, Martin, 1878–
1965. 4. Rosenzweig, Franz, 1886–1929. I. Title.
II. Series: Judaic studies ; no. 8.
BM157.G58   296.3   76–51044
ISBN 0–8173–6904–X

CONTENTS

PREFACE

The impetus for this volume came from some of my former students, most of whom now occupy professorships in Judaic studies throughout the United States. Reluctantly and not without trepidation I agreed to the suggestion and herewith offer samples of studies and articles written in the course of several years.

The selection manifests several areas that have occupied my scholarly and literary interest: some aspects of rabbinic literature (the changing attitude toward Rome, the problem of biblical prophecy, the concept of peace, the concept of sacrifice, the personality of Hillel); an attempt to understand the Book of Job and its place in midrashic interpretation; the Zion motif in medieval literature; the life and thought of Leopold Zunz and the beginning of modern Jewish studies; the Judaic strain in Franz Kafka's reflections on the human condition; some of the concerns of Martin Buber and Franz Rosenzweig; an account of the Frankfurt Lehrhaus. Inclusion of articles written in German was ruled out as impractical; of Hebrew essays only one is presented: an attempt to interpret the last year in the life of Rosenzweig.

Thanks are due to the publishers and editors for their permission to reprint copyrighted materials; to Professor Alexander Altmann for his encouragement; to Professor Leon J. Weinberger, general editor, Judaic Studies, The University of Alabama Press, for his gracious help in planning and producing this volume; and, finally, to my wife, beloved companion since Frankfurt days, who in understanding and devotion—though occasional protest—made my rather arduous schedule of work possible.

N. N. GLATZER

Boston University
October, 1976

1

THE ATTITUDE TOWARD ROME IN THIRD-CENTURY JUDAISM

I

From Daniel to Akiba Judaea lived in the expectation of the impending end of the heathen world and the establishment of the–variously defined–true kingdom "which shall never be destroyed nor . . . left to another people; it shall break to pieces and consume all these kingdoms, but it shall stand for ever" (Dan. 2:44). God was expected to let Israel "judge all the nations according to their desires, and after that they [Israel] shall get possession of the whole earth and inherit it for ever" (Jubilees 32:19); "they shall judge nations, and have dominion over peoples" (Wisdom 3:8); God "will appear to punish the Gentiles . . . and thou, Israel . . . shalt mount upon the necks and wings of the eagle" (Ass. Moses 10:7). The Hellenistic Jews, too, believed, that "when Rome shall rule over Egypt, then the mightiest kingdom of the immortal king over man shall appear" and the Messiah "wield the scepter over all the world."[2] Judah the Galilean and the advocates of the "Fourth Philosophy" believed that "God alone must be their ruler" (Josephus, Antt. XVIII, 1:6). On the basis of this belief Judah organized resistance to Roman rule. The Sicarii endured torture rather than acknowledge Caesar as their lord (War VII, 10:1).

The war of A. D. 66–73 was not between a small province and a mighty empire; here stood kingdom against kingdom, the claim to divinely willed dominion against the rule of an ungodly usurper. Flavius Josephus and Johanan ben Zakkai, each for a different reason, disagreed with Jerusalem's claim and acknowledged Vespasian as the rightful ruler.[3] But in the nation at large the Messianic idea lived on as the hope for a radical change in the historical structure of the world, to be brought about by action, political, spiritual, or both, an action executed by men, God, or both. The ancient Biblical, prophetic, belief in the historic life of nations as the scene where God "does His work" manifested itself, greatly accentuated, in the Maccabean and Roman periods in Jewish history.

When Jerusalem fell, the visions of Fourth Ezra and Baruch preserved the spirit of the imminent Messianic hope. Daniel's "fourth Kingdom" was interpreted as designating Rome (IV Ezra 12:11), whose fall was to occur soon; the Messiah would put to death her last leader and establish a dominion "that will stand forever" (II Baruch 40). This active, political, Messianism motivated the rebellion of Bar Kokhba, whom Rabbi Akiba appears to have acknowledged as the "King Messiah";[4] he expected Hag. 2:6 ("Yet once, it is a little while, and I will shake the heavens, and the earth . . .") to be fulfilled in his era. His opponent, Johanan ben Torta objected to the idea of nearness of redemption ("Akiba, grass will be growing from your cheeks and the Son of David would not be coming").[5] This argument may be considered as pointing to a significant modification of the Messianic theory in the post-Bar Kokhba period. The abandonment or at least weakening, of the belief that Messianic action was at hand and subjugation soon to be turned into triumph implies a change in attitude towards the "fourth kingdom", Rome. The postponement of the Messianic event must be understood as both retraction of Israel's ancient claim to world rulership and admission of Rome to the place originally believed to have been reserved for Jerusalem. This change in the respective historic position of Rome and Jerusalem is related to another issue: the importance of the historic world itself.

Agrippa's speech, as reported by Josephus[6] and Josephus' own address to the defenders of Jerusalem,[7] speeches in which the greatness and the power of Rome are depicted, suggest that that historic world was a God-willed world. It was He who transferred the authority from Israel to Rome. "God, who had given all the nations power in turn, has now settled in Italy."[8] Thus those who "war against the Romans war against God Himself."[9] Jose ben Kisma's appeal to one of the Ten Martyrs of the post-Bar Kokhba period formulates a similar concept: "Don't you know that it is Heaven that made this (Roman) nation to have dominion?"[10] The "firm establishment" of Rome is taken as a proof of its legitimate place within the divine plan. Simeon ben Yohai (mid-second cent.), pronounced foe of Rome, stated that the "greatness of God's name is revealed only when He executes judgment on the sinful nations";[11] however, quoting Ezek. 38:8, he knew, that this will take place only "after many days"; it would nott be "soon."[12] Simon's contemporary, Meir, taught that ultimately, Rome "will return the kingdom to its rightful owner," God,[13] but her present dominion was tacitly recognized. God sees "the kings placing their crowns on their heads and bowing down to the sun" and merely becomes "wrathful."[14] The urgency and imminence of divine intervention appear to be greatly reduced.

Israel's exile and exclusion while the four kingdoms ascend and descend the ladder (the image is borrowed from the story of Jacob's dream) Meir ascribed to her lack of faith in the divine promise of her victorious role in history.[15] Ultimate return from exile was envisaged; but it is the–indefinite–future in which God will again act in the full light of historic events. More and more did the present lose significance as the scene of divine action among the nations and in behalf of Israel. God withdraws into other, more private, realms of Israel's life, where he may manifest his kingship.

Recognition of the reality of Rome's dominion transformed the Messianic concept from activist and militant into passivist and peaceful; from an urgent expectation of change into a distant, quiet, hope; from a history-centered doctrine into a meta-historical one. This shifting of emphasis, with its far reaching consequences for the self-understanding of Israel and its position in the world, in the making for several generations, came to a classic formulation in the third century school of Johanan bar Nappaha of Tiberias. Johanan, who died about 270, exerted a profound influence on a large group of men; his teachings were reported also in the Jewish academies of Babylonia; he laid the foundations of the Palestinian Talmud. Our sources preserve many of his non-legal, haggadic teachings; the relevance, and even accuracy, of the statements vary; some are mere rewordings of older traditions, others, mere applications to the Scriptural text of established hermeneutical techniques; yet much authentic material remains from which to reconstruct the trends of thought of the period. Johanan's teachers were Yannai and Hanina bar Hama, both of Sepphoris (Galilee). Among his disciples were the Babylonian Eleazar ben Pedat and Hoshaya, Abbahu (later head of the school of Caesarea), Levi and Isaac, both great teachers of Haggadah, Samuel bar Nahman of Tiberias, and Abba bar Kahana; to his circle belonged also Simeon ben Lakish. Another important figure of the period is Joshua ben Levi of Lydda, with whom Johanan engaged in learned discussions.

The pages that follow are an attempt to present a selection of the talmudic-midrashic material that illustrates the change in the Judaic image of Rome and in Messianic theory, as well as some major tenets effected by this change. As much as possible the sources will be allowed to speak for themselves.

II

Third-century Rome offers a picture of decline of her former greatness; her northern and eastern frontiers deteriorated, economic life collapsed, literature and art faltered. But the classical concept of Rome's power is preserved in the contemporary Jewish literature, with only occasional hints at her shortcomings.

Daniel saw the "fourth beast" in a separate vision at night (Dan. 7:7), because, so Johanan opined, Rome is as strong as the three other kingdoms combined; according to Simeon ben Lakish, Rome surpasses all in power.[16] Dan. 7:23 is interpreted by Johanan as referring to Rome, "whose power is known to the whole world."[17] Rome is "the beast that dwelt among the reeds" (Ps. 68:30); she attacks valiant nations and appropriates their possessions.[18] At the future judgment over the nations, Rome is presented as boasting of her achievements (roads, baths) and her accumulation of gold and silver.[19] Her power appears to have no limits. In his dream-vision Jacob saw the princes of Babylonia, Media, and Greece ascend the ladder, with the number of steps corresponding to the number of years of their domination over Israel, while the fourth kingdom, Rome, ascended indefinitely. Only the divine voice assured Jacob that this dominion, too, would come to an end.[20] Jacob is presented as praying that the Lord may not further Esau's (Rome's) "evil device" (Ps. 140:8), for "should the Edomite (Roman) Germania go forth they would destroy the whole world."[21] Rome is known to be afraid of "the sons of Barbaria and the sons of Germania" that imperil her boundaries.[22] Yet, "if a man asks you 'where is your God', the answer is: 'in the great city of Rome.' "[23]

The origin of Rome elicited special interest. Her rise was explained and justified in terms of the history of Israel; the religious decline in Israel was held responsible for the foundation of Rome. According to Levi, the city of Rome was established on the day King Solomon wedded Pharaoh's daughter; Romulus and Remus built the first huts in Rome on the day Jeroboam set up the two golden calfs.[24]

The change in attitude toward Rome enabled the third-century talmudic masters to see not merely the might, but also the positive aspects of the empire. "And behold it was very good" (Gen. 1:31) was seen as referring equally to the kingdom of heaven and the earthly kingdom (Rome), to the latter "because it safeguards the right (*dikaion*) of men."[25] The patriarch Isaac was presented as praying that mercy be shown to Esau (Rome), whereupon he is informed by God that "he (Esau) will deal perversely" in the land of Israel; only then did Isaac withdraw his plea.[26] On the other hand, in speaking of the sufferings of the judgment day, Johanan had God say: "These (the Gentiles) are the work of my hands and these (the Jews) are the work of my hands; how shall I destroy the former on account of the latter?"[27]

III

The old notions of the glory and splendor of the Messianic age remained on record in the third century. Jerusalem was to become the metropolis of all lands,[28] her gates to be adorned with precious stones and pearls.[29] The day of return from Exile would be as great as the day of Creation.[30] The six gifts that were taken from Adam at his fall would be restored by the Messiah.[31] Leviathan and Behemoth, food preserved for the Messianic banquet from the days of Creation (IV Ezra 6) reappeared in Johanan's Haggadah after a comparative absence of over a century.[32]

But these texts seem to refer to a far-away future; there is no urgency about the Messianic event; hypothetical speculation pervades the utterances of the masters. The time of redemption was said to be fixed; only a universal repentance of at least one day might hasten the date: so taught Rabbi Johanan.[33] Also: the Messiah would come "only in a generation that is either completely righteous or completely wicked."[34] An air of irreality prevails.

It was therefore futile "to calculate the end"; the resulting disappointment would lead only to the conclusion that the Messiah "will never come."[35] Against all attempts to define the Messianic period, stand the opinions of Johanan and Simeon ben Lakish to the effect that this issue was mysteriously hidden in the heart of God.[36] The only correct attitude toward the Messianic age was that of patient waiting, unhurried expectation.

This trend found expression already in the second half of the second century and was phrased in direct opposition to those masters who based their teaching on Daniel's "until a time and times and the dividing of time" (7:25), as well as to Akiba, who advocated Haggai's prophecy of the impending end (2:6). The only true understanding of Messianism was seen to be that in Habakkuk 2:3: "Though he tarry, wait for him," a sentence that "pierces and descends to the very abyss."[37] This injunction became the directive of Johanan's school and his contemporaries. Joshua ben Levi interpreted Isa. 35:4 as referring to "the hasty ones who try to force the coming of the Messianic end."[38]

The metaphors employed in Scripture to describe redemption (grape-gathering, harvest, a pregnant woman, spices) were understood as a warning against haste: "If any of them are taken prematurely, the owners will get no benefit from them."[39] The exodus from Egypt took place in haste (Deut. 16:3); but in the future redemption "ye shall not go out in haste" (Isa. 52:12).[40] In contradistinction to the apocalyptic yearning expectation of judgment, Johanan dreaded the prospect. Though "the world was created for the sake of the Messiah," he exclaims: "Let him come, and let me not see him!"[41]

The limited duration of the Messianic era was already an old established doctrine.[42] Thus not the Messianic period but the world to come *(olam ha-ba)* that constitutes the true and final redemption is the focus of third-century piety. According to Johanan, the Biblical prophecies refer "only" to the days of Messiah, while the glories of the world to come are known to God alone.[43]

IV

Related to this change in the concept of Messianism is the modification in the concept of exile, dispersion, and suffering. Johanan was well aware of the tragic character of Jerusalem's destruction and exile. He had collected sixty traditions concerning Zion's fall, which he used to relate in interpreting Lam 2:2.[44] When the capture of Israel was reported to the King (i.e. God), "his accounts went into confusion."[45] Yet, as had Johanan ben Zakkai shortly after 70, so did Johanan of Tiberias overcome the crisis. In his thinking the exile of Israel is part of the divine plan, with the destruction of Zion having been contemplated long ago.[46] Together with Eleazar ben Pedat, he stated that while the duration of the Babylonian exile was made known to Israel, no such revelation existed for the present exile, i.e., for the Roman dominion over Palestine.[47] The end was not in sight.

This knowledge of the enduring Roman rule no doubt played a part in Johanan's and his school's choice of Biblical themes for haggadic treatment. The Haggadah of the preceding generations, (especially in the pre-Bar Kokhba period, while discussing a vast variety of motifs, gave special attention to the exodus from Egypt, the crossing of the Red Sea, and the period of the wilderness. These events were interpreted as the clearest examples of God's intervention in Israel's history; as such they implied a promise of, and a pattern for, the redemption from the present exile. The third century teachings, on the other hand, especially those of Johanan and Isaac, while maintaining the older traditions, put greater emphasis on such themes as the Revelation on Sinai, the Temple, Jerusalem, the period of the kings. Greater care was taken with the identification of Biblical names, chronology, and geography of the holy land. The fact of Roman rule accepted, there was a pronounced interest in the past of Israel in its entirety; there was no immediacy of application, no urgency of reference to an expected change in the fate of Israel. The past was elaborated on as the precious possession of the community that, though living in its own land, was in exile; there was time to explore that past. That Israel, in the words of Simeon ben Lakish, does not find rest in exile is indication that sometime it will return;[48] but exile it is, lasting and complete.

Now it became possible to view exile in its positive aspects. Israel had returned to Babylonia, as an estranged wife is sent back to her mother's house.[49] God exiled Israel to Babylonia, because the latter's language was akin to that of Torah.[50] Exile served the purpose of gaining proselytes to Israel;[51] it was a sign of God's mercy, since dispersion helped to preserve the people.[52] In Babylonia, says Levi, Israel worshipped God with their hearts while at Sinai they praised Him only with their mouths (Ps. 78:36).[53] Zion, destroyed, gave rise to more pious men, than she had in her days of glory.[54]

As in the case of exile, positive values were recognized in suffering too. Suffering helped Israel to turn to good ways, said Johanan;[55] it was a community of suffering and deprivation. All Biblical expressions of poverty and privation were understood as referring to Israel,[56] whose exile continues even after the birth of the redeemer, just as Jacob served before he took a wife and remained in servitude after his marriage.[57] However, true distress is only one "that which is common to Israel and to the nations of the world; distress confined to Israel alone is not distress.[58]

V

All attempts at the redemption of Israel in the past Johanan considered to have been failures; since human agencies were employed, redemption could not be final and one servitude led to another. Moses redeemed Israel from Egypt, but she was enslaved again by Babylon. Daniel and his friends were instrumental in redeeming her from Babylon, but then she fell into the power of Elam, Media, and Persia. The redemption from these powers was followed by enslavement in Greece. Freedom from Greece, brought about by the Hasmoneans, was terminated by Rome (Edom). True redemption must, therefore, differ from these temporary reliefs. Thus, Johanan let Israel speak: "We have grown weary of being enslaved and redeemed in order to be enslaved again. We no longer wish to be redeemed by flesh and blood; our redeemer is the Lord of hosts."[59] Israel will be "redeemed of the Lord" (Ps. 107:2)– "and not 'ransomed of Elijah' or 'ransomed of the King Messiah' "; this became the new direction, formulated by Samuel bar Nahman.[60] Not only human intervention, but all vestige of power (a reference, possibly, to the Palestinian patriarchate)[61] and all display of human pride must vanish before the advent of the Messiah can take place.[62]

The critical attitude to man-made redemption led to a disvaluation of prophecy, mother of historic Messianism and of the apocalyptic trends. A number of statements point to the lack of effectiveness of the prophetic activity. Pharaoh's cruel decrees were of greater moment than Moses' prophecies, "because the former brought about the redemption (of Israel) while the latter did not," taught Johanan.[63] Simeon ben Lakish adduced the example of king Ahasuerus, whose evil decree was instrumental in the process of redemption, while the many prophets in the time of Elijah remained ineffective.[64] Similarly, the fact of the Babylonian exile was interpreted as having been a greater force for the people's good than Jeremiah's call to repentance.[65] A more general comment came from Abba bar Kahana: The removal of Ahasuerus' ring (Esther 3:10) achieved more than all the prophets and prophetesses together, "for they were not able to turn Israel to better ways while the king's action was."[66] It was God Himself who acted, through the agency of His choice.

The final judgment would indeed come and re-establish a just order in this world; but Israel was not to engage in revolt against the tyrannical forces. The fourfold "I adjure you, O daughters of Jerusalem" (Cant. 2:7,

3:5, 5:8, 8:4) was interpreted by Levi as God's warning to Israel not to rebel against any one of the "four kingdoms."[67] Only he who stands up against the wave will be swept away by the wave; he who does not offer resistance will remain in place.[68] Israel's exile was caused by her desire to go to war against the nations.[69] It could have been prevented by a non-militant stand. The endeavor of the third-century sages to dissuade Jews from attempting opposition to the Roman rule was based on the doctrine of the peculiarly non-agressive, non-political character of Israel. Passivity extends to the realm of the divine. The demons that were to ward off the Roman attackers of the temple noticed the divine presence "looking on in silence," whereupon they gave way to the enemy.[70]

In the period of Decius (249–251), who demanded Emperor worship, acts of religious coercion became a frequent occurrence. Johanan's answer to such acts was a call to martyrdom. He recorded an earlier decision of the sages in Lydda, according to which martyrdom was to be suffered only where idolatry, incest, or murder was at stake, but he added that under threat of death minor commandments may be transgressed in private, "but in public one must suffer martyrdom even for a minor commandment rather than violate it."[71] However, he who succumbed to the threat and became tainted by idolatry, but who, repenting, responded in prayer, "Amen, May His great Name be blessed" is given pardon.[72]

The "four kingdoms" hold Israel in bondage. In keeping with the traditional tendency to see adversity as punishment for iniquity, the rule of the kingdoms was attributed to Israel's sin at Baal Peor (Num. 25).[73] Yet, both their rule and their ultimate fall appear to have been preordained and part of a precise historic pattern. They are presaged in the story of creation. *Tohu, bohu,* darkness, and the deep were interpreted by Simeon ben Lakish as referring to the four kingdoms, respectively, while "the spirit of God" pointed to the Messianic king; the transfer of authority would come about through repentance (symbolized by "the face of the waters").[74] The prophets allude to the kingdoms (e.g. by the symbol of the four beasts, Amos 5:19),[75] and so does the Psalmist (the four modes of prayer, Ps. 18:7).[76] Thus the presence of the kingdoms was emphasized rather than, as in the book of Daniel, their end.

Though the kingdoms have dominion, Israel "enters them in peace and leaves them in peace."[77] The latter generations of Israel deserve more praise than the former ones, for despite the oppression by the kingdoms, they adhere to the Torah.[78] In the end, Israel will be victorious;[79] Esau's, i.e., Rome's fall will be caused by her pride. "It is a divine law and ordinance *(nomos* and *keleusis)* that he who exalts himself should be punished by fire"; as had Pharaoh, Sisera, Sennacherib, and Nebuchadnezzar of old, so will boastful Rome suffer punishment by fire.[80] It is not rebellion that can free Israel from the subjugation to the kingdoms (and from Gehenna) but, in the words of Johanan, "occupation with the revelation and with the sanctuary."[81]

VI

Following certain traditional teachings, Johanan and his school diverted the attention from a preoccupation with the *eschaton* and the events leading to it and focused it on the inception of Israel's spiritual existence: revelation on Sinai, and its record, the Torah. Nothing that has occurred since Sinai has had the power to alter the position of Torah and revelation. The Law was originally offered to all the nations of the world, but only Israel accepted it; so taught Johanan.[82] In so doing, Israel has served the cause of the world at large; without Torah the world would have returned to the original state of chaos.[83]

At Sinai, Israel underwent a process of purification. There the "filthy lust" that the serpent infused into Eve was removed.[84] Israel is the people's ancient name, taught Joshua ben Levi; the new name acquired at Sinai was "My People."[85] In the dedicated study of Torah, the event at Sinai is being repeated; revelation becomes a continuous process. "He who teaches his grandson Torah is considered receiving it from Sinai," taught further Joshua ben Levi.[86] Similarly, genuine fulfillment of a commandment was regarded as actually receiving it (personally) from Mount Sinai.[87] This much older haggadic motif[88] assumed added relevance in the context of third-century Jewish thought. Study presupposed abnegation of one's self.[89] The student must "render himself naked on behalf of Torah."[90] Then, naturally, social status and position cease to be relevant: "A scholar who is a bastard ranks higher than a high priest who is ignorant."[91]

The concept of the centrality of Sinai and Torah reduced Biblical prophecy to a relative position. In part as an answer to the early Church's emphasis on the prophetic writings, Johanan and his school declared all prophecy to have been contained in the words of Moses.[92] At the same time, not only prophecy but all later developments of Torah, "the minutiae of the scribes and their innovations" were shown to Moses on Sinai.[93] All things of the spirit point to this source, revelation rather than to the end, redemption. The latter is conditioned by the former.

However, Torah isolates Israel. A heathen may be called "wise";[94] but Johanan, contrary to Meir's (2nd cent.) dictum that a heathen who studies Torah is like a high priest (since Lev. 18:5 speaks of men, not of Israelites), considered such a heathen to deserve death.[95] On the other hand, Torah was accessible to proselytes entering the community of Israel, and Johanan seems to have been in favor of proselytism. Abraham's children were said to have been doomed to the Egyptian slavery because he permitted the captured Sodomites to leave (Gen. 14:21) instead of bringing them "beneath the wings of the divine presence."[96]

The ethical teachings of the period, though in principle rooted in older doctrines, have accents and overtones that reflect the sentiment of a community that has relinquished its rôle in historic life. Dearer than the practice of charity *(zedakah)* is the underlying loving concern *(hesed)*, Johanan taught.[97] The judgment over the sinful "generation of the flood" became effective only when it engaged in violence (Gen. 6:13).[98] Man is exhorted to have confidence in divine mercy even if "the sharp sword (of judgment) hovers over his neck."[99] At variance with the traditional stress on man's moral responsibility, Johanan had God say: "Roll the burden of your sins upon Me, and I shall bear them."[100]

Despite the inscrutability of "the rules whereby God guides the world,"[101] man was said to be constantly aware of divine mercy. Johanan pointed to the fact that Scripture mentions God's name only in connection with the good, never the evil; only "the angel of peace and the angel of mercy stand before Him, the angel of wrath is far removed from Him."[102] Even in the moment of wrath He remembers compassion.[103] Mention of the power of God in Scriptures is, according to Johanan, always accompanied by a reference to His meekness.[104] The leading principle in the creation of the world, the guidance of the world, and its future redemption is divine mercy *(rahamim)*; Jose ben Hanina takes this to be the meaning of the threefold "I am" in Exod. 3:14.[105] God's long-suffering encompasses both the righteous and the wicked.[106] Opposing an opinion of Akiba, who denied the generation of the wilderness a portion in the world to come, Johanan remarked: "Here Rabbi Akiba abandoned his loving kindness."[107] Johanan's attitude of mercy in dealing with transgressors motivated his intercession in behalf of Elisha ben Abuya, the apostate (Aher) among the talmudic masters of the second century.[108]   A note of mercy was introduced also into the teachings concerning the relationship of God to the heathen nations. Fully conscious of the differences between Israel and the heathens, Johanan showed regard for them as creatures of God. "God does not rejoice in the downfall of the wicked," he stated, a principle which explained to him why the usual phrase "for He is good" is omitted in reports on Jehoshaphat's battle gainst the Moabites (II Chron. 20:21).[109] The angels that wished to sing a hymn when the Israelites won their freedom from Egyptian bondage were rebuked by God: "The work of my hands is drowning in the sea and you wish to chant hymns?"[110] God was said to sit in judgment over the nations at night (when they sleep and don't commit transgressions), in order "to preserve their existence *(tekumah)*, because God does not desire the fall even of the wicked ones."[111] The blasphemous behaviour of the nations arouses God's ire, but "the Torah enters and speaks in their defence *(sunegoria)*."[112] In the promised future, death will cease not only for Israel but, as well, for the nations of the world, since Isa. 25:8 refers to all mankind.[113]

What preserves the existence of the world is not the power of the kingdoms, not the deeds of the mighty, not even the teachings of the wise, but "the breath of school children in which there is no sin."[114]

VII

Withdrawn from the world, Israel is alone with God. Ps. 4:7 was thus interpreted by Johanan: "Israel says to God: 'We have nothing but the shining of Thy countenance.' "[115] There exists, said Johanan, an understanding *(compromissa)* between God and Israel that neither will be faithless to the other.[116] This covenant, once entered in freedom, is no longer a matter of choice. Only individual Israelites are at liberty to accept or to reject it; the community of Israel is duty bound to recognize the kingship of God.[117] Even against their will, Israel is "My people."[118] His presence with Israel presists even "in the midst of their uncleannesses" (Lev. 16:16).[119] His name is linked to Israel "like a key to a chain," taught Yannai.[120] Not even "an iron wall could separate Israel from her father in heaven," said Joshua ben Levi.[121] On the Feast of Tabernacles, Israel offers seventy sacrifices corresponding to the seventy nations of the world, which is followed by "a simple meal for the King and his beloved friend."[122]

Israel does not aspire to participate in the activities that mark the life in this world. God is presented as having asked Israel: "Do you wish to share with the nations of the world?" But Israel answered: "We have no desire for the dainty portions of the nations . . .; all we desire are Thy commandments."[123]

The "nations" are pictured as trying to dissuade Israel from following their God who "brings upon them pain and suffering"; they invite Israel to join them and become "commanders *(duces)*, prefects *(huparchoi)* and *stratelatai."* But Israel enter their houses of prayer and houses of study, take the Torah, read of the Lord's covenant with them, and are comforted. When the promised end comes, God Himself will marvel at Israel's long patience, but Israel will point to the Torah as the factor that saved them from extinction.[124] This God-centered Israel is eternal, while "the kingdoms come and go."[125]

Third-century Jewish sources, as presented, show an Israel that has overcome the ancient claim to supersede the fourth kingdom by historical means. She has accepted the fact of Rome's rule of this world and has withdrawn into a realm to which the old Messianic categories no longer apply. Messianic protest against Rome and the heathen world was replaced by a life of concentration on Sinai and its message. Historical passivity and the growing disregard of the political world released as its counterpart a process of ever greater introversion. The Messianic idea was reinterpreted as referring to the restoration of the world's disturbed harmony, an act outside Israel's sphere. Exile became Israel's destiny. God Himself is in exile. The same century that witnessed Christianity enter an alliance with Rome and emerge into the bright light of history saw Israel developing a theology of extra-historical existence. The eschatological thinking from Daniel to Akiba was revived in outbreaks of active Messianic rebellions from the early Middle Ages onward; but the later teachings, best represented by Johanan of Tiberias, became the main line of Jewish Medievalism. Both forms of thought were responses to the challenge of Rome and the principle she stood for.

NOTES

1. Abbreviations of talmudic-midrashic works quoted in this and other essays: R. Rabba, i.e., Midrash Rabba to the particular biblical book. – R.Kah.: Rab Kahana. – Midr.Ps.: Midrash on Psalms, or Shoher Tob.– Yer.: Yerushalmi, or Palestinian Talmud. – Sanh.: Sanhedrin. – Meg.: Megillah. – Ab. Z.: Abodah Zarah.
2. Sib. III, 46–49.
3. War III, 8:8–9; Gittin 56.
4. Yer. Taanit 68d.
5. *Ibid.*
6. War II, 16:4.
7. War V, 9:3–4.
8. War V, 9:3.
9. War V, 9:4.
10. Ab. Z. 18a.
11. Lev. R. XXIV, 1.
12. Sifre Deut. Nr. 43.
13. Eccles. R. I, 28.
14. Ab.Z. 4b.
15. Pesikta de R. Kah. 151.
16. Lev. R. XIII, 5.
17. Ab.Z. 2b.
18. Pesahim 118b (Hiyya bar Abba in Johanan's name).
19. Simlai, Ab.Z. 2b.
20. Samuel bar Nahman, Lev. R. XXIX, 2.
21. Isaac, Meg. 6a–b.
22. Hama bar Hanina, Gen. R. LXXV, 9.
23. Joshua ben Levi, Yer. Taanit 64a.
24. Cant. R. I, 42.
25. Simeon ben Lakish, Gen. R. IX, 15.
26. Isaac, Meg. 6a.
27. Sanh. 98b.
28. Johanan, Exod. R. XXIII, 11.

29. Johanan, Baba Bathra 75a.
30. Johanan, Pesahim 88a.
31. Samuel bar Nahman, Gen. R. XII, 5.
32. Baba Bathra 75a.
33. Exod. R. XXV, 16.
34. Sanh. 98a.
35. Jonathan, Sanh. 97b.
36. Sanh. 99a.
37. Nathan, Sanh. 97b.
38. Lev. R. XIX, 5.
39. Midr. Ps. VIII, 1 (anonymous).
40. Samuel bar Nahman, Pesikta de R. Kah. 56b.
41. Sanh. 98b.
42. Sanh. 99a.
43. Berakhot 34b.
44. Yer. Taanit 68d.
45. Yer. Taanit 68c.
46. Lam. R. II, 16.
47. Yoma 9b.
48. Lam. R. I, 30.
49. Johanan, Pesahim 87b.
50. Hanina, *ibid.*
51. Hoshaya, *ibid.*
52. Eleazar ben Pedat, *ibid.*
53. Lam. R. III, 28.
54. Johanan, Pesikta de R. Kah. 142a.
55. Menahot 53b.
56. Johanan, Gen. R. LXXI, 1; Midr. Ps. IX, 12.
57. Johanan, Gen. R. LXX, 18.
58. Johanan, Deut. R. II, 14.
59. Midr. Ps. XXXVI, 6.
60. Midr. Ps. CVII, 1.
61. Hama bar Hanina, Sanh. 98a.
62. Hanina bar Hama, *ibid.*
63. Lam. R. IV, 22.
64. *Ibid.*
65. Isaac, Pesikta Rabbati 136a.
66. Meg. 14a.
67. Tanhuma Buber, Deut., Addition Nr. 3. Similarly Jose bar Hanina: God adjured Israel not to rebel against the nations, and the nations not to enslave Israel too strongly (Ketubot 111a).
68. Levi, Gen. R. XLIV, 18.
69. Pesahim 118b.
70. Joshua ben Levi, Deut. R. I, 16.
71. Sanh. 74a; see also I. F. Baer, "Israel, the Christian Church and the Roman Empire etc.," (Hebrew), *Zion* XXI (1956), 33.
72. Shabbat 119b.
73. Samuel bar Nahman, Midr. Ps. CVI, 7.

74. Gen. R. II, 5.
75. Johanan, Midr. Esther, Introd.
76. Hama bar Hanina, *ibid.*
77. Hanina bar Hama, Cant. R. VII, 1.
78. Simeon ben Lakish, Yoma 9b, against the opinion of Johanan.
79. Joshua ben Levi, Tanhuma on Deut. 27:9; Pesikta Rabbati 49b.
80. Levi, Lev. R. VII, 6.
81. Gen. R. XLIV, 24.
82. Ab.Z. 2b. Comp. Sifre Deut. No. 343.
83. Johanan, Ruth R., Introd. 1.
84. Johanan, Ab.Z. 22b.
85. Pesikta de R. Kah. 108b.
86. Kiddushin 30a.
87. Johanan, Tanhuma on Deut. 26:16.
88. Berakhot 63a.
89. Johanan, Sota 21b.
90. Jose ben Hanina, *ibid.*
91. Johanan, Yer. Shabbat 13c.
92. Isaac and Simeon ben Lakish, Exod. R. XXVIII, 4; Samuel bar Nahman, Exod. R. XLII, 7.
93. Johanan, Meg. 19b.
94. Johanan, Meg. 16a.
95. Sanh. 59a.
96. Nedarim 32a.
97. Yer. Peah 15c.
98. Sanh. 108a.
99. Berakhot 10a.
100. Midr. Ps. XXII, 22.
101. Midr. Ps. XXV, 6.
102. Tanhuma Buber on Lev. 13:2.
103. Eleazar ben Pedat, Pesahim 87b.
104. Meg. 31a.
105. Midr. Ps. LXXII, 1.
106. Samuel bar Nahman, Erubin 22a.
107. Sanh. 110b.
108. Hagigah 15b.
109. Meg. 10b.
110. *Ibid.*
111. Levi, Pesikta Rabbati 167b.
112. Levi, Cant. R. VIII, 16.
113. Joshua ben Levi, Gen. R. XXVI, 3, against the opinion of Hanina bar Hama who restricts deathlessness to Israel.
114. Simeon ben Lakish, Shabbat 119b.
115. Midr. Ps. *ad. loc.*
116. Lev. R. VI, 5.
117. Johanan, Exod. R. III, 7.
118. Hanina bar Hama, Num. R. II, 16.
119. Hanina bar Hama, Yoma 57a.

120. Yer. Taanit 65d.
121. Pesahim 85b.
122. Eleazar ben Pedat, Sukkah 55b.
123. Simeon ben Lakish, Midr. Ps. XXXVI, 6.
124. Johanan, Pesikta de R. Kah. 139b.
125. Isaac, Eccles. R. I. 9.

2

A STUDY OF THE TALMUDIC-MIDRASHIC INTERPRETATION OF PROPHECY

I

Introduction

The critical attitude toward the phenomenon of prophecy, and the attempt to check the unconditional prophetic authority in the name of institutional religion and for the sake of the established law and discipline, is probably older than the Babylonian Exile and the Second Commonwealth. Yet it is that epoch that brings forth a definite turn in the attitude toward prophecy as an authoritative announcement of revelation.

"Since the day when the Temple was destroyed prophecy has been taken from the prophets and given to the wise."[1] In Ezra's system there is no place for new prophecy. The will of God is laid down in the Torah for all future generations. The interpretation of the Law is the task of the scholar to whom the meaning of the divine word is given and not of the prophet to whom God may reveal His secret. The new community is built upon spiritual order to be achieved by all; thus the interference of unpredictable enthusiasm granted a few is excluded.[2] The canonization of the prophetic books that took place in the pre-Maccabean period[3] was said to have been necessitated by the departure of the prophetic spirit from Israel.[4] The written account of prophecy established an additional barrier against a possible appearance of new prophets.

This tendency, however, failed to hinder the rise of ecstatics in times of national peril who claimed the same source of authority as the biblical prophets. Josephus reports many prophets and visionaries who promised liberation from the Roman yoke or predicted the doom of Jerusalem.[5] At times Josephus himself takes on the role of a prophet, speaking as παρακαλῶν εἰς σωτηρίαν.[6]

Much has been said about the Apocalyptic literature which attempted to revive some of the prophetic elements, and which imitated prophetic writings. Here, again, the authority is "the word that calls me and the

Spirit that is spilled upon me" (Enoch 91:1). The essence of the prophetic, or pseudo-prophetic word, is not what should be done but what should be expected in the future. The opposition of the rabbis toward the Apocalyptic groups is well known.

The revival of the prophetic authority in the early Church and the Christian propaganda among the Jews greatly intensified the discussion of problems concerning prophecy among the rabbis. Here the post-biblical Jewish conception of prophecy was brought to completion. In the early Christian communities we find charismatic leadership and growing interest in the prophetic sayings of the Bible. Early Christian writings stress prophetic motives in Jesus' life. The prophets of Israel are understood to have received their legitimacy from Jesus: οι προφῆται, ἀπ' αυτοῦ ἐχοντες τὴν χάριν . . (*Epistle of Barnabas* 5:6). Scriptural prophecy is interpreted as foretelling the coming of Jesus, as condemning the Law and proclaiming a new epoch of faith. Scriptural Law itself is given a spiritual interpretation, supported by sayings of the prophets. Prophecy is taken as the main content of Israel's religion (cf. Justin, *Dialogue,* esp. ch. 52). The prophets appear as demanding the inclusion of the Gentiles within the community of Israel and as calling the Church the true Israel. Thus, in early Christianity, the center of gravity moved from the Law to the prophets (e.g. Justin, *Dialogue,* ch. 7).

The Church itself in its early history—beginning with St. Paul experienced the difficulty of establishing the community upon the foundation of prophecy. Extemporaneous prophecy as an immediate mission from God, founded upon an authority beyond human control, was rivaled by the authority of the Church as a permanent institution headed by bishops and teachers. It became imperative to emphasize the order of the Church and to guard it against outbreaks of the pneuma that might disturb its peace.[7] But the integration of the prophetic sources of religion and the institutional requirements of the Church was an internal problem of Christianity. However, facing opposition, especially from Jewish theology, the Church took it upon itself to represent the case of biblical prophecy and to guard prophetic religion against a faith which it considered to be anti-prophetic.

Prophecy had thus become a controversial topic. The talmudic utterances on prophecy, therefore, do not reflect objective, detached observations. Instead, they constitute critical statements echoing a negative attitude to outbursts of uncontrolled pneuma in the past, on the one hand, and the defense of the Jewish doctrine against the new prophetic movement which disputed the ability of the Jews to understand the words of the prophets, on the other.

The Jewish response to the challenge of the Church was only partly expressed in outright discussions. It is generally accepted[8] that a number of talmudic interpretations and midrashic homilies are the result of polemics against Christian teachings, or attempts to strengthen the faith of those Jews who were exposed to Christian propaganda. Particularly in cities like Caesarea, the residence of the metropolitan of Palestine and Syria and at the same time the seat of the school of Bar Kappara and his disciple Hoshaya, teacher of Yohanan, frequent discussions of theological problems are certain to have taken place.[9]

This study advances the suggestion that these polemics, besides affecting the understanding of single prophetic passages such as that on the Suffering Servant for instance, must also have profoundly influenced the talmudic prophetology as a whole. They must have been a contributing factor towards the deepening of a critical tendency the beginnings of which reach back to periods previous to the Jewish-Christian polemics. Thus the far greater part of the rabbinic response consists of a presentation of the Jewish teachings (supported by Scripture) with a polemic implication, though without direct reference to the Christian doctrine. As this essay primarily intends to describe this talmudic-midrashic concenption of prophecy as a whole, statements that go back to the pre-Christian time are not excluded. Nor does it limit itself to records of discussions between Christians and Jews (which have already been treated by others), including mainly remarks on prophecy and exemplary interpretations of prophetic writings according to Palestinian sources of the second, third, and fourth centuries, in as much as they might reflect a polemical or apologetical attitude. (Some Babylonian talmudic sources are used only by way of comparison). The terms "talmudic" and "midrashic" are used interchangeably. The speakers are briefly identified at first mention.

Before presenting a few typical motives of talmudic prophetology, two points must be emphasized:

Firstly: Talmudic criticism of prophecy by no means lessened the esteem of the prophetic writings. All the books of the canon of Jewish Scriptures were considered of equal importance as the source and the expression of divine Law. As to prophetic teachings—ethical, messianic and theological—it has rightly been maintained that they became part and parcel of the rabbinic doctrine.[10] This study, however,—with one exception—does not intend to interpret the rabbinic discussions of prophetic *teachings*, but is solely concerned with the rabbinic comments on the *phenomenon* of prophecy and on the *form* of religious perception as represented by the prophetic personality.

Secondly: It would be unsatisfactory indeed to state that between the prophetic and the rabbinic views there is merely "a difference in form," and that "the conception of the unwritten Torah is the reproduction of prophecy." It is equally insufficient to say that there is only a difference of method between Ezra and the prophets, but "no difference of principle," unless "principle" is understood in a very general sense.[11] In so complicated a theological problem as prophecy, it would be erroneous to ignore the shift in the scale of values which occurs through the substitution of one "form" and "method" by another. The prophet speaks his word, seized by the hand of God, shocked by the experience of unmediated revelation, stirred by the absoluteness and finality of the divine command. As a result of this experience, the prophet was "under special commission" from God to preach to his people.[12] In assuming that this "form" can be replaced by a less emotional, less revolutionary, less radical "form" without substantial consequences for the "contents," one would fail to understand the nature of prophecy. The problem of prophecy and Talmud cannot be presented merely by employing the principle of a harmless change from one form to another. It can only be approached if allowance is made for a transition in religious thinking, a most decisive turn, not only in the history of Jewish religion, but in the history of religious movements in general.

II

Generalization of Prophetic Experience

The rabbis distinctly consider the prophets as a group which, in past history, took a special place beside the priests and the scribes (e.g., Meir, second century, Sifre Deut. 309). Israel is asked to hearken "to the commandments, to the words of the Torah, to the words of prophecy," etc. (Abba b. Kahana, a disciple of Yohanan, third century, Lam. R., Petiha 1). The psalms composed by Moses "under the order of prophecy" were not included in the Torah, so as not to confound words of Torah with words of prophecy" (Midr. Ps. on 90:1). The phenomenon of prophecy and details of prophetic activity are studied by several teachers. The inauguration of the prophets is discussed, and the messages of different prophets compared.[13] There are comments on the state of consciousness in different prophets,[14] on the field of activity of several contemporary prophets,[15] on their names, places of origin, and family relations,[16] on the collection of prophetical writings,[17] on the chronology of prophets[18] and the order of the prophetic books in the canon,[19] on the style and form of prophetic expressions.[20] The manifold discussions on the subject in talmudic literature show that the rabbis were aware of the particular character of prophecy and that they tried to understand the unique position of the classical prophets.

At the same time, however, the rabbis follow a conception of prophecy as a *universal* revelation of God. The Talmud interchangeably uses the terms prophecy, *Ruah ha-Kodesh*, "the holy spirit," denoting "a universal indwelling of God in the world, his constant self-revelation to man," and Shekhinah, designating the abiding presence of God by the side of man.[21] These terms of divine revelation enable the rabbis to generalize the phenomenon of inspiration. They are described as acting not only in prophets, but in many other persons throughout biblical times. The patriarchs and the four mothers, Tamar, Joshua, Rahab, Samson, Hannah, Samuel's son Joel, David and Solomon, and many others, are considered by the rabbis as inspired by the spirit of prophecy. Divine inspiration is granted now only to individuals, but, at times, to the people of Israel as a whole as long as it deserves this privilege. As a reward for their belief in God, the holy spirit rested upon the Israelites at the Red Sea (Mekhilta on 14:31). The sin of the golden calf, according to Phinehas b. Hama (fourth century), caused the holy spirit in Israel to be replaced by a guiding angel (Exod. R. 32.1). Commenting on Isa. 7:1 and 8:16, Samuel b. Nahman (third century) said that king Ahaz closed down the houses of prayer and the houses of study, so that the knowledge of the Torah may cease and God "withdraw his Shekhinah" from Israel (Gen. R. 41.3). The festival of "Drawing of Water," according to Joshua b. Levi (third century), derived its name from the phenomenon that from there Israel "drew holy spirit" (Yer. Sukkah 55a). Related is a group of midrashic texts which presents the holy spirit as guiding, and revealing divine opinion, criticism, or consolation at certain occasions in biblical times. It is in cases like these that the holy spirit uses Scriptural passages as a form of expression, applying them to these events.[22]

From this more general conception of pneumatic experience, the rabbis challenge the uniqueness of the prophets and the exclusiveness of their visions. They emphasize that, through certain occurrences in Israel's past, God has revealed more of his glory than in the visions of the prophets: e.g., "The maidservant at the Red Sea saw more than Ezekiel and all the other prophets," states Eliezer b. Hyrkanus (first and second centuries). "By the ministry of the prophets" God "used similitudes" (Hos. 12:11); Ezekiel had only "visions of God" (1:1); but the people at the Red Sea, "as soon as they saw Him, they recognized Him" (Mekhilta on 15:2). Berekhiah (fourth century) elaborated upon the same theme: "Moses had to prostrate himself and to supplicate before God" until he was given to perceive divine "resemblance" only "by a sign"; but Israel at the Red Sea was granted unmediated vision (Exod. R. 23.15).

According to the rabbis, the prophets are not the exclusive messengers of God. Aha b. Hanina (third century) has God saying to the prophets: Do you think I have no messengers if you do not accept to be my messengers? In this case I will execute my message "by a snake, by a scorpion, by a frog" (Exod. R. 10.1).

This motive, generalizing the phenomenon of prophecy, did not originate from a polemical intention. It can be assumed, however, that at times it was employed in that spirit. Early Christianity and other prophetic movements stressed the element of inspiration and enthusiasm.

Pneumatic experiences were granted the elevated rank of authoritative prophecies. Men filled with the holy spirit were considered prophets. The rabbis question the absoluteness of prophetic vision. They give prophetic occurrences a more general character, and lessen the difference between prophecy in the strict sense of the word and an expression of the divine presence among men. This enabled them to counteract the revolutionary and challenging position inherent in prophecy, and to refute the charismatic privileges granted to messengers of God in early Christian thinking.

III

The State of Worthiness

"When the last prophets, Haggai, Zechariah, and Malachi, died, the holy spirit departed from Israel."[23] But to the rabbis, the end of the era of prophecy ("holy spirit" in the strict sense of classical prophecy) did not mean the end of revelation or of direct relationship between God and Israel. There were other forms of divine communication with the affairs of men that took the place of original prophecy: holy spirit in a more general sense, awareness of divine presence (Shekhinah), and *Bat Kol*, the "heavenly voice" that from time to time "reveals to Israel things hidden from human knowledge"[24] and announces the will of God . "It was given them to hear by means of the *Bat Kol*."[25]

The talmudic sources tell of some instances where such communication took place after the cessation of biblical prophecy: In the time of the Second Temple, Simeon the Just and Yohanan the High Priest perceived a "heavenly voice" (Tosefta Sotah 13.5-6. Cf. Josephus, *Ant.* 13.10.3). Three and a half years before the destruction of the Temple a heavenly voice admonished Israel to repent, with the words of Jer. 3:14; when no repentance was achieved, the voice called the words of Hosea 5:15 (Lam. R. Petihta 25). A heavenly voice proclaimed that Hillel and Shmuel ha-Katan were "worthy of the holy spirit" (Tosefta Sotah 13.3-4; Yer. Abodah Zarah 42c).[26] The dispute between the schools of Hillel and Shammai, each of whom contended that the Law was in accordance with their views, was solved by a heavenly voice: "Both are the words of the living God, etc." (Erubin 13b). Jonathan b. Uziel, who translated the Prophets into Aramaic, is challenged by a heavenly voice: "Who is it that revealed my secrets to men?" A translation of the Hagiographa is prevented by the interference of a heavenly voice (Megillah 3a). Yohanan b. Zakkai foresees the destruction of the Temple (Yoma 39b). In the century after the destruction of the Temple, Gamaliel II is credited with an utterance inspired by the holy spirit (Tosefta Pesahim 1.27; Yer. Abodah Zarah 40a).[27] After having caused the death of Eleazar of Modiin, Bar

Kokhba perceives a heavenly voice which repeats the prophecy of
Zechariah (1:17) and announces his doom (Yer. Taanit 68df). Both Akiba
and Meir, (second century), are said to have been granted the holy spirit
(Lev. R. 21.7; 9.9). Elisha b. Abuyah, Meir's teacher, hears a heavenly
voice quoting Jer. 3:22 (Yer. Hagigah 77b). Simeon b. Yohai, (second
century), hears a heavenly voice announcing the fate of a bird. In one of
his miraculous actions he is guided by the holy spirit (Yer. Shebiit 38d).
Yohanan derives from Isa. 30:21 the permission to follow the guidance of
a heavenly voice (Megillah 32a). I. Sam. 28:3 spoken by school children,
is taken by Yohanan and Simeon b. Lakish, (third century), as a heavenly
voice intending to inform them of the death of Mar Samuel in Babylonia
(Yer. Shabbat 8c).[28]

There is no doubt that the rabbis were aware of the distinction between the period of Scriptural prophecy and their own time. R. Reuben
(third century) compares the prophetic period to the presence of the king
in the city, the time thereafter to the statue of the king: "The statue
cannot do what the king himself can do" (Cant. R. 8.11). But this "remnant of prophecy," (*ibid.*) though small, was strong enough to support
the consciousness of the rabbis that living revelation is not altogether a
matter of the past and that God speaks to men, not only through the
medium of the Scriptures, but also in direct communication.

The difference, however, between prophetic revelation and revelation
by means of the holy spirit and the heavenly voice is of great importance
for the understanding of talmudic prophetology. The Talmud employs
the motive of the "worthiness" of a man to receive such revelation. A
man is granted the holy spirit by studying the Torah: Joshua b. Levi e.g.,
regarded the presence of God as implied in the presence of the Torah
(Cant. R. 8.13). According to Aha (fourth century) a man becomes worthy
of the holy spirit by devoting himself to study for the purpose of observance (Lev. R. 35.6). Similarly Judan (fourth century): Whoever speaks the
words of the Torah in public is worthy of the holy spirit to rest upon him
(Cant. R. 1.8).[29] The welcoming of one's teacher is "as if he had welcomed the divine presence (Yer. Erubin 22b; cf. Mekhilta on 18:12). The
divine presence is also a result of the observance of the Law and of the
doing of good deeds. In the opinion of Nehemiah (second century),
whosoever accepts one commandment "with faith" deserves that the
holy spirit rests upon him (Mekhilta on 14:31). The giver of charity to the
poor becomes worthy of the divine presence (Midr. Ps. on 17:15).

The presupposition of a state of "worthiness" in the talmudic
prophetology turns divine revelation into a culmination, an end of a
process. It becomes the result of preparation achieved by study and good
deeds, in contradistinction to Scriptural prophecy, where God's call to
the prophet marked the beginning of a process. The prophet was moved

by a divine pathos; he was forced and controlled by "a strong hand"; his mission revolutionized his life. In the talmudic literature, the resting of the holy spirit upon a man means no sudden experience of revelation, overwhelming him by its newness and immediateness.[30] Rather is it an awareness of divine presence, entering the human sphere with the aim to help and to guide. It establishes a more constant sphere of co-ordination and correlation between God and man. It might be assumed that, in these comments on divine revelation, the rabbis, besides having other reasons, were moved also by the desire to challenge the authority of sudden outbreaks of prophetic spirit which intended to give an unex-pected turn to the revealed and established religious order, a motive which occurred in all pneumatic movements and played a great part in the early Christian conception of prophecy.

IV

The Criticism of the Prophetic Personality

The prophets attempted to bring about a change in the life of the people by the proclamation of the word of God. The Talmud emphasizes the fact that this was not a sufficient means to reach the desired aim. It is from this angle that the Talmud, and especially the school of Yohanan, criticizes the activity of the prophets. Moses' prophecy during the forty years did not have the power to bring about Israel's redemption; this (Israel's redemption) was brought about by Pharaoh, who "took off his signet ring from his hand and put it upon Joseph's hand" (Gen. 41:42; Yohanan, Lam R. 4.22). Similarly, Yohanan's colleague, Simeon b. Lakish, contrasts the activity of the prophets of Elijah's time with the action of King Ahasuerus (Esther 3:10) which indirectly caused the redemption of Israel (*ibid*). R. Isaac, a disciple of Yohanan, in a comment on Ps. 137:2, ascribes to the Babylonian Exile the power to lead Israel to repentance, while the prophecies of Jeremiah remained unheeded (Pesikta Rabb. ed. Friedmann 136a).[31] According to Abba b. Kahana, "all the forty-eight prophets and seven prophetesses that prophesied in Israel" were not able to lead them back to the right way, while the decree of Ahasuerus led them back to the right way (Megillah 14a).

In these discussions, the talmudic teachers point to the primarily historic factors that accounted for achievements denied to the prophets. We may assume that the rabbis had knowledge of the fact that the prophets had been instrumental in making Israel conscious of the mean-ing of historic catastrophes. It is all the more significant that they stress the influence of historic events as such and not of their interpretation by the prophets. It might be suggested that the rabbis, particularly in the third century, emphasized the power and authority of *historic reality* in an attempt to counteract conceptions of unconditional authority of the *prophetic word.*

The rabbis consider the authority of the prophet as limited. Yet the prophet as the messenger of the word of God, according to the Talmud, tends to overestimate his power. The rabbis, therefore, have God reprimand the prophets for statements that are interpreted as haughty and self-assured. Levi, a disciple of Yohanan (third century), takes Moses' word to the judges: "And the cause that is too hard for you ye shall bring unto me and I will hear it" (Deut. 1:17) as an expression of self-pride. God, according to Levi, reproaches Moses, telling him that soon he will be confronted by a case which he will not be able to decide, but which could be decided by his pupil's pupil (Num. 27:5). The prophet Samuel, according to Levi, is reprimanded by God for saying: "I am the seer" (I Sam. 9:19). God says to him: I will show you that you are no seer. The words, "For man looketh on the outward appearance but the Lord looketh on the heart" (*ibid.*, 16:7) are understood by Levi as God's corrective answer to Samuel's pride (Midr. Samuel ch.14; Sifre Deut., 17).

The prophets are also shown as failing to understand the true nature of the judgment of God. Jeremiah and Daniel, who witnessed the fall of their nation are, according to Joshua b. Levi, stirred by the victory of the heathens and the enslavement of Israel; in describing the divine attributes, therefore, they change the established formula, Deut. 10:17; Jeremiah omits the attribute of awfulness (32:18); Daniel omits the attribute of might (9:4). Only the Great Assembly that followed the age of the prophets was able to re-interpret God's actions and to re-establish the traditional formula (Yoma 69b).[32]

By pointing to human weaknesses in the prophets and to the limits of their understanding of divine actions, the rabbis pursue the tendency of checking doctrines which recognize the prophet as the central figure in the realm of Revelation and his book as the principal expression of God's will. Against the Christian theory which saw a consequence of Israel's sin in the Law of the Pentateuch (e.g., Justin, *Dialogue* ch. 17) and which placed prophecy and the prophetic books in the center of the Bible, we find a talmudic statement according to which it was only Israel's sin that made it necessary to give them more books than the Pentateuch (Hunia, Eccles. R. 1.34).[33]

V

Prophecy and Law

The prophet speaks because he has heard the voice of God that very hour. The word of God comes unexpectedly, at times against all human anticipation. The power of the prophetic message emanates from this presence of revelation.

In speaking of the prophetic mission, the Talmud repeatedly stresses the idea that only the *delivery* of the message is a matter of "today"; the message itself originated on Sinai and has been waiting for its hour ever since. The revelation on Sinai, the source of the divine Law, is also the source of prophecy. The "great voice" on Sinai (Deut. 5:19) is interpreted by Simeon b. Lakish as the origin of all future prophecy (Exod. R. 28.4). According to Samuel b. Nahman, Moses not only proclaimed his own words but also those of all the later prophets as well (Exod. R. 42.7). Commenting on Deut. 29:14, Isaac says: The messages which the prophets were to prophesy in each and every generation were received on Mount Sinai (Exod. R. 28.4). Isaiah is quoted as having said: I received my prophecy on Sinai but "now the Lord God hath sent me and his spirit (Isa. 48:16), which means that until then he had not been given permission to make his prophecy public (Exod. R. 28.4). The "Merkabah" vision of Ezekiel, according to Berekhiah, had its source in the revelation on Sinai (Cant. R. 1.29). Malachi had been in possession of his prophecy since the revelation on Sinai, but had to wait for this hour to proclaim it (Exod. R. 28.4).

In these comments we may recognize the talmudic criticism of an important characteristic of prophecy: its immediateness, its unforeseen instant breaking into a historic situation. By tracing back the origin of the prophetic message to the revelation on Sinai, the Talmud introduces the element of tradition into prophecy, thus restraining the danger inherent in uncontrolled prophetism. Moreover, in the talmudic emphasis on the connection between the two phenomena—prophecy and Sinai—a polemical tendency becomes apparent. The early Christian interpretation of prophecy saw in Jesus the event to which all the prophets had pointed (e.g., Acts 3:24; Justin, *Apology* 61). Jesus appears as the termination and culmination of prophecy. To see that events have occurred and are occurring as was prophesied appears to Justin as "the greatest and truest proof" of Christianity (*Apology* 30). Thus, in reading the prophets the early Church stressed the element of foresight and prediction. The Talmud criticizes the foundation of this interpretation and, referring to certain aspects in the prophetic books themselves, present the prophets as witnesses to the first revelation of God to Israel. According to the Talmud, the Scriptural prophecies are not essentially predictions but confirmations and elucidations of the work of Moses, in whom were combined the authority of prophecy and Law.

It is not only the source that, in the talmudic conception, is common to prophecy and to Law. Even the task of the prophet is understood to be the same as the task of the interpreter of the Law: to teach the Torah to Israel. The Talmud pictures the prophets as teachers. The purpose of the

prophetic words on future blessings was to foster the study of the Law in
Israel (Samuel b. Nahman, Eccles. R. 1.27).[34] In the talmudic interpretation, prophetic words of general and comprehensive nature are referred
to a specific law or observance. "To walk humbly with thy God" (Micah
6:8), according to Eleazar b. Pedat (third century), means "to escort the
dead to the grave and to lead the bride to the bridal chamber" (Sukkah
49b).[35] "Seek the Lord while he may be found" (Isa. 55:6) leads Abbahu
to the question: "Where is he to be found?" which he answers: "In the
houses of prayer and of study" (Yer. Berakhot 8d). Similarly, to "forsake
the Lord" or, to leave his presence, of which the prophets speak, is
interpreted by the rabbis as disobedience of a certain commandment or
usage.[36] The prophetic phrase, "word of God," is identified with "the
word of the Torah." "I have put My words in thy mouth" (Isa. 51:16),
according to Levi, refers to the Torah (Pesikta ed. Buber 140b).[37] When
the prophet has God say "which I command not" (e.g., Jer. 19:5), the
Talmud adds: "In the Torah" (Eleazar b. Jose, second century, Sifre
Deut., 148).

The same principle underlies the interpretation of the prophetic term,
"knowledge of God." To "(I desire) knowledge of God rather than
burnt-offerings" (Hos. 6:6) Simeon b. Yohai remarks: "The words of the
Torah are dearer to me than burnt-offerings and peace-offerings" (Abot
de R. Nathan ed. Schechter II. 11b). The term Torah or the Torah of God,
when used by the prophet in a broad and extensive sense, is related by
the rabbis to the "Written Law." The term Torot or Torah with the
subsequent synonym is understood as the Written and the Oral Law. If
the parallel part of the sentence contains an unspecified, general term
like "statute," the rabbis offer a specific translation, stressing a concrete
implication.[38] A great many talmudic comments consider the motive,
Torah and study of Torah, to be the implication of prophetic sentences or
phrases of a general theological character.[39]

Here, as well as in other chapters of talmudic interpretation of the
Bible, we find different tendencies at work. Besides the tendency to
arrest anthropomorphism, we can clearly recognize the attempt to counteract pneumatic irrationalism. The rabbis pointed out indefinite,
vague, and more theoretical prophetic terms which lent themselves to
support pneumatic religions, and translated them into concrete demands. Terms like "Knowledge of God," "Covenant," "Way of the
Lord," opened the way to uncontrolled religious emotional experience.
The Talmud, without losing sight of the deeper issues in the relation of
Man to God,[40] stresses "study of the Torah" and "observance of the Law"
as the concrete meaning of "Covenant" and "Knowledge of God," thus
demonstrating the common task of prophet and rabbi.

Closely related is the motive which shows certain prophets as having
instituted some customs and usages.[41] A great number of regulations is

assumed by the rabbis to have been transmitted by Haggai, Zechariah, and Malachi.[42] Yet, in the opinion of the rabbis, the prophet, while interpreting the Law, does not enjoy any privilege qua prophet; he is, like the rabbi, subject to the same statutes that regulate the law-finding procedure. Thus the prophet is not considered the originator of new laws which are not indicated in the Torah, nor has he the right to abrogate or to alter the Law.[43]

As it is the aim of both the Law and prophecy to teach Israel the Torah, the authority of the sage who devotes himself mainly to the Law is considered by the Talmud to be higher than the authority of the prophet who combines other activities with the teaching of the Law. Therefore, according to Tanhum b. Hiyya (third century), the prophet has to prove his authority by a sign or a wonder (Deut. 13:2), "showing the king's seal," while the sage does not need to show the king's seal; he speaks with the authority of the Law (Deut. 17:11; Yer. Berakhot 3b). Prophetic devices, miracles, signs, are not permitted to interfere in the deliberation of the sages or to challenge their vote. In a discussion of susceptibility to Levitical uncleanness of a particularly constructed oven, Eliezer b. Hyrcanus tried to prove his dissenting opinion by many arguments; however, when the sages declined to accept them, he resorted to offering proofs by miraculous deeds and, finally, by a Voice from Heaven. The miracles happened, the Heavenly Voice spoke, confirming Eliezer's viewpoint; but Joshua b. Hananiah arose and exclaimed: "It is not in heaven" (Deut. 30:12); the Torah had already been given at Mount Sinai; we pay no attention to a Heavenly Voice, because Thou hast long since written in the Torah, "After the majority must one incline" (Exod. 23:2; Baba Metzia 59b). The realm of Law is independent. When scholars deliberate a matter of law, no supernatural faculties may interfere. The right to ignore such forces is given the sages— with the revelation on Sinai.

Prophetic qualities, when arising among the rabbis, are ascribed by them to adherence to tradition. At times when sages took the opportunity to foretell the future, they rejected the title of a prophet and explained their power as resulting not from a divine illumination but from following the tradition: "I am not a prophet neither a prophet's son, but I hold this tradition from my teacher. . . ."[44]

VI

The Prophets and Israel

To the prophets the relation of God to the people of Israel was determined by a passionate love. This love, however, was not unconditional.

The center of the prophet's thinking is the divine plan.[45] The self-confident, complacent life of Israel—as of all nations—appears to the prophet as rebellion against God. Israel misinterprets God's love by identifying God with his nation. The pride and disobedience of Israel, or any nation, provoke the judgment of God.[46] The prophet who identifies himself with the divine cause suffers with God the grave disappointment over Israel's sin. He becomes the messenger of Israel's doom. God will not pardon any more (Amos 8:2). The day of the Lord will come upon all proud and lofty ones (Isa. 2:17). God will utterly consume all things from the face of the earth (Zeph. 1:2-7). Man is bowed down but God exalted through justice (Isa. 5:15-16). The prophet's hope that "the remnant will return" and that God will renew his love (Hos. 2:21; Isa. 14:1; 30:18) does not diminish the seriousness and the absoluteness of the prophetic criticism of Israel.

The Talmud, to be sure, takes up this line of prophetic criticism; its statements on the weight of Israel's sin reveal a deep consciousness of the critical position of Israel before God. Joshua b. Levi, interpreting Jer. 3:19, lets God speak to Israel: I wanted to defend you, but you caused me to denounce you and to declare you guilty (Tanhuma ed. Buber II.86). Yohanan reads Malachi 3:5 and exclaims: Is there a remedy for a servant whom his master brings to judgment and hastens to witness against him? (Hagigah 5a). Ammi or Assi (both disciples of Yohanan), in interpreting Ezek. 21:31, lets the angels remind God of Israel's virtue in accepting the Torah on Sinai, but God answers by referring to its sin in having "lowered the exalted and exalted the low" and put the idol into the Temple (Gittin 7a). Abba b. Kahana remarked on Ezek. 16:31: Jeremiah "the son of the corrupted who did righteous deeds" (Rahab) was sent to reprimand Israel, "the son of the righteous who did corrupted deeds" (Pesikta ed. Buber 111b). This definite awareness of sin opens the way to the insight that God's final word is not judgment nor condemnation but salvation. This idea is expressed by Isaac in the form of a dialogue between Abraham and God after the destruction of the Temple. Abraham pleads for Israel in the words of Jer. 11:15, but God rejects every plea in Israel's defense. Only when Abraham finally fears that "there is no remedy for them," a Heavenly Voice quotes Jer. 11:16, interpreting it: "as an olive tree has its future as its end, so is Israel's future at its end" (Menahot 53b).

Yet this prophetic motive of criticism of Israel and of salvation as the *final* act in history is not the only motive in the talmudic discussion of the "Israel" problem. The talmudic teachers challenge the prophetic theme of a possible rejection of Israel and of the catastrophic turn of its history. The talmudic idea of "withdrawal of the divine presence" as the punishment for sin is by no means identical with the judgment proclaimed by the prophets. The relation between God and Israel appears to the rabbis to be of a more steadfast character, not affected by an ever imminent possibility of suspension. The contrast between God and Israel is bridged over by the idea of correlation and harmonious correspondence. The conception of Israel as a cosmic category and necessary condition for the existence of the world, a conception which matured in the talmudic time,[47] did not permit the continuance of the prophetic questioning—not even a temporary questioning—of Israel's right to existence. The idea of sympathy, therefore, that has been observed in biblical prophecy,[48] underwent a significant change in talmudic theology. The prophet participated in the divine feelings and emotions; they were the motives of the prophet's own attitude and action. According to the talmudic thinking, it is God who takes part in the fate of Israel, suffering with them,[49] accompanying them in their exiles,[50] and awaiting with them the day of salvation which will, as it were, redeem divinity itself.[51]

Thus the origin of the prophetic mission, according to the talmudic interpretation, is not primarily to be found in the prophet's participation in God's pathos, but in his direct attachment to Israel, in whose fate God himself participates, even if it be necessary to punish the nation. The "merit of Israel," therefore, becomes a necessary prerequisite of prophetic gifts; the love of Israel, which is unconditional, becomes the source of the prophet's message. "You find everywhere that the prophets prophesy only because of the merit of Israel" (Mekhilta on 12:1). Akiba states that, in all the thirty-eight years in which God's wrath was aroused against Israel, he did not speak with Moses. To which Simeon b. Azzai, Akiba's contemporary, adds: It was not with Moses alone that God spoke only for the sake of the merit of Israel, but with all the other prophets as well (for instance, Ezekiel, Jeremiah, and Baruch) he spoke only because of the merit of Israel (*ibid*). Judah b. Simon, in discussing the initiation of Isaiah, has God take the side of Israel: My children are stubborn and troublesome; do you take upon yourself to be beaten and insulted by them? Isaiah accepts this condition, quoting 50:6 and adds: "I am not worthy to be sent by you to your children" (Pesikta ed. Buber 125b; Lev. R. 10.2).

The prophet's foremost task, according to the rabbis, is not to express God's condemnation of the sin of Israel or to proclaim the divine judgment; instead it is his duty to fight to the utmost for Israel and to advocate the cause of Israel before God, whenever his judgment is imminent. This, also a biblical motive, is emphasized in the talmudic interpretation. Citing the example of Moses, David, and Jonah, Jonathan (second century) maintains: Everywhere you find that the patriarchs and the prophets gave their life for Israel (Mekhilta on 12:1). They suffer whenever Israel suffers, says Jose b. Halafta (second century), commenting on Ezek. 4:9 (Pesikta ed. Buber 71b). According to Simeon b. Pazzi (third century), Isaiah was given "the tongue of the learned" (50:4)—to be the advocate of Israel (Pesikta Rabb. ed. Friedmann 151a). Jeremiah curses the day of his birth (20:14) because he is ordered to bring the cup of God's fury (25:15) to be drunk by Jerusalem (*ibid.* 129af). Levi has the prophet record every good deed that a man did (Lev. R. 34.9). The prophet prays for Israel. Jeremiah and Ezekiel are presented by Nehemiah as having prayed before God that he should not destroy the Temple (Ruth R. 2.2). In the relation between God and Israel, it is the prophet who in a time of crisis pleads with God for Israel's sake, because, in spite of sin, "all that see them must acknowledge them, that they are the seed which the Lord hath blessed" (Isa. 61:9; Exod. R. 46.4).

Guided by this conception of Israel, the rabbis considered a prophet's criticism of Israel as inconsistent with his office. Whenever a prophet reproaches Israel, it is God who takes the side of the nation. He "does not like one who speaks evil of Israel" (Cant. R. 1.39). This motive appears in many versions in the talmudic prophetology. "Slander not a servant unto his master (Prov. 30:10) is interpreted by Simeon b. Pazzi as admonition to the prophets not to denounce Israel before God. Moses is punished for having said, "Hear now ye rebels" (Num. 20:10); Elijah is rebuked by God for having said: "The children of Israel have forsaken Thy covenant" (I. Kings 19:10; Cant. R. 1.39). Hosea is, in talmudic interpretation, reprimanded by God for his failure to reject God's own words: "Your children have sinned," and for his suggestion to exchange the sinful Israel for another nation. The prophet's marriages are not considered by the rabbis as symbols of Israel's faithlessness and rebellion, but as a divine means of educating the prophet toward a deeper attachment to Israel (Pesahim 87a). Isaiah is permitted to state that he is "a man of unclean lips" (6:5), but he suffers punishment for calling Israel "a people of unclean lips" (Cant. R. 1.39).[52] Jeremiah is understood by the rabbis to have reproached God for refusing to pardon Israel's sin (Lam. 3:42), whereupon his prophetic capacity was doubled (Jer. 36:32; Mekhilta on 12:1).

If a prophet is found censuring Israel, other prophets, in the talmudic exegesis, are sent to cancel or restrict that sentence. According to Jose b. Hanina (third century), Moses pronounced four sentences on Israel; but four other prophets (Amos, Jeremiah, Ezekiel, Isaiah) came and revoked them (Makkot 24a). Of the four expressions used by Jeremiah to chastise Israel, one was repealed by Jeremiah himself and others by Moses and Isaiah (Joshua b. Levi and Joshua b. Abin, fourth century, Lam. R. 5.20). This motive sometimes appears in the form of a question put before God asking why he allowed the prophet to reprimand Israel. When God said to Ezekiel: Say to Israel: Thy father was an Amorite and thy mother was a

Hittite (16:3), the "arguing spirit" asked God: If Abraham and Sarah would appear before you, would you insult them thus? (Dimi, fourth century, Sanhedrin 44b).

Prophetic sentences which contain a criticism of Israel, are given by the Midrash and the Talmud an interpretation which limits the scope of the blame, or abolishes it altogether; at times the rabbis even turn the sentence into a testimony of Israel's virtue. By way of exegesis, such sentences are taken to support rabbinic teachings. To Amos' "Are ye not unto Me as the children of the Ethiopians" (9:7) we find the remark: When Israel sins, God calls them Ethiopians (Midr. Ps. on 7:1). Similarly: "As the children of the Ethiopians" you might consider yourself, but "you are unto Me"—children of Israel (Cant. R. 1:35). Or: As the Ethiopian differs by his skin, so Israel differs from all other nations by their deeds (Moed Katan 16b).[53] Hosea's "Ye are not My people and I will not be yours" (1:9) is understood by Hanina b. Hama (third century): Even if you want to separate yourself from me, I shall not share your opinion, but against your will you shall be my nation (Num. R. 2.16).[54] Isaiah's "Children that deal corruptly" (1:4) implies, according to Meir, that though they deal corruptly, they are called "children" (Sifre Deut. 308).[55] Micah's utterance that God will pardon the iniquity "of the remnant of his heritage" (7:18) leads Aha b. Hanina (third century) to the question: Only to the remnant and not to the whole heritage? His answer, based on an exegesis of the word "remnant," eliminates the restriction implied by the prophet (Rosh ha-Shanah 17af).

Like their utterances, so the actions of the prophets, according to the Talmud, were motivated by the task of upholding the honor of Israel. Thus Jonah's reason for going to Tarshish was not "a flight from the presence of the Lord" but an attempt to help Israel. Had he gone to Nineveh and had its people repented, Israel's iniquities would have become visible by comparison with Nineveh, and Jonah would have been the "cause of Israel to be condemned." He therefore fled "outside of the land, where the Shekhinah does not reveal itself." According to Nathan (second century), "Jonah made his voyage only in order to drown himself in the sea." His story is taken as a proof that the "patriarchs and prophets gave their lives in behalf of Israel" (Mekhilta on 12:1).

The prophetic thought of Israel as being forever confronted by the will and the might of God is retained in the Talmud. According to the rabbis, however, Israel's existence is not challenged by God. The theme of "eternal Israel" and of the divine love for Israel, used as a motive in the talmudic interpretation of the prophets, implies to a large extent the polemic answer to the assertion of the Church that God has forsaken Israel and chosen a New Israel. The prophets, upon whom the Church has based its assertion, have been presented by the rabbis, especially in the third century, as spokesmen of the idea that the love of God is unconditional. In the talmudic prophetology, the recognition of this fact becomes the very foundation of the prophetic mission.

VII

Conclusion

For this pre-systematic period of Jewish thought no attempt can be made to synthesize the diversified statements on the subject. It can only be maintained that many of the talmudic-midrashic sayings and interpretations concerning prophecy show a polemic and apologetic attitude towards certain movements, both within and without the Jewish realm, that brought about a revival of prophecy based on the authority of biblical prophecy as well as on a free and sometimes forced interpretation of the prophetic writings. The decisive challenge, however, arose from the propaganda of the early Church and its recognition of the central position of prophecy; its understanding of Jesus as the culmination of prophecy; its conception that prophecy was suspended in Israel, that the prophetic writings imply the abolishment of the Law, that the Law had to be understood prophetically, and that the prophets endorsed the rejection of Israel and the choice of a New Israel.

The talmudic doctrine retained the idea of revelation (as a general, universal phenomenon in Israel), and many of the prophetic teachings, pointing at the same time to certain limitations in the prophetic activity and to certain shortcomings in the prophetic personality. While maintaining that there were forms under which the holy spirit was still active after the cessation of Scriptural prophecy, the rabbis asserted that the resting of the spirit upon man was the result of the study and observance of the Law. The center of all prophecy was understood to be the revelation on Sinai, which had anticipated all future manifestations of the spirit. The prophets are presented as teachers of the Sinaitic Law. The abstract and theoretical postulates of the prophets are interpreted from the point of view of the Law. The prophetic activity is recorded as dependent upon the "merit of Israel," and the prophets are criticised for pronoucements opposing Israel.

These motives are indicative of an attempt to eliminate or at least to restrict the revolutionary, radical, and charismatic elements in prophecy, and thus to counteract the validity of the very basis of the opposing views. Polemics, therefore, increased the critical attitudes of the rabbis towards the phenomenon of prophecy as such. The transformation of the biblical prophet into a teacher and interpreter of the Law becomes a decisive characteristic of talmudic-midrashic prophetology.

NOTES

1. Megillah 17b; cf. Yer. Berakhot 4d; Yer. Megillah 70d.

2. H. H. Schaeder, *Esra der Schreiber* (Tuebingen, 1930), pp. 3, 64 and passim.

3. S. Zeitlin, "An Historical Study of the Canonization of the Hebrew Scriptures," *Proceedings of the American Academy for Jewish Research,* III (1932), 121 ff.

4. L. Ginzberg, *The Legends of the Jews* (Philadelphia, 1928), VI, 448.

5. Antt. XVIII. 4. 1; XX. 5.1; 8.10; Bell. Jud. II. 13.4; 13.5; VI. 5.3.

6. Bell. Jud. III. 8.9; IV. 10.7. Cf. Wilhelm Weber, *Josephus und Vespasian* (Berlin, 1921), pp. 75 ff.

7. I. Cor. 14. Didache 15: 1. Cf. E. Meyer, *Ursprung und Anfaenge des Christentums* (Stuttgart and Berlin, 1923), III, 253 ff.

8. E.g., by L. Baeck, A. Buechler, L. Ginzberg, S. Krauss, A. Marmorstein, S. Zeitlin.

9. Cf. Abbahu (third and fourth centuries), Abodah Zarah 4a on the necessity for the Palestinian Jews to study the Scriptures, because their adversaries urge them to discuss biblical problems; in this respect the Palestinians are said to differ from their Babylonian brethren.

10. Cf. L. Ginzberg, *Eine unbekannte juedische Sekte* (New York, 1922), pp. 265, 275; *Mekomah shel ha-Halakah* (Jerusalem, 1931), p. 11; Ch. Tchernowitz, *Toledot ha-Halakah* (New York, 1934), I, 306; L. Finkelstein, *The Pharisees* (Philadelphia, 1938), II, 463.

11. Travers Herford, *Talmud and Apocrypha* (London, 1933), p. 70; *Pharisaism* (London, New York, 1912), p. 65. An understanding of this problem is shown by J. Z. Lauterbach, "The Ethics of the Halakah," *Yearbook, Central Conference of American Rabbis,* XXIII (1913), 254. Cf. also C. G. Montefiore, *Rabbinic Literature and Gospel Teachings* (London, 1930), pp. 254 F.

12. W. F. Albright, *Archaeology and the Religion of Israel* (Baltimore, 1942), p. 24. Cf H. H. Rowley, "The Nature of Prophecy in the Light of Recent Study," *The Harvard Theological Review,* XXXVIII (1945), 22 ff

13. E.g., Judah b Simon (fourth century) about Isaiah, Micah, Amos: Pesikta ed. Buber 125b.

14. E.g., Jose b. Zimra (third century) and Joshua b. Nehemiah (fourth century), Midr. Ps. on 90:1.

15. E.g., Pesikta Rabb. ed. Friedmann 129b, on Jeremiah, Zephaniah and Huldah.

16. E.g., Yohanan, Lev. R. 6.6; Lam. R. Petihta 24. Cf. Ulla, Megillah 15a.

17. E.g., Yohanan, Cant. R. 4.22. Cf. Megillah 14a and Yer. Megillah 70d.

18. E.g., Baba Batra 14b; Pesikta ed. Buber 128b.

19. Baba Batra 15a.

20. E.g., Isaac (third and fourth centuries), Sanhedrin 89a; Gen. R. 67.9. R. Judah b. Simon, Pesikta ed. Buber 126a; Lev. R. 10.2. Cf. Gen. R. 44.7; Pesikta ed. Buber 117b.

21. J. Abelson, *The Immanence of God in Rabbinical Literature* (London, 1912), pp. 215, 225. Cf. H. Parzen, "The Ruah Hakodesh in Tannaitic Literature," *Jewish Quarterly Review,* N. S., XX (1929–1930), 51 ff.

22. E.g., Bileam's plans are rejected by the holy spirit by quoting Prov. 17:1

(Tanhuma ed. Buber IV, 141). Jephthah's sacrifice was criticised by the holy spirit by quoting Jer. 19:5 (Tanhuma ed. Buber III, 114). At the occasion of the dedication of the Temple and Solomon's prayer, the holy spirit quoted Eccles. 4:2 praising the dead king David (Tanhuma ed. Buber II, 225).

23. Tosefta Sotah 13.2; Yoma 9b; Sanhedrin 11a. In Yoma 21b, the absence of Shekhinah and prophecy is mentioned among the five things that distinguished the Second Temple from the First. In Eccles. R. 12.8, the words, "the spirit returneth to God" (Eccles. 12:7), are interpreted to mean the holy spirit that left the city with its destruction.

24. L. Ginzberg, *The Legends of the Jews* VI, 442, note 36.

25. Tosefta Sotah 13.2.

26. According to the opinion of the sages, Eliezer b. Hyrkanus also was considered worthy of the holy spirit.

27. Tosefta Niddah 5.15 mentions a prediction of Gamaliel II without employing the term holy spirit.

28. *Ibid:* a casual remark by a woman is considered a heavenly voice by Jonah and Jose (fourth century) indicating that the sick Aha was still alive.

29. Cf. the statement of Phinehas b. Jair (second century) according to which the Torah, through different stages leads to the acquisition of the holy spirit and finally to the resurrection of the dead (Abodah Zarah 20b).

30. Cf. Joshua b. Levi: In the first revelation to Moses, God spoke in the voice of Moses' father in order not to frighten him (Exod. R. 3.1).

31. Cf. also Lam. R. 4.22.

32. Cf. Phinehas b. Hama, yer. Berakhot 11c; yer. Megillah 74c.

33. Cf. Adda b. Hanina, Nedarim 22b.

34. Cf. Yalkut Shimeoni on Isa. 64:3.

35. Cf. the same rabbis's comment on Isa. 23:18, Pesahim 118b.

36. See Hoshaiah (about 200) on Jer. 2:5, Pesikta ed. Buber 119 a; Ammi (a disciple of Yohanan and Hoshaiah) on Isa. 1:28, Berakhot 8a.

37. Cf. yer. Taanit 68a.

38. E.g., Judan on Isa. 5:24, Pesikta ed. Buber 121b.; Isaac on Isa. 5:24, Pesikta ed. Buber 121b.; Isaac on Isa. 24:5, Pesikta ed. Buber 98a; Judah the Patriarch (second century) on Mal. 2:6, Yer. Peah 15b.

39. E.g., Eleazar b. Pedat (third century) on Jer. 33:25, Pesahim 68b; Isaac on Isa. 10:27, Sanhedrin 94b; Judah b. Pazzi (fourth century) on Hos. 8:3, Pesikta ed. Buber 121a.

40. E.g., Akiba remarks to Ezek. 36:25 and Jer. 17:13, that Israel in purifying itself stands before God (Mishnah Yoma 8.9). Hela (fourth century) heard a child reading Amos 4:13 and was reminded of man's critical position before God (Hagigah 5b).

41. Cf. Z. H. Chajes, *Torat Nebiim* (Zolkiew, 1836), ch. IX.

42. Erubin 104b; Sukkah 44a; Rosh ha-Shanah 19b; Nazir 53 a; Zebahim 62a; Hullin 137b; Bekorot 58a.

43. Temurah 16a; cf. Chajes, *op. cit.,* p. 18d, and L. Ginzberg, *op. cit.,* VI, 170.

44. Eliezer b. Hyrcanus (first and second centuries), Erubin 63a; Eleazar b. Arakh (first and second centuries) Midr. Ps. on 1:3.

45. Cf. Abraham Heschel, *Die Prophetie* (Krakow, 1936), p. 68 and *passim.*

46. Cf. Reinhold Niebuhr, *The Nature and Destiny of Man* (New York, 1943), II, 25 and *passim*.

47. E.g., Reuben, Berekhiah and Abbahu, Lev. R. 36.4. On the connection of this conception with the ethical view of creation, cf. L. Ginzberg, *op. cit.*, v. 67.

48. A. Heschel, *op. cit.*, p. 70.

49. E.g., Jonathan b. Eleazar (third century) on Ezek. 5:13 (Berakhot 59a); Simeon b. Lakish on Amos 5:1 and Jer. 9:16 (Pesikta ed. Buber 120b); Berekhiah on Isa. 40:1 (Pesikta ed. Buber 128b); cf. Jose b. Halafta (second century), Berakhot 3a.

50. E.g., Simeon b. Yohai on I. Sam. 2:27 and Isa. 43:14 (Megillah 29a); Isaac on Jer. 44:38, Zech. 9:13 etc. (Exod. R. 15.16); Aha on Jer. 40:1 and Ezek. 1:1 (Lam. R., Petihta 34).

51. E.g., Berekhiah on Isa. 62:11 and Zech. 9:9 (Tanhuma ed. Buber III, 71).

52. In these interpretations only the general motivation is important and not the reference to a particular prophet. In other discussions, the same prophet, especially Moses, might be praised for his readiness to fight for Israel. E.g., Pesahim 87b.

53. Cf. Sifre Num. 99. Yalkut Shimeoni on Num. 12:1.

54. Similarly is interpreted Ezek. 20:32.

55. Similarly is interpreted Jer. 4:22 and Ezek. 33:31. Cf. Kiddushin 36a and the opposing view of Judah.

3

THE CONCEPT OF
PEACE IN
CLASSICAL JUDAISM

I

The term classical Judaism will, in this essay, be used to designate the period in which post-biblical, rabbinic Judaism took form. Roughly speaking this era is identical with the talmudic period; more specifically, it commences with Hillel the Elder in Jerusalem (first century B. C.)— himself an heir to the doctrines of preceding generations; reaches its maturity in the teachings of Johanan of Tiberias, in the third Christian century; and comes to a close in the following century.

The biblical term peace, *shalom*, as employed in talmudic and midrashic literature, designates, on the one hand, wellbeing, wholeness, a friendly attitude, and, on the other, harmony between members of a community and between nations. The application of the term to either personal, or communal, or political, or religious life allows those who speak on peace to play on the whole compass of the word. Frequently, whenever one specific aspect of peace is being discussed, the others are implied, or, at least, kept within the range of vision.

II

Before an attempt is made to present classical Judaism's teachings on peace, one must realize that the writings in question contain numerous positive references to war. Biblical literature, with its depiction of both war in the political history of Israel and the vision of universal peace in the messianic future, is the foundation and frame of reference of rabbinic writings. Thus, in these writings, war, too, is accorded attention, even though in many instances merely for reasons of technical exegesis.

God, though One and immutable, is presented as appearing at the Red Sea as a mighty hero doing battle (and at Sinai as an old man full of compassion)[1]. He took the guise of a young man "because in war none is more fitting than a young man"[2]. The words "The Lord is a man of war" (Exod. 15:3) were taken to imply that God taught the art of war to the "experts in war" (Cant. 3:8)[3]. With reference to Deut. 20:10 ff. it is stated that once the obligatory peace overture fails, war becomes a serious pursuit and absence of compassion on the part of the enemy is to be answered in kind[4]. All manner of strategems become permissible in order to reach the objective.[5]

III

Yet, despite the numerous biblical records of successful military operations and references to battle heroes, the writings of classical Judaism consider war objectionable and alien to the spirit of Israel. The province of "the seed of Jacob" is prayer, while "no war is effective unless the seed of Esau [i. e. Rome] has a part in it"[6]. From among the four most useful languages, Latin is said to be one best suited to the conduct of war[7].

The importance of warlike preparations and strategy is underplayed; the preparations are interpreted to be spiritual. That Israel was able "to maintain a firm foothold in battle" is due to "the walls of Jerusalem" (Psalm 122:2), "where students engaged in the study of the Torah"[8]. The phrase, they "that turn back the battle at the gate" (Isaiah 28:6) is understood to refer to the learned debates ("in the battle of the Torah") and to the scholars who spend long hours within the gates of the houses of study[9]. The mishnaic law prohibits going out on a Sabbath "with a sword, bow, shield, club or spear"; Rabbi Eliezer's opinion that these could well be considered a man's ornaments was countered by the Sages: "They are nothing but shameful, for it is written, 'And they shall beat their swords into plowshares . . . nation shall not lift up sword against nation' (Isaiah 2:4)"[10]. Thus, the peace expected at the end of days set a standard for behavior in the pre-messianic era.

IV

Also, in the period under discussion, the comprehension of Israel's past history changed under the impact of the teachings of classical Judaism. Piety, prayer, and study, pacific virtues in classical Judaism, penetrated and transformed the ancient stories of heroism and warlike action. In the new value system, fighters, were at the same time students of the Law. This trend of thinking is best evidenced in the midrashic evaluation of King David. He is presented as both warrior and scholar. His day started with a period of study[11]. "When he was sitting and studying the Torah he was pliant as a worm; when he marched to war he hardened himself like a lance."[12] His kingdom was bestowed on him as reward for his diligence as a scholar[13]. The difference between Saul and David is seen in the former's inability to make his learning accessible to the people and the latter's success in doing so[14]. The angel of death could not approach David "because learning did not cease from his mouth". Only when he paused, could his soul be taken from him[15]. Abishai, one of the heroes in the David story, is said to have outweighed the majority of the learned Synhedrion[16]. Benaiah, one of "the mighty men whom David had", "increased and assembled workers for the Torah"[17]. And in pre-Davidic history, we find Joshua pictured by the talmudic sages as a man "to whom the words of the Torah were precious"[18]. Jacob is said to have conquered the Amorite land not "with sword and bow" (Genesis 48:22) but "with prayer and supplication", as "sword" and "bow" were now understood[19]. Similarly, Abraham's army of "three hundred and eighteen trained men" (Gen. 14:14) appears as composed of men trained in scholarship. Yet, as punishment for Abraham's pressing scholars into war service, his children were made to endure the Egyptian servitude[20].

The idea that life dedicated to the peaceful pursuit of learning is superior to the life spent in war is illustrated by the talmudic legend that makes heathen war leaders who fought Israel, or their descendants, covnerts to Torah. "The descendants of Haman taught the Law in Bene Berak; descendants of Sisera taught children in Jerusalem; descendants of Sennacherib were public teachers of the Law."[21]

V

This negative attitude towards war is, partly, rooted in the prophetic view of the messianic future. Partly, however, the increasing emphasis on peace on the part of classical Judaism in its early development is to be understood as a reaction against acts of cruelty committed by some Hasmonaean rulers and as an answer to King Herod's ruthless administration. During the battles between the two Hasmonaean princes, Hyracanus II and Aristobulus II, Onias, member of the association of peace-loving pious men (Hasidim), refused to pray for the victory of Hyrcanus' forces "since those who stand now with me are Thy people and those that are besieged are also Thy priests"[22]. For his non-intervention in this civil war Onias paid with his life[23].

The Hasmonaean rulers, rejected the Pharisean plea to separate altar and throne[24], and forcibly combined the sacred office of high priesthood with an aggressive policy of conquest and territorial expansion. The descendants of Aaron were no longer "doing the work of Aaron". Shemayah and Abtalion, according to talmudic tradition[25], descendants of the Assyrian king Sennacherib, called themselves "descendants of the heathen, who do the work of Aaron"[26].

It was Hillel the Elder, contemporary of King Herod and a disciple of Shemayah and Abtalion, who attempted to revive the ancient image of non-political, non-militant, prophetic priesthood. "Be of the disciples of Aaron (the priest), loving peace, pursuing peace; be one who loves his fellow-creatures and draws them near to the Torah."[27] This "priesthood of peace", a charge abandoned by the class of ruling priests, is to be made the ideal aim for the nation at large. Charity aims at peace: "The more charity, the more peace."[28] Hillel's concept found its explication in Johanan ben Zakkai, whom tradition calls the youngest disciple of Hillel. Taking his clue from the biblical prohibition of using iron instruments ("thy sword"), in building an altar (Exodus 20:25), Johanan sees the function of the altar as that of serving the establishment of peace between God and man, and encouraging men "to establish peace between man and his fellow-man, between husband and wife, between family and family, between city and city, between nation and nation, between government and government"[29]. Peace among nations is rooted in the practice of peace between man and his neighbor.

The symbol of the first priest of peace remained alive in the generations of scholars after Hillel, and popular stories told in detail of Aaron's efforts as peace-maker[30].

VI

Did the advocacy of peace in classical Judaism imply a peaceful acceptance of the Roman rule? Was not Rome the last of Daniel's "Four Kingdoms" that had to fall before the Kingdom of God could be established? Did not apocalyptic prophecy envisage a great war between the forces of light and the forces of darkness and the abolition of heathenism as a precondition for the rise of the peaceful rule of the "saints of the Most High" who are to receive the acclaim of "all peoples, nations and languages" and last forever? Was not the recognition of Caesar a tacit denial of God as the true King? And, since liberty under God's Kingship alone matters, was not the war against Rome a legitimate war?

This was indeed the political theory of the patriotic revolutionaries known as Zealots and of the adherents of what Flavius Josephus called the "Fourth Philosophy", the theory of all those who joined in the Judaeo-Roman war of 66 to 73 and, later, in the Bar Kokhba rebellion of 132–135. Jerusalem's resistance to Rome was indeed a necessity if viewed within the context of an activist, messianic, philosophy of history. A Jew, faithful to Israel's covenant with God, cannot acknowledge the Lord and, at the same time, give Caesar what is Caesar's.

One of the most significant representatives of the extra-messianic, peaceful attitude towards Rome is the historian Flavius Josephus. He, a priest and scion of the Hasmonaean rulers, was aware of the messianic covenant and of Israel's claim as pioneer of the divine kingdom. But he arrived at the conviction that this covenant, in its precise meaning, no longer held. He realized that Rome was not the godless kingdom destined to fall in the near future; behind Rome's rise to power he detected the working of divine providence. "Fortune has everywhere been transferred to them [the Romans] . . . and God, who had given all the nations power in turn, has now settled in Italy."[31] Thus a war against Rome was a war against God[32]. A vague oracle current in Judaea at the time, mentioned also by Tacitus and Suetonius, to the effect that "a man from [the Jews'] country would become ruler of the world" offered encouragement to the Zealot fighters. To Josephus this oracle denoted "the rule of Vespasian, who was declared emperor while in Judaea"[33]. Josephus' fateful step in surrendering to Vespasian—an act that exposed him to the accusation of treason—must be understood against the background of his historical thinking.

In eliminating the expectation of impending fulfillment of the messianic claim—while retaining the belief in an ultimate messianic future—Josephus interprets Israel as a nation that in its biblical past shunned the use "of weapons and might of hand"[34]. The exodus from Egypt took place "without bloodshed . . . God conducting them as the future guardians of His temple". When the Philistines carried off the sacred ark, Israel "committed the issue to God's decision, themselves employing neither hand nor weapon". In the time of Sennacherib's attack on Jerusalem, Israel's hands "at rest from arms, were lifted up in prayer". In the Babylonian captivity, our fathers did not engage in any action "to shake off the yoke and recover their liberty" but patiently waited for Cyrus to grant liberty to them. Accordingly, Josephus arrives at his conclusion: "No instance can be adduced of our ancestors having triumphed by arms, or failed of success without them, when they committed their cause to God . . . (But) when they took to the field, they were invariably defeated." It appears therefore "that arms have never been granted to our nation; to go to war is to incur inevitable disaster". Israel constitutes a sacred community, inhabiting holy ground. "It is the duty of those who occupy a holy place to commit all to the disposal of God and to scorn human aid."

In Josephus' view, the rule of Rome did not constitute a threat to the Kingdom as represented by Jerusalem, a threat that would have to be averted by a decisive war. Rome ruled the world by the will of God; "without God's aid it would not have been possible to consolidate so great an empire"[35]. Dispassionate comprehension of this fact will safeguard the peace[36]. Jerusalem, on the other hand, was the center of a non-political, religious society,—Josephus calls it a theocracy—wholly dedicated to the worship of the eternal God, to the advancement of order in the world as outlined in the Law of Moses. Its aim is a perfect community of men guided by the universally valid Law. "As God Himself pervades the cosmos, so has our law found its way among all men."[37] Josephus' belief in the depoliticalization of Judaism and of its messianic aim permitted him to work towards peace between Jerusalem and Rome.

He failed; the Zealots continued the struggle to the bitter end. They, too, failed; Rome emerged as the master of *Judaea devicta*. Yet, both

Jewish attitudes, Hillel's and Josephus' on the one hand and the Zealots' on the other, found valiant disciples in the centuries to follow: the latter in the militant messianic movements which renewed the war against the "fourth kingdom", the former in the academies of the talmudic rabbis who, aware of the high price to be paid, became spokesmen for peace.

VII

Like his contemporary, Flavius Josephus, Johanan ben Zakkai is reported to have left the besieged city of Jerusalem and to have appeared before the Roman general, Vespasian, acknowledging his sovereignty and asking his permission to continue his peaceful study of the divine Law in Jabneh[38]. His non-political stand before Vespasian is reminiscent of Hillel's attitude towards Herod. To his disciples, distressed over the loss of the center of worship in Jerusalem, Johanan conveyed the reflection also reminiscent of Hillel's teaching—that acts of loving kindness (*hesed*) constitute an atonement as effective as worship in the central sanctuary[39]. Thus, endeavor on behalf of peace in the realm of interpersonal relationship supplants political action.

Hananya, "the prefect of priesthood", probably the last to hold this office in the second Temple, held peace to be of equal importance as the whole creation[40]. To Joshua ben Hananya (a disciple of Johanan ben Zakkai), who worked for the pacification of the remnant of Judaea after the fall of Jerusalem, tradition attributes a number of statements in praise of peace. Peace, he taught, is the reward for Israel's readiness to accept the Torah; "peace" is the name given to Israel; peace is promised to both the living and the dead[41]. Jose the Galilean, who lived in the period of the Bar Kokhba rebellion, stressed the importance of the law (Deut. 20:10) that a war must be preceded by a peace overture[42]. Both Akiba, martyr in the post-Bar Kokhba persecution, and Ishmael ben Elisha, his learned contemporary, are credited with the statement that even the name of God may be blotted out in water (in the ritual described in Num. 5:11–31) to establish peace between man and wife[43].

Simeon ben Yohai, representative sage of the post-Bar Kokhba generation and a critic of the benefits of Roman civilization, maintained that the blessing of peace contains within it all other blessings[44]. His contemporary, Judah ben Elai, in reviewing the ritual of sacrifices, found their purpose to be the bringing of peace into the world[45]. The activity of the prophets, "who planted the word peace in the mouths of all creatures", had the same aim; so taught another contemporary, Eleazar ben Shammua[46]. Simeon ben Gamaliel II, a descendant of Hillel, the patriarch of this period, considered peace to be one of the three things by which the world is maintained (the others being truth and judgment)[47]. He recalled the ideal image of the high priest Aaron, who gained renown as a peacemaker[48]. In the interest of peace he taught, it is permissible to modify a statement, as Joseph's brothers deviated from the truth (Gen. 50:16) in order to establish peace in the family[49]. Finally, "if one brings peace into his home, it is accounted to him as though he had brought peace to everyone in Israel"[50]. Meir, keen legal scholar and profound thinker of the period, lauded peace as the most beautiful gift of God to the upright[51].

Leader of the following generation was Judah the Prince, compiler of the Mishnah; he advanced the daring dictum that even if Israel should worship idols while preserving peace, God had no power, as it were, over them, "since there is peace among them"; only a divided heart would make them guilty[52]. Another member of the same generation, Simeon ben Eleazar, realized that pursuit of peace requires action. "Let him therefore go forth from his place and move around in the world . . . Seek peace in your own dwelling place and pursue it to another place."[53] Still another contemporary, Eleazar ha-Kappar, preached "the love of peace" and pointed to the priestly benediction that culminates in the blessing of peace (Numbers 6:26)[54]. His son, Bar Kappara of Caesarea, said that even angels, who were free of jealousy and strife, need peace (Job 25:2); how much more then do we, earthly beings who know hatred and enmity, need it[55].

A younger contemporary, Simeon ben Halafta, tried to find in the equal distribution between heavenly and earthly objects in the process of Creation God's plan "to make peace between the upper and the lower spheres"; to complete the harmonious organization of the cosmos, he argued, man is composed of both the lower element (body) and the higher element (soul)[56].

The Mishnah, composed around 200 A. D. and containing the legal, ritual, and ethical teachings of the masters (the "Tannaim") quoted in the preceding section of this essay concludes with the words of Simeon ben Halafta: "The Holy One, blessed be he, found no vessel that could hold Israel's blessing excepting peace."[57]

The following two centuries of active life and thought in Palestinian academies continue the exposition of the peace concept.

Hanina bar Hama, who had studied under Judah the Prince, considers the task of the disciple of the wise "to increase peace in the world"; knowledge, as cultivated by the scholarly "builders of the world", is to be instrumental in the promotion of peace[58].

Hizkiah bar Hiyya, who belonged to the circle of Judah the Prince, recalled the period of Israel's wandering in the desert as a period of dissension and discord; only when the people became peacefully united, were they able to become witnesses of the revelation at Sinai[59]. Peace, he maintained, is an unconditional commandment; other biblical commands are conditional and bound to circumstance (e.g., "if you see" etc.), while of peace it is said: "Seek peace and pursue it"—always[60].

One of the chief spokesmen of third-century Palestinian Jewry, Joshua ben Levi of Lydda, compared the importance of peace to the world to the function of leaven in the dough; without peace, the land would be ruined by the sword and wild beasts[61]. Alexandrai, who handed down teachings by Joshua ben Levi, believed that he who studies the Torah without ulterior motives makes peace both in heaven ("in the Upper Family") and in the family of men ("the Lower Family")[62]. Johanan bar Nappaha of Tiberias, the most important teacher in third century Judaism, considered peace to be a cosmic principle: "Before the Holy One, blessed be He, stand only the angels of peace and angels of compassion; the angels of wrath are far removed from Him."[63]

Johanan's companion, Simeon ben Lakish, counted peace among the divine gifts received by the world[64]. Levi, a disciple of Johanan, conceived of Israel as the bringer of peace to the world[65]. Great is peace, he taught; all divine blessings and promises of salvation and consolation conclude with peace[66]. Yet peace, though of universal significance, must originate in man's heart. In conquering the evil urge, man "creates peace in this world and in the world-to-come"; so expounded Simon, a disciple of Joshua ben Levi.[67].

In the following generation, Jeremiah of Tiberias has God calling Israel "the nation that made peace between Myself and My world; had Israel not accepted My Torah, My world would have returned to chaos"[68]. As Israel is a nation of peace, so God is "the King of peace", in the formulation of Judah bar Simon of Lydda, a contemporary of Jeremiah of Tiberias[69].

These utterances, coming to us from an unbroken tradition of some four centuries, are documents of non-political Judaism in the form it took after the destruction of Judaea. Here Israel apprehends its religious activities as culminating in peace, utilizing the Torah as an instrument of peace and as a blueprint of the worship of God, conceived as a God of peace.

Rabbinic literature, rich and variegated as it is, long resisted attempts at a systematic topical arrangement of its material; there are anly a few exceptions to the rule. It is therefore significant that certain portions within the talmudic-midrashic works can be recognized as anthologies, or remnants of anthologies on peace, a topic that called for special emphasis. Such collections of utterances on peace, or several variations of one and the same maxim, attributed to a variety of teachers, appear in Sifre on Numbers No. 42, Leviticus Rabba IX, 9, Numbers Rabba XI, 16–20, Deuteronomy Rabba V, 12 ff., and in *Perek ha-Shalom*, a late compilation, printed as chapter X of the minor tractate *Derekh Eretz Zuta*. As a rule, the individual sayings are introduced by the words: "Great is peace." Some of the sayings quoted above were taken from these collections and placed in chronological order; others follow, augmented by quotations from other related sources.

The concluding phrase in the priestly blessing, "and give thee peace" (Num. 6:26) is to be understood as "Peace in thy coming, peace in thy going out, peace with all men."[70] Peace is the reward given to repentant sinners, to students and lovers of the Torah, to the humble, and to the charitable[71]. The very aim of Creation is "that there should be peace among the created beings"[72]. A nation is punished by being deprived of peace; the only comfort for fallen Jerusalem is peace[73].

VIII

On reviewing the long list of sayings in praise of peace it may be noted that classical Judaism was mainly concerned with peace in personal affairs, in the sphere between man and man, which was to be an *imitatio* of the peace in the divine realm. Through force of circumstance, Judaism, as represented by the Talmud and the Midrash, had more and more withdrawn from active historical life; thus, little is found in the writings that reflects a stand on peace in inter-nation relationships. Non-political Israel is advised not to resist agression: "If the 'fourth kingdom' (Rome) issues against you harsh decrees do not rebel . . . disobey only if it demands of you to renounce the commandment and the Torah."[74] The midrashic masters note that it is characteristic of Israel to enter in peace the realm controlled by the four kingdoms and to leave it in peace; it is, they say, a nation "in which the peace of Him who is the life of all the world is being maintained"[75]. The accounts of war in Scriptures, they further state, have as their sole purpose only the teaching of the importance of peace[76].

Individual attention was given to the education of a man of peace, a man who would rather "be of the persecuted than of the persecutors"[77]; who "is reviled but reviles not others, who hears himself reproached but answers not, who bears his sufferings in love"[78]; who would prove to be a hero by "making of his enemy a friend"[79]; who would "increase the peace with his brothers, with his relatives, and with every man, even with the heathen in the market place"[80].

In contrast to the extreme messianists who envisaged a fierce war as a precondition for a new, just order of life in the end of days, the teachers of classical Judaism conceived the invention of war a curse in history. Referring to the four kings "in the days of Amraphel" (Gen. 14:1), the Midrash explains: "Before their time there had been no war in the world and it was they who came and introduced the sword and started to wage war. God said: 'You wicked ones, you have introduced the sword, let the sword enter your own heart.'[81] And Moses, credited by the Bible with a number of battles, is pictured as resisting a divine command and as sending a peace embassy to Sihon rather than waging war (Deut. 2:24 ff.), whereupon God Himself confirmed Moses' decree[82]. Also: "After all the evil things the Egyptians did to Israel, Scripture showed compassion on them and bade: 'Thou shalt not abhor an Egyptian because you were a stranger in his land' (Deut. 23:8), but seek peace and pursue it."[83]

The ultimate pacification of suffering humanity was expected in the messianic age. "Three days before the coming of the Messiah, Elijah will call out: 'Peace has come to the world.' "[84] Then swords and other weapons "will not be required . . . they may be compared to a candle at noon"[85]. Peace will be the first word uttered when the Messiah reveals himself; his very name is Peace[86]. The prophetic vision of peace became a central concept in classical Judaism, one of whose masters described the world-to-come by quoting Isaiah (66:12): "Behold, I will extend peace to her like a river."[87]

NOTES

1. Mekhilta on Exodus 15:3.
2. Hagigah 14a.
3. Num. Rabba XI, 6.
4. Tanhuma on Deut. 20:1.
5. Sifre Deut. No. 200.
6. Gittin 57b.
7. Yer. Sotah 21c.
8. Makkoth 10a.
9. Megillah 15b.
10. Mishnah Shabbath VI, 4.
11. Berakhoth 3b.
12. Moed Katan 16b.
13. Aboth de R. Nathan, Second Version, XLVIII, quoting Psalm 119:56.
14. Erubin 53a.
15. Shabbath 30b.
16. Berakhoth 62b.
17. Berakhoth 18b.
18. Menahoth 99b.
19. Baba Bathra 123a.
20. Nedarim 32a.
21. Gittin 57b.
22. Josephus, *Antiquities*, XIV, 2:1.
23. *Ibid.*
24. Kiddushin 66a.
25. Gittin 57b.
26. Yoma 71b.
27. Aboth I, 12.
28. *Ibid.*, II, 8.
29. Mekhilta on Exodus 20:25.

30. Aboth de R. Nathan, First Version, XII; *see also* Tosefta Sanhedrin I, 2 and Perek ha-Shalom.

31. Josephus, *War*, V., 9:3.

32 *Ibid.*, V, 9:4.

33. *Ibid.*, VI, 5:4.

34. This and the following quotations are from *War* V, 9:4.

35. *War* II, 16:4.

36. *Ibid.*

37. *Against Apion* II, 40.

38. Gittin 56a.

39 Aboth de Rabbi Nathan, First Version, IV.

40. Sifre Numbers, No. 42.

41. Perek ha-Shalom.

42. Lev. Rabba IX, 9. V, 14.

43. *Ibid.*, and Deut. Rabba V, 14.

44. *Ibid.*

45. Sifra on Lev. 3:1.

46. Sifre Numbers, No. 42.

47. Aboth I, 18.

48. Perek ha-Shalom. In Tos. Sanh. I, 2, Moses, the representative of stern justice, is contrasted by Aaron, the man of peace.

49. Lev. Rabba IX, 9; other sages quote similar examples from Scripture. *See also* Yebamoth 65b (Eleazar ben Simeon and Nathan).

50. Aboth de R. Nathan, First Version, XXVIII.

51. Num. Rabba XI, 17.

52. Gen. Rabba XXXVIII, 6; *see also* Sifre Numbers, No. 42 (Bar Kappara).

53. Aboth de R. Nathan, First Version, XII.

54. Sifre Numbers, No. 42.

55. Lev. Rabba IX, 9.

56. *Ibid.*

57. Mishnah Uktzin III, 12, quoting Psalm 29:11.

58. The saying appears at the conclusion of the tractates Berakhot, Yebamot, Nazir, Tamid, Keritot in the Babylonian Talmud and at the end of tractate Berakhot in the Palestinian Talmud.

59. Lev. Rabba IX, 9.

60. *Ibid.*, on Psalm 34:15.

61. Perek ha-Shalom.

62. Sanhedrin 99b.

63. Tanhuma on Lev. 13:3.

64. Lev. Rabba XXXV, 7.

65. Cant. Rabba on 7:1, interpreting the name Shulamith (from *shalom*, peace) as referring to Israel.

66. Lev. Rabba IX, 9.

67. Gen. Rabba XXII, 15.

68. Cant. Rabba on 7:1.

69. *Ibid.* on 3:9. On "Peace" as a name of God, *see* Lev. Rabba IX, 9 (Yudan ben Yose).

70. Sifre Numbers, No. 42.

71. *Ibid.*
72. Num. Rabba XI, 4.
73. *Ibid.*, XI, 20.
74. Yalkut Koheleth 978.
75. Cant. Rabba VII, 1.
76. Tanhuma on Lev. 7:12.
77. Baba Kamma 93a.
78. Yoma 23a.
79. Aboth de R. Nathan, First Version, XXIII.
80. Berakhoth 17a.
81. Tanhuma on Gen. 14:1.
82. Deut. Rabba V, 13.
83. *Ibid.*, V. 14.
84. Pesikta Rabbati XXXV.
85. Shabbath 63a.
86. Perek ha-Shalom and Lev. Rabba IX, 9.
87. Lev. Rabba IX, 9.

4

THE CONCEPT OF
SACRIFICE IN
POST-BIBLICAL JUDAISM*

QUEST FOR SUBSTITUTES FOR SACRIFICES AFTER
THE DESTRUCTION OF THE SECOND TEMPLE

After the destruction of the Second Temple in the year 70 and the abolition of the sacrificial cult it became incumbent to substitute a new concept of sacrifice in order to insure the continuity of religious life without a serious brake. The ancient prophets had of course taken up the issue of the ways that truly constituted the will of God.

Thus when one of the disciples of Yohanan ben Zakkai cried out that today, with the Temple in ruins, the means of atonement were annulled, the master was able to comfort him by referring him to a prophetic dictum: "My son, we have another atonement as effective as this: acts of loving kindness, for it is written: 'I desire loving kindness and not sacrifice' " (Hosea 6:6).[1]

However, in the period following the fall of Zion and the termination of the old order, it was not, evidently, sufficient merely to revive the prophetic call to social justice as constituting the true sacrifice. In the era of the Second Temple new religious sensitivities and modes of piety had developed (or were deepened wherever they already existed) that now, after the destruction, had to be assigned a place within a religion that no longer offered sacrificial atonement.

The relevant material is spread over the entire breadth of talmudic-midrashic writings. In addition to anonymous traditions there are statements attributed to Tannaim (e.g., Rabbi Meir and Rabbi Nehemiah), to Babylonian Amoraim (e.g., Rav, Rav Judah ben Yehezkel, Rabba and Abaye) and Palestinian Amoraim (e.g., Bar Kappara, Joshua ben Levi), especially to men affiliated with the school of Rabbi Yohanan of Tiberias (e.g., Abbahu, Hiyya bar Abba, Resh Lakish). The uncertainty of our literary and biographical traditions render impossible more definite attributions.

The new formula that gained momentum as time progressed may be defined as follows: Though actual sacrifices have ceased to exist, other

---

*Based on a paper delivered at the annual meeting of the American Society for the Study of Religion, April 24, 1976.

religious and moral deeds act as their substitutes. Or, to put it differently: Certain, if not all, religious and moral functions were given the rank and status of sacrifices. All of life, it was held, is nothing but a series of offerings to God, attempts to come near to God, be close to God. They are mediators between man and God. God "accepts" the offering, i.e., allows man to come near to him. The root meaning of the Hebrew term for sacrifice, *korban*, to come near, is sensed in many (not all) utterances concerning the new concept of religious and moral functions as equivalent to sacrifices.

A number of specific functions are mentioned in talmudic-midrashic writings as substitutes for sacrifices. The phrase used in most cases is: He who performs this or that act is considered to have brought a sacrifice. There seem to be four categories of such functions: (1) Tenets of Jewish faith; (2) Ritual acts; (3) Ethical deeds; (4) Events in one's personal life.

(1) Tenets of Jewish Faith:

Loving Kindess (see above).

Dedicated study: "In every place offerings are presented unto My name, even pure oblations" (Malachi 1:11) refers to the scholars who study Torah in purity . . . Scholars who study the laws of sacrifice are metaphorically rebuilding the temple . . . He who busies himself with Torah is like a man tendering a "burnt-offering, a meal-offering, a sin-offering, and a guilt-offering" (Lev. 7:37).[2] Reading the laws of sacrifice is equivalent to actually performing the ritual: "Whenever they read it [the order of sacrifices] I will deem it as if they had offered them before me and I will grant them pardon for all their iniquities."[3] In fact the Talmud preserves tractates devoted to a detailed presentation of laws of sacrifices and their discussion in the academies, and the Hebrew liturgy contains lengthy recitations from the talmudic traditions on the subject.

Prayer: The prophetic "we will render for bullocks the offering of our lips" (Hosea 14:3) was understood by the talmudic sages as a reference to prayer as a substitute for sacrifices.[4] Referring to Hosea 14:2, God is made to say: "I do not want your sacrifices and offerings but words [of prayer]."[5] "He who prays in the house of prayer is tantamount to offering a pure oblation."[6] Prayer is mentioned together with the washing of the hands, putting on the phylacteries and the reciting of "Hear O Israel" as being equivalent to building an altar and offering a sacrifice upon it.[7]

Repentance: The Psalmist's words "the sacrifices of God are a broken spirit" (Psalm 51:19) were understood to mean that "if a man repents it is accounted unto him as if he had gone up to Jerusalem and built the Temple and the altar, and offered thereon all the sacrifices ordained in the Torah."[8] "What is the penalty of the sinner?" Wisdom and Prophecy say, recompense; the Law proposes a sacrifice; God, transcending the Law, gives this answer: "Let him repent and he will be forgiven."[9]

(2) Ritual Acts:

Washing of the hands and putting on phylacteries are noted above.

Fasting, diminishing a person's fat and blood, substitutes for the fat and the blood of sacrifice. A sage prays: "May it be Thy will to account my fat and blood which have been diminished as if I had offered them before thee on the altar, and do Thou favor me."[10] Adam is said to have fasted 130 years in atonement for his sin, for acts of self-mortification are equivalent to sacrifice.[11]

Whoever performs the ritual such as the *lulab* and the willow-branch (on the Feast of Booths) "is regarded as though he had built an altar and offered thereon a sacrifice"[12] — though this may not be more than a homiletical statement. Weightier is the observation that after the cessation of the sacrificial worship on the Day of Atonement it is the day itself that brings about atonement:[13] the very day assumes the sanctity of sacrifice and is its equivalent. The leader of prayers is the substitute for the officiating priest in the Temple.[14]

(3) Ethical Deeds: He who observes the laws pertaining to the poor man's share in the crop and other provisions made for the needy (Lev. 23:22) is regarded as a man making his offerings in the Temple before its destruction.[15] "If a man entertains a scholar in his house and lets him enjoy his possessions he is accounted as if he had sacrificed the daily offering."[16] To make a present to a scholar is like offering first fruits.[17] "Whosoever partakes of the wedding feast of a bridegroom . . . and does gladden him . . . is as if he had sacrificed a thanksgiving offering."[18] And in the sphere of personal ethics: "He who is humble of spirit, Scripture regards him as though he had brought all the offerings, for it is said: 'The sacrifices of God are a broken spirit' " (Psalm 51:19).[19]

(4) Events in One's Personal Life: Circumcision is regarded as a mode of sacrifice; indeed, it is a substitute for an offering of thanksgiving.[20] The sages observed a relationship between circumcision, sacrifice and the Day of Atonement. They relate that Abraham's circumcision took place on the Day of Atonement, and upon the spot on which the altar was later to be built in the Temple, for the act of Abraham remains a never-ceasing atonement for Israel.[21] In one's home, it is the table that is an equivalent of the altar. "As long as the Temple stood, the altar atoned for Israel; but now a man's table atones for him,"[22] for at this table he can feed the hungry. Death is understood as sacrifice. "The day of death brings atonement."[23] One of the sages prayed: "May my death be an atonement for all my iniquities."[24] Especially atoning is the death of a righteous man. Such a death "atones like the sprinkling of the ashes of the red heifer."[25] Moses' grave faced Beth Peor so that by his death he might achieve atonement for sins of Israel committed at that location.[26] "Just as the Day of Atonement brings atonement, so does the death of the righteous bring about atonement."[27] A general, summarizing statement:

"All the dead find in death atonement."[28] The highest instance of atoning death is martyrdom. The mother of the seven sons that died "for the sanctification of God's name" (IV Maccabees 8–16) addresses her sons by saying: "My sons, go and say to your father Abraham: 'You brought one offering on one altar, and I on seven altars offered sacrifices.' "[29]

WHAT IS GREATER THAN SACRIFICE?

Our sources relate a number of religious and moral functions that they—in conformity with prophetic teaching—consider "greater than sacrifices." This designation is frequently the result of the sages taking a biblical phrase too literally. On the whole the subjects are identical with the ones discussed so far.

God is understood as saying: "The loving kindness that you show to each other is dearer to me than all the sacrifices that Solomon offered before me."[30] And to David: "Justice and righteousness that you effect are dearer to me than the sacrifices" (of Solomon).[31] The reason given for this preference of justice and righteousness over sacrifices is that sacrifices were operative only so long as the Temple stood, but righteousness and justice are valid both at the time of the Temple and after its destruction. Or: Sacrifices atone only for sins committed unwittingly, but righteousness and justice atone for sins of all categories. Or: Sacrifices are operative only in this world, but righteousness and justice are operative both in this world and in the world-to-come.[32] This homily is based on Proverbs 21:3: "To do righteousness and justice is more acceptable to the Lord than sacrifice." The same biblical verse is paraphrased in the Talmud: "Greater is the practice of righteousness than all the sacrifices."[33] "The iniquity of the house of Eli shall not be expiated with sacrifice nor offering for ever" (I Sam. 3:14). The talmudic sages comment on this: "It will not be expiated 'with sacrifice nor offering' but it will be expiated with the words of the Torah," or, in a different version, "with the practice of loving kindness."[34] Thus the study of Torah and loving kindness rank higher than sacrifice.

The motif of study of Torah as being more valuable than sacrifices appears in a variant text contrasting David's occupation with Torah with the burnt offerings of Solomon.[35] "The study of Torah is superior to the building of the Temple."[36] Similarly, "Greater is prayer than sacrifices."[37] "Chastisements are precious for they bring atonement comparable to sacrifices," which midrashic statement is corrected to read: "Even more, for sacrifices come out of man's property, but chastisements fall upon a man's body."[38]

Unless my research was incomplete, the following motifs seem not to have been considered as equivalent to sacrifices (or even of superior value to sacrifices): Faith itself, the honor due to parents and one's teacher, observance of the Sabbaths and holidays, procreation, visiting the sick, burying the dead, comforting mourners, messianic expectation, and dwelling in the holy land.

Be this as it may, the source material presented so far is, I hope, sufficient to show one of the main trends in post-biblical, rabbinic, Judaism. Sacrifices ceased to exist, but they were replaced by various acts of religious and moral life, acts that brought atonement and were means of coming near to God. The officiating priest was replaced by the pious man, continually building an altar, not of stone, and offering up his gifts—acts of life. Deeds of loving kindness thus cease to be purely interhuman functions, and are more than divine commands to be obeyed; they are sacrifices, in the sense of permitting man to approach God.

Two transformations were achieved. On the one hand: Sacrifice in the old sense was taken out of the circumscribed realm of cult and ritual and was given a broader implication. Now, study, prayer, charity, and loving kindness, etc., are accounted as sacrifice, or better, they are new forms of sacrifice. On the other hand: Religious and ethical actions were given a higher status by being elevated to a position of idealized sacrifice.

REEVALUATION OF BIBLICAL SACRIFICES

The process of finding substitutes for sacrifices after the cessation of the Temple cult did not lead to a diminution of the value of these defunct sacrifices. In the religious imagination of post-biblical Israel they continued to exist, and, understandably, they gained in significance. Thus we have a large number of talmudic-midrashic texts that, some more clearly than others, testify to the persistent quest for inner meanings inherent in biblical sacrifices, beyond the functions assigned to them in the relevant biblical texts, such as atonement or reparation.

Adam is put into the Garden of Eden "to till it and to keep it" (Gen. 2:15). This is read by the Midrash as an allusion to sacrifices, i.e., the first man is given the command to offer sacrifices.[39] The ladder in Jacob's dream (Gen. 28:12) symbolizes the stairway to the altar; "set upon the earth"—the altar; "and the top of it reached to heaven"—the sacrifices, the odor of which ascended to heaven; "and behold the angels of God"—the High Priests.[40] Jacob is shown in his dream the Temple built, sacrifices being offered and the priests officiating.[41] King David, who was not permitted to build the Temple, is comforted by God: "Even though you will die, never shall your name be removed from my house; at every sacrifice there will be sung psalms of yours."[42] Temple and sacrifice are eternal.

Among the birds only doves and pigeons, persecuted creatures, are eligible as sacrifices; so "man should always strive to be rather of the persecuted rather than of the persecutors."[43] Sacrifical regulations contain moral teachings.

The cultic term "sacrifice of peace-offerings" (Lev. 7:11) is understood to imply that it "makes peace between the altar, the priests and Israel . . . it brings peace to all."[44] Not only peace-offerings make peace; "the service in the Temple in general brings blessing to inhabitants of the world and the rains come down in season."[45] The rebuilding of Zion and Jerusalem is due to the merit of burnt offerings,[46] It is the merit of Torah and the merit of sacrifices that saves a person from punishment in hell.[47] "Precious are sacrifices; through them God fulfills the will of the righteous."[48] "God yearns for the priestly blessing"—this notion is read into, or read out of, Numbers 6:27.[49] "Priests are compared to angels," indeed, "they are called angels."[50] From among the various types of sacrifices God is said to hold dearest the offerings of thanksgiving.[51]

Sacrifices are one of thirteen biblical items that are connected with the name of God.[52] The divine name used with reference to sacrifices is the tetragrammaton itself, rather than any of the substitutes.[53]

Meaning, beyond what is indicated in the biblical accounts, is expressed in the following talmudic text: On the seven days of the Feast of Booths seventy offerings were made in behalf of the seventy heathen nations. When the heathens destroyed the Temple they destroyed the atonement that was made for them.[54]

Traditionally, Jewish children start their biblical study with Leviticus (and not with Genesis). The reason is given in the Midrash: "Because young children are pure, and the sacrifices are pure; so let the pure come and engage in the study of the pure."[55]

MICHAEL THE GREAT PRINCE

The high position in the religious imagination of the talmudic sages accorded to the biblical Temple, priesthood, sacrifices, is particularly evident in traditions about Michael "the great Prince" (Daniel 12:1), Israel's guardian angel. In the fourth of the seven heavens, called Zebul (Habitation), "there is located the heavenly Jerusalem and the Temple and the altar are built, and Michael stands and offers up thereon a sacrifice."[56] In one of the late midrashic versions Michael is called high priest and the nature of his sacrifice is specified: "What does he sacrifice? The souls of the righteous."[57] Here the Hebrew term for sacrifice, *korban*, may still have—or have again—the root-meaning of being near, bringing near. Michael lets the souls of the righteous be brought near to God.

A different nuance is stressed in yet another version of this midrash. We hear of the heavenly tabernacle (that corresponds to the tabernacle on earth) wherein the mystical "youth" (*naar*) "whose name is Metatron (a secret name of Michael) sacrifices the souls of the righteous to atone for Israel in the days of their exile."[58] Here the motif of "bringing near" is combined with the motif of atonement.

The man who "wrestled with Jacob until the breaking of the day" (Genesis 32:25) is considered by the Midrash to be the angel Michael. When he touched Jacob's hollow of the thigh and wounded him (verse 26), God is said to have said to Michael: "Did you do right in making my priest a cripple?" Michael replied: "But am not I your priest?" Whereupon God replied: "You are my priest in heaven, he is my priest on earth."[59]

Michael's heavenly priesthood occupied the minds of periods beyond the one we are dealing with. What concerns us is the importance accorded by the Midrash to the symbolism of sacrifice and sanctuary. In the messianic time the above-noted heavenly altar will descend from on high to Jerusalem.[60]

When the generation of those who returned from the Babylonian Exile began to build the Second Temple, "How did they know where to build the altar? said Rabbi Eleazar: 'They beheld the altar all built, and Michael, the great Prince, stood by it, sacrificing on it.' "[61]

THE SACRIFICE OF ABRAHAM

Among the biblical accounts of sacrifices there is one of outstanding significance in talmudic and later Hebrew literature: the sacrifice that Abraham was ready to make in offering up his son Isaac. This act becomes a major motif and symbol. The text (Genesis 22) is the scriptural reading on the second day of the New Year's festival. The merit of this act endures throughout time. Abraham is understood as saying: "May God regard this as though I slaughtered my son before Thee."[62]

Both Abraham and Jacob spent time outside the land of Israel; Isaac, however, was not given permission to leave the land. Why? God said to Isaac: "You are an unblemished burnt offering, which, if it goes on the other side of the Veil [in the sanctuary], becomes disqualified."[63]

The ram's horn that is sounded as a part of the New Year's liturgy represents symbolically the horn of the ram offered by Abraham in place of Isaac. The reason for this solemn ritual: "So that I [God] may remember in your behalf the sacrifice of Isaac son of Abraham."[64]

SUMMARY AND CONCLUSION

Post-biblical Judaism was greatly concerned with the orderly functioning of religious life; here standards tended to become more and more fixed and binding. However, in matters of thought, faith, religious reflection we find greater informality, variety of opinion and of idiom.

Thus, in the history of post-biblical Jewish views on sacrifice, we encounter side by side both a glorification of biblical sacrifices *and* attempts to broaden the scope and meaning of sacrifice in order to include many religious and moral actions. And, although enough equivalents were found, the hope persisted that the sacrificial worship would one day be reinstituted.

The change from the biblical concept of sacrifice to the post-biblical Judaic views is a remarkable chapter in the history of religion. Whatever the ancient sacrifices meant—expiation, gift, communion with God— there was enough in the institution and/or the performance of the cult to arouse prophetic criticism. "I am full of the burnt-offerings of rams, and the fat of beasts; I delight not in the blood of bullocks, or of lambs, or of he-goats" (Isaiah 1:11). And the psalmist echoed this criticism: "Sacrifice and meal-offering Thou hast no delight in" (Psalm 40:7). "For thou delightest not in sacrifice . . . thou hast no pleasure in burnt-offering (*ibid.*, 51:18). The fourth book of the Sybilline Oracles rejects "all temples and altars, . . . befouled with constant blood of living things and sacrifices of four-footed beasts" (27–30).

The Essenes expressed their piety not in the sacrifice of animals but rather in sanctification of mind;[65] they claimed to possess holier means of purification than sacrifices.[66]

The biblical prophets, wisdom teachers, psalmists, and some sectarians prepared the way for a radical transformation of the concept of sacrifice in the direction of a religion of the heart, of a life of loving kindness, with the goal of reaching "a nearness of God" (Psalm 73:28). This process culminated in the talmudic-midrashic attitude to sacrifice.

NOTES

1. I Abot de R. Nathan IV.
2. Menahot 110a.
3. Taanit 27b.
4. E.g., Pesikta de R. Kahana 165b.
5. Exod. Rabbah XXXVIII, 4.
6. Yer. Berakhot 8d.
7. *Ibid.*, 15a.
8. Lev. Rabbah VII, 2.
9. Yer. Makkot 31d.
10. Berakhot 17a.
11. Erubin 18b.
12. Sukkah 45a.
13. Sifra, Ahare VIII.
14. Yer. Berakhot 8b.
15. Sifra, Emor X.
16. Berakhot 10b.

17. Ketubot 105b.
18. Berakhot 6b.
19. Sanhedrin 43b.
20. Pirke R. Eliezer IX.
21. *Ibid.*, XXVIII.
22. Berakhot 55a.
23. Mekhilta, Yethro II.
24. Berakhot 60a.
25. Moed Katan 28a.
26. Sotah 14a.
27. Lev. Rabbah XX, 7.
28. Sifre, Shelah 112.
29. Gittin 57b, and parallels.
30. Yalkut Shimoni Hosea 522.
31. Yer. Berakhot 4b.
32. Deut. Rabbah V, 3.
33. Sukkah 49b.
34. Yebamot 105a.
35. Shabbat 30a.
36. Megillah 16b.
37. Berakhot 32b.
38. Midrash Psalms XCIV, 2.
39. Genesis Rabbah XVI, 5.
40. *Ibid.*, LXVIII, 12.
41. Sifre, Korah 119.
42. Pesikta Rabbati II, 4.
43. Baba Kamma 93a.
44. Tanhuma Tzav IV.
45. I Abot de R. Nathan IV.
46. Tanhuma Tzav XIV.
47. Yalkut Shimoni Pekude 415.
48. Midrash Tadshe 14.
49. Sotah 38b.
50. Numbers Rabbah XVI, 1.
51. Tanhuma Tzav VII.
52. Tanhuma Yelamdenu Behaalotekha XI.
53. Sifre, Pinhas 143.
54. Sukkah 55b.
55. Leviticus Rabbah VII, 3.
56. Hagigah 12b, Menahot 110a, Zebahim 62a.
57. Midrash Aseret ha-Dibrot I.
58. Numbers Rabbah XII, 15. I am grateful to Professor A. Altmann for a discussion of this motif.
59. Yalkut Shimoni Vayishlah 132.
60. Midrash Aseret ha-Dibrot.
61. Zebahim 62a.
62. Midrash Aggadah, ed. S. Buber, p. 53.

63. Genesis Rabbah LXIV, 3.
64. Rosh ha-Shanah 16a.
65. Philo, Probus XII.
66. Josephus, Antiquities XVIII, 1, 5.

5

HILLEL THE ELDER
IN THE LIGHT OF THE
DEAD SEA SCROLLS

It is still too early to evaluate the significance of the Dead Sea sectarian writings in relation to contemporaneous normative Judaism. As matters stand today, we have learned of some of the sect's teachings, its institutions, and its organizational detail. But as long as the history of the sectarian movement cannot be written, consideration of its relationships to the official Judaism of the period must remain fragmentary and provisional.[1] One point, however, can be made with a degree of certainty: Official Judaism must have noted the exodus from Jerusalem and must have taken a stand on the phenomenon; the zeal and determination of those who joined the New Covenant invited response, or criticism. Such reasoning becomes particularly pertinent if we keep in mind that much of the thought, discipline, and way of life of the Early Hasidim (fourth and third centuries) found its way into the Essene order and related groups.[2] This hypothesis granted, it can be said that primarily those among the leading teachers in Jerusalem, whose concern was the cultivation of the ancient *hesed*[2a] ideal paid attention to the Dead Sea brotherhood.

The talmudic tradition was aware of a critical *caesura* in the Judaism of the early Maccabean period. Joseph, son of Joezer, described as "the *hasid* (pious) in the priesthood,"[3] is considered the last in the long chain of teachers "who studied the Torah like Moses our master; from his time on, the Torah was no longer studied in this manner."[4] Also: "The scholars up to the days of Joseph, son of Joezer, were all without reproach; from his time on that could not longer be said."[5] The crisis to which the Talmudic tradition alludes appears to have been overcome with the appearance of Hillel the Elder, who about 30 B.C. became the leading teacher in Jerusalem. In summing up his life's work, the rabbinic sources compare Hillel to Ezra the Scribe: both were active in periods when "the Torah was forgotten from Israel" and had to be reestablished.[6]

The question arises whether Hillel, and his school, in attempting to reform religious life in Jerusalem, took into account the fact that not insignificant groups of Judeans had withdrawn into the wilderness "to prepare the way for the Lord." A brief analysis of some of Hillel's teachings, and the sayings and deeds attributed to him and his school, may lead us in the direction of an answer, however preliminary.

Hesed. If the connection between Early Hasidism and the sect is accepted, then the not too frequent, but emphatically stressed, term *hesed,* and the references to the love for *hesed (ahavat hesed,* Mic. 6:8) in the Manual of Discipline[7] are no coincidence. It can be argued that the sectarians tried to realize the *hesed* ideal which was focal in the early hasidic communities. The social regulations and communal character of sectarian life make such a supposition probable, even though the sect did not call themselves *hasidim.*[8] However, the Manual speaks of "a covenant of *hesed*" into which those dedicated to following God's laws shall be brought.[9]

An examination of the terminology employed by the talmudic accounts of Hillel's teachings and his mode of life, and of the selection of scriptural verses applied to him, reveals a preference for the terms *hasid* and *hesed.*

" 'A man of mercy *(ish hesed)* benefits himself'[10]—this refers to Hillel the Elder."[11] Referring to his soul, Hillel said: "I am going to do kindness *(hesed)* to the guest in the house."[12] In discussing the issue of the Day of Judgment, the School of Hillel pointed to the divine attribute of mercy *(hesed).*[13] A leading saying of Hillel's on the importance of learning reads: "An ignorant man cannot be a *hasid.*"[14] His reason for teaching "every man" is that even "the sinners, when drawn to the study of Torah, became parents of righteous men, *hasidim,* and worthy people."[15] When Hillel died, his disciples enumerated the master's three characteristics: "the *hasid,* the humble man, the disciple of Ezra."[16] Johanan, son of Zakkai, whom tradition regards to be Hillel's chief pupil, took as his motto, after the destruction of the Temple, Hosea's: "I desire mercy *(hesed)* and not sacrifice."[17]

In addition to direct references to the *hesed* motif there are stories of Hillel's life which illustrate his hasidic tendency. Returning from a journey he heard cries in the vicinity of his house, but he trusted in the Lord that the cries did not come from his house.[18] In contradistinction to the School of Shammai, which from the first day of the week prepared for the coming Sabbath, the School of Hillel was wont to quote: "Blessed be the Lord, day by day he beareth our burden."[19] And whereas the School of Shammai, for the sake of truth, described a bride "as she is," Hillel's disciples described every bride as "beautiful and graceful" and led the Sages to the formulation: "A man's heart should always be outgoing in dealing with people."[20]

During the "ceremony of Water-Drawing," held on the second day of the Festival of Booths, in which Hasidim and "men of good works" actively participated, Hillel is said to have admonished the easygoing and encouraged the contrite by saying that the people's joyful homage is dearer to the Lord than the praises of myriads of angels.[21] To his wife, who gave to a poor man a meal prepared in honor of a guest, he said approvingly: "All you have done was done for the name of Heaven."[22] A once wealthy, but now impoverished, man he provided with a horse and a servant; one day, when he could find no servant, he himself "ran before the poor man for three miles."[23] A hasidic trait is manifest also in Hillel's word on humility: "My humiliation is my exaltation; my exaltation is my humiliation."[24]

It is possible that Hillel, who was naturally inclined toward Hasidism, consciously cultivated the hasidic form of religion in Jerusalem in order to counterbalance the sect's emphasis on *ahavat hesed.* He might even have felt that the sectarians, by their extreme exclusiveness, deviated from the doctrines of Early Hasidism, and that only through contact with the simple people in Jerusalem could the ancient teachings be restored.

Study. The Manual of Discipline speaks of the rule that in a congregation of ten men "there shall not cease to be a man who expounds the Torah (*doresh*[24a] *ba-torah*) day and night, continually. . . ."[25] In addition, the community is to spend a third of the night in reading the Book, expounding the Law, and worshiping together.[26] "The way of the Lord"[27] to be cleared in the wilderness is interpreted to mean "the study of the Torah (*midrash ha-torah*) as He commanded through Moses, to do according to all that has been revealed throughout time and as the prophets revealed by his Holy Spirit."[28] Those "who choose the way" will be guided with knowledge and instructed in the secrets of marvel and truth so that they may walk perfectly each with his fellow in all that was revealed for them.[29] All those "who have offered themselves for his truth" have the duty to "purify their mind (or knowledge) in (or by) the truth of the laws of God."[30] This tenet makes study a pursuit of central importance for the Covenanter. The people of Israel are called, among other things, "the people of the saints of the covenant, taught in the law."[31]

The Teacher of Righteousness is looked upon as the man whom God has given a heart "to interpret all the words of His servants, the prophets"[32]; God had made known to him "all the secrets (or mysteries) of the words of the prophets."[33] The sectarian group is led by an "expounder (or searcher) of the Torah" (*doresh ha-torah*), who is called the Star and to whom Num. 24:17 is applied.

We knew already from Philo that the Essenes devoted much time and attention to study, especially on the Sabbath: "In synagogues . . . they sit decorously . . . with attentive ears; then one takes the books and reads aloud and another of especial proficiency comes forward and expounds what is not understood."[34] A "holy congregation" is to Philo a group "in which it is ever the practice to hold meetings and discussions about virtue"[35] as documented by the Torah. The study of the Torah should not be a mere application of the ear, but an understanding with the mind.[36]

It is true that there was a long tradition of study in postexilic Judaism.[37] But, with some notable exceptions, this endeavor, as far as the Law is concerned, was cultivated by the priests and directed mainly toward a mastery of established traditions; if held in ever present readiness, these could be applied to any given situation. Although the traditions were ultimately based on *midrashim,* the chief concern of the schools was the correct preservation of the teachings, and their value lay in their practical application.

In the sectarian writings, however, we find (besides interest in the pragmatic side of scriptural exegesis) an emphasis on study for its own sake, on nonpractical, pure study, on study that approaches the character of worship.

It is this type of learning that found its way back to the Jerusalem schools through the activity of Hillel. Through Hillel the study of the Torah became an issue of great religious significance. It became a prerequisite of piety (*hasidut*).[38] It was understood as leading to life: "The more Torah, the more life . . . he who has gained knowledge of the Torah, has gained life in the world-to-come."[39] Study, therefore, was not to be postponed: "Say not: 'When I shall have leisure I shall study'; perhaps you will not have leisure."[40] Stagnation was impermissible: "He who does not increase (his knowledge) causes it to decrease."[41] The process of study had to be continual. Asked to explain the difference between the expressions "the righteous" and "he that serveth God" and their antithesis "the wicked" and "he that serveth him not" in Mal. 3:18, Hillel interpreted both "he that serveth him and he that serveth him not" as referring to people who were perfectly "righteous" in their actions; "he that serveth him not," however, was the man who had studied ("repeated his chapter a hundred times") but ceased to do so; only he who studied without cessation was the one "that serveth God."[42]

Long before Hillel there were students who received the teachings from their masters; Ben Sira uses the terms *beth ha-midrash,* house of instruction, and *yeshibah,* which, later, came to mean an academy of learning. But only in connection with Hillel do our sources first speak of a true community of disciples[43]; of a master's use of everyday events to start a conversation of religious or ethical importance[44]; of attempts to spread knowledge of the Torah beyond the immediate circle of disciples,[45] as an expression of love for one's fellow men. Be the function of the *sons* of Aaron the priest what it may, the task of the *disciple* of Aaron is defined by Hillel as "loving peace, pursuing peace, loving one's fellow men, drawing them near to Torah."[46]

This development can be interpreted as introducing, or reintroducing, into the Jerusalem school an element which was being cultivated in the sectarian community. However, in defining the method of reading

Scriptures and determining the laws, Hillel differed from the usage of both traditional Pharisaism and the sect.

When, after an absence of years, Hillel reappeared in Jerusalem, he was invited, as a former student of Shemaiah and Abtalion, to quote a decision in a ritual question to which the Elders of Bathyra knew no answer. Instead of referring to a tradition, he employed hermeneutical rules (*middot*), logical principles of interpretation. This approach failed. "He sat and expounded (*darash*) to them the whole day long but they did not accept" his teachings. Finally, Hillel added: "I have received this tradition from Shemaiah and Abtalion." That authority was accepted.[47]

This talmudic report shows that Hillel's stress on *midrash* was a decisive one. It has been pointed out that only in Hillel's time did study become increasingly methodical, and the logical categories by which the Torah was to be expounded broadened.[48] The *midrash* method, with its constant reference to the text itself, resulted in the elimination of any authority which resisted rational examination; knowledge of the meaning of the scriptural word was no longer confined to the man to whom, as to the Teacher of Righteousness, God revealed the mysteries. It resulted, furthermore, in the restriction of the power of tradition as sole authority in the law.

Hillel's School in which rabbinic modes replaced older Pharisaism, combined the theoretical, logical reading of Scripture with a worship-like, inherently religious, "learning." The *midrash* cultivation of the sect seems accepted; in the method of *midrash*, however, Hillel differed from the sect.

The Poor. The Essenes are known to us as "despisers of riches."[49] The biblical term "the poor of the flock" is applied to members of the sect, "they that give heed unto Him."[50] Love of riches is a feature of the "men of the Pit."[51] A fragment of a commentary to Ps. 37 refers to the sectarians as "the community of the poor."[52] The laws of the sectarian group include one "to strengthen the hand of the poor and the needy."[53]

Hillel's personal regard for the poor is part of his hasidic outlook on life. What interests us more is his concern with the status of the poor in the official Judean community and in Jerusalem. In his school, Hillel opposed the Shammai trend which, continuing an older Pharisaic tradition, wanted school admissions restricted to students who, besides being wise and modest, came from good families and were rich. Hillel maintained that "everybody should be taught,"[54] rich and poor.

In discussing religious usage, Hillel was spokesman for the poor, or, at any rate, for the less privileged group, of the Judean population, while the Shammai school represented the interests of the conservative well-to-do.[55] According to Hillel, the benedictions sequence at the home service on the eve of the Sabbath or of a festival should be based on the living conditions of the poor; the Shammai school set the order according to the pattern of the well-to-do.[56] The so-called New Year for fruit trees is, according to Hillel, observed half a month later than the date set down by the Shammai school[57]; Shammai's regulation was based on the experience of the rich, who had better fields and gardens, the fruits of which matured earlier than the fruits in the gardens of the poor; Hillel's later date was for the accommodation of the poor. A quantity of food sufficient for a single meal is required for a ritual (known as *Erub tabshilin*) performed on the eve of a festival which is followed by a Sabbath; the Shammai school required two courses, the minimum apparently, of a rich man's meal; the Hillel group ruled that one course was sufficient, because that was the customary meal of the poor.[58] Hillel accepted the benediction over bread as a blessing over the entire meal, for the bread was the main dish of the poor. The Shammai school, with the meal of the rich in mind, ruled differently.[59]

The actual care of the poor was an integral and undisputed part of the biblical tradition and needed no special emphasis. The adjustment of the minutiae of ritual life to the standards of the poor and the humble—due, no doubt, to a genuine internal development within Pharisaism— served, in Hillel's day, to counteract the sect's claim to being sole champion of the poor against the world of the rich.

The Intermediate Group. The polarity between the wicked, usually identified with the prosperous, and the righteous, usually detected among the poor and the humble, is not new in Judaism. However, in the period of Alexander Jannaeus, tension between the "sinners" and the "righteous" assumed extreme proportions. In sectarian thinking the world is to be understood in the light of an absolute dualism between good and evil. Against the vast realm dominated by sin stand the sons of the New Covenant, "the Elect of Grace." The Covenanter is obligated "to love everything that He has chosen, and to hate everything that He has rejected."[60] The Book of Enoch mirrors most forcefully the radical position of the "righteous" and their hope for the utter destruction of the sinners.[61]

It is against this background that a discussion on the Day of Judgment by the schools of Hillel and Shammai should be read.[62] Referring to the division in the Book of Daniel between those who "shall awake to everlasting life" and those doomed "to everlasting abhorrence,"[63] the schools assigned the "perfectly righteous" to the first group, the "perfectly wicked" to the second. However, they introduced the concept of an "intermediate group," people in whom good and evil are mixed and who, technically, are in an equilibrium. The strict Shammaiites insisted that such people would have to taste the fire of punishment (Gehenna) before being allowed to rise again, "for the Lord . . . bringeth down to the grave and bringeth up."[64] The lenient Hillelites maintained that the Lord who is "full of mercy *(hesed)* inclines the scales of judgment toward mercy"; i.e., there is no Gehenna for the "intermediates"; it was in their behalf that David said: "I was brought low and he saved me."[65]

It is obvious that in this discussion it is not the difference of opinion between the two schools that is of primary importance, but their postulation of the existence of an "intermediate group." This new doctrine reads like a response to the sharp juxtaposition of the righteous and the wicked in the Book of Enoch, the *Habakkuk Commentary* from Qumran, and other writings. Without denying the existence of the wholly wicked (who deserve their punishment), the schools of both Hillel and Shammai, in keeping with the *hesed* idea, restored the average man to his rightful place in the community and in theological thought. The term "intermediate," or "average," is used again in the Hillel texts in connection with his student body. Hillel designates as his successor not a member of the sixty outstanding disciples, but one from among the remaining twenty, whom he terms "average," or "intermediate."[66]

"For the better order of the world." The drive for the wilderness which motivated the sect is echoed in the Psalms of Solomon. The pious found that "there was not . . . one that wrought in the midst of Jerusalem mercy *(hesed)* and truth." Therefore, "they that loved the synagogues of the pious *(hasidim)* fled from them" and wandered in deserts "that their lives might be saved from harm."[67]

It was one of Hillel's principles not to separate from the community but to work within its framework. Our sources remember Hillel for his endeavors to improve the social conditions of the community and for initiating special legislative measures *(takkanot)* in its behalf ("for the better order *(tikkun)* of the world").[68] Adopting a Hellenistic institution, he introduced the *prosbul,* a ruling protecting the creditor against cancellation of a debt in the Sabbatical year and the borrower against possible resistance of the lender.[69] Another legal enactment concerned the sale of houses in a walled city; buyers of such houses used to circumvent the law of redemption by the original owner within a year[70] by absenting themselves around the time when that original owner was expected to make his bid. The ruling introduced by Hillel allowed the original owner to deposit the due amount in the court of law and thus obtain the right to renewed ownership.[71] We also hear of Hillel's effective opposition to certain Sages, whose inconsiderate ruling would have made bastards of some Alexandrians.[72] A legislation regarding usury was designed to prevent a lender from possible exploitation of a carelessly made arrangement at the time of the loan; precaution must be taken, Hillel ruled, that not even in minor transactions "they be found partakers in usury."[73] The School of Hillel, prompted by the Shammaiites, solved the awkward position of a man "who is half bondman and half freedman" by compelling the master to set him free and turn the remaining obligation into a bond of indebtedness.[74] The motivation for this law is, again, given as "for the better order *(tikkun)* of the world."

Thus—in a period in which many felt that Judean society was doomed and the only possible life would be to follow the orders[75] of "the exiles of the desert"[76]—Hillel's tendency seems to have been the correction of existing deficiencies, prevention of misuse of existing laws, restoration of the original meaning of the statutes, and work for a better functioning society.

Proselytes. The Damascus Document counts the proselyte *(ger)* among the groups of which the community is composed.[77] The duty of helping the poor and the needy is extended to the *ger,* which may refer to the stranger.[78] The Manual of Discipline does not mention the proselyte as a part of the community. Millar Burrows holds that the term *ger* in the Damascus Document may possibly refer only to probationary candidates for membership.[79] The spirit of exclusivism in the sects makes it improbable that the proselyte was considered a desirable addition to the community.

Hillel, on the other hand, is known as having had a friendly attitude toward proselytes. Our texts, which mingle facts with legend and stress primarily Hillel's forbearance as against Shammai's sternness, nevertheless reveal a pronounced interest in keeping the doors open for the Gentile. Hillel is said to have accepted a heathen who agreed to conversion only if taught "the whole Torah while standing on one foot," and another who originally refused to accept the Oral Law as valid.[80] Hillel even admitted a candidate who immodestly aspired to the office of high priest.[81] A later story refers to the two sons of the latter proselyte as "Hillel's proselytes."[82]

In all the instances mentioned, Shammai, representing a more conservative trend within Pharisaism, is said to have instantly rejected the prospective converts.[83] Even though Hillel's position is not unique in Pharisaic tradition, it acquires special significance in a period in which the Dead Sea sect considered an exclusive attitude necessary for the proper observance of Torah.

Messianism. Expectation of the coming of a Messiah, of the end of days, the tribulation to precede the end, of life in the world of light—all these have an important place in the sectarians' thinking. The Covenanters were to play a decisive role in the final drama: "Into the hand of his elect will God give the judgment of all the peoples and by their chastisement all the sinners of his nation will be punished."[84]

In the Hillel texts there is no reference to the messianic idea. There is mention of retributive justice on earth[85] and an affirmation of the life in the world-to-come, a portion of which is to be gained by the study of Torah.[86] The silence on messianism in a period in which it was a burning issue cannot be adequately explained by the paucity of our sources. It can be assumed that, in concentrating on learning, on *hesed*, on the reconstruction of the Pharisaic community, Hillel counteracted the challenge of eschatological thought. As quite indirect evidence, the fate of Jonathan, son of Uzziel, Hillel's distinguished disciple, may be cited. Jonathan, whom the sources made also heir to the prophetic tradition of Haggai, Zechariah, and Malachi, is said to have undertaken an Aramaic translation *(Targum)* of the prophetic books. A Voice reprimanded him for having "revealed God's secrets to mankind." He defended his work as being done "that dissension may not increase in Israel." When, continuing his labors, he came to the Book of Daniel, with its allusions to the messianic end, the Voice issued again and said: "No more!"[87] In this legendary report in which much is questionable, an antimessianic tendency in the Hillel circle seems at least indicated.

Contacts. Provided the preceding points are sufficient to suggest that Hillel had knowledge of the sectarian development, the question comes to mind whether he may have had direct contact with the Covenanters. Our sources speak of a Menahem who preceded Shammai as Hillel's associate. A difference of opinion persisted for generations on the question whether the customary laying of hands on the head of the sacrifice may, or may not, be performed on a festival (to which, with one exception, the same prohibition of work applies as to the Sabbath); only "Hillel and Menahem did not differ."[88] Then, however, "Menahem left his office and Shammai took his place."[89] Among the answers to the question "Whither did he go?" it is recorded that "he went over from one principle to another"[90]; that is, as some scholars interpret it, he left the Pharisees and joined the Essenes.[91] It is indeed possible that our Menahem is identical with Menahem the Essene who predicted a great future to young Herod and whom Herod rewarded by honoring all the Essenes.[92] A personal contact between Hillel and a representative of a sectarian group, or even a community, is not out of the question.

There may have been a period in Hillel's life spent in preparation for his Jerusalem activities. The gap between the time he spent in the School of Shemaiah and Abtalion[93] and his appearance before the Elders of Bathyra[94] has been explained by an assumption that he had gone back to his native Babylonia. More probable—yet by no means certain—would be to suggest that he studied the religious situation wherever he could best observe it. A legendary description of his learning suggests the widest possible range of observation and interest.[95] A Baraitha lets Hillel distinguish between "a generation to which the Torah is dear" when it is appropriate to spread its knowledge and a period in which it is more advisable only to gather.[96] At an enigmatic gathering of the Sages in the upper chamber of one Gurya's house in Jericho, a heavenly voice issued proclaiming that there was among those assembled "one who would be worthy of the holy spirit but his generation is not worthy of it." Thereupon all eyes were fixed upon Hillel the Elder.[97]

These statements, however vague, may reflect Hillel's situation before he returned to Jerusalem to start his work in "re-establishing the forgotten Torah." An early rabbinic source sees Hillel's activity as beginning "one hundred years before the destruction of the Temple,"[98] i.e., at 30 B.C., which roughly coincides with the earthquake in the spring of 31 B.C.,[99] a significant event for Judea proper and apparently also for the Dead Sea community.[100] It is difficult to decide whether this is more than a coincidence.

Summary. There are indications that in his teachings and activities Hillel the Elder took notice, among other religious and social issues of his time, of some doctrines and institutions current in the sectarian movement. Such reference may be found in his concept of learning, in his application of the *hesed* principle, and in his special regard for the poor. Shammai, in contradistinction to Hillel, represented, on the whole, the established traditions. Hillel's emphasis of an "intermediate group" may have been an attempt to counteract the sectarian dualism of good and evil. Hillelite institutions "for the better order" of society may, among other considerations, have been motivated by desire to counterbalance the sectarian drive to the desert.

Hillel's friendly attitude toward proselytes can be read in the context of his nonexclusivist concept of Torah and the community of Israel. The absence of the messianic motif in Hillel's thought may be due to an awareness of the perils dormant in an eschatological world outlook; the place of messianism is taken by the concept of the life in the world to come.

It is therefore possible that, in addition to other factors, Hillel—while adopting some of the sect's teachings, especially those it preserved as heirs to pre-Maccabean Early Hasidism—attempted to reform Pharisaic Judaism as an answer to the challenge of the sectarian movement. Here emerges classical, rabbinic, Judaism.

True, Hillel's activity can be interpreted against the background of the religious, social, and political conditions in Jerusalem proper and in the official centers of Judaism. Singly, every source reference can be understood as referring to conditions created by the Sadducean opposition, by the Jerusalem priesthood, by the Herodian rule, the older traditions, etc.

Such a procedure, however, would rest on the assumption that those concerned with Torah, and foremost among them Hillel the Elder, ignored the movement which created the sect and wrote off its members as heterodox extremists not worthy of consideration.

Yet, the approach I have chosen remains as a possibility. Were Hillel a mere cultivator of established traditions, it would be precarious, without explicit textual evidence, to presuppose his regard for conditions outside his immediate group. But Hillel was very early recognized as a second Ezra and many of his teachings and actions show a reformatory spirit. To such a man a wider view and a more general concern must be attributed. Then, however, a reading of the texts, as here attempted, suggests itself. Even so, no one point should be pressed; a revaluation of detail should be expected.

NOTES

1. On some significant parallels between the sectarian and rabbinic writings, see S. Lieberman, "Light on the Cave Scrolls from Rabbinic Sources," *Proceedings of the American Academy for Jewish Research*, 20 (1951), and "The Discipline in the So-Called Dead Sea Manual of Discipline," *Journ. of Bibl. Lit.*71 (1952).

2. See I. F. Baer, "The Historical Foundations of the Halacha," *Zion* 17 (1952); "The Ancient Hassidim in Philo's Writings and in Hebrew Tradition," *Zion* 18 (1953); *Israel among the Nations* (1955), all in Hebrew.

2a. This Hebrew word has many shades of meaning when translated into English: mercy, kindness, steadfast love, etc. Therefore it is used in its transliterated form in this essay. The adjective form is *hasid* (pl. *hasidim*) and often means "pious." [*Ed. note*]

3. Mishnah Hagigah II. 7.

4. Temurah 15b.

5. *Ibid*. Another report, referring to the martyrdom of the Sages under Alexander Jannaeus, says, "the world was desolate until Simeon, son of Shetah, came and restored the Torah to its former authority" (Kiddushin 66a).

6. Sukkah 20a; a third period of decline was said to have ended by Hiyya and his sons.

7. ii, 24; v. 4, 25; viii, 2; x, 26. See Brownlee's trans., Appendix B.

8. I. F. Baer pointed to a possible relationship of the name *essenoi* to *essenes*, the Artemis priests of Ephesus who took upon themselves "to live as Essenes (*esseneuein*) in purity and piety." "The Historical Foundations of the Halacha," *Zion* 17 (1952), pp. 43 f.

9. i, 7–8.

10. Prov. 11:17.

11. Lev. Rabbah XXXIV. 3.

12. *Ibid*.

13. Tosefta Sanhedrin XIII. 3; Rosh ha-Shanah 16b quoting Ex. 34:6, a verse rarely cited by the Tannaites.

14. Aboth II. 6.

15. Aboth de R. Nathan I, ch. III.

16. Yer. Nedarim 39b; Sanhedrin 11a.

17. Aboth de R. Nathan I, ch. IV.

18. Berakhoth 60a, quoting Ps. 112₇.

19. Betzah 16a, quoting Ps. 68:20.

20. Kethuboth 16 bf.

21. Mishnah Sukkah 53a; Yer. Sukkah 55b; Aboth de R. Nathan II, ch. XXVII.

22. Derekh Eretz VI.

23. Kethuboth 67b.

24. Lev. Rabbah I. 5. Cf. Mt. 23:12; Lk. 18:14.

24a. *Doresh* = he who expounds. *Darash* =he expounded. From the same stem comes the noun *midrash* = commentary. [Ed. note]

25. vi, 6–7.

26. vi, 8–9. Sir. 51:23, "Spend the night in my *beth ha-midrash*" cannot be understood literally.

27. Is. 40:3.

28. 1 QS viii, 14–16.

29. *Ibid.*, ix. 18–19.

30. *Ibid.*, i, 11–12.

31. 1 QM x, 10.

32. 1 QpHab ii, 8–9.

33. *Ibid.*, vii, 4–5.

34. *Probus* 80–82, in the translation by F. H. Colson. The motif of concentrated study and exposition, and "transmitting the knowledge of the laws from husband to wife, from father to his children, from master to his slave" as in Philo's idealistic sketch of the Mosaic constitution; *Hypothetica* 7, 13.

35. *Quod Deus Sit Immutabilis* 24.

36. *De Specialibus Legibus* 4, 26.

37. E.g., "Raise up many disciples," attributed to the men of the Great Assembly (Aboth I. 1); Abtalion's admonition to the wise (*ibid.* II).

38. Aboth II 6

39. *Ibid.*, 8. This is possibly the earliest reference to the connection between the pursuit of learning and man's part in the world-to-come. The term "gain life in the world-to-come," used by Hillel, also Aboth de R. Nathan II, ch. XXVI.

40. Aboth II. 5.

41. *Ibid.*, I. 13.

42. Hagigah 9b. Some scholars have doubted the identity of Hillel in this text with Hillel the Elder.

43. Hillel recognized among his students thirty, like Moses, worthy of prophecy, thirty, like Joshua, worthy of miracles, and twenty "average" men. Sukkah 28a.

44. E.g., Lev. Rabbah XXXIV. 3, on the duty to care for one's body "since man has been created in the divine image," and on the soul as a guest in the body.

45. Aboth de R. Nathan II, ch. XXVI.

46. Aboth I, 12.

47. Yer. Pesahim 33a.

48. L. Ginzberg, "The Significance of the Halachah for Jewish History," *On Jewish Law and Lore* (1955), p. 95; Ginzberg lets this development start with "the great expounders" Shemaiah and Abtalion.

49. Josephus, *Bell.* 2, 8, 3.

50. CD, vii, 20c. For the relationship between poverty and piety, see e.g., Ps. Sol. 10:7.

51. 1 QS ix, 21 f. See also 1 QpHab xii, 6 where the members are called "the poor ones" (*ebyonim*).

52. Fragment A, col. II.

53. CD vi, 21, and xiv, 14.

54. Aboth de R. Nathan I, ch. III.

55. L. Finkelstein, *The Pharisees,* applies to the two groups the terms "Plebeians" and "Patricians," respectively.

56. Mishnah Berakhoth VIII, 1. This and the following interpretations of the laws follow Ginzberg, *op. cit.,* pp. 104 ff.

57. Mishnah Rosh ha-Shanah I. 1.

58. Mishnah Betzah II. 1.

59. Mishnah Berakhoth VI. 5.

60. 1 QS i, 3–4.

61. E.g., 94:8, 10; 95:7; 96:1; 98:3, 10, 13; 99:10–16; 102:4; 103:3; 104:2.

62. Tosefta Sanhedrin XIII. 3; Rosh ha-Shanah 16b f.

63. Dan. 12:2.

64. 1 Sam. 2:6.

65. Ps. 116:6.

66. Sukkah 28a; Yer. Nedarim 39b.

67. Ps. Sol. 17:17ff.

68. Gittin 34b.

69. Mishnah Shebiith X. 3.

70. Lev. 25.

71. Mishnah Arakin IX. 5.

72. Baba Metzia 104a.

73. Mishnah Baba Metzia V. 9.

74. Mishnah 'Eduyot I. 13.

75. 1 QS uses the term *tikkun* (spelled with a *kaf*), viii, 13 and *passim.*

76. 1 QM i, 2.

77. CD xiv, 4, 6 (ed. Rabin, p. 69).

78. *Ibid.,* vi, 21 (ed. Rabin, p. 25).

79. *The Dead Sea Scrolls,* p. 263.

80. Shabbath 31a.

81. *Ibid.*

82. Aboth de R. Nathan I, ch. XV.

83. Hillel is said to have generally displayed a nonrestrictive attitude; he is pictured standing at the gate of Jerusalem, trying to convince "people" going out to work that they would do better to forsake their worldly interests and devote themselves to the Torah. Aboth de R. Nathan II, ch. XXVI.

84. I QpHab. v, 4–5.

85. Aboth II. 7.

86. *Ibid.,* 8; Aboth de R. Nathan II, ch. XXVI.

87. Megillah 3a.

88. Mishnah Hagigah II. 2

89. *Ibid.*

90. Yer. Hagigah 77d.

91. Ginzberg maintains that there was already a spiritual affinity between him and the Essenes even before he joined them; and that there was the Essene influence upon him that motivated his concurrence with Hillel's opinion regarding the sacrifice ritual, *op. cit.*, p. 101.

92. Josephus, *Ant.* 15, 10, 5.

93. Yoma 35b.

94. Yer. Pesahim 33a.

95. Soferim XVI. 9.

96. Berakhoth 63a.

97. Tosefta Sotah XIII. 3; Sotah 48a.

98. Shabbath 15a.

99. Josephus, *Ant.* 15, 5, 2.

100. C. T. Fritsch, "Herod the Great and the Qumran Community," *Journ. of Bibl. Lit.* 74 (1955), pp. 175 f.

6
FAITH AND ACTION

The relationship between the ideal and the real, the awareness of God (faith) and of the responsibility towards the world (action), concerns us both as historians of religion and, simply, as human beings living today. And just as one often wishes that modern man apply historical perspective to his thinking, so should one expect a theologian to be fully conscious of the needs of modern man.

In the modern age Judaism has often been presented as a religious community that considers faith to be a private affair of the Jew; its nature and scope are said not to be really relevant so long as right action directed to the needs of the day results. Practice, it is argued, is the essence, whereas one theory can easily be replaced by another. The ideological background of charity may be of historical interest; what matters is the exercise of charity.

This view may, in devious ways, be traced back to Moses Mendelssohn, the father of Jewish Enlightenment in the eighteenth century. In his *Jerusalem* (1783), Mendelssohn pleaded emphatically for a distinction between, on the one hand, eternally valid truths that are based on reason and are not given to man through some supernatural revelation and, on the other, laws and commandments which, in Judaism, are the contents of divine revelation. Thus, Mendelssohn opined, Judaism is not revealed faith but a revealed order of life, revealed legislation.

This theory seemed to confine Judaism to the realm of ritual functions, of ceremonials commemorating events of the past, of rules for individual and social behavior, while, at the same time, permitting the Jew to feel at one with the Christian in belonging to the "universal religion of humanity" which is grounded in reason. Mendelssohn pointed with pride to the fact that classical Judaism knew no articles of faith, that faith was never considered as binding religious convictions, theories, and principles. Only laws were so regarded.

It is essential to realize that Mendelssohn did not propound this view as an historically objective analysis of traditional Judaism. His theory of Judaism—based partly on Leibniz's division of truths into rationally arrived at eternal ones and historically conditioned temporary ones—was his critical reaction against both a state and a church which interfered with the freedom of belief and thought. He pleaded for a separation of church and state and for freedom of conscience in the institutions of religions. In this respect Judaism seemed to him to be a pioneering philosophy.

We shall not maintain that Mendelssohn's theory was accepted and followed by the succeeding generations. His definition underwent considerable modifications. However, what remained was fateful separation between religious teachings and religious action, or, in other words, between beliefs held by Jews and actions undertaken by them. Quite frequently the opinion was expressed that Judaism was a religion of the deed, visible and measurable, while Christianity, in its various forms, emphasized faith, inward orientation. Since a half-truth is intellectually more confusing than an outright distortion, the matter warrants closer analysis.

The Biblical prophets advocated a subtle relationship between the theoretical and the practical in religion, between the knowledge of the Lord and the exercise of justice in the reality of life. What is "knowledge of the Lord?" asks Jeremiah. It is to know "that I am the Lord who exercises mercy, justice, and righteousness in the earth, for in these things I delight" (*Jeremiah* 9:22 ff). Thus "knowledge of God"—this sublime term in religious thought—is understood to refer not to the divine essence, not to divine attributes, but to the divine concern with the world of man, a knowledge that must lead to man's following in these very ways of God. Later in his book, Jeremiah criticizes the king of Jerusalem and evokes the image of the king's father who "judged the cause of the poor and the needy," adding: "Is not this to know Me, saith the Lord" (*ibid.*, 22:16). In other words: Only merciful action in the world leads to the knowledge of God, and, in turn, such knowledge is to be manifested in merciful action. The two are interdependent and cannot be separated.

The Messianic king of the future is described by Isaiah as filled with "the spirit of knowledge and the fear of the Lord"; thus equipped, he will "with righteousness judge the poor and decide with equity for the meek of the land" (*Isaiah* 11:2–4). And men "shall not hurt nor destroy . . . for the earth shall be full of the knowledge of the Lord" (*ibid.*, 11:9). This knowledge cannot but inspire men to cast out wars, bloodshed and injustice; at the same time, such activity on behalf of fellow-man and society cannot but lead to the knowledge of what is higher than man.

In my view, it would be factually incorrect to see the essence of Biblical prophecy in its peculiarly intense and all absorbing God-experience, or solely in the actual, practical content of the prophets' speeches. Both belong together; the one is conditioned by the other.

How did post-Biblical Judaism, and especially the Talmudic literature, view the relationship between faith and works? Since all later developments in Jewish thought (prior to the Emancipation) refer back to the Talmud, examination of this material is of interest.

The first generations after the fall of Jerusalem in 70 C.E. formulated our problem as follows: "What is more important, study or action?"—a formulation in which "study," being a mode of worship, referred both to inner piety and to acquisition of knowledge. Rabbi Tarfon, who lived in Jerusalem before its fall and in Lydda thereafter, thought action to be more important. He stated that the divine glory (the *Shekhinah*) came to rest upon Israel only after they had "done work" (erecting the desert sanctuary.[1] Rabbi Akiba, leading sage of the Bar Kokhba generation, responded by pointing to study as the more important endeavor. The issue was discussed by the elders present and a decision reached to give preference to study—"because it leads to action."[2] By stressing this interrelationship, the elders avoided the danger that either of the two components, study or action, could be considered in isolation and as separable from the other.

But learning, knowledge, principles, faith had to be translated into practice; they were not allowed to outweigh practice. The opposite balance was advocated as the ideal. Hanina ben Dosa, a mystic known for his intense piety in that period, put it in these words: "He whose deeds exceed his wisdom, his wisdom shall endure; but he whose wisdom exceeds his deeds, his wisdom will not endure."[3] Another contemporary, Eleazar ben Azariah, compared the man whose deeds exceed his wisdom to "a tree whose branches are few but whose roots are many," so that "no wind can stir it from its place."[4] It is to be noted that, contrary to expectation, not wisdom and learning, not faith and theory, are here symbolized by the image of "roots" but deeds. They, the deeds, are the roots that secure the strength of the tree and its branches, i.e., beliefs, principles, faith, wisdom, learning.

This attitude to faith and works, theory and practice, was maintained by the following generations of scholars, both in Palestine and in Babylonia. The man who devoted himself to mere theory but ignored practice was not considered worthy of having been created. While the one who studied with the intention of supplementing his knowledge by action was worthy of the holy spirit.[5] Study was understood as a profoundly religious function, an act of faith. However, in the last-quoted statement the gift of the holy spirit is granted only if knowledge is consummated in action.

Unrealized study is sterile. It has been taught: "He who says that he is only concerned with the study of the Torah has no (reward even for the study of the) Torah; because only what is accomplished in action is also achieved in study; without action there is no achievement in study."[6] "He who busies himself solely with the study of the Torah is as if he had no God."[7]

Or, in another formulation: A man who has learning without the supplementary factor, active piety ("the fear of Heaven"), "is like a treasurer who has the inner keys but not the outer keys: how shall he enter?"[8] Similarly, using the image of the gate for learning and theory and the image of the court for piety and practice, one of the Talmudic masters proclaimed: "Woe to him who has no courtyard, yet makes a gate for it."[9] Both images imply that practice is the way to theory, that action leads to faith, and that self-sufficient theory is insufficient. Thus the Talmud arrives at this conclusion: "The goal of wisdom (*hokhmah*) is man's turning (to God) and good deeds," so that no man be found who "engages in all types of study and then strikes his father and mother, his teacher and one who is greater than he," for Scripture, in speaking of the "fear of the Lord," stresses doing and not learning (Psalm 111:10)[10].

In view of the sacred character of learning in Talmudic Judaism, this strong emphasis on works, action, fulfillment of the law as inseparable from study, as both basis and goal of study, appears to be polemical in character. In part, at least, it seems to be directed against the Paulinian doctrine of the contrast between "the law of works" and "the law of the faith," the justification by faith "without the works of the law," of the establishment of the law through faith (*Rom.* 3:27–31). Pointing to the example of Abraham (*Gen.* 15:6), Paul rejected the "justification by works." "To him that worketh not, yet believeth in him that justifieth the ungodly, his faith is reputed to justice . . ." (*Rom.* 4:5). "For as many as are of the works of the law, are under a curse" (*Gal.* 3:10). In answer, it may be suggested, the Talmudic masters who came in contact with the Paulinian theory felt the need to stress in the faith of Israel the essential character of works, good deeds, observance of the law. These teachings were accepted as basic, even in periods and places where the Paulinian criticism of the law and the value of works was not acute, or no longer acute.

However, it would be erroneous to assume that this accent in Judaism on the deed and on practice originated solely in polemic response to Christianity. This historical condition was only the occasion for a reformulation of the prophetic definition of the "knowledge of God," which, as we have seen, was intimately bound up with the exercise of justice.

The Talmudic view on the subject is best expressed in a reflection on *imitatio Dei*. "Be thou like Him," taught Abba Shaul in the generation after the Bar Kokhba rebellion. But how can this be done? "Just as He is gracious and merciful, so be thou gracious and merciful."[11] And the Deuteronomic command "to walk in all His ways" (*Deut.* 11:22) was defined as man's duty to emulate the actions of God: His loving concern, His justice with men, His kindness in all His doings.[12]

We are now in a position to answer the question: What is the meaning of human activity, of man's involvement in the various forms of ethical, social, and cultural work? What prompts man to action? According to classical Jewish teachings man, through his productive activity in the world, furthers the work of divine creation. God created the world, but it is man's responsibility to help in the continued process of creation. In so doing, man becomes "a participant with the Holy One, blessed be He, in the work of creation."[13]

In the case of the other two central concepts of faith, revelation and redemption, man is recipient; he may, and indeed must, prepare himself for both, but both revelation and redemption are *granted* to him; in creation, in the world's growth and development, man is active partner. The word of God that reaches man in revelation is to enable him to perform his constructive work in the world, whose purpose it is, step by step, to perfect and make ready the world for the Kingdom of God, i.e., for redemption. The work of man, his action in the world, is motivated, even justified, by his knowledge of the divine origin of the world and his faith in its God-given purpose. His action connects him with both. It is the medium through which Torah, faith, learning, rise above the level of theory, *theoria*, mere vision.

Medieval Jewish philosophers tended to cultivate the type of man whose mind is utterly absorbed by what they called "knowledge of God," a man who realizes that it is only his intellect that joins him to the divine source of intellect. Such life requires seclusion, retirement, and as limited association with others as possible. Moses Maimonides, the most influential Jewish thinker of the Middle Ages, considers the aim of religious life to be such a state of communication with God, "undisturbed by any other thing." Having reached intellectual perfection, a person's mind will be with God "even while speaking with others, or attending to his bodily wants . . . even while his body is in the society of men." In order to find Biblical support for his theory, he presented the patriarchs and Moses as men who were "exclusively filled with the knowledge and love of God" even when engaged in ruling others and fulfilling their tasks in the world. "Only their bodily limbs were at work, while their heart and mind never moved away from the name of God." Such freedom from worldly involvement and concentration on the exercise of the intellectual and rational faculties earn man the grant of divine providence and freedom from evil; "worldly matters" separate man from God and expose him to chance and evil.[14]

Here, meaningful action is restricted to prayer, reading of the Law, observance of the commandments, which are the means of "filling our mind with the precepts of God and freeing it from worldly business."[15] However, this withdrawn love of God is, in Maimonides' view, within reach of only a few individuals. Humanity at large lives in a different order. Like Greek and Moslem thinkers, Maimonides was aware of the need for a harmonious society and a well-established state, headed by a perfect ruler.[16] Plato's advice that the kings should be philosophers reappears in Maimonides; the scholar and the prophet (in a special Maimonidean sense) bear responsibility for adequate leadership in the state. The faith, knowledge and wisdom of the man of the spirit is to be translated into service and active concern for the fellow-man whose well-being depends on good government and a just society. Indeed, the very end (and climax) of the *Guide of the Perplexed* reaches back to the prophetic definition of the "knowledge of the Lord" as the knowledge that the Lord demands "mercy, justice and righteousness in the earth" (*Jer.* 9:23) and declares that intellectual perfection is to be expressed by, and translated into, moral action. Thus man will "imitate the ways of God."[17]

For the community of Israel, Maimonides composed a Code (*Mishneh Torah*), which comprises the entire life of the individual, the family, the nation, covering all its aspects—philosophical, religious, ritual, ethical, juridical, and institutional. This is a world of action, in contradistinction to his delineation of the world of the perfect and pure intellect. What motivates this action becomes explicit in the concluding chapters of the work, in which Maimonides describes the hoped-for future, "the days of the Messiah." He sees a world of nations at peace, and among these nations the restored kingdom of Israel; wars are no more, oppression has ceased, and famine has been conquered throughout the world, the necessities of life being readily available to all; it is a world filled with "the knowledge of the Lord."

Is the Messianic organization of humanity at peace man's ultimate hope? Maimonides' answer is in the negative. Ultimate happiness comes to man only in the immaterial post-historical (or meta-historical) world-to-come, for which the Messianic order of things is but a period of preparation.[18]

Maimonides' teachings are in many ways indicative of the mood of the Jewish Middle Ages. Life was lived between the two poles of faith and action. Whatever action was possible in a world that imposed severe limitations on groups such as the Jewish one did not permit the positing of a religious theory that would put much weight on human activity. Community institutions, it is true, were maintained with considerable care; social, ethical, and ritual laws called for active hands and minds. And even mystics adhered to the norms of a non-mystical society. But the intellectual, spiritual aspects of faith offered disproportionately more in scope and profundity than the realm of action. God's purpose seemed to be more adequately fulfilled in worship, in learning for its own sake, and in ever deeper intellectual knowledge of God.

This state of affairs accounts for the thinly veiled tension in Maimonides' work between the life of action, even political action, as realized in the Messianic era, and the pure life of faith as lived in the stillness of philosophic contemplation and fulfilled in the spiritual world-to-come.

The process of living in tension between the two poles of faith and action continued, with varying emphases, into the seventeenth and eighteenth centuries. There were extreme phenomena designed to break the tension. The Messianic movements, culminating in the outburst of Messianism that is associated with the name of Sabbatai Zevi in the seventeenth century, attempted to channel pent-up faith into revolutionary action and to bring about a radical change in the order of life, personal and national. On the other hand, the tradition of rabbinic learning produced the type of dedicated, selfless, ascetic scholar who found his bliss in the exploration of the laws and, ultimately, in the ever clearer understanding of the word of God as recorded in the Torah. The world mattered little; the rectification of its ills and, finally, its redemption would come in God's good time.

Between these two extremes we find a variety of types who attempted with greater or lesser success to co-ordinate faith and action. Our literature is a record of such attempts, some deeply sincere, others woefully artificial, still others again pathetically naive.

The entire scheme and its underlying tendencies called for an over-all change when Enlightenment set in in the eighteenth century and the slow process of civil and political emancipation in the nineteenth. It was in this situation that Moses Mendelssohn raised his still small, yet mighty, voice to which we referred at the outset of this paper. I hope our analysis of the classical Jewish heritage up to Mendelssohn enables us to realize both the extent of Mendelssohn's departure from tradition in separating faith from action and the historically conditioned need for such departure.

The men who accepted Mendelssohn's challenge, fighters for emancipation, advocates of social reforms in the Jewish community, pioneers of modern, especially historical, Jewish scholarship, were at the same time pioneers of a new Europe, spokesmen of a secular, liberal, progressive, democratic society, a commonwealth freed from the shackles of dogmatism and clericalism and dedicated to the pursuit of humanism and the good life which is common to all. This new European humanity existed, of course, more in the vision of a minority than in the reality of social and political life. But to the modern Jew this vision and a fraction, however small, of corresponding reality offered a frame of reference in which he could make the transition from the medieval to the modern world. He entered this new world as a man freed from the separating, isolating, divisive tendencies of classical Jewish religion and emphasizing instead its universalist, humanist elements. He believed that a similar liberalizing process was taking place in the Christian world. Consciously or unconsciously, he disregarded the fact that this new Europe was a Christian Europe, however liberalized Christianity had become. The Jew interpreted modern Europe and the modern Western world in general as a realm of action, of productive effort, as an era of growth and advancement in all fields of human interest. Religion was expected to affirm and to accentuate this effort at progress, rather than act as a force that relativized it, that pointed to a suprahuman, extra-historical frame of reference.

In rereading Jewish history the modern Jew, as best exemplified by the literary historian Leopold Zunz, tended to emphasize those periods in history during which Jews actively participated in the cultural, literary and scientific enterprises of the world at large, periods that could be interpreted as times of free intellectual intercourse and reciprocal influence. Zunz declared the religions concept of revelation to be a divisive factor; "rather do I see," he said, "everywhere only emanations of one and the same world spirit *(Weltgeist).*"[19] Abraham Geiger, leading liberal theologian, stressed the concept that Judaism had its roots not in the Middle Ages but in antiquity and that its religion has always represented activity, life, and knowledge, as opposed to "a brooding spirit and dark faith."[20] Heinrich Graetz, celebrated Jewish historian, maintained that the Jewish idea of God who reveals Himself finds its historic realization in an "adequate state constitution," so that "the God-idea is at the same time an idea of a state." Therefore, strictly speaking, Judaism is not a religion (that is, a system of beliefs) but rather the law of a state *(Staatsgesetz).*[21]

Thus everywhere in modern Judaism we find the accent on action, on realization of what was deemed beneficent for the commonweal, and emphasis on organized society, the state, and, in a larger sense, the historic world, which makes such participation of the Jew possible.

The tension between faith and action, between the ideal and the real, has been resolved by reducing faith to an inconsequential entity. Mendelssohn's definition of Judaism (whereby the term "revealed legislation" was interpreted to connote action sanctioned by religion) has indeed become the basis for modern Jewish life. To be sure, there is traditional Judaism that perpetuates the pre-Mendelssohnian trends; there is Franz Rosenzweig's call to return to the classical purity of faith; there is Martin Buber who demands that all deeds be done in the conscious presence of the divine Thou. With these and similar exceptions, we find ourselves in a situation where faith and action move more and more apart. A modern Jew readily understands the need for action, social, communal, and, in the sphere of religion, the need for organizational action. He understands, and he responds. But he does not seem to feel the need to go back to the foundations upon which the structure of action rests. Action is bound to the present and to the immediate, foreseeable, future. Faith is, in addition, both historical and visionary; it establishes a perspective by preserving the experience of the past and cultivating a trust in the future. Faith maintains that God is holy, and that "He shows Himself holy in righteousness" (*Isa.* 5:16); that man is but a creature, yet one created in the image of God. It is this perspective, this frame of reference for human action, that is being revoked by the separation of action from faith.

If Judaism is to remain a view of God, world, and man, then the fundamental concept of a relationship between faith and action, newly defined, would have to be revitalized; what Mendelssohn had separated would have to be reunited. And Judaism must remain a philosophy of life not merely for its own sake but for the sake of the world in which we live. The modern Jewish religious thinker is a member of the thinking religious community in the Western world, and its concerns are his. Our common concern is man's condition in a rapidly changing world. Advocates of both scientific and traditional culture, both technologists and humanists, are accountable for the type of man and the type of society that are in the process of formation. The "mutual incomprehension" of which C. P. Snow speaks will have to be overcome, together with the neutralism of the one side and the traditionalism of the other, if indeed we wish to preserve the freedom of the individual, a fair balance between the control of the elemental forces and the control of oneself, a balance between specialized research and the unity of knowledge. The alternative is not just an unfortunate tension in the Western world, but the growth of demonic powers and the prospect of self-destruction.

The increasing technicalization and mechanization of vast areas of life threaten the reduction of man to an insignificant, exchangeable, nameless, impersonal being, a cipher to be fed into computers. If faith has not merely an historical but also a current meaning, i.e., if we permit faith to be a challenge in our lives, then all the efforts of scientists and non-scientists, theologians and non-theologians, are needed to help safeguard the non-technical, non-mechanical, irreplaceable element in man: his personality. Man must free his action from being tied to the moment; a wider perspective is needed for meaningful work. Behind practical social action we ought to rediscover and redefine the image of man to whom this action is directed; behind practical organizational endeavor we ought to rediscover and redefine the image of the community for which this endeavor is intended. The image of man as created in the image of God and the image of the community whose members truly communicate with each other, these are not issues of action but of faith. While former generations had to be instructed to progress from faith to action, modern man must learn to translate action into the language of faith.

NOTES

1. I Abot de R. Nathan XI.
2. Kiddushin 40b.
3. Abot III, 12.
4. *Ibid.*, III, 22.
5. Lev. Rabbah XXXV, 6.
6. Yebamot 109b.
7. Abodah Zarah 17b.
8. Shabbat 31b.
9. *Ibid.*
10. Berakhot 17a.
11. Shabbat 133b.
12. Sifre, Ekev 49.
13. Shabbat 10a; Gen. Rabbah XLIII, 8.
14. Guide of the Perplexed III, 51.
15. *Ibid.*
16. *Ibid.*, II, 40.
17. *Ibid.*, III, 54.
18. Mishneh Torah, Hilkhot Melakhim XII, 4–5; Hilkhot Teshuvah VIII, 7–8, IX.
19. *Leopold Zunz—Jude, Deutscher, Europäer,* ed. N.N. Glatzer, Tübingen, 1964, p. 186.
20. A. Geiger, *Das Judentum und seine Geschichte,* Breslau, 1871, III, p 157ff.
21. H. Graetz, "Die Konstruktion der jüdischen Geschichte," *Zeitschrift fur die religiösen Interessen des Judentums,* III, 1846, pp. 15ff. English in *Ideas of Jewish History,* ed. Michael A. Meyer, New York, 1974, p. 224.

7

"KNOWEST THOU. . . ?" NOTES ON THE BOOK OF JOB

With chapter 31, Job concludes his challenge to God. "Here is my mark, let the Almighty answer me. . . . I will declare unto Him the number of my steps, as a prince I will enter His presence" (31:35, 37). In the course of his argument Job has spoken of "the terrors of God" that "set themselves in array" against him (6:4); he has pointed to God as the cause of evil ("While Thine eyes are upon me, I am gone," 7:8); and he has portrayed God as having set a watch over Job, as scaring him with dreams (7:12, 14). God is said to be the cause of destruction of innocent and wicked alike; it is He who handed over the earth into the hands of the wicked (9:22, 24); He oppresses and despises His creatures, and shines "upon the counsel of the wicked" (10:3). Even if man be righteous, he cannot lift up his head (10:15). God "shutteth up a man and there can be no opening"; He controls "the deceived and the deceiver" (12: 14, 16). He makes judges fools and the men of trust He deprives of speech (12: 17, 20). He hides his face and holds Job for His enemy; he puts Job's feet in the stocks and watches all his paths, so that "man wastes away like a rotten thing" (13:24, 27); He destroys the hope of man (14:19). In His wrath He has torn Job, hated him, gnashing at him with His teeth. He has cast him into the hands of the wicked and broken him asunder; He runs upon him like a warrior (16: 9, 11, 12). Job cries out, "Violence," but "there is no justice." God has kindled His wrath against Job and counted him "as one of His adversaries" (19: 7, 11). He has estranged Job from his kinsfolk and his friends, even from his servants (19:13 ff.). God's presence inspires terror and dread (23:15); He has deprived Job of his right (27:2); his cry receives no answer from God, who has "turned to be cruel" to him and who persecutes him with His mighty hand (30:20 f.). Towards the end of his argument Job speaks of the "destruction from God" that threatens him, and "by reason of His fear I could do nothing" (31:23).

In this argument, God and Job appear as antagonists. God exists and He has brought Job into being. But in the situation in which Job finds himself there is no breakthrough to this hostile, estranged divinity. The issue at stake does not seem to be Job's affliction; his personal calamity is but a part of a general picture: a world without order and justice, a society in which the wicked rule, unchallenged from above. The divine care and concern with man, posited and defended by Job's friends, is rejected by him as contrary to his experience. Though both parties live in the same world, he sees what they fail to see. The friends' judgment of events is rooted in the firm basis of tradition, of concepts established by religion as true, whereas Job speaks from a radically different background. This essay will attempt, however tentatively, to inquire into the background of Job's rebellious utterances, in which God and world appear in such sharp opposition to man and which express his utter isolation.

To find the clue to the motif behind Job's defiant stand we may do well to examine the key terms employed by the author in the presentation of his subject.

Elihu, introduced by the author (or the editor of the final version of the book) after Job had concluded his argument, appeals to "men of understanding" who will agree with him that "Job speaketh without knowledge" (34:35). He accuses Job of multiplying words "without knowledge" (35:16). He himself, Elihu, will fetch his knowledge from afar (or, with Tur Sinai, will carry his knowledge far away), while disobedient men "shall die without knowledge" (36:3, 12). God is great "beyond our knowledge" (36:26); His deeds in the realm of nature (in the description of which Elihu anticipates God's own revelation in chapters 38 *et seq.*) are great, but we cannot "know" (comprehend) them (37:5).[1] He bids Job consider the wondrous works of God "who is perfect in knowledge," taunting him twice with the question of whether he had knowledge in the field of nature (37: 15, 16), adding ironically: "Let us know what we shall say unto Him" (or, according to Tur Sinai, "unto it," *sc.* the dark clouds) (37:19). Elihu's speech concludes on the note that God rejects the "wise at heart" among men (37:24).

It seems, therefore, that it was the proud affirmation of knowledge on the part of Job that provoked the divine anger and became the barrier between creator and creature. A closer reading of Job's own speeches suggests that Job's claims were indeed based upon the assumed possession of knowledge, whereas the friends disputed his possession of it, holding that knowledge is with God, not with man.

In the first cycle of speeches, Bildad's resigned insight, "For we are but of yesterday, and know nothing" (8:9) while God is eternally just (8:3), is countered by Job: "I know that it is so,—how can man be just with God?" (9:2) Here the doubter and rebel gives an ironical twist to the pious man's faith; the former says what he does because he "knows."[2] And what is yet unknown to him, he demands to know: "Make me know why Thou dost contend with me" (10:2).[3] He reminds God of His creation and life-granting action, adding, proudly, "I know that this is with Thee" (10:13). Zophar tries to make Job aware of the "deep things" and the "purpose of the Almighty" which leave man impotent to "do" or to "know"; it is God who "knows" (11:7, 8, 10). Job counters: "Who knoweth not such things as these?" (12:3),[4] and "What ye know, do I know also" (13:2). But this equality of knowledge is but in appearance; it is only Job's knowledge that drives him "to reason with God" and to argue his ways before Him (13:3, 15). He is sure of his ways: "I know that I shall be justified" (13:18).

At the start of the second cycle of speeches, Eliphaz accuses Job of "windy knowledge" (15:2) and rejects the notion that Job possesses wisdom acquired in the secret council of God, a knowledge unattained by the friends (15:8 f.) Bildad adds a description of the downfall of the wicked: "This is the place of him that knoweth not God" (18:21). In answer, Job wishes his friends to "know" that God has wronged him (19:6). As for himself—"I know that my vindicator liveth" (19:25); Job's deepest hope, like his innocence and his notion of evil in the world, is a matter of knowledge.[5]

Zophar's conviction of just retribution is conveyed to Job as a matter of sound "knowledge" (20:4). Job rejects the dogma of the misfortunes of the wicked, pointing to the prosperity of those who "desire not the knowledge of God's ways" (21:14). The enigmatic verse, "Will any teach God knowledge" (21:22) is either Job's quotation of an argument of the friends who discuss his claim to knowledge (F. Hitzig, Tur Sinai) or it means: Can any man explain on behalf of God the injustice meted out to human kind, depicted in the following verses (B. Duhm, Ehrlich). In either case, the key word is *knowledge*.

In the third cycle of speeches Eliphaz unjustly attributes to Job, the knower, the notion that God does not know ("What doth God know?," 22:13; comp. *Ps.* 73:11). His friend's admonition to return to God evokes in Job the image of a God who conceals Himself, who eludes man: "Oh that I knew where I might find Him" (23:3); if he indeed would reach His presence, he "would know the words which He would answer me" (23:5). But though "He knoweth the way I take" (23:10), i.e. although He is aware of my innocence, He prevents those "that know Him" from seeing His days (24:1)—if it is exegetically possible to read chapter 24 as a continuation of 23.

Thus it appears that underlying the argument of the dialogue is the question of whether Job has knowledge of the ways of God—for only on the basis of such knowledge could he have uttered invective and made his passionate pleas—or whether such knowledge is not accessible to man, the latter being the position held by the friends.

The cycles of the discourses of Job and the friends are appropriately followed by the poem on wisdom (28). This chapter, which "contains no single *obvious* connection with the stage of the debate now reached,"[6] has been conceived by some interpreters to be a later addition to the book of *Job*. But if our suggestion of the knowledge-motif in the discourses is correct, the poem on wisdom, regardless of its literary origin, is in its right place. It refers both back to these discourses, which raise the problem of human knowledge, the forward, subtly presaging the answer announced in the speeches of Elihu and finally given by the voice from the whirlwind. Many are man's achievements in the material world, the poem declares. But as to "wisdom"—a term which to the author denotes not prudence, practical, or applied sagacity, but true wisdom, "knowledge"—"man knoweth not the price thereof" (28:13; Greek: *the way thereof*), only "God understandeth the way thereof, and he knoweth the place thereof" (28:23). Such wisdom remains with God; it is not communicated to man. Man's wisdom is no more than "the fear of the Lord—and to depart from evil" (28:28), traits that characterised Job in the happy days (1:1), before he had met with adversity and realised the unjust order in the world, and had rebelled in reliance on his own possession of "knowledge," and had thus encountered as his antagonist Him "who is perfect in knowledge" (37:16).

When the Lord appears to answer Job, the text again uses "knowledge" as a central motif. The divine speeches unfold the wonders of creation. However, the literary form chosen by the author is not that of an objective presentation, but a series of questions addressed to Job, disputing his ability to know and to act. Divine justice is not argued or interpreted; rather, man's access to knowledge is denied by implication. Apparently, then, this is what is at stake: it is the claim to knowledge that has been at the base of Job's rebellion.

The key word is placed at the very outset of the speeches: "Who is this that darkeneth counsel by words without knowledge?" (38:2). Continuing on the note of Elihu's concluding statement (37:24), Job is asked about the earth's foundation, if indeed he has "understanding," if he "knows" (38:4 f.). He is asked about the "recesses of the deep" "if thou knowest it all" (38:18). About light and darkness—"thou knowest, for thou wast then born" (38:21), a reproach reminiscent of 15:7 and 20:4. Pointing to the stars, God asks: "Knowest thou the ordinances of the heavens?" (38:33), and turning to the animal kingdom: "Knowest thou the time when the wild goats . . . bring forth? Does the hawk soar by thy wisdom?" (39:1, 2, 26). Man's inability to know is related to the limits set upon his ability to act (38:12, 16, 20, 22, 31–35, 39; 39:1 f., 9–12, 19 f., 27; 40:9, 25–32).

The issue of human knowledge *versus* divine knowledge is now settled. The fourfold[7] use of the key word in Job's answer to the Lord's speeches reveals the author's intention to have his hero realise that "knowledge" is the true issue between him and his God. By now, Job's knowledge is but an awareness of his own limitations. "I know that Thou canst do everything" (42:2). It is man who, "without knowledge," attempted to obscure the purpose of God (42:3) and who "uttered that . . . which he knew not" (42:4). Knowledge is with God; Job who, out of presumption, attributed to himself the possession of knowledge, can now but pray that God grant him knowledge: "I will ask Thee and do Thou make me know" (42:4)—thus turning God's taunting question (40:7) into a humble quest addressed to Him.

II

Some commentators have suggested that the book of *Job* contains allusions to the Adam story in *Genesis* or, possibly, in some ancient poetic version of the Pentateuch. *Job* 12:7–10 seems to refer to an ancient legend about Adam's conversation with the animals.[8] The expression "first man" in 15:7 is interpreted by some as a reference to the myth of a primeval man.[9] The phrase *ke-'adham* in 31:33 may mean "like (ordinary) men" or may allude to Adam's concealment of his transgression. Less probable is Tur Sinai's proposal to see in the conclusion of the poem on wisdom (28:28) a reference to Adam—plausible only in the context into which the commentator places the poem.[10]

Can it be maintained that, beyond these probable references, the author (or the final redactor) of the book of *Job* as a whole wished to allude to the story of Adam's daring appropriation of knowledge of good and evil, by which he antagonised divinity and incurred trouble and, finally, death? The parallels in both the story of Adam and the drama of Job point in that direction. Eve's prompting of Adam to disobey the divine command is paralleled by the suggestion of Job's wife that he "blaspheme God and die" (2:9). The serpent of *Gen.* 3 reappears as Satan in *Job*. The change in Job's fate once his afflictions evoked in him the ability to "know" evil around him, which in turn aggravated his misfortune, corresponds to the change in Adam's lot caused by his acquisition of "knowledge"; granting the obvious differences between the two stories, in both instances the loss of innocence, "knowledge," and estrangement from God are interrelated. Adam (and Eve) receive the announcement of God's wrath; Job experiences this wrath throughout the poem. "To dust thou shalt return" (*Gen.* 3:19) is paralleled by Job's reference to "dust and ashes" in his final confession (42:6). The motif of death in the Adam story recurs numerous times as a central element throughout Job's speeches, from the curse of the day of his birth (chapter 3) to his final cognition, "I know that Thou wilt bring me to death" (30:23). Commencing his answer to Job, God asks, "Where wast thou . . . ?" (38:2), echoing His question to Adam, "Where art thou" (*Gen.* 3:9). The panorama of the created world, spread out before Job's eyes, yet excluding man from the picture, corresponds to Adam's exclusion from the paradisiac world, originally created for his sake.

If these parallels and references are not merely coincidental, it may be surmised that the author of the book of *Job* (or its final redactor) wished his readers to notice the correspondence between the heroes of the two stories. In the internal history of the Bible, Adam, man, expelled from Paradise, is progressively recalled into the presence of the divine, in Noah, in Abraham, in Moses; and "the knowledge that is forbidden" and death-causing is reformed into a knowledge that is revealed, granted, and life-giving. As against this theory of man, the author of Job presented his hero as the man who remained "Adam," the being who by arrogating "knowledge" became fully man, and who upon that knowledge based his judgments, expectations, and claims. Like Adam, whose fate it was to undergo suffering as a consequence of knowledge, Job experiences the interdependence of the two factors up to the point when a divine revelation teaches him to see himself in the context of a wider, extra-human, universe, and to recognise the limits of his knowledge before God, who, in spite of Adam's deed, still remains the Lord of knowledge.

III

The medieval Jewish Bible-exegetes and religious thinkers interpreted the book of Job primarily as an argument about providence and God's concern with individual man, His goodness, and man's central position in the world.[11] However, among the other themes recognised by the interpreters as germane to the book, is the theme of knowledge. This is especially true of the conception formulated by Moses Maimonides (1135 1204), who discussed Job in his Guide III, 23–24. Maimonides finds it noteworthy that the text speaks of Job's ethical conduct but makes no mention of wisdom. "Had he been wise he would not have been in doubt about the cause of his suffering."[12] Only after "he had acquired a true knowledge of God" (yedi'ah 'amittith) did he realise that "there is true happiness in the knowledge of God" (yedi'ath ha-Shem), attainable by all "who know Him" (she-yeda'o), a condition that cannot be upset by earthly affliction.[13] Thus, according to Maimonides, the book of Job demonstrates man's progress from ignorance and the wrong type of knowledge ("imagining God's knowledge to be similar to ours"[14]) to the stage of knowing God, a knowledge which leads to the love of God.[15]

Man's limited knowledge is also an aspect of the Job interpretation by Joseph Kara (11th–12th century). Human understanding "is like nothing compared with His wisdom." Though God's ways are intended for the welfare of man, they are, nevertheless, beyond human comprehension. It is man's error to approach the problem of divine rule as if "he were God's partner in the work of creation."[16]

In his commentary on Job, Abraham ibn Ezra (1092–1167) singled out the recurrent phrase "knowest thou?" as the main point in the divine speeches and as the argument that brought about Job's submission and

helped him to overcome his rebellious self-pride (*gobhahh libbo*).[17] Similarly, Samuel ben Nissim Masnut of Aleppo (13th century), in his *Midrash Sefer 'Iyyobh Ma'ayan Gannim*, interpreted chapters 38 *seq.* as having
the aim of making Job "realise that he has no knowledge and that he is
unable to fathom the ways of God." He found peace only after "he has
been made to know what he has not known."[18] Bahya ben Asher ibn
Halawa (Spain, *d.* 1340) likewise traced Job's rebellious assertions back to
his lack of knowledge, maintaining at the same time that Elihu's observations are rooted in wisdom. In the end Job, in Bahya's view, realises that
he is unable to know the wondrous ways of God "unless He, in His
mercy, makes them known to him." Now, Job says, "I have attained to
prophecy and I know that You exist and know. . . ."[19]

Levi ben Gerson (Gersonides, 1288–1344), in his classical commentary
on *Job*, ascribes chapter 28 to Job. In so doing, he makes Job the spokesman for the high value of wisdom and for the notion that only God
"knows the complete essence of wisdom" —an understanding that Job
reaches only towards the end of the stormy disputes.[20] Somewhat
weaker is the argumentation of Joseph Albo (*ca.* 1380–*ca.* 1445), whose
Job arrives at the idea of God's supreme knowledge by way of logical
deduction from His power as it is displayed in creation.[21]

These references (and more could be added) indicate that the tradition
of medieval Jewish Bible-interpretation was aware, though not centrally,
of the motif of knowledge in the book of *Job*. The book was interpreted as
reaching its culmination in the demonstration of the perfect knowledge
that is God's, which, by more or less evident implication, serves as a
radical correction of man's ability to "know." Maimonides is alone in
using the concept of knowledge as the key to the interpretation of the
entire *Job* complex.

IV

Like the motif of knowledge, so the motif of the Adam-Job correspondence did not escape the attention of some readers of the book, Jewish,
Christian, and Moslem. The emphasis varies according to the observer's
religious tradition and theological tendency. Yet even an exposition that
points to a *contrast* between Adam and Job is of interest. What is significant is that the exploration of either of the stories has evoked a reference
to the other.

In the course of its multifarious discussion of the book of *Job*, the
Midrash in interpreting *Job* 9:35, makes Job argue that he has not fol-
lowed the example of Adam "who listened to the words of his wife."[22]
The Targum to *Job*, in its original version, saw in *Job* 28:7 an allusion to
Eve and the serpent, an observation that the later reviser eliminated from
his text.

In his *Expositions on the Book of Psalms,* St Augustine (354–430), refers to Satan who "took away everything" from Job but left him his wife. "Merciful do ye deem the devil, that he left him a wife? He knew through whom he had deceived Adam."[23] Similarly, St Chrysostom (*ca.* 344–407) interpreted the role of Job's wife as an accomplice of Satan, whom he quotes as saying: "For if even out of paradise I cast mankind by her means, much more shall I be able to trip him (Job) up on the dunghill."[24] The examples of Adam and Job serve Chrysostom as indication that Satan "both accuseth God to man and us to God."[25]

In a homily "on the power of man to resist the devil,"[26] Chrysostom compared the temptation of Adam, whom the devil "attacked by means of mere words," to the trial of Job, who was "attacked by means of deeds," i.e., by the calamities that befell him. Adam was deceived and conquered by a serpent; Job's tempter was a woman, his wife, who "was far more persuasive" than the serpent, and yet she did not prevail. The preacher exhorted his audience to avoid imitating Adam, whose indolence caused him many ills, and to "imitate the piety of Job" who emerged "the conqueror throughout": in the course of his dispute with the Deity Job overcame the notion that "the just God who had in every way been served by him, was at war with him." Similarly, in a homily "concerning the statues,"[27] Chrysostom compared Adam in paradise and Job on the dunghill; the former had provoked God and lost his paradisiac state, the latter had risen in piety and "all things reverted to him with greater glory than before." In another connection both Adam and Job appear as "enjoying great dignity and proclaimed by the God of all," and because of this honour are ready targets for Satan.[28]

In a Moslem version of the folktale of Job,[29] which goes back to Wahb (*d.* A.H. 110, = 728–9 C.E.) and Ka'b-el-ahbar (*d.* A.H. 32, = 652–3), Satan (*Iblis*) boasts about the power given him over Job's possessions and declares that only once before had he enjoyed such power, namely, when he expelled Adam from paradise.[30] When Job's trial was over, the angel Gabriel gave him a fruit from paradise and Allah clothed him in garments taken from paradise.[31] In the Moslem legend of Job, related in Tha'labi's *Book of the Stories of the Prophets,* and discussed by D. B. Macdonald, Satan is counselled to apply to Job the technique he used in enticing Adam.[32]

The *Zohar* reads *Job* 1:21 ("Naked came I out of my mother's womb, etc.") as a parallel to Adam's and Eve's "knowledge" of their nakedness (*Gen.* 3:7); the garments in which a man ascends to the other world are made out of "those days in which he acted virtuously and did not sin"; both Adam and Eve's and Job's "nakedness," therefore, refer to their sinful state.[33] Shemtob ben Joseph Falaquera (13th century), in his commentary on Maimonides' *Guide,* quotes the saying of Rabbi Simeon ben Laqish[34] who identifies Satan with the Evil Inclination and the Angel of

Death in this form: "Satan, the Evil Inclination and the tempter of Eve are all one."[35] Zerahiah ben Isaac ben She'alti'el of Barcelona (13th century), in his commentary on *Job*,[36] drew a parallel between the book of *Genesis* and the book of *Job*. Both fall into two parts. To the story of Adam, Eve, and the serpent corresponds to the story of Job and Satan; both stories are followed by a second part which deals with issues of faith, providence, understanding, and right behaviour. At the base of this observation is the talmudic notion that Moses was the author of both "his book and the book of *Job*"[37]; to Zerahiah, however, this notion suggested a deeper, thematic relationship between the two works. The above-mentioned Bahya ben Asher ibn Halawa also assumed that there was a correspondence between the book of *Job* and *Genesis*. Both books, he postulated, concern themselves with the creation of the world, with the issue of divine providence and retribution; and both the story of creation and the book of *Job* avoid the tetragrammaton and use instead the name *'elohim*, which denotes the quality of divine justice.[38]

The suggestion advanced in this article, that the author of the book of *Job* wished to turn the reader's attention to the motif of knowledge (human knowledge *versus* divine knowledge) is not founded upon the references to it in later literature; to an even lesser degree is the tentative note, that the book of *Job* alludes to the story of Adam, dependent on such references, significant as these are. Our reading of the *Job* text is based on a form-critical approach, or more specifically, on the guide provided by the text in its use of the key term *yada'*, *know*, and its synonyms. And if the assumption is permissible that the author of the book of *Job* was conscious of the story in *Gen.* 3, the implication is not that "knowledge" in both *Job* and *Gen.* 3 mean in reality one and the same thing; but merely that the author of *Job* read *Gen.* 3 in the light of his own problem, and that he intended to resolve in his book the issue raised by the Adam story. Adam, who was made to believe that, by eating from the Tree of Knowledge, he would become "as God, knowing good and evil," is here, in Job, led to the realisation that he does not know: that knowledge belongs to God. If at all correct, the reading of the book suggested here would help to underline its character as a work that is at once genuinely Hebraic and universally human.

NOTES

1. "That all men may know it" (37:7) is obscure.
2. On the problem of similarity between 9:2 and 4:17–19 (Eliphaz), see Tur Sinai's comments on both passages. See also F. Stier, *Das Buch Ijjob*, Munich, 1954, p. 282.
3. Cf. 13:23: "Make me know my transgression."
4. Cf. also 12:9.

5. But the Ugaritic phrase, "And I know that the powerful baal liveth" (C. H. Gordon, *Ugaritic Handbook*, Rome, 1947, p. 138) suggests that a liturgical formula underlies 19:25a.

6. S. R. Driver and G. B. Gray, *The Book of Job* (International Critical Commentary), Edinburgh, 1921, p. 233.

7. Or threefold, if we exclude 42:3a as a variant of 38:2.

8. Tur Sinai *ad loc.*

9. Cf. Driver and Gray, *op. cit.*, p. 134.

10. Tur Sinai *ad loc.*

11. On this subject, see the present writer's "The Book of Job and Its Interpreters" in *Studies and Texts* (ed. A. Altmann), vol. III, Philip W. Lown Institute of Advanced Judaic Studies, Brandeis University (Harvard University Press), 1966, p. 197f.

12. *Guide to the Perplexed*, III, 22.

13. *Ibid.*, III, 23.

14. *Ibid.*

15. *Ibid.*

16. Kara's *Job* commentary was published in the *Monatsschrift für Geschichte und Wissenschaft des Judentums* V–VII (1856–8). See comments on *Job* 37:18 and 24; 36:26 and 29.

17. Appendix to the commentary on *Job*, towards the end.

18. *Majan-Gannim, Commentar zu Job*, ed. by Solomon Buber, Berlin, 1889, comments on *Job* 38:1 and 42:2.

19. *Kad ha-Qemah*, ed. by Hayyim Breit, Lemberg, 1880, 74a and 76b.

20. Commentary on *Job, ad loc.*, especially "the Discourse as a Whole."

21. *'Iqqarim* IV, 10.

22. *Gen. Rabbah*, 19, 12, ed. Theodor-Albeck, p. 181, 1. 4 f., ed. Wilna f. 44a col. ii, quoted also by Samuel ben Nissim Masnut in his *Job* commentary, *Ma'ayan Gannim, ad loc.*

23. P. L. 36, 660; *A Select Library of the Nicene and Post-Nicene Fathers of the Christian Church*, vol. VIII, ed. by A. Cleveland Coxe, New York, 1888, p. 221, comment on *Ps.* 56.

24. *Homilies on First Corinthians, op. cit.*, vol. XII, ed. by T. W. Chambers, New York, 1889, p. 166. P.G.L. 61, 237, *supra*.

25. *Homilies on Second Corinthians, loc. cit.*, p. 284. P.G.L. 61, 402, *med*.

26. *A Select Library of the Nicene and Post-Nicene Fathers of the Christian Church*, vol. IX, New York, 1889, pp. 191–7, especially 194 (translated by T. P. Brandram). P.G.L., 49, 269, *supra*.

27. *Ibid.*, p. 369. P.G.L., 49, 66. Another juxtaposition of Adam and Job appears in the author's treatise "To Prove that No One Can Harm the Man Who Does Not Injure Others," *ibid.*, p. 273.

28. *Homilies on the Gospel of St Matthew, op. cit.*, vol. X, New York, 1888, p. 80. P.G.L., 57, 209, *supra*.

29. Naftali Apt, *Die Hiobserzählung in der arabischen Literatur*. Erster Teil. Kirchhain, N. L., 1913. University of Heidelberg Dissertation.

30. *Op. cit.*, p. 38; German tr., p. 15. Comp. also Duncan B. Macdonald, "The Original Form of the Legend of Job," *American Journal of Semitic Languages and Literatures*, XIV, 1898, p. 146.

31. Apt, *op. cit.*, p. 65; German tr., p. 28.

32. Macdonald, *op. cit.*, p. 157.

33. *Zohar* I, 224a, on *Gen.* 47:30. English tr., by H. Sperling & M. Simon (Soncino Press), ii, 1932, p. 319.

34. Babylonian Talmud, *Babha Bathra* 16a.

35. Commentary on the *Guide* III, 22.

36. Published by Israel Schwarz in his *Tikvath 'Enosh*, Berlin, 1868, pp. 167–293.

37. T. B. *Babha Bathra* 14b.

38. *Kad ha-Qemah*, ed. Hayyim Breit, Lemberg, 1880, 68a.

8

THE GOD OF ABRAHAM AND THE GOD OF JOB: SOME TALMUDIC-MIDRASHIC INTERPRETATIONS OF THE BOOK OF JOB

The person of Job and the biblical record fascinated the talmudic-midrashic sages and occasioned a relatively significant amount of interpretative and hermeneutic utterances. However, except for a small collection of their sayings in T. B. *Bava Bathra* 15a–16b, and a section in the Jerusalem Talmud (*Sotah* 20cd), the material on Job is scattered throughout the vast stretches of the Talmud and the various *midrashim*. A *midrash* to *Job*, no longer extant, is mentioned in *Yalqut Shim'oni* 897; and some fragments of a *midrash* to *Job* were published by S. A. Wertheimer. On the surface, no coherent picture of Job emerges from the available material; various strains of traditions are represented. But the nature and the quality of the talmudic-midrashic reflections on Job allow us to assume that there once existed a larger corpus of material, and that our extant *midrashim* are but fragments of a larger whole.

Among the subjects, issues, and motifs discussed are the days of Job's accusation and the meetings of the heavenly councils,[1] the duration of Job's ordeal,[2] his life span,[3] his period in history,[4] the authorship of the book of *Job* and its position in the Hagiographa.[5] There are references to the liturgical uses of the book,[6] to certain verses in it as bases for legal decisions,[7] and to a targumic version of *Job*.[8]

Job is viewed by some as one of the "seven prophets who prophesied to the heathen",[9] and as "a righteous heathen",[10] who however became involved in the plan to destroy Israel in Egypt.[11] A prominent motif is Job as a scapegoat, to keep Satan busy at the time of the exodus.[12] Job's friends, too, were, according to early opinion, heathen prophets,[13] who instructed Job in various doctrines;[14] they were rewarded for their visit to Job.[15] A proverb is quoted: "Either a friend like the friends of Job or death."[16] Elihu is given special consideration;[17] rather than criticise Job's views of God, he declared his praises, leaving it to Job to be more specific.[18] Yet, noting the debates recorded in the biblical text, it is said: "As long as Job stood against his friends and his friends against him, the atmosphere of stern divine justice prevailed. . . . As soon as they made peace with each other and Job prayed for his friends, God returned to him."[19] A lone view appears in the saying: "Job never existed at all, but is only a typical figure" (*mashal*),[20] or in the version of Simeon ben Laqish: "Job never was and will never exist."[21] A high point of exegesis is attained when the Community of Israel finds itself symbolically represented in the tragedy and triumph of the sufferer. "I am the man" (*Lam.* III: I) is paraphrased to mean: "I am Job." Israel addresses herself to God: "I am Job; what Thou hast brought upon Job Thou hast brought upon myself. . . ."[22] The prophet Jeremiah is made to compare the chastisement of Zion to that of Job, and to see in the consolation of Job a prefiguration of Jerusalem's consolation.[23]

I

Job the Saint in the Testament of Job

Beyond these issues of interpretation, the early commentators faced one substantive question: what was Job? A saint, as the first two chapters of the biblical book indicate ("The Lord gave, the Lord has taken away" I:21)? Or a rebel, as the central part of the book presents him ("Thou destroyest the hope of men" XIV:19)?

It seems that *originally* it was Job that perfectly pious man who took the centre of the stage, a view best represented by the so-called *Testament of Job.* This work was first published by Angelo Mai in 1833 based on a Greek manuscript in the Vatican Library.[24] Kaufmann Kohler reissued Mai's text with an English translation and notes.[25] Emil Schürer considered the Testament to be a Christian work,[26] while Friedrich Spitta[27] and Kohler[28] maintained its Jewish character.

In the *Testament,* Job undertakes to destroy the image of the Satan, worshipped by the people in his town. Satan, in turn, wages war against Job. He accepts the challenge: "I shall from love of God endure until death all that will come upon me and I shall not shrink back." All misfortunes fall upon Job, and his wife urges him to curse God and die. Job answers her: "Together with thee I will sustain the evil which thou seest, and let us endure the ruin of all that we have." Satan realises that he cannot defeat Job, and he yields to him. Job bids his children: "Now my children, do you also show a firm heart in all the evil that happens to you, for greater than all things is firmness of heart."

Three kings come to comfort Job. They are overwhelmed by his fall from his former estate, and cry and lament. Job says to them, "be silent and I will show you my throne and the glory of its splendour: my glory will be everlasting. The whole world will perish . . . but my throne is in the upper world. . . . Kings perish and rulers vanish, and their glory and pride is as the shadow in a looking-glass, but my kingdom lasts forever and ever. . . ." The kings become angry at Job's repudiation of earthly rule, but he continues to express his views: "My heart holds fast to heaven, because there is no trouble in heaven. . . . Who understands the depths of the Lord and of his wisdom to be able to accuse God of injustice?"

Zophar mentions that they had brought physicians to cure him, to which Job rejoins, "my cure and my restoration come from God, the maker of physicians". Elihu appears on the scene, "imbued with the spirit of Satan" and speaks hard words. But God manifests Himself to Job and declares that Elihu "had spoken not as a man, but as a wild beast". When the friends finally realise their error, God pardons them "through his servant Job", but He "did not deign to pardon Elihu" for "he has loved the beauty of the serpent."

An account of Job's restoration is missing in the extant *Testament*. The hero, restored to his former estate, addresses his children: "Do not forsake the Lord. Be charitable towards the poor; do not disregard the feeble. Take not unto yourselves wives from strangers." At the end there "came He who sitteth upon the great chariot and kissed Job. . . . He took the soul of Job and soared upward". He was buried and "received the name of the good who will remain renowned throughout all generations of the world". This concluding phrase of the *Testament* is identical with the final line in the Greek "colophon" to *Job*: 'It is written that he will rise up with those whom the Lord will reawaken."

It may be suggested that the *Testament of Job* was used in efforts to win converts to Judaism. But even if it was so used, it goes back to a genuine Jewish view of the hero. The proselytising tendency may have influenced the style and tenor of the work, but its main thesis—the unshakeable faith of Job, his saintliness in the face of adversity—is Jewish.

We possess a Hebrew text which was composed under the influence of the *Testament of Job* and its glorification of the hero.[29] This is an addendum to a MS of *'Avoth de-Rabbi Nathan* found in the Vatican Library.[30] In the text Job, whose trial lasted one year, is subjected by Satan to a series of misfortunes, but he remained loyal to God and "acknowledged and praised Him for all his attributes". "In that hour all the world came to realise that there was none like him in all the earth." At this point Satan is rebuked and cast down from heaven. God assembles all the angels and praises Job for his total devotion and sinlessness. The angels pray on behalf of Job and God has compassion on him, heals him, and blesses him twofold at the end of the twelve months.

This tradition of Job the humble, patient saint, true worshipper of God, was maintained by the early Christian church: by the Apostle James (*Epistle of James* v:11), by the First Epistle of Clement to the Corinthians (*I Clement* xvii) where Abraham, Job, and Moses are seen as examples of humility; later, the tradition appears in the Syrian version of the *Apocalypsis Pauli*,[31] in the *Apostolic Constitutions*,[32] and it is maintained by Bishop Theodore of Mopsuestia.[33] Moreover, Islamic sources and later traditions contain various versions and formulations of the biblical folk-tale of Job and its Jewish elaboration best preserved in the *Testament of Job.*

II

Job the Saint in Talmudic-Midrashic Tradition

In the talmudic *'aggada* and *midrash* the tradition of the blameless and saintly Job is continued. This continuation is significant, for it was strongly counteracted by an interpretative tendency of a different kind, shortly to be considered.

A *midrash* contained in the Wertheimer collection extols Job's charitable deeds. He admonishes a man in need: "Forever trust in the Lord's mercy and grace; He has not forsaken you and He never will." In his own suffering Job was upheld by the blessings of those to whom he had given aid and hope. Thus "the blessing of him who was about to perish came upon" him (XXIX:13).[34] The dominant motif is the hero's purity and saintliness.

Job is pictured as one of the four "who by themselves learned to know God", the others being Abraham, King Hezekiah, and the Messiah.[35] His name was one of the seven that was said to have been engraved on the seven branches of the golden candlestick in the Sanctuary.[36] Contact with him brought beneficence: "Whoever received even a small coin from Job, it became a blessing unto him."[37] Like Noah and Daniel, "he lived to see a new world".[38] "His prayer was pure."[39] He "made an hedge about his words" just as did Adam, Moses, the prophets, and God Himself.[40] He "sheltered his generation like a tree",[41] he "was generous with his money",[42] he helped widows and orphans,[43] he "fed and sustained others",[44] "his doors stood wide open", he "brought comfort to sufferers",[45] "to the blind and deaf and lame",[46] "and justice to the poor".[47]

Our texts go beyond such specific acts of ethical behaviour. Rava has Job try "to exculpate the whole world" by insisting that God has designed his creation as it is and thus had predetermined man's deeds. The charitable determinist had to be reminded that though God did create the evil inclination in man, He also created Torah as its antidote.[48] His submission is stressed: "If a poor man withstands the test without rebellion he receives a double portion in the world to come." An example of this tenet is Job, "who suffered in this world and whom God repaid in double measure".[49] The implication of this utterance is that Job suffered without rebelling. In a midrashic text Job affirms that since his happy past had not led him to forget God—as it is wellbeing that brings it about that man forgets God—how should chastisements—which normally make a person humble—provoke him to rebel? "Which teaches us that the righteous gladly accept the allocation of chastisements, as they happily accept the allocation of goodness."[50] The sages did not fail to note Job's defiance in the biblical text, but, so they teach us, "a man is not held responsible for what he says in distress",[51] i.e., Job's harsh utterances are outcries of anguish but not voices of rebellion.

What about Job's wife? In the biblical story she counsels Job to "curse God and die" (ii:9) and is reprimanded by him. In the midrashic tradition she is presented in a positive light. The biblical text lets Job use the plural when he says, "What! shall *we* receive good at the hand of God and shall *we* not receive evil?" (ii:10) — thus, says the *midrash*, Job includes her in his piety.[52] A *midrash* interprets the wife's advice "curse God and die" to mean: "Pray to God that you may die so that you leave the world as an upright and just man" before you face sin and suffering. "Indeed, it is unthinkable that he was a worthy person and his wife was not."[53]

In these characterisations of Job little attention is paid to his rebellious outbursts, or his blasphemous assertion that God terrorises man. Job appears as blameless, indeed a paragon and example of piety.

III

Job and Abraham: Two Figures of Saintliness

I now venture to suggest that the figure of the saintly, uncomplaining, humble Job existed side by side with the figure of Abraham, who was called friend and lover of God. Both Abraham and Job were known as men who turned against the idolatry of their fathers and who found the one God; both found in Satan an obstacle to their work; both had their doors open to strangers; both were singled out to undergo the test of perfect faith, and both were to serve as examples of piety for future generations in Israel, and equally for those who joined themselves to Israel's religion.

The glorification of Abraham seems older, and seems to have been the pattern for the glorification of Job.[54] But what matters is that at one time there existed the two great examples of faith: Job *and* Abraham. Abraham's greatness is extolled in the *Testament of Abraham*, the *apocryphon* preserved in two Greek versions first published by M. R. James,[55] and in the *Apocalypse of Abraham*, an *apocryphon* of which the original was probably Hebrew, preserved in old Slavonic and first issued in German by G. Nathanael Bonwetsch.[56]

In the *Testament of Abraham*, which concentrates on the death of Abraham, the hero is introduced as "the beloved friend of God, the friend of strangers"; he witnesses the trial of a soul whose sins and good

deeds were equal; his prayer rescues the soul.[57] Since he himself has
"never sinned, he shows no pity for robbers and adulterers, but learns
that God who made the world takes no delight in destroying any".[58]
Abraham intercedes for 7000 servants who had died and they are restored to life.[59] The hero, who has avoided death several times, finally
surrenders. He kisses the hand of death and dies. His soul adores God,
who orders that it be taken to Paradise to be with the righteous and the
holy.[60]

The *Apocalypse of Abraham,* written around the end of the first century
B.C.E., introduces the hero as an iconoclast and the proclaimer of the true
God. In the second part of the book, elaborating on *Gen.* xv, "God lifted
Abraham above the firmament" and told him "to look down upon the
world beneath". The *midrash,* too, contains this motif, but the *Apocalypse*
goes into greater detail. The holy man is being disturbed by Azazel; but
this "seducer of mankind" is told "leave this man alone, thou canst not
lead him astray, thou canst not tempt the righteous". Abraham ascends
to the seventh heaven, where he beholds the divine throne. He learns
that man has free will and may choose his way; he is told of the future
sufferings of the people of Israel and of the messianic redemption, the
end of the sufferings under the four empires, and the return of Israel to
their land.

Thus the *Testament of Abraham* and the *Apocalypse of Abraham* on the
one side, and the *Testament of Job* on the other, present us with two
ancient heroes, both iconoclasts; both sinless; both resisting Satan; the
one, Job, the man of faith, the other, Abraham, the patron of Israel. The
glorification of Abraham, which started very early in the popular literature, is continued into the classical *midrash* and beyond; there is no need
to elaborate on it here. As far as Job is concerned, we have seen that there
is a trend in midrashic literature that maintains the "Job the saint" motif.
However, the co-existence of the two paradigmatic heroes, Abraham and
Job, raised a problem in the course of time: are the two of equal stature, or
in one subordinate to the other? Furthermore, could the tradition that —
besides Moses — there existed *two* exemplary men of faith, maintain
itself for any length of time? And again, does the "Job the saint" view do
justice to the text of the biblical book of *Job?*

IV

Job Compared with Abraham

We consider first the comparison of Abraham with Job, or Job with
Abraham, according to the talmudic-midrashic tradition.

In the heavenly assembly Satan states that he has found none as
faithful as Abraham, whereupon the Lord asks him whether he has

considered Job "for there is none like him on the earth" (i:8).[61] Here Job appears as the Lord's favourite. Some sages held that in comparing Abraham with Job, the latter should be ranked higher than Abraham.[62] R. Yohanan of Tiberias is credited with the remark that of Abraham it is said that he feared God (*Gen.* xxii:12), whereas beyond the fear of God greater praise is accorded to Job in 1:8.[63] If so, how comes it that God allowed Satan to destroy Job? In commenting on the second scene in heaven, in which God again tells Satan of Job's piety, Yohanan says: "Were it not expressly stated in Scripture we would not dare to say it. [God, in permitting Job to be destroyed without cause, is] like a man who allows himself to be persuaded against his better judgment."[64] Thus the honour of Job is affirmed even against the judgement of his Creator.

According to others, Job and Abraham were of equal rank. If "love of God" is faith's highest rank, then both Abraham and Job are viewed as enjoying equal status. Just as the term "fearing of God" used in the *'Aqedah* story (*Gen.* xxii:12) implies Abraham's love of God, so "fearing God" in the opening sentence of *Job* indicates his love of God.[65] Joshua ben Hyrcanus interpreted xiii:15 ("Though He slay me yet will I wait for him") to imply that Job served God from love. But since the reading of *lo(')* is in doubt ("I will wait for Him" or "I will not wait"), there occurs the verse: "Till I die I will not put away my integrity from me" (xxvii:5) — "teaching that Job acted from love." The text ends on a dramatic note: "Who will take away the dust from thine eyes, Rabban Yohanan ben Zakkai — for all thy days thou didst expound that Job served the Holy One, blessed be He, from fear only [based on 1:1], and has not Joshua, thy disciple's disciple, now taught us that he acted from love?"[66]

That Abraham and Job were viewed as parallel figures is indicated by a *midrash* that makes Abraham plead with God after the *'aqedah* never to test him again. God accepts the plea, and admits that "sore afflictions and additional trials should have come upon Abraham, but they will not come back". The afflictions, the *midrash* adds, are "those very ones that came upon Job."[67]

Yet this discussion of fear *versus* love, and the attempt to prove that Job served God from love, has a distinctly polemical ring. Apparently, the idea of the two holy men, both of them lovers of God, was challenged by those sages within the midrashic realm who concentrated on the figure of Abraham and rejected the *Testament of Job* and related traditions. The reasons motivating this rejection may have been subtleties of religious thought, exegetical disquisition (attention to the context of the book of *Job* and its passages recording Job's rebellious outbursts), acceptance of the *Testament of Job* tradition by sectarian groups, or a combination of these reasons. Be this as it may, many midrashic utterances oppose the glorification of Job and suggest the lowering of his status below that of Abraham's, whilst entering upon a critical evaluation of Job's own stand.

Seemingly, the sages critical of Job felt that Abraham's name had to be protected against the competition of Job. Satan himself is pictured as safeguarding the memory of Abraham. "When Satan saw God inclined in favour of Job, he said: 'Far be it that God should forget the love of Abraham'."[68] Hence Satan's accusation (and, in a comparable situation, the provocation of Hannah by Peninah) had "a pious intention". Our source quaintly adds: "When 'Aha ben Jacob offered this exposition in Papunia, Satan came and kissed his feet"[69] in gratitude. Thus the notion suggests itself that there was something in the tradition of the saintly Job—a saint despite his rebelliousness—that exercised a considerable attraction. Hence, devotees of the aggadic Abraham—a figure of a more normal saintliness—feared that the memory of Job would obscure that of Abraham. These sages had therefore to focus attention on the negative features in the Job story, in an endeavour to enhance the glory of Abraham over against Job. Here a different picture of Job emerges.

V

Job Viewed as Inferior to Abraham; Job the Rebel

In the critical view of these sages, Job lagged behind Abraham and could not measure up to him. Whilst Job refrained from looking at other men's wives (xxxi:i), Abraham did not look even at his own.[70] In the Sodom story Abraham had but cautiously raised the question of divine justice, but it was Job who flatly asserted "it is all one, He destroyeth the innocent and the wicked" (ix:22).[71] Of the four men mentioned as having been smitten by God, Abraham is counted among those who reacted benignly; Job alone rebelled and asked, "What have I done unto Thee?" (cf. xiii: 23).[72] Abraham praying for Abimelech is considered as representing compassion, whereas Job, in his relation to his friends throughout the dialogue, is viewed as representing arrogance.[73] When the sufferings befell him Job turned to God, pointing to the hungry whom he had fed, the thirsty he gave to drink, the naked he had clothed (xxxi:17, 20). This challenge finds a midrashic answer: God says to Job, "thou hast not yet reached half the measure of Abraham."[74] Eliphaz is made to say to Job: "Are your deeds like those of Abraham? He was tried ten times and stood up to them all . . . while you faced one trial only."[75]

In the view of this group of sages, Job is reprimanded for having rebelled and having "cried out against the attribute of justice". "Doest thou perhaps consider thyself greater than [Adam and] Abraham [and others] who were tried and punished and who remained silent [thus demonstrating their love for God]?" Had Job overcome his resentment and not rebelled, he would have attained the level of Abraham and the other patriarchs, and to the phrase: "God of Abraham, Isaac, Jacob" would have been added "and the God of Job".[76] As matters stand, however, because Job had not acted in accordance with the ideal of the *Testament of Job,* his name could be linked neither with the name of God, nor with the name of the patriarch whose fear of the Lord was in reality love for Him. Thus in the *baraita* of the seven kinds of Pharisees, Job represents "the Pharisee from fear" while Abraham symbolises "the Pharisee from love, the most beloved of them all".[77]

It may be seen, therefore, that what this cluster of accounts proffers is not simple homiletics, but rather a polemic designed to counteract the view of the *Testament of Job* and related *'aggada,* and to remove the hero from close proximity with Abraham. The sages of the critical school realised that Job, far from being a saint, was indeed a rebel and a blasphemer. Listed by some as a heathen, he had originally been a pious man; but the chastisements that afflicted him disconcerted him, and "he begun to curse and to blaspheme".[78] Whereas the prophets of Israel approached God with supplications, Job, the most righteous among the Gentiles, could not but "address God with reproaches".[79] Rabbi Eliezer ben Hyrcanus points to ix:24, saying that Job "sought to turn the dish upside down", i.e., to challenge providence.[80] To Rava, Job's outburst implies that though "he did not sin with his lips" (ii:10) "he did indeed sin within the heart".[81] Rav condemned Job for "making himself the colleague of heaven" (with reference to vi:2) and for forgetting that a servant may not argue with his master.[82] The aggadist Levi quoted ix:22 as a frivolous utterance, for which Job deserved punishment.[83] When suffering came upon Job, he rose against God's stern justice: "O that I knew where I might find Him" (xxiii:3); this, in the biblical text, has no blasphemous connotation, but it is understood by the *midrash* as a word of protest.[84] The sequel, "that I might come even to his seat" is expanded by the *midrash* to be read as Job's attack on the Almighty: "If He is in the palace above, I shall come even to his seat; if He is in the palace below, I shall come even unto his seat."[85] Job, wishing to know where he "might find Him" is to be compared (says the Midrash) "to a palace soldier who, being drunk, kicked at [the door of] the prison *(fulakē)* and allowed prisoners to escape; he threw stones at the bust *(ikonin)* of the governor of the city, cursed the magistrate and said: 'Show me where the governor of this city lives, and I will teach him justice'."[86] Another midrashic text compares Job's pretension to have reached a deep understanding of God's works (quoting xxiii:5) to the claim of "a man with a slave's chain around the neck *(kollarion)* who would say: 'I know what is inside the king's residence *(praitorion)'*."[87]

In this group of *midrashim* Job is viewed not only as being less saintly than Abraham, less God-loving than the patriarch; he is plainly a rebel, arrogantly rising up against the divine rule, attempting to be "a colleague of heaven" rather than its servant. The style of the *midrash* is less

102   *Essays in Jewish Thought*

lofty than the style of the biblical dialogue, but the effect is the same: Job appears as an antagonist of God.

VI

The Toning Down of Job's Rebellion; the God of Job

There is, however, one significant difference between the biblical and the midrashic account both of Job's protest and of the divine attitude to the protester. The biblical dialogue lets Job rage and rave and storm. God remains silent up to the point in ch. xxxviii where, against all expectation, He deigns to answer "out of the whirlwind". And this "answer", though addressed to a human person, is the word of a distant all-powerful deity that asks man, "Do you know?" Can you act in the context of this vast, majestic creation?

In the midrashic texts the rebellious Job is made conscious of rather different attributes of the deity: it is the God of the psalmists and the talmudic sages who offers the answer. And with it, the rebellion of Job loses much of its fury. His defiance is toned down, softened, and its thrust weakened.

First, in the *midrash* God does not let Job wait whilst He remains icily silent up to the very end of the drama. The midrashic Job, who suspected that a whirlwind caused God to confuse *'Iyyov*, Job, and *'Oyev, enemy* (referring to ix:17) is given an immediate answer "out of the whirlwind": the *'aggada* has God go into great details, proving patiently from a number of natural phenomena that He does indeed exercise individual providence and care; there is no haphazardness or confusion in nature— "shall I then confuse *'Iyyov* and *'Oyev*?"[88] Job's protestations are answered as they occur, and the response comes from a caring, benevolent deity.

Thus, in the parable of the drunken palace soldier, the rebel is shown the governor in action, imposing sentence *(katadike)*, and is prompted to confess that he "was drunk and had little realised the power of the governor", and to ask to be forgiven.[89] Another midrashic text has God ask Job: "Job, why do you get up and say, 'O that I knew where I might find Him?" (xxiii:3). Whereupon God points to a certain feature of his work, in order to convince Job of the futility of his pursuit.[90] The rebellious outcries of the solitary sufferer in the biblical text are thus reduced in their scope by the rabbis. The sufferer is listened to, and his words find response. Rage is replaced by a series of arguments. God attempts to win Job's understanding.

One way of toning down the singular, astonishing rebelliousness of Job as it appears in the biblical book, and of reducing the harsh impact of its account, was to interpret Job's lot as having been predestined. What

happened to him was neither chance nor the result of God's enmity; all
was part of a meaningful, divinely ordained scheme. In the words of
Yohanan of Tiberias, Job was destined *(methuqqan)* to suffering, just as
Abraham was destined to lead the world to repentance, Adam to die,
Cain to banishment, Moses to redeem Israel.[91] Seen in the perspective of
other biblical events, equally predestined, Job's case loses its poignancy.

A similar effect of toning down the harshness of the book was achieved
by viewing Job under the aspect of the duration of his judgement.
According to Rabbi 'Aqiba this judgement lasted twelve months, just as
long as the judgement of the generation of the deluge, that of the Egyptians, the future judgement of Gog and Magog, and the judgement of the
wicked in Gehenna.[92] Again the focus of attention is shifted from Job's
singular case on to a secondary feature, here the duration of the trial,
wherein Job is not alone but one in a series of biblical examples. (There is
about a score of instances in which Job is listed as one in a line of biblical
episodes, but they do not add any new note to our argument.)

In place of the aura of estrangement between Job and God in the
biblical text of the dialogue, in the *'aggadah* God gently asks Job, "What
doest thou wish, poverty or suffering?" to which the hero replies: "Lord
of the universe, I am ready to accept all the troubles in the world, but not
poverty."[93] The biblical Job could not have been asked such a question,
nor could he have been given a choice between troubles.

The biblical text of the story presents us with a progression of horrors
that overwhelm the unsuspecting Job. On the other hand, the aggadist
Levi informs us that by punishing Job's animals first, then his servants,
then his children, and last of all Job himself, God revealed Himself as
"the Lord of Mercy, who does not inflict suffering on human beings
first."[94]

Job's protest against God oppressing and despising the work of His
hand (x:3) is a fierce indictment of divine rule. The *midrash* changes that.
According to Resh Laqish, Job's "inquiry" refers to a particular instance.
It refers to the embryo conceived in adultery, whose features God shapes
in the likeness of the adulterer. Job turns to the Creator: "Is it consistent
with thy dignity to stand between adulterer and adulteress?" God must
have taken offence at that, for He replies: "Job, you really owe Me an
apology", and explains to Job the correctness of his action in exposing
the adulterer.[95] Thus Job is seen not as protesting against general oppression and injustice, but as merely raising a problem which, with the
patient help of God, can be calmly resolved.

The biblical Job exclaims: "If my land cry out against me . . ."
(xxxi:38). In the *midrash*, God takes exception to Job's saying *"my* land",
whereupon Job informs Him that his phrase has been misunderstood.[96]
We find ourselves on a plane where a discourse can take place between
man and God, and where man is in no way obfuscated by his Maker's

word or action. The God who in the biblical book overwhelms Job by his power—and his judgement—becomes, in aggadic thinking, a God who "never [fully] displays his strength towards any of his creatures, for He . . . comes to each one according to his strength".[97] It is in this sense that the Lord's speeches from the whirlwind are expounded in the *midrash*. They are not read as what they are manifestly intended by the biblical text to be, or as a critique of Job's arrogance and presumption "to know"; they are interpreted as further documentation of God's goodness and concern for man. "At times the world and its fullness cannot contain his glory, yet at times He speaks to man from between the hairs of his head",[98] a play on the words *se'arah (whirlwind)* and *sa'arah (hair)*. The silent God of the book of *Job* is countered in Talmud and *midrash* by the God who speaks as soon as the human voice reaches Him. In another comment on the whirlwind the *midrash* points to the beneficence of the divine act of homoeopathic healing: Job was smitten with the whirlwind (ix:17) and was answered and healed by the whirlwind (xxxviii:1).[99]

The motif of healing and restoration is evident also in a midrashic interpretation of the opening phrase in God's speech: "Gird up thy loins like a cock [eagle]" (*ke-gever*, xxxviii:3). In the *midrash* these words lose their foreboding quality, and read (with reference to *Psalm* ciii:5): "Like an eagle which has lighted upon a dungheap and shakes itself clean, so Job shook himself free of suffering and was renewed."[100] This restoration does not occur, as it does in the biblical text, after Job's submission, but is implicit in the opening section of the divine address to him.

Job exclaims: "O that I knew where I might find Him" (xxiii:3). God answers, "Where wast thou when I laid the foundation of the earth" (xxxviii:4), which the sages interpret as the Lord's *immediate* reply, rendered in a spirit of patience and one of personal concern; there is no rebuke of human presumption (which the biblical text implies).[101]

Job's suffering leads him to search for God in every direction — forward, backward, on the left hand, on the right, but to no avail: "I cannot behold Him, . . . I cannot see Him" (xxiii:8 f.). Then God addresses Himself to him: "Why do you weary yourself? I am revealing Myself to you." The Lord was indeed speaking to him "forth of every hair on his head", with reference to xxxviii:1[102] Again, ch. xxiii — the midst of Job's fierce argument — and ch. xxxviii — the Lord's answer — are brought close together; the terse, cold, and strangely neutral tone of ch. xxxviii is transformed into an expression of divine concern for Job's anguish. The distant God of the book of *Job* becomes the God of the rest of the Bible and of the sages, a benevolent, responding, and caring deity.

The talmudic-midrashic concept of God required a radical reinterpretation of the God-idea in the Book of *Job*. The book had to be adapted to a theology of faith, concern, trust, and communication between God and man. Correspondingly, the change in the God-concept called for a change in the Job-concept. We have seen how "Job the saint" was replaced by "Job the rebel". Nevertheless, the rebelliousness of this Job had to be toned down, if he was to confront the benevolent, caring God. No longer was it possible to assume an overall antagonism between Job and his God. Instead protest, though retained, had to be greatly modified. This, then, becomes the authoritative picture of Job in the midrashic realm.

If my analysis and attempt at reconstruction are correct, the following main points emerge from the available material, part of which consists of fragments only.

1. There is the motif of Job the saint, based on the first two chapters of *Job* and represented mainly by the *Testament of Job* and related *'aggada*. This Job is a figure paralleling the picture of Abraham, as represented mainly by the *Testament of Abraham*, the *Apocalypse of Abraham* and related *'aggada*.

2. Objection is raised to a Job that would rival the piety of Abraham — an objection to a Job-picture that had started to play a role in the imagery of nascent Christian theology. Such objection, possibly combined with an attempt to do justice to the biblical book of *Job* as a whole, led to the depiction of Job as a rebel against the divine rule.

3. However, since the view of the God of Job as documented in the biblical text was unacceptable to the talmudic-midrashic sages and had to be modified to conform to the theological sensitivity of the age, the concept of Job the rebel likewise had to be modified. His rebelliousness becomes intermittent, preliminary, and subject to correction by a benevolent deity. He is not a sinner, but rather a human being in error, requiring guidance. Against this background it was Rabbi Yohanan who took Job as an example of a man who "goes through life with a good name and with a good name departs from this world".[103]

It was with these attitudes to the book of *Job* and to its hero that the Talmud and *midrash* laid the foundation for the mediaeval Jewish interpretation of the book.

NOTES

1. Targum to 1:6; "Jerusalem" Targum to I:6 and II: 1.
2. Mishnah, *'Eduyyoth* II:10; *Lamentations Rabbathi* I:40.
3. *Genesis Rabbah* I.XI:4; cf. also LVII:4.
4. T. J. *Sotah* 20C et seq.; *Genesis Rabbah* LVII:3; T. B. *Bava Bathra* 15a.
5. T. J. *Sotah* 20d; T. B. *Bava Bathra* 14b.
6. T. B. *Ta'anith* 30a; Mishnah, *Yoma* I:6.
7. *Leviticus Rabbah* VII:3; T. J. *Sotah* 20d; *Genesis Rabbah* LXIV:5.
8. T. B. *Shabbath* 115a.
9. T. B. *Bava Bathra* 15b.

10. T. J. *Sotah* 20d; cf. *Genesis Rabbah* LVII:3.
11. T. B. *Sotah* IIa; *Sanhedrin* 106a; *Exodus Rabbah* I:9.
12. *Exodus Rabbah* XXI:7.
13. T. B. *Bava Bathra* 15b.
14. *Ibid.* 16a; *Leviticus Rabbah* IV:6; *Tanhuma, Qedoshim,* 15.
15. *Eccles. Rabbathi* VII:4.
16. T. B. *Bava Bathra* 16b.
17. T. J. *Sotah* 20d; cf. T. B. *Bava Bathra* 15b.
18. *Exodus Rabbah* XXXIV: 1
19. *Pesiqta Rabbathi,* XXXVIII.
20. T. B. *Bava Bathra* 15a.
21. T. J. *Sotah* 20d; cf. *Genesis Rabbah* LVII:3.
22. *Lamentations Rabbathi* III:I; *Pesiqta de-R. Kahana,* XVI.
23. *Pesiqta Rabbathi* XXVI, end; *Pesiqta de-R. Kahana,* XVI.
24. *Scriptorum Veterum Nova Collectio,* Rome, VII, I. In 1897, M. R. JAMES issued an edition based on a Paris manuscript: *Apocrypha Anecdota* II (*Texts and Studies,* ed. by J. A. ROBINSON, vol. I). See most recently I. JACOBS, "Literary Motifs in The Testament of Job", JJS XXI, 1970, pp. I ff.
25. *Semitic Studies in Memory of Alexander Kohut,* Berlin, 1897. SEBASTIAN P. BROCK, *Testamentum Iobi,* edited with an introduction and apparatus criticus (Pseudepigrapha Veteris Testamenti Graece, vol. II), Leiden, 1967.
26. *Geschichte des jüdischen Volkes,* 4th ed., Leipzig, 1909, p. 406.
27. *Zur Geschichte und Literatur des Urchristentums,* III:2, Göttingen, 1907.
28. *Jewish Encyclopedia,* VII, pp. 200 ff.
29. See E. URBACH, *Hazal,* Jerusalem, 1969, p. 362, note 71.
30. Published as *Addendum II* to Version A of the work, ed. S. SCHECHTER, Vienna, 1887, p. 164.
31. *Apocalypses Apocryphae Mosis, Esdrae, Pauli, Johannis,* ed. C. TISCHENDORF, Leipzig, 1966, pp. 66 f.
32. *The Ante-Nicene Fathers,* ed. A. ROBERTS and J. DONALDSON, New York, 1913, VII, p. 482.
33. G. D. Mansi, *Sacrorum conciliorum nova et amplissima collectio,* Venice, 1759–1798, IX, pp. 223 ff. Cf. MIGNE, P.G.L., 66, 697.
34. *Leqet Midrashim* to *Job* XXIX:13.
35. *Numbers Rabbah* XIV:2.
36. *Targum Sheni* I.
37. T. B. *Pesahim* 112a.
38. *Tanhuma, Noah* 5.
39. *Exodus Rabbah* XII:4.
40. *Avoth de-R. Nathan,* A, ch. I.
41. T. B. *Bava Bathra* 15a.
42. *Ibid.,* 15b; *Megillah* 28a.
43. T. B. *Bava Bathra* 16a.
44. *Genesis Rabbah* XXXI:9.
45. *Genesis Rabbah* LXVI:I.
46. *Tanhuma,* ed. BUBER, *Wa-Yishlah* 8.
47. *Pesiqta Rabbathi* XXXII.
48. T. B. *Bava Bathra* 16a.

49. *Exodus Rabbah* xxxi:3.

50. *Leqet Midrashim* to *Job* ii:10.

51. Rava; T. B. *Bava Bathra* 16b.

52. 'Abba bar Kahana; *Genesis Rabbah* xix:21.

53. *Leqet Midrashim* to *Job* ii:9.

54. See Ephraim Urbach, *Hazal*, Jerusalem, 1969, pp. 361 f. I. Jacobs, *op. cit.* (p. 43, n. 1), pp. 4 ff.

55. In J. A. Robinson, *Texts and Studies*, vol. ii, Cambridge, 1893.

56. In *Studien zur Geschichte der Theologie und Kirche*, ed. G. N. Bonwetch and R. Seeberg, i, Leipzig, 1897. The old Slavonic version was published by N. Tichonrawow, Petersburg, 1863, and about the same time by J. Sreznewskij.

57. *Recension* A,§§ xii ff.

58. *Ibid.*, § x.

59. *Ibid.*, § xviii.

60. *Ibid.*, § xx.

61. T. B. *Bava Bathra* 15b.

62. It is interesting to note that while the Midrash compares Job with Abraham, the biblical work employs the Adam motif. See "Knowest Thou . . . ? Notes on the Book of Job" in the present volume.

63. T. B. *Bava Bathra* 15b.

64. *Ibid.* 16a.

65. R. Me'ir, T. B. *Sotah* 31a; Tos. *Sotah* vi, i. The *Tosefta* prefixes this text with a statement of Ben Pathuri referring to xxvii: 2: "A man does not make a vow by the life of the king unless he loves the king." Cf. also T. J. *Sotah* 20c.

66. Mishnah, *Sotah* v, 5.

67. *Numbers Rabbah* xvii:2.

68. Levi; T. B. *Bava Bathra* 16a.

69. *Ibid.*

70. Rav; *ibid.*, 16a.

71. Levi; *Genesis Rabbah* xlix:17.

72. *Midrash Psalms* xxvi: 2; in some manuscripts attributed to 'Aqiba; cf. *Semahoth* viii, 2.

73. *Pesiqta Rabbathi* xxxviii.

74. *'Avoth de-R. Nathan* A, ch, vii.

75. *Tanhuma*, ed. Buber, *Wa-Yishlah* 8.

76. *Pesiqta Rabbathi* xlvii.

77. T. J. *Berakhoth* 14b.

78. T. B. *Bava Bathra* 15b.

79. Yohanan; *Deut. Rabbah* ii:3, quoting *Job* xxiii:4.

80. T. B. *Bava Bathra* 16a; Joshua ben Hananiah, the other party to the discussion, stated that "Job was only referring to Satan". The same argument concerning ix:24 is taken up by the fourth century Babylonians, Rava and 'Avayye.

81. *Ibid. Genesis Rabbah* xix:2 in the name of R. 'Abba.

82. With reference to ix:33; T. B. *Bava Bathra* 16a.

83. *Genesis Rabbah* xlix:17.

84. *Exodus Rabbah* xxxi: 11; *Pesiqta Rabbathi* xlvii; *Pesiqta de-R. Kahana* xxix.

85. *Tanhuma*, ed. Buber, *Bereshith* 13.

86. *Exodus Rabbah* xxx:8.

87. *Tanhuma, Qedoshim* 15.

88. T. B. *Bava Bathra* 16a f.

89. *Exodus Rabbah* xxx:8, quoting xix:4.

90. *Pesiqta de-*R. *Kahana* xxix.

91. *Genesis Rabbah* xxx:8; Midrash *Esther Rabbathi* vi:3: a parallel source, *Exodus Rabbah* ii:4 has different examples, omitting Job; cf. *Tanhuma, Shemoth* i: "Sufferings had to occur, and Job was predestined that they should come through him."

92. Mishnah, *'Eduyyoth* ii, 10; *Lamentations Rabbathi* i: 40 quotes this mishnah, adding the longer periods of judgement of Nebuchadnezzar and Vespasian.

93. *Exodus Rabbah* xxxi: ii.

94. *Leviticus Rabbah* xvii:4 and *Ruth Rabbathi* ii:10.

95. *Leviticus Rabbah* xxiii:12.

96. *Tanhuma, Re'eh* 15.

97. *Exodus Rabbah* xxxiv: i.

98. *Genesis Rabbah* iv:3.

99. *Mekhilta* to *Exodus* xiv:24.

100. Midrash on *Psalm* ciii:8.

101. *Exodus Rabbah* xl:3.

102. *Pesiqta Rabbathi* xlvii. cf. *supra,* p. 55, n. 4.

103. T. B. *Berakhoth* 17a.

9

THE BOOK OF JOB
AND ITS INTERPRETERS

This series of colloquia deals with transformations of Biblical motifs. If we apply the term "motif" to the Joban theme of the innocent sufferer who rises in rebellion against a seemingly unconcerned, unjust, arbitrary God, whom in the end he encounters as the Creator and Lord of the universe, then indeed the history of the interpretation of the Book of Job discloses a variety of types into which the figure of Job was transformed.

It should be said at the outset that the figure of Job, more so than others in the Bible, lent itself to a considerable diversity of interpretations. The reasons for this are to be sought in the variety of views exposed in the Book itself, in its position in the Biblical canon, and, last but not least, in the multifariousness of motifs employed in Talmudic-Midrashic literature in its presentation of Job[1] — a literature that assigns Job to diverse historical periods, and even permits the assumption that "Job never existed but is only a symbolic figure."[2] There are various opinions concerning the origin of Job, Hebrew or gentile, the purpose of his sufferings and the meaning of his query to God, the role of Satan, and the character of Job as compared with that of Abraham. Such latitude permitted remarkable freedom of interpretation and provoked the conception of a number of self-contained compositions in which Job appears as a symbolic representation of a particular attitude to God and world. As in the Biblical text, the change in Job's attitude is induced by the speeches of the Lord, whose argument was anticipated in the speeches of Elihu. In the exposition of these speeches, the medieval interpreters displayed their skill in adjusting the Biblical text to their own philosophical or theological opinions. Rarely was there an attempt to realize the radical nature of the Divine "reply" to the quest of Job; the difference between the view held by the author of the Book of Job and the views of the medieval commentators was too vast to allow serious consideration of the former.

The focusing of attention on the folk story of Job, of which the first two chapters and the prose conclusion are a part, gave rise to a literature in which Job became the symbol of a saint who remains steadfast throughout his sufferings. Though not in the mainstream of tradition, this treatment is, nevertheless, important in the context of Job interpretation. Some aspects of such a reading of Job are to be found in the commentaries such as Rashi's, Saadya's and Samuel Masnut's.

The major trend of Jewish tradition is represented by the Bible commentators and religious philosophers who acknowledge some form of rebellion, heresy, or, at least, an imperfection on the part of Job; in their interpretations the hero's reform, or conversion, appears then in an exposition of the speeches of Elihu (chapters 32–37) and of God (chapters 38–41).

Apart from these presentations, the cycle of themes is to be considered that forms the Zoharic interpretation of Job. There is also a transformation of the Job motif in the Sabbatian theology,[3] which, however, will not concern us here.

The entire literature covers a wide range of types, from Job the saint, via Job the rebel, Job the dualist, the man lacking in knowledge, the Aristotelian denier of providence, the man confusing God and Satan, the determinist, the man who failed to give Satan his due, Job the scapegoat, to Job the prototype of the Sabbatian Messiah. This study will survey extra-Talmudic Jewish literature, from the "Testament of Job" to about 1600. Obviously both survey and analysis will be extremely brief.

I

Job the Saint

The best documentation of Job as saint is the so-called "Testament of Job." Its Hebrew original, composed probably in the first pre-Christian century, is lost; two Greek versions, which incorporate later changes and additions, each represented by one manuscript, became known in the nineteenth century.[4]

The Job of the "Testament" is not on trial because of a pact between God and Satan. This Job, or Jobab, King of Edom, had destroyed a venerated idol, the handiwork of Satan. He knew that by this action he would provoke the wrath of Satan and invite countless afflictions upon himself; he knew as well that God would restore his fortune if he endured. He was ready. "I shall from love of God endure until death all that will come upon me and I shall not shrink back." The friends, fellow kings, seeing Job's misfortune, lost their faith, but Job rose to the defense of God. He rejected the ministrations of physicians, asserting that his cure would come from God. He prohibited a search for the bones of his children, declaring, "They are in the keeping of their Maker." Elihu's role in the "Testament" differs radically from the role assigned to him by the mainstream of traditional interpretation. In the "Testament" Elihu is "imbued with the spirit of Satan."[5] Yet, in passages reminiscent of the Elihu speeches in the Book, he chastises Job for his self-pride. Finally God appears "from a whirlwind and clouds" (as in the Septuagint to 38:1) to pardon the three friends and to condemn Elihu, "for he has loved the beauty of the serpent." Job is returned to his original state.

Job as the exemplar of perfect faith appears also in *Aboth-de-Rabbi*

Nathan (Version I, Addendum II). The version of the Job folk tale as related there is a compilation from various sources. As in the Biblical story, Satan is given permission to test Job's faith; as in the "Testament of Job," the hero remains steadfast, "acknowledging and praising the Lord for all his attributes," until "all the world believed that there is none like him in all the land." "He has not sinned, not even with the words of his mouth and has not turned his heart" from God. This latter motif seems to be a repudiation of the tradition (*Baba Bathra* 16a) that Job, though he "did not sin with his lips," as the Biblical text indicates (2:10), did sin with his heart. The tradition upholding Job as a symbol of unquestioning faith had to assert itself against the tendency of those interpreters who were impelled to insist on the sinfulness of Job in order to justify the acts of God.

The conclusion of the Job story in *Aboth de-Rabbi Nathan* comes from a third source. Satan, who has failed to alienate Job's faith, was condemned by God and cast down from heaven. God in his mercy cures Job, whose afflictions last one full year — symbolic of a perfect unit of time.

The early Christian church seems to have followed the motif of Job the saint. The Epistle of James, head of the Church of Jerusalem, cites Job (and the prophets, but not Jesus) as prototypes of patient endurance (5:11). The Syriac version of the "Apocalypsis Pauli" of the end of the fourth century points in the same direction.[6] In it, Satan tries daily to seduce Job into apostasy, but Job remains constant in his faith and love, expecting his recompense in the World to Come.

Bishop Theodore of Mopsuestia (died 428), disciple of Diodorus of Tarsus and the most influential teacher of the school of Antioch, speaks of an "outstanding and much esteemed story of the saintly Job, retold orally by everybody in a similar form, not only among Israelite people but also by others."[7] He believed this popular tale of Job the saint to be the true story, adjudging the Biblical Book of Job to be a mere literary product created by an author anxious to display his knowledge and to gain repute. The speeches attributed to Job by the Biblical author, Bishop Theodore considered unbefitting a man "who mastered his life with great wisdom and virtue and piety."

Of interest is also the Moslem version of the folk tale of Job the saint, which is documented by two late manuscripts, one dating from about 1785, the other from about 1840; both, apparently copied in Egypt, are based on a single original.[8] One of the manuscripts refers to Wahb and Ka'b-el-ahbar as the authorities for the tale; both were Yemenite Jews, converted to Islam. Wahb died after A.H. 110, Ka'b in A.H. 32.[9] In this tale, Satan (Iblis), angered by the lack of veneration accorded him by Job and his wife, receives permission to test Job's faith. This motif for Satan's action is reminiscent of the reason given in the "Testament of Job" and, as we shall note later, by the Zohar.

Job's faith is unshakable. Iblis finds him in a mosque, praying: "Behold, the misfortune that Thou hast brought upon me only served to increase my gratitude and my patience," an attitude by which he acknowledges the example of the prophets and messengers of God. He calls himself "the servant of his Master and His messenger" and proclaims his readiness to satisfy his hunger by calling upon His name and his thirst by praising Him. As in the "Testament of Job" the hero refuses to be cured by a physician. God Himself, partly through the mediation of Gabriel, cures Job by a fruit from Paradise — a quince — and paradisiac garments.[10]

II

The medieval Bible exegetes, who confronted the Book of Job in its entirety, could not concentrate on the motif of Job the saint, which confines the reader's view to the prose story and the epilogue of the Book. The medieval commentator had to do justice to those portions of the Book in which Job appears to be challenging God's justice, to regard Him as hostile to man, and as unwilling to give answer to man's insistent queries. In describing Job's character, the commentator had to decide what measure of rebellion to ascribe to Job, or, as was the case in many commentaries, what tradition with regard to Job's rebelliousness to follow, or whether to remove the stigma of rebellion in order to absolve a Biblical hero from offending divinity. Obviously, the point of view assumed by the commentator determined the details of his exegesis.

In the sections that follow some of the main medieval views of Job will be reviewed as they appear in the commentaries.

1. Job the Imperfectly Pious Man

The view of Job as imperfectly pious is best represented by Rashi (Rabbi Solomon ben Isaac, 1040–1105), who seems to have composed his Job commentary in the latter part of his active life; the master's hand stopped at 40:20; his commentary was completed by others and the entire work emended by disciples and copyists.[11]

Rashi's Job did not dare to rise in protest against divinity. His fear of God, though imperfect (comment on 1:2), was deep-seated. In his comments on chapter 9, Rashi greatly modified Job's rebellious utterances. Rather than expressing Job's protestation, this chapter, in Rashi's opinion, denotes Job's submission in a spirit of fear of God. Thus, to the text, "God will not withdraw his anger" (9:13), Rashi added the words, "from fear of man"; to the text, "Yet would I not believe that He would hearken unto my voice" (9:16), he added, "because of my fear of Him, and how could I not fear Him"; to the text, "Though I be righteous, mine own mouth shall condemn me" (9:20), he added, "fear [of Him] would silence my voice." On 13:15 Rashi commented: " 'Though he slay me' I shall not separate myself from Him and I shall always trust in Him; therefore, there is no rebellion and transgression in my words." And on the verse that follows he commented: "As I am wholly with Him, so is He salvation to me," referring the word *hu* not to the second part of the verse, but to God.

Yet, Job's piety was imperfect. He said that God "destroyeth the innocent and the wicked" (9:22) and asked God not to let the Divine terror make him afraid (13:21). Worse still, he had talked too much and by his verbosity he had upset God's plan "to have the divine name rest upon him" (comment on 38:2). These imperfections required correction; this was achieved by Elihu's remark on man's insignificance in the cosmos (comment on 33:12) and by God's reference to Abraham, whose piety was perfect because unquestioning.[12]

Another example of an interpretation of Job as the symbol of an imperfectly pious man is the Job commentary of Joseph Kara, the northern French Bible exegete (eleventh to twelfth century).[13] His Job, though on the whole a just man (comment on 12:4), is helpless before the evil urge and conscious of his sinfulness before God (comments on 7:20 and 9:20). He wonders why the all-knowing God had to test him[14] of whose trust in Him He must have been aware (comment on 13:15). Yet, despite his suffering, he feels certain that God will be his salvation (comment on 13:16). Elihu extols both God's independence from man's actions and His compassion for man (comments on 35:9f. and 36:26). "Your suffering came upon you to save your soul from darkness . . . He reproves you because He loves you" (comment on 33:24). The speeches of God elaborate on Elihu's statement on Divine independence (comment on 38:4ff.) and His concern with His creation. "I am full of compassion for the beasts and animals that live in deserts and I feed them, and all the more for man created in [My] image and likeness" (comment on 38:26f.). This is a Job who had no reason to rebel, for he never really doubted God's providence. It required but little effort to dispel his confusion and restore his perfect faith. The problem of evil was not an issue in Kara's commentary.

A similar interpretation of Job as imperfectly pious is provided by *Ma'ayan Gannim*, a midrash on Job by Samuel ben Nissim Masnut of Aleppo, who is known to have been visited by Judah al-Harizi in the second decade of the thirteenth century.[15] This work[16] is, except for the author's own notes, largely a compilation from the Targum (in its two versions),[17] Talmud and Midrash, Ibn Ezra, and, to a large measure, Rashi.[18]

Masnut's Job was allowed by God to be tested by Satan, who feared that Job's piety might cause God to forget the piety of Abraham (compare *Baba Bathra* 14b). Throughout his ordeal Job remained a man of faith. His harsh, provocative statements — for example, in chapter 9 Masnut attributes to events of the past, to Pharaoh (verse 4), to Sodom and Gomorrah (verse 5), and the like. Historically localized, the verses bespeak the well-ordered and purposeful Divine power, rather than a blind, terrorizing force. For his description of Job's deep faith, Masnut borrowed extensively from Rashi's commentary.[19] It is a humble, self-effacing Job that he presents. "I do not rely on my prayer and on myself, because I am not worthy that He answer me and hearken unto my voice" (comment on 9:16). "I cannot justify myself in order to accuse Him, because He is high above all glory and praise" (comment on 9:22). Thus the commentary turned Job's assertion of the utter futility of man's argument into a pious person's humble recognition of God's mercy. Job's friends were unable to stand their ground before God (comment on 27:2); their apparent justification of God was, in reality, heresy (comment on 32:4).

It was only his suffering that led Job to believe that God considered him to be His enemy (13:24). According to the Talmudic dictum, a sufferer is not to be held responsible for his outbursts (comment on 28:26). Yet Job's failure to understand God's ways called for rectification. The Lord's address "made him realize that he had no knowledge and that he was unable to fathom the ways of God" (comment on 38:1). Once "he had been made to know what he had not known," Job regretted his doubts that had interfered with his piety and his repentance was complete (comment on 42:2). Addressed by God, he reached "true understanding" (comment on 42:6).[20]

Compositions such as Rashi's, Kara's, and Masnut's failed to achieve an internal unity. They describe Job as a completely devout man, then establish, somewhat arbitrarily and inconsistently, his error, in order to justify the obvious correction that is the purpose of the Lord's speeches. One notes that the authors would have preferred to concentrate on the piety of Job. It is the evidence of the text that compelled them to picture this piety as imperfect.

2. *Job the Rebel*

The interpretation of Job as a rebel, a doubter of Divine justice in the distribution of good and evil, is most poignantly presented by Abraham ibn Ezra (1092–1167). His commentary on Job, written in Rome about 1140, made abundant use of his predecessors; he followed Saadya Gaon in some one hundred instances (though he quotes him only six times); in his explanations of words he is dependent on Jonah ibn Janah, whom, however, he mentions only once.[21] Profiat Duran complained that Ibn

Ezra "composed attractive works," but that "there is not much in them that is new."[22] What is, however, novel in Ibn Ezra's commentary on Job is his remark that much of the difficulty in interpreting the text stems from the fact that our Book is a translation (comment on 2:11).[23] Moreover, it is remarkable that, especially in his lengthy epilogue to the commentary, Ibn Ezra manifested a profound interest in the book as a whole, over and above exegesis, and let himself be guided by its insight, even where this insight was at variance with his own philosophy.

In Ibn Ezra's view Job became a rebel, protesting against the unjust Divine rule, when he, an innocent man, was made to suffer; consequently, he could not but think that God considered man to be His enemy. He was unable to believe that in afflicting a righteous man a just God could have a purpose in mind. It was Elihu who prepared the way for Job's conversion from a rebellious skeptic to a humble man of faith; he accomplished this by making Job aware of the mysterious essence of the acts of God both in nature and in the human world; man must suffer and be silent.

Elihu's argument was perfected in the speeches of the Lord. Whether or not he was fully conscious of the importance of his observation, Ibn Ezra pointed to the key phrase in these speeches: "Knowest thou . . . ?" —a question addressed to man, who in self-pride has arrogated to himself knowledge. The references in these speeches to the mighty creatures were intended, according to Ibn Ezra, to demonstrate man's limited dominion on earth, and, by implication, his impotence in confronting the higher realms.

Ibn Ezra's own view on evil—namely, that it is occasioned by the imperfection of matter and that God is the author of good only—did not enter into his discussion of Job. Rather, he emphasized the limits of human knowledge, which prevent man from comprehending the universe he inhabits. It is the presumption of knowledge, he argued, that posits certain aspects of existence as evil and that results in skepticism.

Job as rebel against God appears also in the work of Nahmanides (Moses ben Nahman, 1194–1270?), both in his Job commentary[24] and in his treatise *Sha'ar ha-Gemul,* which is the concluding chapter of his *Torath ha-Adam.*[25]

In the view of Nahmanides, the afflicted hero (who could not realize that his faith was being tested) assumed that man's fate is not directed by God but determined by the constellations; God considers man too insignificant to merit His attention; He is too great to be concerned with man.[26] Therefore, Job concluded, both the righteous and the wicked are at the mercy of chance (commentary, preface to chapter 3, and comments on 9:2 and 9:22). He admitted the proposition that Divine providence extends only to the species, desiring their preservation, but not to the individual man, who is too lowly in God's eyes.[27] Job "was inclined to heresy"[28] and rebelled against a God who ignored individual man and allowed Job, a righteous man, to meet an undeserved fate.

In his answer to Job, Nahmanides differed significantly from Ibn Ezra. Whereas the latter pointed to the limits of human knowledge, Nahmanides, the mystic, referred the rebel to a "world of souls" (*'olam ha-neshamoth*) in which the ills of the material world would be resolved. With the mystic's caution he alluded to the transmigration of souls, "a deep mystery" accessible not to a thinker but to the initiate alone.[29] By focusing attention on the soul—over which Satan has no dominion, as our author interprets Job 2:6—Elihu impelled Job to realize that the thesis of the undeserved suffering of the righteous man could not be maintained (commentary, introduction and comment on 33:30). Man's soul thus having been taken care of, Job apprehended that God "watches over His world and exercises providence over it." Indeed, "all terrestrial beings have been created for the sake of man, because none of them know the Creator but he" (comment on 36:2). Of Job's three friends it was Zophar (in modern opinion, the least profound of the three) who contributed to the solution of the problem created by "the prosperity of the wicked": all existence evidences both "manifest wisdom" and "hidden wisdom" and no man can pass judgment on the affairs of the world; the good fortune of the wicked may be a sign of the Creator's mercy.[30]

While Zophar and Elihu suggested nonrational notions ("the world of the souls" and "hidden wisdom"), the speeches of God offered what must have appeared to Nahmanides to be logical proof. God's account of the marvels of creation—intended in the Biblical text as a repudiation of man's proud assertion of knowledge and power—was understood by Nahmanides as giving Job proof of providence and the good order and guidance in the universe at large and as intended to convince Job by inference that, this being the case, there must be still greater design and purpose in the creation of the higher being, man; the details of this order, however, must remain a mystery which human reason cannot penetrate.[31]

Job, according to Nahmanides, is the symbol of a man whose rebellion resulted from his attempt to explain good and evil by his own reason. Gradually he was made aware of the aspect of the mysterious in the world and he "returned to his Creator," perceiving that everything is under a rule of righteousness and mercy.[32] Accepting as a basis that which he could grasp through reason, he discerned measure and justice in "what is distant and hidden."[33]

Nahmanides' reading of Job reappeared in *Kad ha-Qemah*, a manual of religious thought by the Spanish Bible commentator Bahya ben Asher ibn Halawa (died 1340).[34] The idea of the transmigration of souls, to which Nahmanides referred with considerable caution and subtility, appeared in Bahya's argument quite explicitly formulated.[35]

Transmigration, according to Bahya, implies special providence and establishes man as being superior to other creatures, who were created but for the sake of man. To know this is true wisdom, in the name of which Elihu speaks,[36] while Job, rebellious by denying providence, "multiplieth words without knowledge" (Job 35:16).[37] Elaborating on Nahmanides' interpretation of the speeches of God, Bahya understood them as revealing both the Divine attributes of mercy and of justice, the former in chapters 38 and 39, the latter in chapters 40 and 41, which describe the giant creatures, Behemoth and Leviathan. As does transmigration, so too creation, depicted in the speeches of God, implies providence, both universal and individual.[38]

The rebel in Job was converted by the gift of knowledge. After having been confronted by Elihu and the Lord, Job realized that he could not have knowledge of God's wonders "unless He, in His mercy, makes them known to him."[39] The emphasis by Bahya on the motif of knowledge, clearly intended by the Biblical text, is significant; it was often overlooked in medieval Jewish exegesis.[40]

Rebellion against a God who withholds His providence from individual man is the motif also of the Job interpretation of Meir, son of Isaac Arama (1460–1545), in his *Meir 'Iyyov*. This commentary on Job was completed in 1505–1506, some thirteen years after the author and his father, exiles from Spain, found refuge in Naples.[41] According to Arama, who on this point follows an established pattern, Job's affliction impelled him to abandon his original faith[42] and adopt the "despicable belief" (*ha-'emunah ha-megunah*) in an unconcerned God.[43] After Elihu's powerful assertion of providence[44] came the definitive answer from God.[45] In contradistinction to the Greek mode of thinking, says Arama in interpreting chapters 38 and those that follow, Creation testifies to Divine closeness to, and concern for, all creatures, and especially for man.[46] In this exposition Arama, following older traditions, is aided by the rendition of Job 38:36, *batuhoth* by "reins," and of *sekhvi* by "heart," implying that the very existence of a thinking being is proof of God's nearness to man's intellectual self.[47] In response Job bows to this supreme evidence of providential care inherent in creation and sustaining the universe.[48]

It may be suggested that the author's experience of the expulsion of 1492 determined his choice of the Book of Job as the first of his commentaries, to be followed by interpretations of Psalms, Isaiah, Jeremiah, Canticles, and the (unpublished) commentary on the Pentateuch. Arama was, no doubt, searching for an affirmation of his own faith and of its source, the element of the personal concern of God—and read this faith into the majestically neutral, objective speeches of God. Thus, to him, the Book of Job is "in its beginning, its end, and all of it [dedicated to the] fear of Heaven."[49]

3. Job the Dualist

Since human suffering cannot be ascribed to God, "who is good and who causes good," the existence of a second god must be assumed, a god who is the origin of evil and who works destruction, especially if aided by the constellations and not opposed by the good God. In the opinion of Obadiah Sforno (*circa* 1475–1550), Job symbolizes this trend of thinking. In his commentary on Job, *Mishpat Sedeq*,[50] Sforno presented a Job who rises in anger against this good God, Who, because of His greatness, disregards the rights of human kind and thus fails to interfere with the evil force.

Again the answer[51] was provided in chapter 38 and those that follow, which Sforno, like others before him, interpreted as testimony not of God's wondrous majesty, but of His concern for individual man. This concern is manifest in the grant of the power of intellect to man (by which he becomes similar to his Creator)—a motif emphasized by Gersonides and Joseph Albo—and in God's exercise of individual providence, which is not bound to the laws of nature. God removed Behemoth and Leviathan to faraway regions, for otherwise man would have been unable to cope with them. The nonmechanical and seemingly unjust administration of retribution is a means of safeguarding man's freedom of choice. By such clarification God convinced Job that there is no "evil god who causes all ills." God "delighteth in mercy."[52] However, evil has its rightful place in the universe (comment on 40:5), since everything issues from the one, good God, who comprises both good and evil (comment on 42:2). The answer to the problem of evil suggested by dualism is refuted by the providential revelation of the one God.

III

The medieval Jewish philosopher who dealt with Job as a theological problem enjoyed greater freedom than the Bible commentator, who, in addition, was responsible for the very text of the Book. However, no clear-cut dividing line can be drawn between the two: Saadya, for example, was both commentator and philosopher. But it can be stated that in such cases the author's philosophical concerns determine his work as exegete; the philosopher's freedom of movement, however circumscribed, is discernible in his commentary. Again, as in the case of the Biblical expositors, so too in the works of the philosophers, Job became a symbol of distinct approaches to the problem of evil and to divine justice.

1. Job the Pious Man in Search of an Answer

Saadya Gaon (died 942), deeply concerned with the purity of the God concept, could not admit the notion of rebelliousness in his presentation of Job. His translation and interpretation of the Book of Job, which is one of the parts preserved from his *tafsir*, bears the title *Kitab al-Ta'dil* (Book of Theodicy),[53] in which the all-pervading, unlimited grace (*djud*) of God is to be demonstrated. Neither Job nor his friends doubted the justice of God.[54] Only, as had Moses and Jeremiah before him, Job wanted to be informed of the cause of his affliction. But, like them, he did not receive a direct answer (comment on 37:24). "God is too lofty and exalted in His power to answer man word for word" (comment on 33:13–15). God is completely independent of man; neither will man's good deeds profit, nor his iniquity harm Him (comment on 35:12–15). In his speech, God used the image of Leviathan as indication of His unlimited power. Job was impelled to realize that human knowledge is unable to fathom "the subtle rule of the Wise, exalted be He, and His affairs" (comment on 42:6). By scrupulously avoiding anthropomorphisms[55] and by using various exegetical devices, Saadya kept his good, just, and gracious God far removed from unseemly contact with the human world.

We note that Saadya did justice to the original meaning of Job 38 and the following chapters, a section which many commentators turned into a document of individual providence. In fact, Saadya tended to interpret the entire Book in the light of its concluding speeches. Job the pious man did not question Divine justice and providence but sought knowledge; the answer, therefore, was but a reference to the source of all knowledge.

Saadya returned to the Job problem in chapter five of his *'Emunoth ve De'oth*.[56] The suffering inflicted on the pious man is to be understood as punishment for whatever transgressions he committed, or, as in the case of Job, as a test visited upon a man whom God knows beforehand to have the strength to bear it and remain faithful. Such a trial "enables mankind to realize that God has not chosen a pious man gratuitously."[57] Job passed the test. Unlike the Biblical Job, Saadya's did not rise in protest against a seemingly unjust God; his confidence in God remained unshaken throughout his trials. His only wish was to know the reasons motivating Divine acts.[58] As a man of faith[59] he found no difficulty in realizing the incompatibility between Divine knowledge and human knowledge.[60]

2. Job the Man Lacking True Knowledge

Moses Maimonides (1135–1204), who devoted to an analysis of the Book of Job chapters 22 and 23 of the third book of his *Guide to the Perplexed*,[61] observed that the text (1:1) ascribes to Job uprightness and

ethical virtues but not wisdom and intelligence. His denial of a just rule
in the universe and the perplexity engendered by his afflictions were
consequences of his lack of wisdom. Satan was identified by Maimonides with the evil inclination[62] which is present in man from birth
onward.[63] Job's error, instigated by Satan (from the root *satah*, "turning
man away from truth and leading him astray in the way of error"), was
thus indicative of the stage in life when wisdom is not yet in evidence.
Lacking wisdom, knowing God only from tradition, and confused by his
misfortune, Job viewed God as contemptuous of man, laughing at the
trials of the innocent, and permitting the wicked to prosper.[64] The good
inclination, that force by which man may overcome "Satan," the evil
drive, comes only when the mind is developed. Consequently, "as soon
as he [Job] had acquired a true knowledge of God, he avowed that there is
undoubtedly true felicity in the knowledge of God," which "no earthly
trouble can disturb."

Elihu is depicted by Maimonides as introducing the concept of the
angel's intercession on behalf of a person in peril, which he designates as
the principal objective (*ha-kavvanah*) of Elihu's speech.[65] One gains the
impression that Maimonides considered such an interceding angel to be
the counterpart of Satan, the adversary and evil inclination. If this impression is correct, the transformation of Job the wisdomless to the
intellectually mature Job ready for the knowledge of God could then by
symbolized by the replacement of the angel of error and accusation by
the angel of intercession.[66]

In addition, Elihu, in his discourse on the observation of nature as
leading to a comprehension of God's rule in the universe, prepared Job
for the prophetic revelation (*nevu'ah*) in chapters 38 on. These speeches
aimed at communicating the radical difference between God's creation
and human production, between God's rule, providence, and intent,
and the corresponding human faculties. Intellectual maturity is attained
once man has freed himself from "the error of imagining God's knowledge to be similar to ours." True human wisdom leads to a humble
acknowledgment of the uniqueness and incomparability of Divine
knowledge. It is this recognition that enables man to bear suffering and
evil, and that silences his doubts about "whether God knows our affairs
or not, whether He provides for us or abandons us."

Like Saadya before him, Maimonides did not attempt to interpret
chapters 38 on as inferring individual providence. Rather, in close attention to the text's intent, he tried to remove the issue of providence from
the realm of human concern. In this reorientation of human thought he
saw the source of what Job, who feared the Lord, was wanting before his
conversion: the love of God.

Maimonides' interpretation of Job was made use of by Zerahyah ben

Isaac ben Shealtiel of Barcelona (thirteenth century), author of a Job commentary, written in Rome in 1290-91.[67] In a fairly extensive introduction he states that he was prompted to write his commentary by the fact that none of his predecessors went beyond a literal interpretation of the Book.[68] Paradoxically enough, this declaration is followed by a digest of Maimonides' discourse on the various philosophies represented in the Book—a discourse with which our author wholeheartedly agreed.[69] Possibly Zerahya's most interesting point, not borrowed from Maimonides, is his perception of the parallel structure of the Book of Job and Genesis.

3. Job the Aristotelian Denier of Providence

In making Job and his friends representatives of various schools of thought on the subject of providence, Maimonides assigned to Job the role of advocating the views of Aristotle,[70] in a strange combination with the notion that Job, before his conversion, was lacking in knowledge.

The parallel between Job and Aristotle, whose God had no knowledge of particular incidents, was more definitely elaborated by Gersonides (Levi ben Gerson, 1288-1344), mathematician, astronomer, and exacting follower of Averroës. To the Book of Job, to which he was particularly attracted, Gersonides devoted an extensive commentary[71] and an analysis in part four of his *Wars of the Lord*.[72]

The Aristotelian view, Gersonides postulated, commends itself because of the human experience of the "faulty management," the "imperfect order of events" (*ro'a ha-seder*): that is, the suffering of the righteous and the prosperity of the wicked; the alternative view would be the attribution of injustice to God. However, in following Aristotle, Job displayed a tendency to heresy and rebellion (commentary on chapter 37, general principles). For, if man is abandoned to the fate that emanates not from God but from the order of the heavenly spheres—that is, from the universal laws of nature—then incapacity and deficient power must be ascribed to God, Who was not able to create a more perfect order (commentary on chapter 40, preface).[73]

The way out of this dilemma was indicated by Elihu, Gersonides thought. The Divine purpose is indeed the "bestowal of good," but the actual determination and order of good and evil God left to the functioning of the heavenly bodies. However, He endowed man with reason, which effects a measure of union with the Active Intellect; this serves as protection against evil happenings. The stronger man's attachment to reason, the greater is his potential protection. In addition, there are direct acts of Divine providence, independent of the prearranged order of the heavenly bodies — a fact that Elihu failed to consider (commentary on chapter 33, general principles).

After an extensive analysis of Elihu's arguments,[74] Gersonides was comparatively brief in his comments on the speeches of God. He concentrated on the meaning of Behemoth and Leviathan; their exaggerated description, he contended, was intended to demonstrate "that God is not incapable of giving to every creature the highest possible measure of good" (commentary on chapter 41, the discourse as a whole).

All that Job needed was a revision and a qualification of his Aristotelianism, not its abandonment.[75] His sin was light; had he heeded the chastisement and surrendered, he would have realized that God extends providence to "intellectual man" (*ha-'adam ha-maskil*) according to the degree of his intellectual union with God (commentary on chapter 37, general principles). Finally he realized this, without being forced to surrender his correct assumption, namely, that "Divine providence does not pertain to individuals — as far as the majority of men is concerned" (commentary on chapter 42, end).

The Biblical drama of rebellious man who defied his God as being hostile to humanity is here reduced to an account of the conversion of an Aristotelian with a strong Jewish consciousness to a faithful follower of Gersonides.

4. Job as Confusing the Work of God and the Work of Satan

The above view was presented by Simeon ben Semah Duran (1361–1444) in his commentary on Job, *'Ohev Mishpat,*[76] and in a short account in his religio-philosophical work *Magen 'Avoth.*[77] In his interpretation the sufferings of Job were instigated by Satan; it was not God who planned these sufferings, "for He is good to everybody and will give [man] only what is good."[78] But Job, uninformed about the true cause of his trouble, accused God of injustive and imputed to Him a hostile attitude toward man.[79]

It was Elihu who instructed Job in the difference between God's ways and man's, in the peculiarity of Satan's doings, and in the work of the interceding angel, who is the counterpart of Satan.[80] Elihu's arguments silenced Job and made him repent.[81] Having been granted knowledge of what is eternal, Job "renounced the life of this world—where both material bliss and calamity are matters of no consequence."[82] According to Duran, the Book of Job "hints at the full recompense which is to come in the world to come, with the resurrection of the dead and in the days of Messiah."[83] Assuming the existence of this vastly expanded universe with the accent on the beyond, it was easy to affirm unlimited providence, which, Duran believed, "the Book of Job attempts to prove."[84] Also, in such a universe it was not difficult to distinguish between the circumscribed regimen of evil and the limitless, eternal realm of good, between the work of Satan and the work of God.

5. Job the Determinist

It has long ago been demonstrated that, as was the case with other aspects of Simeon Duran's philosophy, his discourse on providence[85] was taken over by Joseph Albo (1380?–1445?). In his *Sefer ha-'Iqqarim*,[86] IV, 7–16, Albo, without mentioning his source, followed not only the details of Duran's argument but also his formulation.[87] However, in his analysis of Job, contained in the fourth, and concluding, part of *'Iqqarim*, Albo deviated from his *Vorbild*. Like Nahmanides and Gersonides before him, Duran turned Job into a symbol of a man who believed that good and evil in life are determined by the heavenly bodies (IV,5). There is a preordained order of things (IV, 18), he argued, and neither man's righteous conduct nor prayer will counteract the unchanging law that rules the world. Though he affirmed the notion of God's knowledge—a changeless knowledge—Job denied God's providential care for the world, because he was painfully aware of the "imperfect order of events" (*ro'a ha-seder*), a term we encountered in Gersonides' argument.

What convinced the determinist's mind of his error? According to Albo, it was not the veritable manifestation of God, creator of the universe, but the compelling character of logical proofs, "arguments for providence, found in this book [of Job] and elsewhere." Here, the medievalist embarked on a lengthy presentation of "three kinds of proofs": the first, "derived from general things," consisted of two arguments (IV, 8), the second, "derived from special and particular events in human life," consisted of three arguments (IV, 9), and a third, "derived from the intellect," consisted of two arguments, the second of which had two forms (IV, 10). In the course of this detailed analysis, Albo (interpreting Job 38:28) argued that "the existence of rain cannot be ascribed to nature" but demonstrates special providence (IV, 8). By interpreting (like others before him) the word *sekhvi* in Job 38:36 as "the intellectual power in man" (*ha-koah ha-sikhli she-ba-'adam*) and *batuhoth* as an allusion to the *prima intelligibilia*, or axioms, Albo was able to point to the gift of reason as designed by God to elevate man above the animals mentioned in the context: incontestable proof of Divine grace and providence (IV, 10). It would contravene reason to assume that God, who has the power to lead man to perfection, would not come to the aid of man who has the potential of intelligence. Indeed, all is encompassed in providence, even "all evil that comes to the righteous is due to providence" (IV, 10). Divine power is the guarantee of divine providence.

The more deep-seated reason why, according to Albo, Job required the discipline of logical arguments is to be found in the fact that he served God not out of love but for reward; throughout his defiant speeches, Job justified Satan's suspicion, his certainty even, of the true nature of Job's piety (IV, 7).[88] In Albo's view, only the attitude of being the servant of

God for love of Him, as Abraham was, can silence the doubts concerning the just rule of the world and the seeming dominance of evil; only this ultimate—unquestioning—trust prepares man for the realization that "all the good that comes from God is due purely to His loving kindness, and is not compensation for one's good deeds" (IV, 16). In contradistinction to Abraham, Job, who feared God, had to be dealt with on the level of rational argumentation. However, once he comprehended the extent of God's knowledge and power, Job found peace (IV, 10), and the former determinist turned into a man of faith.

IV

The Zoharic literature offers a series of Job interpretations which, at several points, show material affinity to the Talmudic-Midrashic observations on the subject,[89] while at the same time retaining their—at times daring—originality. The Zoharic reflections — scattered over the entire work and only loosely related to each other — deal primarily with the Job of the folk story, rather than with the Job of the dialogue. The figure of Satan is greatly in the foreground. Most of the tests attempt to understand Job in the context of the reality of evil, as represented by Satan, the "other side," in order to probe into the deeper reasons for Job's fate, and to determine his place in the cosmic drama of the fall and redemption.

The brief analysis that follows is restricted to the main part of the Zohar; the *Midrash ha-Ne'elam, Ra'ya Mehemna,* and the *Tiqqune Zohar* were not considered.

1. Job the Man Who Failed to Pacify Satan

In one of the principal Zoharic compositions on the subject, Job symbolizes the man who failed to be "cognizant of both good and evil." Cognizance of evil is demonstrated by permitting a portion of one's sacrifice to go to Satan, "the other side."[90] Job offered burnt offerings ('*oloth*; Job 1:5), a sacrifice that ascends in its entirety to heaven; this is taken to imply that he tendered no portion to the "other side." Had he satisfied Satan's due, the "unholy side" would have separated itself from the holy, and by so doing have prmitted the holy side to rise undisturbed to the highest spheres; the "other side" would then have been unable to prevail against him. Since Job failed to appease Satan, God himself let "justice be executed" on him and suffered Satan to take what was his due. "As Job kept evil separate from good and failed to fuse them, he was judged accordingly: first he experienced good, then what was evil, then again good. For man should be cognizant of both good and evil, and turn evil itself into good. This is a deep tenet of faith."[91]

2. *Job the Scapegoat*

Another Zoharic interpretation points to Satan's arraignment of Abraham for having substituted an animal sacrifice for the offering of Isaac, a transaction at variance with the law in Leviticus 27:10. Recognizing Satan's right, God apportioned to him the heathen branch of Abraham's family, the house of Uz, descendants of Abraham's brother Nahor. Job, hailing from the land of Uz, deserved to be given into the power of Satan. For, as counselor to Pharaoh, he had advised the Egyptian ruler to deprive the Israelites of their possessions and to subject their bodies to heavy toil, without, however, exterminating them. He was judged according to his own scheme: his possessions and his body were given to the power of Satan, who was, however, bidden to "spare his soul" (Job 1:12). Therefore, Job, the schemer against Israel, serves as a scapegoat to be thrown to Satan, when, on the Day of Judgment, he rises to accuse Israel. Satan's attention is diverted and he leaves Israel in peace. This can be compared "to a shepherd who throws a lamb to a wolf in order to save the rest of the flock."[92]

In a Zoharic discourse on the Day of Atonement, Satan is presented as attempting to hinder God in effecting Israel's crossing of the Red Sea. Satan declares that the period of servitude originally specified had not yet passed and that Israel is unworthy of entering the Holy Land. To placate him, God allows him to occupy himself with Job in order to leave His children unharmed. The simile of the shepherd and the wolf is again quoted. "Thus, while Satan was busy with Job, he left Israel alone and they were not accused."[93]

3. *Job the Isolationist*

Still another Zoharic observation situates the story of chapter 1 of Job at a time when the world was judged and its fate depended on but one person to turn the scale in either direction. Satan, eager to denounce the world, was maneuvered into concentrating on Job. The latter was singled out because he "was known to be apart from his people"; his separation from the community made him a target for accusation "in the upper realm."

Job's reaction to the ensuing trials proved Satan to have been partly right in doubting his victim's piety. "He did not sin with his lips" (Job 2:10), "but he did sin in his mind, and later also in his speech." However, "he did not go so far as to attach himself to the 'other side,' " and this steadfastness in resisting Satan saved him in the end.[94]

4. Job's Suffering as a Sign of Divine Love

The Zohar presents Elihu as a descendant of Abraham and also as a priest and descendant of the prophet Ezekiel; his exemplary behavior earned him the honorable name, "man" (Adam).[95] In a remarkable note on Job 34: 10f. the Zohar has Elihu discourse on Divine justice and mercy in the governing of the world and on the meaning of suffering that befalls a righteous man. Such suffering is declared to come "from the love which God bears for him; He crushes his body in order to give more power to his soul, so that He may draw him nearer in love."[96]

The motif of suffering as a path to the love of God appears also in *Helqat Mehoqeq*, the Job commentary of Moses ben Hayyim Alsheikh (*circa* 1508–1600).[97] In commenting on Job 33:17, Alsheikh has Elihu extol the merit of suffering, which aids man in overcoming sin, in acquiring humility, and in escaping the punishment of hell.[98] Furthermore, a world in which the wicked would meet with Divine repudiation and the just with approval would make piety a matter of expediency; the dominant motivation for goodness would be "fear of God." Only the apparent imbalance in the relationship between human action and Divine response is the proper background for selfless faith.[99]

To summarize our review: the central figure in the Book of Job lent itself to a great variety of transformations. Poets, commentators, and philosophers depicted Job as reflecting their own doubts and beliefs, their quests and hopes. He was seen variously as a symbol of sainthood, of rebellion against the unjust order in life, of confusion about providence, of human imperfection, of a man in error concerning the nature of evil, or as a scapegoat. Very few commentators were guided by the Book itself; among them was Maimonides, who pointed to the theme of knowledge as a central motif of the Book.

Knowledge as the central theme of the Job poem was also recognized by Saadya, ibn Ezra, Nahmanides, and Bahya ben Asher. As we have seen, it was Saadya who grasped the original meaning of chapter 38 and the following chapters. A very few (for example, Saadya and Maimonides) escaped the temptation of forcing upon the speeches of God a declaration of individual providence. On the other hand, Saadya was not ready to permit the text to manifest the rebelliousness of Job.

On the point of individual providence the difference between the concept of God as maintained by the author of the Book of Job and that maintained by the commentators becomes especially evident. Like the Talmudic interpreters of Job before them, the latter could not possibly accept the idea of a God whose universal power, as displayed in Creation, would not imply concern for man. He could not remain inaccessible, impenetrable. The God Who, in the text, *asked* questions of Job, was made to *answer* Job's question.

The figure of Elihu deserves special mention. Whereas in the "Testament of Job" he is depicted as inspired by Satan, he figures prominently in most commentaries; it is he who answers Job, preparing the ground for the appearance of God. In the Zoharic tradition he becomes the spokesman for the redemptive quality of suffering.

In general the interpreters who based their Job on the hero of the folk tale or on the haggadic exposition of Job did not feel called upon to account for the hero's conversion following the speeches of Elihu and the Lord.

The interpreters who did not impute rebellion to the Job of chapters 3ff. or who underplayed his rebellion read the speeches of Elihu and of the Lord as providing the necessary minor correction in the hero's views of God.

Those who did recognize the rebellion of Job under trial transformed the converted Job into a symbol of true philosophical enlightenment, of perfect knowledge; they rarely approached the radical position of the text, which presents Job as humbly acknowledging his own inability to know, silent before God, knowing only that He knows.

NOTES

1. Especially BT *Baba Bathra* 14b–16b; Mishnah *Sotah* V, 5: BT *Sotah* 31a; PT *Sotah* 20d; *Tanhuma Noah* 5, *Tanhuma Vayera* 5; *Tanhuma* (ed. Buber), *Vayishlah* 8, pp. 116f.; *Sifre* 32, on Deut. 6:5, ed. Friedmann, 73a; *Pesikta Rabbati* 165a; *Genesis Rabbah* XLIX, 17, *Numbers Rabbah* XIV, 7; *Deuteronomy Rabbah* II, 3; *Aboth de-R. Nathan* II, 14, 43 and 45.

2. *Mashal hayu*; BT *Baba Bathra* 15a.

3. See Hayyim Wirshubsky, "Ha-theologia ha-shabtait shel Nathan ha-'Azati," *Keneseth*, 8: 235f. (1943), and G. Scholem, *Be-'iqvoth ha-mashiah* (Jerusalem, 1944).

4. "Testament of Job," edited and translated by K. Kohler, in *Semitic Studies in Memory of Alexander Kohut* (Berlin, 1897).

5. Cf. PT *Sotah* 20d, where Elihu is identified with Balaam.

6. Given in English in Constantin Tischendorf, *Apocalypses Apocryphae* (Leipzig, 1866), pp. 66f.

7. G. D. Mansi, *Sacrorum conciliorum nova et amplissima collectio* (Venice, 1759–98), IX, 223–225.

8. Naftali Apt, *Die Hiobserzählung in der arabischen Literatur. Erster Teil* (Kirchhain, N. L., 1913). Published dissertation, University of Heidelberg.

9. Duncan B. Macdonald, "Some External Evidence on the Original Form of the Legend of Job," *American Journal of Semitic Languages and Literatures*, 14:146, n. 6 (1898). Macdonald offers a translation of the Arabic story of Job in Tha'labi's

"Stories of the Prophets" (early eleventh century), partly based on traditions that originated with Wahb and Ka'b.

10. The combination of the Job theme with one or another motif of the Biblical Adam story appears too frequently in the Job literature to be dismissed as a coincidence. The nature of the relationship between the two complexes and its relevance to the interpretation of the Book of Job would require a separate study.

11. The problem of the variant readings has been discussed by Isaac Maarsen, "Raschis Kommentar zu Sprüche und Job," *Monatsschrift für Geschichte und Wissenschaft des Judentums,* 83: 442–456 (1939).

12. In Rashi's interpretation of Job 38:2, Job says: "Had I known your plan I would not have multiplied words!" Whereupon God reminds him of Abraham "who did not know [My plan] yet stood the ten [trials]." Another significant reference to Abraham is Rashi's comment on 1:6–7, where Satan's accusation of Job is understood as motivated by the Tempter's meritorious desire to protect the memory of Abraham's righteousness (cf. BT *Baba Bathra* 15b).

13. Most of Kara's commentaries on Biblical books were soon forgotten, and they have been published only in the modern period. The commentary to Job was printed from a manuscript containing the major parts of the commentaries, written in Rome at the end of the thirteenth century and acquired in 1853 by the Breslau Jewish Theological Seminary. It appeared in *Monatsschrift für Geschichte und Wissenschaft des Judentums,* volumes 5–7 (1856–1858); unfortunately, the text was carelessly copied and the reading presents unnecessary difficulties.

14. Job's suffering as a test of his piety is the interpretation also of *Sefer Hasidim,* 1512.

15. *Tahkemoni* (ed. Paul de Lagarde, 2nd ed., Hannover, 1924), XLVI, 173.

16. *Majan-Gannim, Commentar zu Job* (Berlin, 1889), edited by Salomon Buber from a manuscript in the Bodleian Library. Leopold Zunz lists the author in his *Literaturgeschichte der synagogalen Poesie* (Berlin, 1867), p. 597, incorrectly quoted by Buber as *Zur Literatur und Geschichte* (introduction to *Ma'ayan Gannim,* VI).

17. The original version of the extant Targum, composed in Palestine probably in the fourth or fifth century, reduced the impact of provocative or obscure passages of the text by referring them to events of the Biblical past or by reading into them meanings suggested by rabbinic thought. This version was revised in the eighth or ninth century by a translator who planned to restore the plain meaning of the text, at least in the case of crucial sentences. His work is evident in forty-six places, where the older version is replaced by the reviser's own, to which, in most instances at least, he appended the original rendition, marking it *targum 'aher.* Four verses record a third rendition. Cf. Wilhelm Bacher's discussion of the two versions in "Das Targum zu Hiob," *Monatsschrift für Geschichte und Wissenschaft des Judentums,* 20:208–223 (1871). Bacher (pp. 283f.) suggested that the author of the revision lived in Italy.

18. In some of his own notes, Masnut draws upon his knowledge of Arabic. His reliance, in the main, on the Talmudic-Midrashic material justifies his calling his book a midrash; indeed, it takes the place of a classical midrash on the Book of Job. Masnut mentions the rabbinic authorities by name, but gives no references to sources.

19. Cf. Rashi on 9:4, 5, 11, 13, 15, 16 whose terse notes he expands. For Masnut on 9:22, *ba'averah,* read with Rashi *ba'avurah.*

20. The friends were reprimanded, for they did not undergo a change of heart, but continued their arguments against Job (comment on 42:7).

21. Julius Galliner, *Abraham ibn Esra's Hiobkommentar auf seine Quellen untersucht* (Berlin, 1901), pp. 18, 30, *et passim*.

22. *Ma'ase 'Efod*, p. 44.

23. Ibn Ezra states this in conscious opposition to the Talmudic opinion that attributed the authorship to Moses (BT *Baba Bathra* 14b).

24. Published in the rabbinical Bibles (Venice, 1517, and Amsterdam, 1724–27).

25. First published in Constantinople in 1519; *Sha'ar ha-Gemul* appeared in separate editions in Naples in 1490, and Ferrara in 1556.

26. The extensive introduction to the commentary places the Job issue into the context of the general problem of Divine providence. Since the Torah postulates God's providential knowledge and care for the individual, a tenet that is, however, often contradicted by human experience, Scripture was bound to deal with the problem. In Psalm 73 the solution is left in a state of ambiguity, whereas the Book of Job contains the full answer. Following the Talmudic tradition, Nahmanides considered the Book to be the work of Moses, who wrote it on command from God, just as he wrote the Book of Genesis.

27. *Sha'ar ha-Gemul* (Ferrara, 1556), p. 11.

28. *Ibid.*, p. 15.

29. Cf. Nahmanides' similarly veiled reference to transmigration in his commentary on Gen. 38:8.

30. *Sha'ar ha-Gemul*, pp. 12–14. Among the parallels between this treatise and the Job commentary are the references to Psalm 73; to the fate of Rabbi Akiba; to the influence of constellation on human life; to the essential difference between the issue of "the righteous man who suffers" and "the wicked who prospers," and to the solution proposed by Elihu. One of the major differences is the evaluation of the Lord's speeches.

31. *Sha'ar ha-Gemul*, p. 16.

32. *Ibid.*, pp. 16f.

33. *Ibid.*, p. 17. In his article "Über die Authentie des Commentars Nachmani's zum Buche Job" (*Monatsschrift für Geschichte und Wissenschaft des Judentums*, 17:449–458 [1868], Zacharias Frankel noticed some discrepancies between Nahmanides' Job commentary and his other writings and concluded that this commentary was the work of a later mystic who ingeniously used the master's style and attributed it to him. Frankel thought to have found convincing proof for his assertion in Nahmanides' failure to formulate Elihu's theory in *Sha'ar ha-Gemul*, whereas the commentary is more explicit on this point. From a remark of Gersonides in the introduction to his Job commentary (to the effect that, except for Maimonides, no interpreter had analyzed the opinions posited in the Book of Job) Frankel concluded that the author of the pseudo-Nahmanides, who did offer such an analysis, must have written after Gersonides. But, as already pointed out by Bela Bernstein (*Die Schrifterklärung des Bachja b. Ascher ibn Chalawa und ihre Quellen* [Berlin, 1891], p. 15, n. 36), Frankel's argument is refuted by the testimony of Bahya ben Asher, who used Nahmanides' commentary in his own *Kad ha-Qemah* and, being close to Nahmanides' period and his doctrines, must have been sure of the identity of the true author. As to Frankel's other

charge: the change in the measure of reluctance to reveal what is hidden should not be found astonishing in the writings of a mystic. Nahmanides' Job commentary is quoted also in *Sefer ha-Emunoth* by Shemtov ibn Shemtov (Ferrara, 1557), VII, 3.

34. *Kad ha-Qemah*, a critical edition by Hayyim Breit, based on manuscripts in Oxford and Parma (Lemberg, 1880).

35. *Kad ha-Qemah* 73b. For Bahya's reference to Nahmanides as his source, see 68a. He took over Nahmanides' introductions to, and interpretative summaries of, the Book's sections, while omitting the exegesis of the text.

36. Elihu, like the friends and Job himself, came from the seed of Abraham, "the root of faith" (*Kad ha-Qemah* 69b, 73a.)

37. *Kad ha-Qemah* 74a.

38. *Ibid.*, 74b–76a.

39. *Ibid.*, 76a, commenting on Job 42:4.

40. Equally significant is the remark that the Book of Job corresponds to the Book of Genesis; both teach the creation of the world and providence; both refer to God predominantly as *'elohim,* thus emphasizing the attribute of Divine justice. Bahya ben Asher's *Sova' Semahot* (Amsterdam, 1768), presented on the title page as a commentary on Job, is only an abridgment of certain sections of *Kad ha-Qemah* and the author's *Shulhan 'Arba'*, an ethico-religious treatise.

41. The date appears in the concluding note to the book, printed in Salonica in 1517. The references that follow are according to the Venice edition of 1567.

42. Arama interpreted Job 19:25 as referring to Job's faith during the years of well-being and the rest of the sentence as indicating his current state.

43. *Meir 'Iyyov* 57b f. In Arama's interpretation, Eliphaz considers Job's suffering as either a test of piety or a chastisement for sins, since no man is perfect; the suffering of the pious is, therefore, a providential act and rebellious man is simply in error (*Meir 'Iyyov* 18a f. on Job 4 and 5). Bildad goes a step further by denying that there is ever a case of a righteous man suffering without reason (*Meir 'Iyyov* 23b on Job 8).

44. *Meir 'Iyyov* 93b and 111a.

45. After Elihu's defense of providence no further argument was needed, Arama maintains; God appeared only in response to Job's quest to be addressed by his Creator.

46. *Meir 'Iyyov* 111a f.

47. *Ibid.*, 115a.

48. *Ibid.*, 122a.

49. *Ibid.*, concluding note.

50. *Mishpat Sedeq* (Venice, 1589), printed together with Simeon Duran's *'Ohev Mishpat.*

51. The friends, according to Arama, explained Job's fate as vicarious suffering for the sin of his generation, or as punishment for his lack of loving-kindness toward the poor or chastisement for his presumptuous wish to reason with God, or as occasioned by the sin of Adam or "the instigation of the serpent." Elihu argued that God deviates from the course of nature in order to fulfill the needs of man, who is the purpose of creation; the mighty movements of the spheres are designed to benefit man, transitory though he be (*Mishpat Sedeq,* introduction).

52. *Mishpat Sedeq,* introduction, 3b–6a.

53. A critical edition, by Joseph Derenbourg, with notes by W. Bacher, appeared as volume V of the *Oeuvres complètes de R. Saadia* (Paris, 1899). For a critical analysis of the translation, see Roman Ecker, *Die arabische Job-Übersetzung des Gaon Saadja ben Josef al-Fajjumi* (Munich, 1962). Cf. also Erwin I. J. Rosenthal, "Saadya's Exegesis of the Book of Job," *Saadya Studies* (Manchester, 1943).

54. The three friends, however, maintain a narrow view of suffering (which, according to Saadya, may befall one for the sake of moral and intellectual instruction, or as an act of purificiation from sin, or as a test and examination of faith). Only Elihu, who pointed to "test and examination" as the cause of Job's suffering, had the correct concept. Saadya considered the three speeches of Elihu (Job 32–35) to be the answer to three speeches by Job (comment on 35:16).

55. In circumventing anthropomorphisms, Saadya went far beyond the Targum, which he used and on which he was in a large measure dependent. Cf. the list in Rosenthal, pp. 188–191. However, Abraham ibn Daud (*Ha-'Emunah ha-Ramah* [Frankfurt am Main, 1852], p. 89) found that "the interpreter" was not thorough enough. Jakob Guttmann, *Die Religionsphilosophie des Abraham ibn Daud* (Göttingen, 1879), p. 31, identified "the interpreter" as Saadya.

56. This chapter circulated in the Middle Ages as a separate treatise, known as *Sefer ha-Teshuvah* (The Book of Repentance).

57. *'Emunoth ve-Deoth* (ed. D. Slucki, Leipzig, 1864), p. 87. Saadya continues by saying that God would not have chosen a man unable to endure the test of suffering; a pious man's status among his fellow men rises once his faith is proved firm against the challenge of seeming injustice.

58. As in the *tafsir*, so here too Saadya maintains that there is no Divine answer to a quest such as Job 10:2; only when suffering is meted out as punishment is the definite reason revealed to man or nation, as the case may be.

59. See esp. Saadya's rendition of Job 13:14, 15, and 19.

60. The Bodleian manuscript (Neubauer 125) which contains Saadya's Job translation and commentary includes, in addition, a second Arabic translation of some 600 of the 1070 verses of Job and an Arabic commentary of some 140 verses from the first half of the Book: remnants of the work of Moses ben Samuel ha-Kohen, called ibn Gikatilla. Wilhelm Bacher published these texts, which previously had been confused with those of Saadya (*Festschrift zu Ehren des Dr. A. Harkavy* [St. Petersburg, 1908], pp. 221–272). Moses ha-Kohen's commentary was used by Abraham ibn Ezra, in a number of passages, in the latter's Job commentary.

61. Maimonides believed he had offered an exhaustive and final elucidation of the idea contained in the account of Job (*Guide*, III, 22, end). For one of his chief observations he claimed prophetic inspiration (*kidemut nevuah*) (*Guide*, III, 22, middle).

62. *Yeser ha-ra'*; BT *Baba Bathra* 16a.

63. *Aboth de-R. Nathan* I, 16.

64. Job's and his friends' opinions on providence correspond, in Maimonides' view, to the theories of the various schools of thought: Job's view parallels the opinion of Aristotle; Eliphaz' insistence on strict justice is the view of the Torah; Bildad's defense of the theory of reward and compensation suggests the doctrine of the Mutazilah, and Zophar's recourse to the Divine will as the source of all events coincides with the view of the Ashariya (*Guide*, III, 23).

65. Maimonides opined (*Guide*, III, 23) that in Elihu's speech were intermingled ideas already expressed by the previous speakers, in order "to conceal the opinion peculiar to each speaker" from the sight of the ordinary reader.

66. Maimonides made a point of calling both Satan and the two inclinations "angels" (*Guide*, III, 22, end).

67. Published by Israel Schwarz in his *Tikvat 'Enosh* (Berlin, 1868), pp. 167–293.

68. *Ibid.*, pp. 170f. The commentary contains critical remarks against Abraham ibn Ezra's and Nahmanides' interpretation of Job.

69. The author tried to understand Maimonides' reluctance to reveal to the ordinary reader the true meaning of Elihu's view beyond proferring a slight hint (*remez rahoq*); he himself, however, felt inclined to lift the veil somewhat (*Tikvat 'Enosh*, Zerahya's comment on 32:3). On the nonesoteric level, Elihu in rejecting Job's denial of providence, affirmed divine concern for human beings, both during their lives and thereafter (comment on 34:21f.).

70. See my Note 64.

71. Written in 1326; published at Ferrara in 1477 and Naples in 1486 and included in the rabbinical Bibles. An English translation, with introduction and notes by Abraham L. Lassen (*The Commentary of Levi ben Gersom [Gersonides] on the Book of Job*), appeared in New York in 1946. This translation has been used in the present chapter.

72. *Milhamot' Adonai*, completed in 1329. Published at Riva di Trenta in 1560. The references in the present chapter are to the Leipzig edition of 1866. Direct quotations from the *Wars* are found in the commentary. In the introduction to the commentary, the author refers to the treatment of the central theme in the *Wars*, and in the *Wars* he refers to his analysis in the commentary (*Wars*, IV, 2, p. 155). In the introduction to the commentary, Gersonides states that the Job interpretations of his predecessors (except that of Maimonides) hindered rather than advanced his understanding of the Book; they failed to "direct the explanation of the words in accordance with the meaning of the contents."

73. The friends represent current popular opinions, Gersonides thought. Eliphaz affirmed individual providence but admitted that some suffering is caused by man's defective knowledge and some good is due to accident. Bildad believed that everything comes from God, but that men lack adequate understanding of what is really good or evil. Zophar questioned man's ability to judge the character of the righteous and the wicked correctly. Job rejected these affirmations of God's justice as mere assumptions.

74. According to Elihu, the sin of Job consisted in negating the value of man's following in the ways of God—a view that leads to a paralysis of social life and intellectual perfection. The divinely established order in the universe reflects His "justice, equity, goodness and grace." God, mighty and wise in the work of Creation, cannot be considered to be less effective in dealing with the comparatively simpler issue of "bringing good to the good and evil to the evil" (commentary on chap. 34, general principles). Elihu justified Job's affliction as a providential measure, intended to free him "from his tendency toward rebellion" (commentary on chap. 37, general principles).

75. In ascribing chap. 28 to Job, Gersonides has Job acknowledge the ultimate value of wisdom; its essence being known only to God, it is accessible to men in a

measure dependent on the degree of their closeness to God. Though both the righteous and the wicked are alike in matters of external success, only the former attain eternal happiness, which is wisdom and understanding; this state is to be reached by the fear of the Lord and by avoiding evil (commentary on chap. 28, the discourse as a whole, and the general principles).

76. *'Ohev Mishpat,* written in 1405, was published at Venice in 1589 and in the rabbinical Bible (Amsterdam, 1724–27).

77. Completed in 1425.

78. *'Ohev Mishpat,* introduction, chap. iv, end.

79. *Ibid.,* comment on 9:24.

80. It can be assumed that in the concept of the Intercessor as the force opposing Satan, Duran followed the suggestion of Maimonides.

81. *Magen Abot* (Leghorn, 1785), 33b.

82. *'Ohev Mishpat,* comment on 42:6.

83. *Ibid.,* 204b.

84. *Ibid.,* introduction, chap. viii.

85. *Ibid.,* introduction, chaps. ii–iv and xiii–xvi. In his edition of *'Iqqarim* (see Note 86), IV, 49, n. 5, Husik refers erroneously to *Magen Abot;* read *'Ohev Mishpat.*

86. Completed (according to Zacuto) in 1425 and published at Venice in 1485. Isaac Husik published a critical edition and English translation (*Sefer ha-'Iqqarim, Book of Principles,* by Joseph Albo, 4 vols. [Philadelphia, 1929–30]).

87. Heinrich Jaulus, "R. Simeon ben Zemach Duran. Ein Zeit- und Lebensbild," *Monatsschrift für Geschichte und Wissenschaft des Judentums,* 23 (N.S., 6): 447–463 (1874). Already Jacob ibn Habib and Isaac Abravanel had referred to Albo's borrowings. See Manuel Joel, *Don Chasdai Creskas' religionsphilosophische Lehren* (Breslau, 1866), p. 76f.

88. Had Job been a servant of God out of perfect love and not merely "a God-fearing man," then, Albo thinks, Job would have accepted his suffering "gracefully, for the love of God" and the question of reward and punishment and the underlying issue of providence would not have arisen (IV, 11). He would have understood the happiness of the wicked and the misfortune of the just as being ultimately justified (IV, 14 and 15). Albo lists "four reasons or explanations for the prosperity of the wicked and four for the instances of evil befalling the righteous" (IV, 13).

89. E.g., the juxtaposition of Job and Abraham, the national origin of Job, his position at the court of Pharaoh, the New Year as the day of the assembly in heaven, one year as the duration of the trial, the play on the words *'Iyyov* and *'oyyev* ("Job" and "enemy"), the exegesis of Job 2:10. On the Zohar's literary sources, *see* G. G. Scholem, *Major Trends in Jewish Mysticism* (New York, 1954), pp. 172–176.

90. In the Zohar's interpretation of Gen. 4:8, Cain sacrificed mainly to the "other side," rendering his gift unacceptable to God, while Abel brought his offering mainly to God and spared only "the fat thereof" to the "other side" (Zohar, II, 34a).

91. Zohar, II, 34a.

92. *Ibid.,* 33a. Another account speaks of Job as a righteous man among Pharaoh's advisers, one to whom Exod. 9:22 refers, and who was impelled to

suffer together with the Egyptians, because under certain conditions "the righteous are punished for the guilt of the wicked." It was to this fact that Job referred
in his speech, 9:22 (Zohar, II, 52b f.).

At variance with the Biblical characterization of Job's wife (Job 2:9f.), Zohar,
III, 5a, speaks of her as being as God-fearing as her husband; it was because of
her that he was called "great" (Job 1:3).

93. Zohar, III, 101b. A different role is assigned to Job in a brief discourse on
Job 1:6. As in the Targum and elsewhere in the Zohar, "the day" is interpreted as
the New Year and Job is understood to have been "smitten to make atonement for
the sins of the world" (Zohar, III, 231a).

94. Zohar, II, 33b.

95. *Ibid.*, 166a f.

96. *Ibid.*, I, 180a f.

97. Appeared at Venice in 1603. Alsheikh accepted the traditional notion that
Job lived at the time of the exodus from Egypt and was used by God as a scapegoat
to pacify Satan (*Helqat Mehoqeq* 4a, commenting on Job 1:7).

98. *Helqat Mehoqeq* 79a. The problem of the suffering of the just and the
prosperity of the wicked would be resolved in the World to Come (*ibid.*, 23b, on
Job 9:22).

99. *Helqat Mehoqeq* 91a, on Job 37:22. In Alsheikh's view, Job exemplifies such
faith. Commenting on Job 13:15, he has Job express his conviction that the Lord,
who sees the heart, is aware of his uprightness (35a). Job's wish that his words be
written in a book (19:23) Alsheikh interpreted as referring to the book of the
Torah (51a f.). His slight imperfections were corrected by the redemptive experience of suffering (101b, commenting on Job 42:2).

10
ZION IN MEDIEVAL LITERATURE PROSE WORKS

In the period of Western European Emancipation important spokesmen for a Europe-Centered Judaism declared that Jews no longer considered Zion their concern.

Abraham Geiger, outstanding advocate of Reform in the mid-nineteenth century, interpreted Judaism as a universal religion and ethics of humanity which cannot be reconciled with a national existence and national aspirations. Thus only after the abolition of the independent state in Zion, could the Jew assume the historic role of representing an abstract, all-comprising, faith. Modern Jewry will have to discard the last remnants and symbolic remainders of a national past and the last shreds of hope for a revival of Zion, before unrestricted Jewish religious universalism can become reality. We do not wish to return to Zion; the earth is our home.

This attitude, though it adduced biblical prophets for its support, indicated a radical break with the thinking of classical Judaism. What had happened was more than a change of emphasis. It is still too early to determine how far-reaching this break was. The meaning of this change within Judaism can be better understood if the idea of Zion in medieval Hebrew thought is considered. Here, Exile and the restoration of Zion appear as the central facts in the inner life of the Jew. Literature records what can be expressed in words. Thus the religious philosopher Saadia (9th-10th cent.): "Our Lord has informed us through His prophets that He will deliver us from the state in which we find ourselves now; that He will gather our dispersed from East and West and bring us to Zion and settle us there permanently."[1]

Dispersion was considered an abnormal state. Hasdai ibn Shaprut, the tenth century Spanish statesman and lover of Hebrew learning, writes: "We who were many are now few, and are fallen from our high estate and dwell in Exile. We have no answer to those who say to us daily: 'Every people has a kingdom, but you have none.' "[2]

At times, what was beneath the surface broke through with the strange power of the paradox: "The destruction of the Temple was not a reality, the foundations of Zion never fell into the power of other nations; God has treasured up the stones of Jerusalem and hidden them from the sight of men; a day will come and the ancient stones will be revealed and found in their former position."[3]

The radical "no" to Zion, pronounced by Western European Emancipation, is here countered by determined, and, at times, radical, affirmation. Before analyzing this affirmation in some detail, let us review some of the more pronounced attempts to bring about redemption and a Messianic return to Zion.

I. ATTEMPTS AT REDEMPTION

About 720 Sharini (Serenus) appeared in Syria and proposed to free Palestine from the Mohammedans. A generation later Abu Isa of Ispahan, Persia, and his disciple Yudghan, rose to free the Jews from Exile and to reestablish Zion. The 12th century saw the rise of David Alroy in the East and in the 11th-12th centuries a number of Messiahs in the West: in Fez, in Cordoba, and in France. In the year 1121 a Messiah appeared in the land of Israel by the name of Solomon, who envisaged an impending ingathering of all Israel in Jerusalem. In 1172 a Messiah whose name we do not know stirred the Jews in Yemen to hopes of a return to Zion.

A mystic Messiah appeared in the person of Abraham Abulafia of Saragossa; he went to Rome to sit among its poor and the rejected, as tradition depicts the Messiah of Israel; for the year 1290 he expected the beginning of the era of redemption. He was followed by his disciple, Abraham, the prophet of Avila, who waited for the redemption to begin in 1295.

The year 1391 was a year of widespread destruction for Spanish Jewry; the following year a Kabbalist, Moses of Castile, was supposed to become the divine instrument of redemption. Isaac Abarbanel who witnessed the expulsion of the Jews from Spain in 1492 was convinced by his interpretation of the Book of Daniel that the redemption would come in 1503. The year before, Asher Laemmlein, encouraged by the Messianic writings of Abarbanel appeared as the forerunner of the Messiah. Also at the beginning of the 16th century, a young woman of a Spanish Marrano family testified that the king Messiah had appeared to her and had made her a messenger of the approaching redemption. In 1524, David Reubeni, an adventurous Oriental Jew, arrived in Rome to win Pope Clement VII for a plan of a reconquest of Palestine from the Turks. Soon, Reubeni was joined by Solomon Molcho, a Spanish marrano who lived in Messianic visions of the fall of Rome and the rise of Israel in Zion.

The 16th century mystics in Safed perceived signs of the impending redemption of Zion; the disciples of the saintly Rabbi Isaac Luria believed that their master was himself the Messiah, son of Joseph, who was to precede the Messiah, son of David. Don Joseph Nasi of Constantinople, who started to rebuild Tiberias in 1565 with the thought of establishing a Jewish colony, aroused in the faithful the belief that this plan would lead to the coming of the Messiah.

The most fateful Messianic movement in Jewish history, centered around Sabbatai Zevi, coincided with the aftermath of the Chmielnitzki catastrophe in Poland (1648–9) and the devastation of central Europe during the Thirty-Years-War. The Messianic year was expected to come in 1666 and Jews everywhere in the world impatiently awaited the end of the Exile and the start of new life in Zion redeemed.[4]

As late as 1840 we find a group of enthusiasts—the so-called Tarniks—in Eastern Europe who expected the redemption to occur in that year. Here ends the epic only partly retold, of the expected return to Zion which started to occupy the mind of the people since the early Middle Ages.

All these attempts ended in failure. It would be historically wrong to say that all those who put their trust in the Messiahs without ever reaching Zion found their way back to the organized Jewish community in Exile. The aftermaths of the so-called pseudo-Messianic movements form a tragic chapter in Jewish history, and Hebrew literature displays an understandable reluctance to go beyond allusions in dealing with this issue.

However, the very recurrence of Messianic leaders, visionaries or psychopaths, coupled with an ever-renewed belief in elaborately calculated "Messianic years," illustrate the force of the Zion idea in Jewish history. If, in an attempt to analyze the attitudes to Zion, we shall speak of five main types, we readily admit that they are interrelated and that, at various points, they overlap and blend in the fancy of the people. Yet, this should not prevent us from a description, however tentative, of the major trends as they confront us in the writings of the Jewish Middle Ages (which extend far beyond the medieval period in the West).

We find some —mainly in the East—to whom Zion was the land to be reconquered by a Messianic action which was to take place within the framework of history; others—mainly in the West—were engaged in a mystic vision of the redemption without, however, losing sight of the concreteness of Zion; still others, non-Messianists, non-mystics, attempted to return to Zion as individuals or in small groups of dedicated men. And there were those who placed Zion within a structure of thought that seemed to give preference to values considered higher than Zion, namely, Sinai, Torah and the World-to-Come. Finally, there were those who assimilated all the motifs, all the apparent differences and contradictions, into one great— and very simple—concept of Zion, as both ideal and reality, fact and faith in one.

All these thinkers, visionaries, and men of action left an echo of what moved them in chronicles, travelers' notes, letters, biblical commentaries, rabbinic responsa, legendary accounts. In reconstructing their thinking, we come face to face with a picture of strange grandeur; find ourselves in the presence of a drama of a people in Exile who, generation after generation and through many different roads, attempt a return to Zion. The expulsion from Zion could not destroy the validity of Zion.

II. THE RECONQUEST OF ZION (MILITANT MESSIANISM)

Our first inquiry will be into the Zion idea inherent in the Messianic movements which—as we have seen—rose time after time. In most of these movements the faithful rallied around a Messianic leader, who, as part of his mission, proposed to free the land of Israel and to reestablish Zion. What is the driving force behind medieval Messianism? Is it the desire of the persecuted group to free itself from oppression? Or a romantic striving for the revival of a glorious past? Let us consider the medieval Messianic *midrashim* which deal with this aspect of Zion, e.g., *The Book of Elijah, The Book of Zerubbabel, The Revelations of Simeon ben Yohai.*

The Book of Elijah,[5] written early in the seventh century, a period of wars between Persia and Rome, views these clashes as directly related to the final attack of Gog and Magog on Jerusalem, an act, which must precede redemption. "Then Messiah appears and God, aided by him, wages war against all the nations." Israel's rise is bound up with the fall of the godless empires. *The Book of Zerubbabel*[6] expected the coming of the Messiah in 638, when the Persian empire fell and Islam rose to power in the East. This world-historical event becomes the background for the activity of the Messiah, called Menahem ben Amiel. He will fight against Armilus, the last of the kings who went to war against Jerusalem, Armilus will be defeated and "the saviors shall go up to Mount Zion to rule Mount Esau and the kingdom shall be the Lord's."[7] The little book with its mixture of apocalyptic visions and political motivation became a basic text for later Messianic literature.

The first part of *The Revelations of Simeon ben Yohai* comes to us from the early Islamic period. The unknown author interprets the historic role of Islam as the power divinely appointed to break the rule of Rome and prepare the way for Israel's return to Zion.[8] In this connection, a *responsum* by Rab Hai Gaon (940–1038), dealing with the redemption of Zion, should be mentioned. Here, based on older documents, the first redeemer, the Messiah son of Joseph, is to slay the Edomite governor of Jerusalem. "When the nations of the world hear that an Israelite king has risen in Jerusalem they will expel the Jews from their midst. . . . They will say: Since you have your own king, you shall not remain in our countries. . . . Many Jews will leave the covenant of Israel and join the nations. . . ." The drama of redemption unfolds and finally Israel is united in Zion, joined by the nations that survived the wars. "And when they will appear before the King Messiah, he will order them to cease using swords and resorting to wars." This political aspect of redemption is followed by a supernatural vision of a new heaven and a new earth.[9]

In these writings, redemption and the return to Zion are placed squarely in the midst of history. Wars between the nations of the world are of immediate relevance to the future of Zion.[10] God did not withdraw into a beyond with the fall of Jerusalem; He still acts within world-history and uses political means for the sake of Zion. The place of Israel is within the frame of history, the wicked empires of the heathens will run their course and vanish, whereupon Israel is to establish the kingdom of God on earth; the servitude to the empires must, therefore, come to an end and Israel return to its historic rôle in Zion and in the world. Thus, the Messianic movements are political actions, historical movements in the strict sense of the term, although supernatural aspects enter the overall picture. Israel's withdrawal from active history, the abandonment of the world as the scene of history, is of a temporary nature and not final; Zion is not merely a place of refuge for a persecuted minority, not only the religious center of Judaism, but the historical response to the challenge of Edom, Rome, the fourth of the Empires; Zion is destined to replace the tyrannies of the world by the authentic kingdom. The return to Zion is the return to historical action. The Messiahs through the ages demonstrate the urgency of this idea.

III. ZION IN HEAVEN AND ON EARTH (THE ZOHAR)

The motif of the activist, militant Messiah enters even the type of medieval writing where one would least expect it: mystical literature. In the *Zohar*, the Messiah appears in a dual rôle: as the man of suffering and as the man of war. Jerusalem destroyed causes a critical disunity in the world; her restoration will effect the harmony even within the Deity. The drama of the fall and the restoration of Zion takes place simultaneously on two levels, one upper, one lower.

As the suffering servant the Messiah hears of "the pain and affliction of those who suffer for their belief in the unity of God," he "weeps aloud and enters a certain Hall of the Afflicted; there he takes upon himself all the pains and sufferings of Israel. For as long as Israel was in the Holy Land, the Temple service averted afflictions from the world; now it is the Messiah who keeps them away from mankind."[11]

The suffering redeemer becomes the fighter against the world of wickedness and an avenger of his people. "The kings of the world rise to fight against him and even in Israel there will be come wicked ones joining in the battle against the Messiah.

"The Messiah lifts up his eyes and beholds the Patriarchs visiting the ruins of God's Sanctuary. He beholds mother Rachel with tears in her eyes. The Holy One tries to comfort her, but she refuses to be comforted.

"The day comes when a flame of fire shall be burning in Great Rome/ Constantinople/; it will consume many towers and many of the powerful shall perish then. The kings will take counsel together and issue many decrees to destroy Israel. The Messiah beholds the picture of the destruction of the Temple and of the saints who were martyred there. And the sintly fathers will arise and gird the Messiah with weapons of war. Then he will take ten garments of holy zeal and go into hiding for forty days and no eye shall be permitted to see him."

"The Holy One shall behold the Messiah thus adorned and He will kiss him upon his brow and set upon his head the crown that He Himself had worn when the children of Israel were freed from Egypt. Then the Messiah will enter one of the sanctuaries, and behold there angels who are called 'the mourners of Zion' weeping over the destruction of the Temple; they shall give him a robe of deep red that he may commence his work of revenge."

"After having been crowned on high, the Messiah shall be crowned on earth near the grave of mother Rachel. To her he will offer happy tidings and comfort her, and now she will let herself be comforted and will rise and kiss him."

"His army will consist of those who are diligent in the study of the Torah, but there shall be only few such in the world. Yet his army will gain strength through the merit of little children at school and through the merit of the infants for whose sake the Divine Presence dwells in the midst of Israel in Exile. For it is the young ones and the infants that will give strength to the Messiah."

"On that day the Messiah will begin to gather the exiles from one end of the world to the other." The events of the liberation from Egypt will repeat themselves.[12]

The new Zion will restore the glory of the old. For "since the destruction of the Temple, blessings had been withheld from the world, both on high and here below, so that the lower forces were strengthened. . . . When the Temple was destroyed and the people driven into dispersion, the Divine Presence took one last look at the Holy of Holies and left her home to accompany Israel into Exile."

When she had entered the lands of dispersion she learned how the people were oppressed and trodden under foot by the heathen nations. "But the day comes when the Holy One will recall the Community of Israel and the Divine Presence will return from Exile, restore the Sanctuary, build the city of Jerusalem and raise Israel from the dust."[13]

If we compare this picture of the redemption of Zion with the militant Messianism of *The Book of Elijah, The Book of Zerubbabel, The Revelation of Simeon ben Yohai*, we see that the mystics were concerned not only with the historic wrong committed by the Empires of the world, and with the restoration of Israel's place in history, but also with the healing of a cosmic wound. It is not only Israel that needs Zion; the equilibrium of the world depends on Zion; a new Zion will end the separation between God and his world. Not only Israel's exile will end, but universal exile. Redemption of Zion has a cosmic meaning.

There is enough in such writing—which was quite popular with not insignificant groups within the Jewish people—to divert the mind from the realm of doing into the realm of supernatural vision. But the careful reader will sense between the lines the power to transform heavenly visions into concrete, even revolutionary, action in behalf of an earthly Zion.

IV. ZION AS A PERSONAL SOLUTION OF THE GALUT PROBLEM (JUDAH HA-LEVI)

Zion, as we continue our reading of medieval literature, was not only fought for by militant Messianism, not only longer for in mystic vision. Equally important, Zion was reached by those who saw in it the place where a Jew might find his personal solution of the Galut peoblem and reenter the covenant with his God. This view is best represented by Judah Ha-Levi (c. 1080-c. 1141), who recognized both the historic and the universal role of Zion but who confronted the collective action of the Messianists and the mystics with his personal commitment. At the basis of Judah Ha-Levi's thought is the ancient Hebrew concept of the interrelationship between Israel, its God, and its land. The covenant between God and Israel—the central fact of Jewish faith—requires for its realization a place on this earth. This concept Judah Ha-Levi presents in his poetry, in his book, the *Kuzari*; he attempts to realize it in his very life. The king of the Khazars, voicing the attitude of many, accepts the fact of the relationship between God and the people of Israel, but questions the rabbi on the necessity of the *land* of Israel.

Answering, Judah Ha-Levi makes his classic declaration: The Holy Land is the only place on earth in which the divine element (*ha inyan ha-elohi*), can manifest itself; prophecy is possible only in this land, or with reference to this land. Ha-Levi removes the early history of mankind, Adam, Cain and Abel, from the legendary nowhere and everywhere, and places them in the historic realm of Zion.

The conflict between the brothers Isaac and Ishmael, Jacob and Esau, was not, he claims, about material prosperity, but about the blessing connected with this land. Both Ishmael and Esau (who later came to be regarded as symbols for Islam and Rome) inherited worldly power, but the covenant with God remained with Isaac, Jacob and his descendants. Moses' prophecy is connected with Mount Sinai—which to Judah Ha-Levi is part of the Holy Land. The revelation took place on Sinai, i.e., outside the limits of Palestine, which earlier sages have taken as a symbolic indication of the supra-national, universal character of the Mosaic revelation. But Judah Ha-Levi, without minimizing the universal meaning of Torah, insists on the proximity of Sinai, mount of revelation, and Zion, center of the religious universe of faith.

Thus, Ha-Levi continues, Zion is destined to guide the world to the truth. And, indeed, not only the children of Israel, but sons of other nations, Persians, Indians, Greeks, offered sacrifices in Jerusalem. Even today, all nations make pilgrimages to this land.

Turning from the past to the present, Ha-Levi lets the king express what he himself felt so keenly: if Jerusalem is the sacred place on earth for all monotheist religions, if Israel in the past desired to remain in it, if Israel believes that the Divine Presence will return there, if it truthfully recites the prayer, "Have mercy on Zion, for it is the house of your life," if all this is so, how is it that you don't do all in your power to live there? This question, which reaches deep into the historic tragedy of the Jewish people, Ha-Levi does not answer by an apologetic reference to adverse political conditions (an easy thing in the period of the Crusades), nor by a theological reference to a plan of salvation which might impose our waiting for the right moment. Judah Ha-Levi sharply criticizes his people for the sluggishness of their response to the call of God's land. The failure to return he calls Israel's sin. The reestablishment of the covenant between God, Israel, and the land did not, and does not, depend on historical forces or on an inscrutable will of God, but on the people's decision to enter this covenant. "The divine spirit only gives man as much as he is able to receive."[14]

The covenant is still binding: in Zion only God can be worshipped in freedom. "Functions of faith will be perfect only in Zion"; "Heart and soul are pure and immaculate only in the place which we know had been chosen by God." Zion serves to remind men of, and to move them to, the love of God. If all Israel would yearn deeply for its land, even though it lies presently in ruins, Jerusalem would be rebuilt.[15] It is this desire to free oneself of the sin of Exile, that prompts Judah Ha-Levi to leave his family and friends, his native land and his medical practice, and to start his travel to Zion.

The poet in Judah Ha-Levi does not remain arrested in a blissful vision of Zion, the thinker does not find rest in his knowledge of the Covenant. He does not wait for a Messiah to prepare the way to Zion. Since Zion is the solution of the religious and of the Galut problem—both are related—the Jew, according to Ha-Levi, is obligated to seek this solution as an individual, representing the people of Israel in the solitude of his personal life.

Thus, Judah Ha-Levi exemplifies the faithful who before him, and after him, singly, or in small groups, attempted to go to Zion, without waiting for a Messiah to lead them.

There is a vast literature of letters and reports by such travelers.[16] Of the many *aliyot*, "ascents" to Zion, let us mention the three hundred or more French and English rabbis who went to Zion in 1211, to anticipate there the coming of redemption.

A brief reference to the most distinguished thirteenth-century rabbi in Germany, Meir of Rothenburg, is apposite here. It was this master of Halakhah who decided that "it is permissible to leave one's teacher (in the land of Israel) and to go to the diaspora in order to study Torah," and that "it is not permissible to leave one's teacher in the diaspora and to go to the land of Israel."[17] This *responsum* shows how central appeared to him a Jew's obligation to study the Torah. Yet the other center was Zion. Like Judah Ha-Levi before him, Rabbi Meir planned, therefore, to leave his native land and settle in Zion. He was caught on the way and, on order of the Emperor, confined in a fortress for the rest of his life.

The travelers to Zion were motivated not solely by a wish to anticipate the redemption in Zion. The land had not only a future. Its past was within reach; it lived on in the present. And there was a present.

As to the past, that lived on in the present. A good example of this is Obadiah of Bertinoro's "Letter from Jerusalem."[18] It communicates the excitement of the fifteenth-century Jew on finding that the spot where the angels appeared to Abraham was *still* called Mamre; that the valley Eshkol outside Hebron still bore that name; and that the grapes in the valley to *this day* excelled in size the grapes anywhere else. There were not only the graves of the patriarchs, sages and saints; by going to Zion, the Jew found himself in living contact with a past which, in his intellectual and religious life, never ceased to be a present.

As for the present, the travelers to Zion felt that he was returning to the land which was still his home. The changes in the official control of the country were never fully recognized; historic facts were not considered quite relevant.

From the second half of the ninth century we have this document: "It is a rule with our rabbis that there is not one man in Jewry who has not four cubits of ground in the land of Israel. And should it be said that that land was seized by Gentiles several generations ago, we answer, that it was established by our masters that the land cannot be seized and the tenure of Israel continues valid."[19]

The question whether Zion can ever be possessed by other nations already occurs in Rashi's (1040–1105) biblical Commentary. This classical work starts out almost demonstratively with the declaration—based on an older midrash—that the Holy Land, like all lands, is the Lord's, and that it was His will to take Canaan away from the hands of the seven nations and to give it to Israel. It has been suggested[20] that this nationalist comment on the cosmological, universalist, first sentence of Genesis illustrates Rashi's reaction to the contemporary Christian claim of the Holy Land as their inheritance. In 1064—Rashi was then 24 years old—thousands of Christians from the vicinity went on a pilgrimage to Jerusalem. Later, Rashi must have known of the preparations of the Crusaders to reconquer Jerusalem. The earlier Christian idea of a heavenly Jerusalem was now supplemented by an intense interest in the earthly Jerusalem. It was, therefore, the proper time for Rashi to reaffirm the ancient Jewish belief that persisted in spite of a full millennium of Galut: God has given us the land, it is ours. Ultimately, Israel will return to Zion and Jerusalem will be the city of the righteous.[21]

V. SINAI VERSUS ZION (MAIMONIDES)

The centrality of Zion, encountered so far in medieval Hebrew thought is counterbalanced by another idea: the devoted study of the Torah, which reenacts the event of Mount Sinai, makes the student worthy of the World-to-Come. The going back to Sinai frees the Jew from involvement in historic action and from the shocks of defeat by historic forces. By adhering to Sinai—an event preceding historic life in Zion—and preparing himself for the World-to-Come, the Jew is enabled to transcend the fate of life within history. History remains the frame of political activity, but more important than the rises and falls in history is the rise in man's intellectual perfection which is achieved by the study of Torah.

The outstanding exponent of this view is Moses Maimonides (1135–1204), who in his writings most clearly distinguished between the Messianic era and the World-to-Come. He lived in a period of decisive changes in the political structure of his native Spain and of Egypt, his adopted country. The world-historical struggle between Edom and Ishmael, Christian Rome and Islam, in which the Holy Land was significantly involved, led many Jews to believe that the hour of Messianic redemption had arrived. The wars of the great powers, it was felt, were a prelude to a radical change in the position of Israel in the world. The Moslem empire was believed to be the fourth of the empires, which according to the Book of Daniel, have to run their course in history before the Messianic empire of Israel is established in Zion.

Maimonides, who suffered with Israel, and shared its hopes for the liberation of Zion, opposed, nevertheless, both the *emphasis* on the Messianic turn of events, and the focal position which the anticipated return of Israel to the stage of history had assumed in the hearts of the people and many of its leaders.

His *Mishneh Torah* wherein he embodied the beliefs and the laws of Israel, Maimonides concluded with two great chapters on the Messianic age. "The Messiah will arise and renew the kingdom of David's house; he will rebuild the Temple in Zion and gather the dispersed of Israel. . . .

Do not think the Messiah will have to perform signs and miracles . . . Do not think that in the Messianic age anything in the world's order will be changed, or that an innovation will be introduced into creation. . . . Before that time a prophet will arise to guide and to prepare Israel; his only desire will be to establish peace in the world. . . . The sages and the prophets did not wish for the Messianic age in order to achieve dominion over the world, or to attain material advantage and ease. . ."

While painting this picture of a united humanity centered around a rebuilt Zion and dedicated to the knowledge of the Lord, Maimonides almost unobtrusively injects the remark that this radical turn in the human cosmos and in world history is not final. For the people of Israel the Messianic age is primarily a period of opportunity "to study Torah and wisdom without disturbance and interference, so that Israel be worthy to enter the life of the World-to-Come."[22] In this last of the fourteen books of the *Mishneh Torah*, he refers his reader to the first, where he gives a more detailed disquisition on the goal of the wise man and the true Israelite. That goal is the perfection of intellectual life and the worship of the Creator out of loving devotion; nothing else matters in the material world.

In his *Epistle to Yemen* Maimonides points to Sinai, the mount of revelation, as the central event in Judaism; whether Sanai is, as to Judah Ha-Levi, part of the territory of the land of Israel is irrelevant to him. The term "World-to-Come," he adds, is not to be understood as a world which does not exist at present and is to come only after this world has passed. This true world is with us right now, and we partake in it if we choose a life of Torah and wisdom. The present state of the historical world hinders the pursuit of this kind of intellectual life. As the center of a peaceful world, the new Zion will create the foundation for such true advancement of man. No pseudo-Messianic shortcuts will lead to Zion. And Zion is not an end in itself, because the end of man is not in history; but within this limited, yet real, material, historical world of peoples, the road to perfection leads through Zion.

On the level of day-to-day practice, this system of values, giving preference to Sinai over Zion, is expressed—to quote one out of many sources—in an opinion of Rabbi Hayyim Kohen (12th century) that "today there is no religious obligation to live in Zion . . . since we are not able to observe all the laws of the Torah connected with the land."[23] Here we may recall the *responsum* by Rabbi Meir of Rothenburg, who permitted a student to leave the land of Israel if it would benefit his studies of the Torah, but did not allow a student to leave his studies in the diaspora in order to settle in Zion.

The same Meir of Rothenburg criticized the eschatological ideas of the mystics of his time and opposed indiscriminate emigration to Zion.[24] To the question of why the Babylonian Talmudists (Amoraim) did not leave to settle in the land of Israel, he gave the answer that there the cares of a livelihood would have diverted them from the study of the Torah.[25]

Incisive criticism of those who, in their zeal for Torah, had neglected work for God's Kingdom in Zion can be found in a midrash that refers to earlier manifestations of this neglect. Here, God addresses himself to "the righteous ones in every generation": "O ye righteous ones, you deserve thanks that you have waited for my Torah, yet you did not wait for my Kingdom. He, however, who did wait for my Kingdom, I myself will be his witness to the good. So did those Mourners for Zion who suffered with me because of My desolate Sanctuary; now I will be their witness."[26]

VI. THE COVENANT WITH ZION (NAHMANIDES)

A combination of emphasis on the World-to-Come, as in Maimonides, and longing for the restoration of Zion, as in Judah Ha-Levi, is to be found in the 13th century Spanish mystic, Bible commentator, and physician, Moses ben Nahman, or Nahmanides. He believed that, though the final aim of our existence should be the World-to-Come, we must, nevertheless, adhere to the belief in the redemption in Zion; through the Zion idea we bear witness against powers in history, Spain and Rome. Only in the God-chosen land can we concentrate on undivided devotion to the Torah, that cannot be attained in Exile. Only in Zion will we be able to prove the truth of our religion to the nations of the world, Spain and Rome.

Messianism, according to Nahmanides, is the expression of our striving for the nearness of God, and, at the same time, the assertion of our wish to prove to our adversaries the truth of our cause.[27]

The spiritual aspect in Nahmanides' Zion concept may at any moment turn into an acceptance of Zion in all its concreteness, an acceptance comparable to Judah Ha-Levi's.

Nahmanides transforms a word of God to Moses, spoken in the particular situation of the conquest of Canaan, into a positive commandment valid at all times. He interprets the verse, "And you shall take possession of the land and settle in it, for I have given the land to you to possess it,"[28] as follows: "In my opinion this is a positive commandment; the Israelites are bidden to settle in the land. . . . ; they should not despise the inheritance of the Lord. Should they decide to go and to conquer Babylonia or Assyria or any other country and settle there, that would be a transgression of a divine commandment. Our sages have extolled the obligation to reside in the land of Israel and have considered it unlawful to leave the land; they have called rebellious a wife that refuses to follow her husband to the land of Israel; they have enjoined upon a husband to follow his wife to the land of Israel;[29] but here in this verse we have a definition of this duty as a positive commandment, as it occurs in other places also, such as:[30] 'Behold, I have set the land before you, go in and take possession of the land.' "[31]

The land of Israel is "our land," says Nahmanides, and no other nation may find a home there. In the verse, "And I will devastate the land, so that your enemies who settle in it shall be astonished at it," which the biblical text lists among the punishments for Israel's disobedience, Nahmanides reads "a happy message for all the exiled, namely, that our land does not accept its enemies. You will not find in the whole wide world a good and wide-stretched land, settled since ancient times, yet lying waste like the land of Israel; this is indeed promising for us for it reveals that since we left the land no other nation could be accepted there; all tried to settle there but none succeeded."[32] The commentary from which we quoted, was completed by Nahmanides in the land of Israel, to which he emigrated following the religious disputation in Barcelona in 1263.

In Nahmanides we behold a harmony, not at all consciously intended, yet fully accomplished, between the elements of mysticism and historic orientation, the concept of the World-to-Come and the act of returning to Zion. Although our literature documents these elements of the Zion idea in relatively distinct forms, it is the blending of beliefs and hopes, action and passion, that is characteristic of the medieval Jew. Thus it is fitting to conclude this essay with Nahmanides who represents this union.

From Jerusalem which had just been devastated by the Mongols, he writes to his son: "What shall I tell you about this country? It is barren and abandoned. To describe it briefly: the holier the places, the more waste. . . . But in spite of this destruction, the land is still blessed. . . . May He who constrained us to see Jerusalem destroyed, also grant us the joy of seeing it rebuilt and restored when the glory of His Presence returns there."[33]

The few examples from medieval Hebrew literature extant are expressions of considerable forces of intellect and emotion, indications of an awareness of historical phenomena, and of the perils involved in political action, documents of rebellion and faith, emanating from Zion. Most of this power and passion was directed into other intellectual or political pursuit in the course of Western European Emancipation; some of the classical Zion-centered energy entered modern Hebrew literature and the modern, largely secular, movement to rebuild Zion.

NOTES

1. *The Book of Doctrines and Beliefs,* ch. VIII.
2. Letter to the king of the Khazars.

3. *Zohar* II, 240b; *Emek ha-Melekh*, 65.

4. The Frankist movement cannot be considered here.

5. A. Jellinek, *Beth ha-Midrash*, III, Leipzig 1855.

6. *Beth ha-Midrash*, II.

7. Obadiah v. 21.

8. *Beth ha-Midrash*, III.

9. B. M. Levin, *Otzar ha-Geonim*, Sukkah.

10. Even the approaching Mongol invasion of 1237–1240 found a Messianic interpretation especially since 1240 coincided with the Hebrew year 5000, or the beginning of the sixth, and final, period in the pre-Messianic history of the world.

11. *Zohar* II, 212a.

12. *Ibid.*, II. 7b–9a.

13. *Ibid.*, I, 134a. For the Zohar quotations, see also *Commentary*, XXI (1956), pp. 365ff.

14. *Kuzari* II, 8–24.

15. *Ibid.*, V, 22–27.

16. Part of these writings were collected by Abraham Yaari in his *Iggerot Eretz Yisrael*, Tel Aviv 1943, and analyzed by Jacob David [Kurt] Wilhelm in his *Dor Dor ve-Olav*, Jerusalem 1946. See also *Roads to Zion*, edited by Kurt Wilhelm, New York 1948.

17. *Tashbetz*, No. 564f.

18. *Iggerot Eretz Yisrael*, p. 142.

19. M. Asaf, *History of Arab Rule in Palestine* [Hebrew] Tel Aviv 1935, p. 83.

20. Bernard D. Weinryb, "Rashi Against the Background of his Epoch," Rashi Anniversary Volume, American Academy for Jewish Research, New York 1941, p. 42.

21. Commentary on Isaiah 4:3.

22. Hilkhot Melakhim XII. 5. Cf. also Commentary on Mishnah Sanhedrin X, article 12.

23. *Tosafot*, Ketubot 110b.

24. *Tashbetz* No. 247 and 559–562.

25. *Ibid.*, No. 564. f.

26. *Pesikta Rabbati* XXXIV.

27. *Sefer Ha-Geulah*, London 1909, pp. 20–21.

28. Numbers 33:53.

29. Ketubot 110b.

30. Deuteronomy 1:8.

31. Commentary on Numbers 33:53.

32. Commentary on Leviticus 26:32. Cf. Maimonides, *Mishneh Torah*, Hilkhot Abodah Zarah X. 6.

33. Appendix to the *Commentary on the Pentateuch*, Lisbon 1489.

11

THE BEGINNINGS OF
MODERN JEWISH STUDIES

Our inquiry into the beginnings of modern Jewish studies is in effect an attempt to analyze the most significant intellectual movement of Western Judaism in the recent period of history.

We shall take the term "beginnings" to refer roughly to the four decades between 1818, the date of publication of Leopold Zunz's *Etwas über die rabbinische Literatur*, and about 1860, the period that saw the beginning of the publication of H. Graetz's *Geschichte der Juden* (1853), the publication of Abraham Geiger's *Urschrift und Übersetzungen der Bibel*, I. M. Jost's *Geschichte des Judenthums* (both in 1857), Zacharias Frankel's *Einleitung in die Mischna*, and Zunz's *Die Ritus der synagogalen Poesie* (both in 1859). Around 1860, as Franz Rosenzweig expressed it, "the movement had run its course; having attained political emancipation, German Judaism sank into a postprandial doze," to be awakened only by a wave of anti-Semitism and, spiritually, by the Zionist movement.[1] Naturally, however, our review will have to consider both the developments which preceded and those which followed this period.

I

It is well to keep in mind that scholarly investigation of Judaism did not start in nineteenth-century western Europe but has had a long history.

One could point to the beginnings of scientific treatment of Hebrew grammar (as a discipline independent of the Masorah but influenced by Islamic linguistics) in Sa'adia Gaon (tenth century); in the contributions to Hebrew grammar by Karaite scholars; in Sa'adia's disciple, Dunash ben Labrat, who examined the Biblical text from the philological viewpoint; in Judah ibn Kureish of North Africa, an older contemporary of Sa'adia, who probed the relationship between Biblical and Rabbinical Hebrew and Arabic and stressed the linguistic study of the Targum; in Hayyuj (about 1000 c.e.) and Jonah ibn Janah (eleventh century), who can be credited with laying the foundation for a scholarly Biblical exegesis. In his commentaries on Isaiah and the Psalms, Moses ibn Gikatilla of Cordova (eleventh century) introduced historico-critical discrimination. Abraham ibn Ezra (twelfth century), who learned a great deal from him, insisted on the *peshat* to the exclusion of other methods of interpretation, which led some scholars to regard him as a father of modern Biblical studies.

A discernment of some of the social, economic, and psychological factors at work in Jewish history is evident in the *Shebet Yehudah* of the ibn Vergas (fifteenth to sixteenth century), and historical and literary criticism in the *Me'or 'Enayim* of 'Azariah dei Rossi (sixteenth century). Simone Luzzatto of Venice, in his *Discorso circa il stato degli Hebrei* (Venice, 1638), exhibits an understanding of the political and economic conditions of Europe and an insight into the peculiarities of Jewish communal life in the Diaspora.

Scholarly approach to the Talmudic literature can be dated as far back as Hai Gaon (tenth to eleventh century), whose commentary on the Mishnah, of which only fragments (in addition to quotations in the *'Arukh*) are extant, utilizes the author's historical, archeological, and philogical (Arabic and Aramaic) knowledge. We also have fragments of his *Kitab al-Hawi*, a lexicon of difficult words in the Bible, Targum, and Talmud. Textual criticism in the realm of Talmudic literature was the concern of many premodern scholars. We mention only Solomon Luria (1510–1573), who, using older sources, attempted in his *Hokhmath Shelomoh* to correct the numerous copyists' errors of many generations that had distorted the text. The Cracow edition of the Talmud (1616–1620) contains the corrections according to Luria's glosses. There is a history nine centuries long of Talmudic methodology, which may be considered another chapter in the prehistory of modern Judaic studies. The search for chronological order and clarification of terminology in the vast Talmudic materials, which started with the *Seder Tanna'im va-Amora'im* in the ninth century, came to a temporary conclusion in the encyclopedia (*Pahad Yizhaq*) of Isaac Lampronti (1679–1756). This work started to appear in 1750. Elijah, the Gaon of Vilna (1720–1797), has been called the father of Talmud criticism. In the words of Louis Ginzberg, "The Gaon was bold enough to declare that the interpretation of the Talmud must be based on reason and not on authority." This "emancipation of tradition" as far as the texts are concerned made the application of critical principles imperative. Revised texts and a comparative study of related literature led the Gaon from "external" to "internal" criticism.[2]

In the state of transition from the old, classical to the modern, critical Judaic studies, objective research (especially in the origins of halakah) was hampered by doctrinal considerations and by the desire to defend Israel's tradition. Jacob Zebi Meklenburg (1785–1865), in his *Ha-Ketab veha-Qabbalah*, still maintained that the details of the Oral Law could be harmoniously discovered in the text of the Written Law. Zebi Hirsch Chajes (1805–1855) set out to prove that the Law, both Written and Oral, issued in a single Divine revelation, and that historical development could be spoken of only with regard to non-Pentateuchal statutes.[3] Samuel David Luzzatto (1800–1865) deeply resented the seeming lack of personal involvement on the part of Western Jewish scholars who, he said, studied Judaism "as other scholars explore the antiquities of Egypt and Assyria, Babylonia and Persia."[4] He defined true Jewish scholarship as learning based on faith.[5] Solomon Judah Rapoport (1790–1867) pointed to the scorn of gentile scholars at the historical illiteracy of Jews.[6]

II

Against the representatives of religion-accentuated and -directed scholarship the new school of learning, best represented by men such as Zunz, Jost, Steinschneider, and Geiger, stressed complete freedom of interpretation, as well as freedom from the possible application of the results of scholarship to the conduct of life. In a footnote to his programmatic treatise of 1818, Zunz hastened to say that the study of Jewish literature was not meant "to offer a norm [or direction] for our own judgment."[7]

A main link connecting the old, classical and the new, critical form of Judaic research was Talmudic lexicography, the attempt to list and expound the rich and variegated linguistic material of the Talmudim and the Midrashim. Best known is the *'Arukh* of Nathan ben Yehiel of Rome (completed in the beginning of the twelfth century), a work that utilized Geonic and later sources. Later scholars (Elijah Levita, David de Pomis, Benjamin Mussafia, David ha-Kohen de Lara [author of *'Ir David* and *Kether Kehunah*], and others) compiled either new lexicographical lists or supplements to the *'Arukh*. The Christian Hebraist Johannes Buxtorf the Elder (1564–1629) used the *'Arukh* in addition to the writings of Elijah Levita as a source for his *Lexicon hebraicum et chaldaicum* (Basel, 1607). Toward the end of the eighteenth century, Isaiah Berlin (or Pick) wrote a commentary on the *'Arukh* that remained a fragment.[8] In 1812 there appeared the *Or Esther* of Simon and Mordecai Bondi of Dresden, a not very successful lexicon of the Greek and Latin words in the Talmudic midrashic writings.[9] Moses Landau of Prague (1788–1852), a grandson of Ezekiel Landau, issued in 1819–1824 a new edition of the *'Arukh*, under the title *Ma'arkhe Lashon*. The Zunz-Ehrenberg correspondence reveals the eagerness with which the appearance of this work was anticipated in learned circles. Alas, Landau's work, which does not even mention the author of the original *'Arukh*, proved a failure. It was this publication that aroused the ire of S. J. Rapoport and prompted him to write his biography of Nathan ben Yehiel, a masterpiece of historical criticism.[10] The original *'Arukh* was also the key to Zunz's ingenious reconstruction of the *Pesiqta de Rab Kahana*, a major feat in the early period of modern Jewish studies.[11]

Before analyzing the new trend of Jewish studies, a seemingly technical point should be briefly mentioned: the status of libraries and collections of books and manuscripts within reach of Jewish scholars.[12] The

Gaon of Vilna, who so strongly emphasized correct readings, may not have seen more than half a dozen manuscripts in his field.[13] Early editions were hardly available to him; the Polish and Russian libraries owned very few Hebrew books of note.

The son of the Gaon of Vilna, Rabbi Abraham, was the author of *Rab Pe'alim* (which, incidentally, remained unpublished for eighty-five years, appearing only in 1894). It enumerates works of midrashic and rabbinic literature known only from quotations and it was to serve as a guide in the search for these lost writings. In this work the son continued the father's quest for texts and still better texts, a direction followed by other scholars who were influenced by the Gaon, among them Avigdor of Slonim, commentator on the Tosefta, Enoch Zindel, commentator on several Midrashim, and especially Raphael Rabbinovicz (1835–1888), author of *Sefer Diqduqe Soferim, Variae Lectiones in Mischnam et in Talmud Babylonicum* (1867 et seq.); Rabbinovicz' work was based upon a unique uncensored manuscript (Codex Hebraicus 95) of the Babylonian Talmud he had found in the royal library at Munich. The importance of this manuscript, written in 1342, had been recognized a century and a half before Rabbinovicz by Nathan Weil, the author of *Qorban Netan'el,* but nobody had paid attention to Weil's project.

In the West there were some Hebrew collections in French and Italian libraries, but Jews were not allowed to use them. The first Jew to be granted admission to a public library appears to have been Hayyim Joseph David Azulai, who in 1755 and 1778 visited the Bibliothèque Nationale in Paris and happily saw many Hebrew manuscripts there in various fields.[14]

Leopold Zunz (1794–1886) received his first intimation of the existence of a comprehensive Hebrew literature from Johann Christoph Wolf's *Bibliotheca hebraea* (1715–33). That this work was more than a supplement to Bartolocci's *Bibliotheca magna rabbinica* is due to Wolf's utilization of David Oppenheim's (or Oppenheimer's) book and manuscript collection, which was brought to Hamburg before its acquisition by the Bodleian Library in 1829.[15] Zunz first consulted the Oppenheim library in Hamburg in 1828, some four years before he mapped out in his *Gottesdienstliche Vorträge* a literary history of the Midrash in its broadest sense. But it was not until 1846 that he was able to undertake a trip to the British Museum in order to study its Hebrew manuscripts, and not until 1855 a trip to Oxford and Paris as well as London; a trip to the de Rossi collection in Parma followed only in 1863; the Vatican Library, with its hundreds of Hebrew manuscripts, was closed to him. In an impassioned appeal to "the people of Italy" he urged the overthrow of the Pontifical State, in order to advance the course of European humanity and at the same time open the gates of the Vatican Library to Jewish scholarship.[16]

To enable him to write his history of Hebrew liturgy, Zunz for years dispatched to his friends urgent pleas, at times bordering on imposition, for help in looking up quotations in early editions of books deposited in local libraries and for the acquisition of *mahzorim* and *selihot* in various imprints and for various rituals.

The chief spokesmen for modern Jewish studies conceived of their task not in terms of "contributions toward . . . ," "comments on . . . ," but in terms of major, comprehensive projects. Zunz, in 1825, drafted a plan of a four-part work on the *Wissenschaft des Judentums,* and in 1829 he prepared an extensive introduction to the *Wissenschaft;* S. J. Rapoport planned a *Toldedoth Anshe Shem* and a complete '*Erekh Millin;* Abraham Geiger conceived of a scholarly history of Judaism in the Biblical and Talmudic period, and Zacharias Frankel a history of halakah. What they managed to produce were preliminary essays, or, at best, elaborations of parts of the original plans. It is important to realize, however, that the concept of modern Jewish studies called for a transformation of Jewish learning from a literature of glosses, commentaries, bibliographical lists, and collections of chronographical materials into comprehensive presentations of Judaism as found in its literature, its philosophy, and its history—manifestations of the new vistas of learning, marked by scholarly objectivity, broad scope, meaningful context, proper form and style, and—respectability.

There was one field in particular which suffered gross neglect: Biblical, and more specifically, Pentateuchal studies. Zunz started his *Gottesdienstliche Vorträge* with an analysis of the Book of Chronicles; although he had a strong interest in Bible studies,[17] he concentrated on Hebrew liturgy. Zacharias Frankel dealt with the Septuagint and Alexandrian hermeneutics, but his chief concern was Talmudic literature. Abraham Geiger's *Urschrift* began with the Return from Exile. Heinrich Graetz contributed commentaries to, and articles on, various Biblical, mainly non-Pentateuchal, books, but his magnum opus was his *History,* which includes a history of the Biblical period. S. D. Luzzatto did include the Pentateuch among the Biblical books which he interpreted, but he abstained from exercising criticism on them, a criticism he applied (with great caution) to post-Pentateuchal books and with full academic freedom to medieval literature and Hebrew philology.

Not even the vast complex of Biblical law, largely overlooked by the schools of Biblical criticism, received much attention from Jewish scholars, with the exception perhaps of S. L. Saalschütz, author of *Das Mosaische Recht* (1848). Max Wiener suggested that the cause of this self-limitation was "the after-effect of the traditional belief in inspiration."[18] Wiener's suggestion provides a partial explanation, but more important, in our opinion, was the wish to avoid a field so strongly related to issues of faith, the discussion of which would have created friction with Christian scholarship.

III

The field of study that more than any other reveals the radical change between the old learning and modern Jewish scholarship is Jewish history. We shall concentrate on this one aspect of our subject.

The first attempt to understand Judaism in terms of history was made by a man who could examine Judaism only from the outside and in terms familiar to his own world: Jacques Basnage (1653–1725), the French Protestant who after the revocation of the Edict of Nantes tasted some of the bitterness of exile. He recognized the existence of Jews in history and realized that Josephus' account could be continued into his own days; accordingly, the title of his work includes the phrase, *pour servir de Suplément & de Continuation à l'Histoire de Joseph.*

To Basnage, the history of the Jews was the story of a sect, a sect that "was rejected because it had rejected Jesus."[19] Beyond this, even the enlightened, well-educated Basnage could not go. But the mere fact that Judaism could be treated in historic terms, and Jews as a group with a coherent and comprehensible history, was of enormous significance, insofar as it permitted the Christian reader to understand Israel in non-dogmatic terms. Basnage's work formed the basis for the works of Christian Hebraists, among them the Silesian pastor Christian Unger and the above-mentioned Johann Christoph Wolf.

Not for another century did the Jews themselves feel the need of presenting their story in terms of history. Of Basnage's contemporaries only Moses Hagiz took notice of the former's work.[20] Moses Mendelssohn and the period of Jewish enlightenment had little use for historical thought. But once the step had been taken toward history, it was not only historicity that began to matter, and not merely historic continuity and exposition of meaning that was suggested by the historic view. The modern students of Judaism were concerned as well with the place the Jewish people and Judaism occupied within *world history.* Hegel had presented Judaism as a child of the Orient, and by so doing he removed it from the historical scheme in the West.[21] Jewish historians had to take a stand on this crucial issue before they could proceed with the technical aspects of historical research.

The predominant philosophy in this new trend in Judaic studies is best described as historicism. Karl Löwith[22] has demonstrated the ever-growing historicism in the various disciplines. By the mid-nineteenth century Christian dogmatic theology had become history of dogma, economics had been replaced (by Karl Marx) by a materialistic philosophy of history, philosophy had turned into history of philosophy, and biology into the Darwinian history of evolution. The permanent, the absolute, the universally true was replaced by "time and motion, the process of history,"[23] the relativity of truth, a series of events determined by their place in the ever-changing historical course and reduced in their importance because of this determination. Hegel still maintained "a concept of philosophy as a science of the absolute and considered meaningless a merely historical treatment of philosophical issues." But his successors turned his casual dictum that "philosophy does not leap across its time" into a historicist dogma which implies that "a respective thought may be true and reasonable in its time but turns untrue and unreasonable in the following period of time."[24]

This historicistic mode of thinking (which, for lack of a better term, we may call a "functional," "practical," or "lower" historicism) provided a ready answer to the quest of *Wissenschaft des Judentums* in its first generations. The issue of doctrine, of the binding character of tradition, of truth, could be safely excluded from the investigation. Establishment of the historical roots of religious observances helped in the introduction of synagogal and liturgical reforms, in which the early advocates of *Wissenschaft* were interested. Not only so radical a reformer as Abraham Geiger but such a reforming traditionalist as Levi Herzfeld as well was guided by the idea of historical origins. Zacharias Frankel's Breslau School was based on a positive historical orientation. Historicism as applied to the messianic idea helped Zunz to keep the eschatological dynamite from exploding in his structure of Judaism, which he presented as a movement toward humanism, progress, democracy, and Europeanism. It also sustained his views of the European revolutions, especially the revolution of 1848, as messianic events.[25] It assisted him also in wrestling the interpretation of Judaism from the hands of theologians and philosophers of religion, placing it in the hands of historians. "The history of the post-Talmudic age is not merely a history of religion or church history [*Religions- oder Kirchengeschichte*]; having as its subject a people, this history displays a national character," said Graetz,[26] immediately qualifying his statement by stating that the normal prerequisites of a nation had, in the case of Israel, been supplanted by "spiritual life" (*geistige Potenzen*). Despite this admission and despite occasional references to it and glimpses of understanding, religious thought was excluded from the scope of coherent scholarly investigation. What really mattered was the historical framework and the categories of historical thinking.

Some explanation of this reluctance to deal with religious thought was offered by Zunz in a letter in which he referred to Ludwig Steinheim's *Die Offenbarung nach dem Lehrbegriff der Synagoge:* "I cannot agree to the hostile division between revelation and paganism; rather do I see everywhere only emanations of one and the same world spirit [*Weltgeist*]; only in the phenomenal world are there antagonisms, even contradictions, but philosophy resolves them. . ."[27]

To simplify: since religious thought lacks an objective foundation and makes for divisiveness, it is better left with the theologians and sermonizers and should not become a subject of scholarship, Zunz felt. It was the tendency of the period to demonstrate points of contact between Israel and the world, even a close relationship between the two, a task undertaken by what may be called "ideological," "theoretical," or "higher" historicism.

In contradistinction to "lower historicism," by means of which time-honored institutions, usages, and beliefs were presented in the relative positions they occupied in the context of history, it was the intention of "higher historicism" to establish Judaism as an integral part of world history. This almost dogmatic construction came to occupy the status previously held by religion. The preoccupation with status in history obstructed the vision from a perspective based on an authentic examination of the internal history of Judaism. It may be mentioned in passing that once before, in Jewish Hellenistic literature, attempts had been made to present the history of the Jewish people as part of world history. In both instances apologetics was engaged in at the expense of legitimate self-interpretation and the energies spent on the one field were lost to the other.

The historicistic position found its classical expression in the works of Zunz, Jost, Geiger, and Graetz. It was here that the difference between the older forms of Jewish scholarship and the new trend in Judaic studies became most obvious.

Zunz's "Etwas über die rabbinische Literatur" ("Notes on Rabbinic Literature"), written by the twenty-three-year-old student in 1817 and published in 1818, is on the surface a program of work that awaits the *Wissenschaft*. On a deeper level, however, it is an attempt to break down the confines and limitations of traditional, rabbinic, classical Judaism and to posit a concept of Judaism that includes all, or most, aspects of human thought. Zunz held that European literature was steadily replacing Hebrew literature. Even what had been written in the Hebrew language in the last fifty years—that is, since the time of Mendelssohn—he wrote, was but a "preparation for a time in which rabbinic literature [a term Zunz applied to the entire body of post-Biblical writings] will have ceased to exist."[28] Neo-Hebraic literature "is being carried to its grave," he said, and therefore "it is upon scholarship to render account of the process that has come to a close. No new publication of importance is expected to interfere with our survey."[29]

What was this survey to encompass? In addition to the Bible (which,

Zunz states parenthetically, is not confined to the Jewish people but which "became the foundation of the Christian states"),[30] in addition to theology, law, ethics, history, philology, et cetera, there are fields that concern the Jew "as an earth-dweller": mathematics, geography, astronomy, chronology, natural history and medicine, technology, commerce, music, and so on. Thus Hebrew literature, far from being narrowly parochial, is testimony to a full, normal, human civilization. As such, Zunz continues, knowledge of Judaism viewed in its totality—and historical *Wissenschaft* alone can afford us this view—is a contribution to universal human knowledge, which is "the most noble aim [*der nobelste Endzweck*] of man."[31] True knowledge is the awareness of the relationships between the particular and the universal and the conception of the place the singular occupies in the total; scholarship teaches us how the detail emerges from its isolation to become "an integral part of the spiritual creation" of humanity.[32]

To advance this theory Zunz had to break with the scale of values of classical Judaism, to which a Biblical commentary or a halakic work was central and a Jew's treatise on a medical subject peripheral. Zunz superimposed the concept of literature (in the sense of a multifaceted body of writings) on Hebrew letters, just as he forced the writings of the Jewish community out of their seclusion into the wider framework of world literature.

In criticism it must be said that, though there were many significant relationships between Jewish and Christian writings in the Middle Ages, as well as a considerable body of Jewish contributions to the various fields of general knowledge, the Jews never defined their intellectual endeavors as contributions to a world literature. If pressed for a definition, they might have construed their work as a search for the meaning of the Scriptural word or of the ramifications of the basic code of laws.

In reinterpreting the literary history of Israel according to the scale of values of the new Europe, Zunz anticipated the guiding principles of the Verein für die Cultur und Wissenschaft der Juden. In the year following the publication of "Etwas über die rabbinische Literatur," Eduard Gans, a leading figure in the Verein, gave his interpretation of the concept of the new Europe. That new Europe, according to him, represented the creative incorporation of the great historic forces—the Ancient Near East, Hellas, Rome, and Christianity—and their achievements: monotheism, the concepts of beauty, freedom, the state and society, and philosophy. These forces were not independent entities; they survived and reached their true significance as parts of an organic whole. It was incumbent upon Judaism, too, to surrender its independence for the sake of the greater European realm; the Jewish world was not to vanish but to become absorbed by the European ("nicht 'untergehen,' aber in die europäische [Welt] 'aufgehen' "). On another occasion, in 1821, Gans called upon the Verein to help tear down the wall that had until then separated the Jewish world from the European.[33] Europe as a new historical entity, a realm of liberal cooperation, free from medieval narrowness and dogmatism: such was the concept that inspired both the theoretician Gans and the literary historian Zunz.

In Zunz's view the Jew represented the spirit of enlightened Europe long before the modern period. The exclusiveness of the medieval Jew was but the unavoidable reaction to persecution. In his treatise "Die Namen der Juden,"[34] Zunz defended the universal, nonreligious character of given personal names and explained the existence of "synagogal names" as occasioned by "the growing pressure on the part of Christians," which led the Jews "to isolate themselves within the confines of their customs."[35]

In his essay "Zur Literatur des jüdischen Mittelalters in Frankreich und Deutschland,"[36] Zunz pointed to the medieval Church "that had absorbed the life of the Europeans while excluding the Jews," a condition that forced the "Jewish church" to "turn all thought and feeling into religion, that is, into exclusiveness [*in ein religiöses, das ist in ein ausschliessendes*]."[37] Thus, the Jew's interest in religion was merely defensive; if circumstances permitted, his concerns would have been those of nascent Europe, Zunz thought. Israel's centuries-old literary history provided the proof of her ability to cooperate with Western humanity, and, what was more, of her comprehension that she was nothing more than a part of this humanity. Consequently, the Jew was no novice in the new historical structure, Europe.

The concept of the interrelationship of Jewish and world literature—not as one of the historical factors but as the basic fact—was reaffirmed by Zunz in the introductory chapter to his *Zur Geschichte und Literatur* (1845). In this work the Jew is presented as being, by means of his literary activity, "most intimately connected with the culture of Antiquity, with the origin and growth of Christianity, with the scientific activity of the Middle Ages," so that his literature aptly "supplements general literature." Though an indigenous organism, Jewish literature should be dealt with in accordance with the laws applicable to literature in general; conversely, an understanding of Jewish literature aided in the understanding of all literature. This universal character of literature, the concept that the parts are but organic components of a whole, was not yet recognized by men, said Zunz, but it should be our task to advance to such understanding.[38] For the Jews it should be a matter of self-respect to join in the life of new Europe, fully conscious of their place and function in the past.[39]

Zunz found strong evidence of the Jews' universal, extranational, extrareligious interests in their broad intellectual life under Islam.[40] This reasoning of Zunz (and of the many who followed his example) displays a personal value judgment rather than objective scholarship. If the emphasis on religious topics in one part of the world is occasioned by the social and political conditions in that part of the world, then the same measurement must be applied in explaining more comprehensive concerns in another part of the world. Either both prove or neither proves the inherent, objectively discernible nature of the Jew. Zunz's argument postulates *one* manifestation of the Jewish spirit as the only truly valid one and poses the theory of an organic world literature in the Middle Ages while admitting its unreality. This type of argumentation strengthens our suspicion of a gross disparity between Zunz's technical mastery of his material and his historicistic speculation. Zunz, who gave the most careful attention and the most untiring devotion to the minutiae of the texts, who in his endless lists, registers, and bibliographical references offered an example of critical acumen and scholarly exactitude, became vague, hypothetical, and subjective in his historical interpretation. In the former activity we see the scholar, steeped in the Hebrew material, using modern methods of textual criticism, analysis, and organization, in the latter, the apologist, herald of a new Europe, advocate of human rights and emancipation, constructing a scheme of history to support and justify his claim.

In his introduction to the *Gottesdienstliche Vorträge* (1832), the aim of research appeared to Zunz to be, in addition to scholarship, public recognition of Jewish rights (Zunz used the singular, *Recht*) and "the winning of the favor of those in power and the good will of sensible men."[41] Scholarship was expected to serve as the most honest method of appeal, as the best possible proof of the Jews' right to be counted.

I. M. Jost (1793–1860) published his first presentation of Jewish history in 1820–1828 in nine volumes; this was followed by a second, popular, presentation in 1831–1832. The earlier work was supplemented by a history of the 1815–1845 period in three volumes, which appeared in 1846–47. A final three-volume *Geschichte des Judenthums und seiner Secten* appeared in 1857–1859.

Jost was keenly conscious of the fact that up to his day the Jews had been living in a state of exile from world history. Now it was no longer the exile from Jerusalem that was painfully felt but the state of exile within the European community. Only recently had the Jews become aware of the radical changes in the society around them. Jost called 1815 "the year of birth of the new development [in the life] of the Israelites in Europe."[42] Hostility and rejection on the part of the surrounding world, he wrote, had now given way to true brotherly love;[43] the doors of the Middle Ages had been closed and the portals of a new Europe opened.[44] It therefore became necessary to "mediate between Synagogue and world culture [*Weltbildung*]," a task in which Mendelssohn pioneered.[45]

Looking back at the period preceding the change in climate, Jost found that Jews had failed to participate in the issues of the world (*Weltbegebenheiten*); they did not feel the need of "inner advancement" in education; the "Talmudists, the only teachers of youth, stood outside the present time, living in an imaginary world." With the onset of the new era, which, according to Jost, called not for the liquidation of "religious peculiarities" (*kirchlicher Eigentümlichkeiten*) but for reconstruction, it became essential "to retrace the process of history in order to understand the course of Judaism."[46] In this need Jost recognized the origin of "scholarly elucidation of Judaism."[47] Therefore, modern Jewish, and especially historical, scholarship was to him a means for the solution of problems arising from the confrontation of traditional Judaism and modern Europe.

Abraham Geiger (1810–1874), leader in the movement for religious reforms, is best known for his *Urschrift und Übersetzungen der Bibel* (1857), a study of Biblical criticism and developments in Judaism in the period of the second Temple. His view on Jewish history is recorded in his lectures on *Das Judentum und seine Geschichte* (1864–1871). Judaism, according to him, had a history in the true sense of the word; it had proved to be an active, salutary force in world history, mostly in contrast to other forces in history. It entered world history by means of Christianity; Jesus was "the proclaimer of the Jewish teachings to the world."[48] But this event did not terminate the activity of Judaism in world history. It next contributed the weapons for combating the spiritual servitude and priestly hierarchy that had developed within Christianity.[49] Non-Judaic religions and movements might or might not be able to break with the dogmatism and narrowness of the Middle Ages without losing their identity, Geiger thought. Judaism would and should undertake this battle against medieval thought, especially since its roots are not in the Middle Ages but reach back into antiquity, and its religion has always represented activity, life, and knowledge as opposed to a brooding spirit (*müssiges Grübeln*) and dark faith (*dunkeles, finsteres Glauben*). Judaism, which even in the medieval period lived within humanity (*innerhalb der Menschheit*), though isolated and persecuted, would now be called upon to live in close contact and in freedom with humanity.[50] Thus Geiger presented Judaism as a community whose destiny it was to cultivate what was common both to classical Israel and to Europe.

In this interpretation of Jewish history and Western history in general Geiger displayed a disregard both of the self-interpretation of the West, especially of the "historic school," which emphasized the medieval roots of the modern period, and of the self-interpretation of medieval Judaism.

He overemphasized the importance of Judaism for the West and, at the same time, underplayed the historic position of Christianity. This fateful misreading of Judaism as well as of history was Geiger's response to those historians of the West whose philosophy of history postulated an exclusion of Israel from the sphere of world history.

Heinrich Graetz (1817–1891) was less extreme than Zunz in his view of the relationship between Israel and the European world, but his theory was more comprehensive than Zunz's. In his *Die Konstruktion der jüdischen Geschichte,*[51] written as an ideological background to his magnum opus, *History of the Jews* (1853–1876), he maintained that "the totality of Judaism is discernible only in its history."[52] The central idea of Judaism, he argued, the idea of God Who reveals Himself, finds its historic realization in an "adequate state constitution" so that "the God-idea is at the same time an idea of a state."[53] Therefore, Judaism is, strictly speaking, not a religion (that is, a system of beliefs), but rather the law of a state (*Staatsgesetz*), to be fully realized in the Messianic period. The elements of religion and politics merge and form a union.[54]

In his emphasis on the historical, political character of Judaism, Graetz opposed the Christian philosophy of history for having relegated "some stray details of Jewish history to the margin of the annals of world history" while denying post-Biblical Israel "the possession of history in the higher sense of the word."[55] In fact, however (he states), Judaism "produced an active history" together with its passive history of martyrdom.[56] The Diaspora put Judaism squarely into history and the life-process of the world (*Weltleben*); it followed during its wanderings the trend of developments in world history, although, thanks to the isolating force of Talmudism, it preserved its identity.[57] In the Middle Ages life appeared to have come to a standstill; but Judaism was only seemingly dead (*Scheintod*); it was, rather, going through a period of "hibernation that enabled Israel to enter the dauntless world-history race with its younger and luckier rival."[58] Judaism's variegated course through the ages seemed to Graetz to suggest that the ultimate task of Judaism was "to organize a religious state constitution, one which is aware of its . . . concatenation with the world at large."[59]

This eloquent "construction" manifests Graetz's desire to present the Jews not merely as a people possessing a history but as one of the forces in world history. The first was taken for granted; the second had to be affirmed. Graetz could achieve such affirmation only by ignoring the vast difference in implication between a historically viewed life of a people and sovereign, political action and interaction, struggle for power and dominance, that might or might not become a force in the political structure of the world, or, at least, in the nineteenth century, in the

Western world. Thus his use of the terms *Weltleben* or *Allerweltsleben*, which points to the political as one of the components of Judaism, cannot but mislead the reader.

Furthermore, the assumption of a role for Judaism in world history was made by Graetz only at the expense of the historic place of Christianity. *Der Bibelsche Orient,* attributed to Hakam Isaac Bernays, propagated Israel's "world-historic task of being an apostle to the nations."[60] In support of this position, Graetz claimed that this tenet had stood the test of history; "the European and Asiatic nations have been rescued from darkness through the light borrowed from Judaism."[61] But, it seems to us, that while the Jewish origin of Christianity is beyond question, utilization of this fact to support a claim to Judaism's taking part in world history is of very doubtful relevance. Theological and historical categories do not mix too well. Concerning the issue in question, history seems to prove the opposite of what Graetz and others expected.

Finally, Graetz admitted a duality of tendencies within Jewish history: one, the creative "life in the world," the other, the conserving, isolating tendency of Talmudism. He suggested a dialectical relationship between the two. However, such a conception obscures the fact that in many phases of Jewish history Talmudism was more than "an armor against alienation";[62] it was a self-sufficient world in which the Jew explored the word of God, lived in accordance with His law, and needed nothing more: an utterly unhistorical, undialectical world.

In Graetz's scholarly work, his *History,* he was able to overcome the historicistic claims of his programmatic essay. References to "intimate contact with eventful world history" are still to be found,[63] but enough is said to indicate the decidedly nonpolitical character of the Jewish community. Under the impact of the extant material, Graetz's treatment presents Jewish history as cultural or intellectual, rather than political, history.[64] He sees world history undergoing radical changes while Judaism "remained constant, allowing merely for modification of external forms."[65] The term "world history" is retained but given a symbolic, internalized meaning: "Jewish history of seventeen centuries presents world history in miniature; the Jewish people is a universal people, being everywhere at home because it has nowhere a home";[66] Jewish literature, because of its many contacts, is a world literature in itself.[67]

Thus Graetz was able to bridge the gap between his theory of history and the writing of history. In the work of Zunz, the corresponding gap between his theory of history and his history of Hebrew literature is spanned by the assumption that it is Hebrew literature that "manifests the great laws of history"[68] and that by means of its literature Judaism partakes in the "universal intellectual movement" (*totale Geistes-bewegung*).[69] What concerns history in the strict (and the only valid) sense of the word, Zunz realized, is that "a nation *in partibus* does not perform deeds" and thus has no history.[70] Zunz privately called the Jews "the canteenmen and clowns dragging along everywhere in world history,"[71] a sharp and incisive statement that considerably modifies his high-sounding historicistic claims.

In this discussion of the beginnings of modern Jewish studies we notice the difference in quality between exact research and the inquiry into the philosophy of Jewish history. In matters of exact research—Rapoport's biographies, Zunz's studies on the Midrash, homilies, and liturgy, the works of Solomon Munk on medieval Jewish philosophy, of Zacharias Frankel on Biblical exegesis and the Mishnah, of Moritz Steinschneider on bibliography, of Graetz on history, and especially his excursuses—we encounter objective, honest, and to a high degree successful attempts to deal with at least some aspects of Judaica. In this field modern Jewish scholars continued the scholarly heritage of the pre-emancipatory period. The philological, critical, and analytical methods had improved under the influence of general scholaship, but Jewish scholarship as such moved and advanced within a long tradition of research and learning, as well as within a long tradition of assimilating the intellectual apparatus of other cultures and applying it to Jewish thought and studies. In this realm the modern Jewish scholar was completely at home.

In contradistinction to exact research, the quest for a philosophy of Jewish history constituted a definite departure from the thinking of the past. The motifs of classical thought about the meaning of Israel—exile, suffering for the love of God, *galut* as punishment and purification, as a preparation for the world to come, messianic redemption—lost their relevance. The religious inquiry, an inquiry from within, was replaced by a historicism that attempted to view Jewish history from without. In order to retain the right to exist in the present, Judaism had to be explained in terms of world history, as a community of universal historic significance.

Here the Jewish scholar entered a foreign domain. Modern thinking in the field of world history had its own tradition: Christianity, which, reinterpreted, lived on in secular formulations. The Jew entered this domain without a tradition of his own, at the same time ignoring the existing Western tradition, or at least underplaying its implications. He was a *homo novus* in search of a home in a world that was not yet ready to grant him this privilege. Theories about the position of Judaism in world history helped the modern Jew to overcome his feeling of isolation in the new world. The obstacle to sober, patient scholarship resulting from such theories has been removed only in the present century, when the philosophy of Jewish history has achieved its own and regained balance and perspective.

NOTES

1. Franz Rosenzweig, "Hermann Cohens jüdische Schriften," *Kleinere Schriften* (Berlin, 1937), p. 307.

2. L. Ginzberg, *Students, Scholars, and Saints* (Philadelphia, 1928), p. 135.

3. Z. H. Chajes, *Mebo' ha-Talmud* (Zólkiew, 1845), chap. i.

4. S. D. Luzzatto, letter to Rapoport, June 5, 1860, *Iggeroth Shedal* (Przemyśl, 1882), p. 1367.

5. *Ha-hokhmah ha-meyusedet 'al ha-'emunah.*

6. S. J. Rapoport, introduction to the biography of Nathan ben Yehiel, *Bikkure ha-'Ittim* 10:3–6 (1829).

7. Leopold Zunz, *Gesammelte Schriften* (Berlin, 1875), I, 5.

8. *Hafla'ah she-ba-'Arakhin,* ed. R. W. Günsberg (Breslau, 1830).

9. See B. Beer, "Die neuere jüdische Literatur und ihre Bedeutung," *Monatsschrift für Geschichte und Wissenschaft des Judentums,* 3:249ff. (1853).

10. *Bikkure ha-'Ittim* 10:7–79 (1829).

11. Leopold Zunz, *Die Gottesdienstlichen Vorträge der Juden* (Berlin, 1832), chap, xi.

12. See Zunz, "Bibliographisches," *Zur Geschichte und Literatur* (Berlin, 1845), pp. 230–248.

13. On this and the next items, see S. Schechter, *Seminary Addresses* (Cincinnati, 1915), pp. 183–186.

14. H. J. D. Azulai, *Ma'agal Tob,* ed. A. Freimann (Berlin, 1921), pp. 34, 122, 124, 163.

15. On the history of Oppenheim's library, see Alexander Marx, *Studies in Jewish History and Booklore* (New York, 1944), chap. xiv.

16. "Die hebräischen Handschriften in Italien," *Gesammelte Schriften,* III, 1–13.

17. Leopold Zunz, "Bibelkritisches" (1873–1874), *Gesammelte Schriften,* I, 217–270.

18. Max Wiener, *Jüdische Religion im Zeitalter der Emanzipation* (Berlin, 1933), p. 230.

19. Heinrich Graetz, *Geschichte der Juden,* X (1868), 317.

20. *Ibid.,* p. 319, n. 1.

21. Heinrich Graetz, *Die Konstruktion der jüdischen Geschichte* (Berlin, 1936), p. 94. The work originally appeared in *Zeitschrift für die religiösen Interessen des Judenthums,* vol. 3 (1846). English: *Ideas of Jewish History,* ed. M. A. Meyer (New York, 1974). pp. 219 ref.

22. Karl Löwith, "Die Dynamik der Geschichte und der Historismus," *Eranos-Jahrbuch* 21:229 (1952).

23. *Ibid.,* p. 230.

24. *Ibid.,* pp. 230f.

25. See N.N. Glatzer, "Zunz and the Revolution of 1848," *Year Book,* Leo Baeck Institute, 5:122–139 (1960). Included in the present volume.

26. Graetz, *Geschichte der Juden,* vol. V, introduction.

27. May 1, 1836; *Leopold Zunz: Jude-Deutscher-Europäer,* ed. N. N. Glatzer (Tübingen, 1964), p. 186.

28. Zunz, *Gesammelte Schriften,* I, 4.

29. *Ibid.*

30. *Ibid.*, p. 1.

31. *Ibid.*, p. 27.

32. *Ibid.*, p. 28.

33. *Rede bei der Wiedereröffnung des Vereins.* . . , *18. Oktober 1821* (Hamburg, 1822).

34. *Gesammelte Schriften*, II, 1–82.

35. *Ibid.*, p. 19.

36. *Zur Geschichte und Literatur* (Berlin, 1845), pp. 22–213.

37. *Ibid.*, p. 159.

38. *Ibid.*, pp. 1f.

39. *Ibid.*, p. 17.

40. *Ibid.*, pp. 158f.

41. Zunz, *Gottesdienstliche Vorträge*, p. xii.

42. I. M. Jost, *Neuere Geschichte der Israeliten* (Berlin, 1846), pp. 1f.

43. *Ibid.*, p. 3.

44. *Ibid.*, p. 6.

45. *Ibid.*, p. 8.

46. I. M. Jost, *Culturgeschichte zur neuern Geschichte der Israeliten* (Berlin, 1847), p. 5.

47. *Ibid.*

48. Abraham Geiger, *Das Judenthum und seine Geschichte* (Breslau, 1871), III, 6.

49. *Ibid.*, pp. 5f.

50. *Ibid.*, pp. 157ff.

51. Cited in Note 21, above.

52. Graetz, *Die Konstruktion der jüdischen Geschichte*, p. 8.

53. *Ibid.*, p. 15.

54. *Ibid.*, p. 17.

55. *Ibid.*, p. 49.

56. *Ibid.*, p. 50.

57. *Ibid.*, pp. 51–54.

58. *Ibid.*, p. 50.

59. *Ibid.*, p. 96.

60. Graetz, *Geschichte der Juden*, XI, 431.

61. *Ibid.*

62. *Ibid.*, p. 54.

63. *Geschichte der Juden*, V, 3.

64. *Ibid.*, p. 6.

65. *Geschichte der Juden*, IV, 2.

66. *Ibid.*, p.3.

67. *Ibid.*, p. 4.

68. "Über die . . . hispanischen Ortnamen," *Zeitschrift für die Wissenschaft des Judenthums*, 1:116 (1823).

69. Leopold Zunz, *Zur Geschichte und Literatur* (Berlin, 1845), p. 3.

70. Leopold Zunz, *Literaturgeschichte der synagogalen Poesie* (Berlin 1856), p.1.

71. Letter to S. M. Ehrenberg, July 29, 1851; *Leopold Zunz: Jude-Deutscher-Europäer* (see above), pp. 332 f.

12
LEOPOLD ZUNZ AND THE REVOLUTION OF 1848

With publication of four letters by Zunz to the Ehrenbergs

Zunz's political speeches, given at various literary organisations in Berlin, a selection of which he published as an appendix to the first volume of his *Gesammelte Schriften,* inform us of what he expected from the democratic movement in Germany, and in Prussia in particular. He advocated the right of the people "to have an ethical will," to express and to exercise it in freedom; such a will had to be able to resist the traditional powers of nobility, clergy, and bureaucracy, and, in addition, to resist any constitution in the formulation of which it had not participated. Such a constitution therefore as that imposed (*oktroyiert*) by King Frederick William IV (December 5, 1848) was meaningless, for a nation that has come of age must enjoy full equality; it cannot be subjected to the will of the ruler. The State must represent the organic life of a free people, a people composed of mature, ethically-inspired human beings; democracy is but the realization of the universally human. It is permissible for a religious creed to be active in the home and in the community of the faithful, but it is not permissible for it to influence, in the form of a religious organisation, the political structure of the nation. "The Constitution knows only one religion: justice. As long as justice is upheld, not only the Church but also the people, united in the State, will be filled with the divine spirit. Wherever justice, freedom and harmony dwell together, there is the kingdom of God" (December 3, 1861).[1]

These tenets, for which Zunz fought in 1848–49 and again after the resignation of Frederick William IV and the beginning of the New Era in 1858, are, naturally, based on the ideas of equality and liberty as promulgated in the course of the French Revolution. In an address of July 5, 1865, entitled "Revolution,"[2] Zunz pointed to the covert ("invisible") revlution of modern thought in Holland and England that led to the world outlook of such men as Leibniz and Spinoza, Lessing and Kant. It was the attempt, he said, of the forces of reaction to suppress the teachings of these men and what they implied for humanity at large that provoked the revolution of 1789. However, he continued, this revolution was merely the beginning of a movement which had not yet run its course. The ideas of the French Revolution had penetrated the rest of Europe and other parts of the world; "modern Italy and South America are products of the French Revolution; its effects are felt in Algiers, Tunisia, Egypt, and Turkey; the 1808–1815 regeneration of Prussia is rooted in the ideas of restoration of the human person (*menschlichen Seins*) and of equality of right as opposed to [the claims of] antiquated institutions." Prussia's present constitution, he declared, followed, in its essence, the principles of the National Assembly of 1789, but for the ideas of 1789 to be realized universally, "another world revolution in Europe" will be required. The revolution will come to an end with the establishment of a *Rechtsstaat* in the whole of Europe.

Such was Zunz's political credo. But the role these ideas and beliefs played in the context of his personal life, how much his intellectual existence depended on their realization, we learn not from his addresses but from his letters. In these private communications over the decades we are able to follow Zunz through the years of rising hopes, growing doubts, renewed expectations, and of final disillusionment and resignation.

The letters show Zunz at the peak of his political excitement in March, 1848. His elation is evident in his style, which seems to lose its customary laconic quality and terseness. In the report which describes the events as they occur, observation is intermingled with hearsay; it is not, however, the authenticity of every detail that matters but Zunz's intense interest in the people's revolt against the ruling class and its army and in the initial success that augured well for the popular movement. However, it is noteworthy how much information of current happenings reached Zunz and with what interest in details he followed the political events both in Berlin and in the various German lands. A previous unknown piece of information is provided by Zunz's reference to his call, made at a street demonstration, for "weapons and a national guard, twenty thousand men strong," and to the response of another demonstrator. In the post-script to the letter of March 19, we meet Adelheid Zunz,[3] shaken by the external evidence of popular fury, worried about the welfare of her family, but, naturally, less involved in the political events themselves.

In letters by I. M. Jost to S. M. Ehrenberg, the Frankfurt scholar and friend of Zunz expressed his regret at the latter's outspoken stand in favour of the democratic movement, a stand by which he "will forego the sympathies of the statesmen" and jeopardize his chances for a career in public life. Zunz was proud to state that Jews had taken part in the street fighting and some had made the supreme sacrifice; Jost voiced his annoyance at "clumsy revolutionism of so many young men from Jewish communities." Zunz genuinely believed that the underprivileged were justified in fighting openly for human rights and civil liberties, and that the Jews were free to take a stand; Jost attributed the improvement in the Jewish position "not to the progress of [political] understanding or legislation, but to German Catholicism which took us in tow."

We turn to the Zunz letters for an indication of the meaning the Revolution of 1848 and the events leading to it had for him. In a considerable number of letters we encounter the use of Messianic terminology. The urgency with which Zunz refers to Messianism makes it impossible to interpret these phrases as mere figures of speech. In December 1830, he refused to attach undue significance to the polemics around Abbé Chiarini and his *Théorie du judaisme,* "since according to all signs of the times, the Messiah is on the way." In August 1831, he noted that "in the whole of Germany the press awakens, the *geulah* [redemption] is near." The events of the pre-1848 period—the victory of the liberal party in Switzerland and the defeat of the Catholic *Sonderbund,* the improvement of political conditions in both Rome and London—evoked from him the statement: "Thus let us not lose hope in the growth of Messianism and, braced up by it (though at times weakened), continue our work to the best of our abilities, everyone within the reach of his hands" (December 1847). He looked forward to a visit by Julia Ehrenberg[4] as much as to "the Messianic time, which may come as a surprise any day, any hour, and bring us happiness' (February 1848). In March, 1848, he felt that "the blood-stained Day of Judgment is at hand for the oppressors of so many nations. . . . The moneyed aristocracy, the bureaucracy, black clericalism, Metternich's diplomacy—they all are shaken by fever; the Day of the Lord is near." In April, 1848, he dismissed some molestations of the Jews, because, despite them "our case has definitely gained a victory in civilized Europe and out of this conviction let us, next Passover, celebrate the redemption." A letter of June, 1848, concludes with the wish "that we correspond with each other until the redemption comes."

When reaction came, Zunz tried to hold on to his political beliefs. It could not have been otherwise, for his expectations had in them the zeal and the poignancy of Messianic hopes. In July 1851, he wrote: "Besides, nothing has changed in my way of life and I am still awaiting the Messiah." A year later, he reaffirmed his expectation of the Messiah, adding: "The Redeemer is perhaps nearer than one thinks" (July, 1852). He expressed the wish soon to behold the Prophet Elijah announcing the fall of Gog and the imminent redemption (July, 1852). "Since the Messiah and revolution always come unexpectedly, we could still live to see the rulers 'by the grace of God' subsisting on charity—*bimherah beyamenu* [soon, in our own days], Amen" (August 1852). He cried a *pereat* to the tyrants, and stated that, obviously, he has "nothing to do with government authorities, courts, and Maecenases, thus sharing the lot of millions who hope for the redemption" (October 1852). Since, according to Jewish legend, "the Messiah dwells before the gates of Rome," Zunz had "all the hope that he will soon march into Rome and destroy the black brigade" (February 1853). In August 1854, while working on his *Die synagogale Poesie des Mittelalters,* he spoke of the "falsehood, stupidity, violence" prevalent in European affairs, but nevertheless asserted that he had not lost hope; "I even believe that I have contributed a little stone to the Messianic Temple with my book" (August 1854). In a letter of June, 1861, he recalled the Paris insurrection of June, 1848, cruelly suppressed by Louis Cavaignac: "On this day Cavaignac, out of love for a theoretical republic, actually destroyed freedom; maybe the restorer [of that freedom] is being born today; he could then, in 1889, continue the [activity of the year] 1789."

These quotations—and many more could be added—speak a clear language. The letters offer the personal background of Zunz's political orientation. To Zunz, the European revolution is the fulfillment of eschatological expectation; it is the Messianic event. Zunz, of course, was not the only one in his period who tended to see the realization of the Messianic hope in the steady progress of western humanity, and in the advance of liberalism. But in the case of Zunz, who more than others realized the scope and the depth of the tradition of Jewish Messianism, this identification carries greater weight. In his mouth, the use of the term Messiah is free from homiletic superficiality, so frequently encountered in the period.

However, to the Jew who made the classical tradition of Israel his own, Messianism denoted the intervention of God through His "anointed one," offering a radical resolution of issues human, social, political, that the normal historical process failed to resolve; it denoted, as well, the finality of this achievement thus bringing to an end all previous attempts at reform. In the history of Jewish dispersion, the Messianic vision served as an absolute and ideal goal that regulated the Jew's attitude to the process of the world's history. It prevented him from accepting as final an answer which, owing to the nature of human history, would prove to be fragmentary, limited, relative. It taught him to wait. The so-called pseudo-Messianic outbreaks were the not infrequent instances of loss of nerve and the breakdown of the reserves instilled by classical Messianism.

Zunz could wait no longer. In a letter to M. Isler (February 1837), he explicitly disavowed such "distant" Messianism: "The gazing into a remote future to which the Messiah has accustomed the Jews, this I have completely discarded." He expected the Revolution to bring Messianic fulfillment. He hoped for a development that would "soon, in our own days", or, at least, in a foreseeable future, lead to a complete termination of what he termed the "medieval" system, and for the rise of democracy, an essentially new era of the freedom of man and the union of nations. Thus, the events of the French Revolution, of 1830 and 1848, became paramount in Zunz's historical and political orientation. The 10th of August 1792, the day of the storming of the Tuileries, was a sacred day in his private calendar; in a note written in 1856 he called it "the birthday of democracy." The Revolution in its various forms provided Zunz with the clue to the riddle of events. In 1861 it seemed to him that "we face a war or a second edition of 1789." Two years later he felt that "we move with quick steps toward 1789." A letter of March 18, 1863, is dated "1848 + 15." Unshakable was his trust in the ability of historical circumstances to bring about a revolutionary change in the political attitudes of Europe, a trust based on his conviction that we had entered the Messianic era. Indeed, in his mind, the vision of a new Europe had replaced that of the new Jerusalem in the Messianic prophecies of classical Israel. The religious and emotional content of the latter was, in Zunz's thinking, transferred to the former.

The struggle for Jewish emancipation could not be more than a single item in the scheme of things envisaged by Zunz. In speaking of this emancipation, Zunz again used Messianic terminology. As early as 1823, he wrote of the internal preparation needed before the government could decide to change the civic status of the Jewish community. We need, he said, "good schools, good teachers, capable rabbis, a valiant leadership; once we have them, the Messiah will not fail to come." In 1830 he expressed joy over the "progress of constitutional liberty that will spell the defeat of the bigots, the Jesuits, and the tyrants, in which, too, I envisage the redemption of the Jews" (September 1830).—Since in the eyes of Zunz the issue at hand was nothing less than redemption, he could not be expected to be satisfied with a working political compromise, the grant of a modest place in a many-layered society, and the opportunity to make a contribution to its growth.

His fervour and total dedication to the cause of revolution explain the depth of Zunz's disappointment when his Messianic hopes were not fulfilled and he could not help seeing the forces of reaction growing stronger after 1848–49 and remaining in power even after the New Era dawned in Prussia. The letters show us a man torn between hope and despair. Zunz could not adjust himself to the circumstances created by the regained strength of the old powers, by the re-institution of bureaucratic mediocrity, and, politically, by Russia's dominating voice in Central European affairs. Zunz could not admit defeat; he believed rather that "only seemingly have we retrogressed, in reality we have made progress" (March 1849). Finally, the signs of the changed times grew more and more pronounced and challenged the optimism of Zunz, who remained a revolutionary in the secret recesses of his heart. He pictured the possessors of political power in the various countries in alliance with each other "for the dissemination of slavery and stupidity" (March 1849). In April 1850 he sneered at the recent (March 20) proceedings of the Erfurt Parliament; "I fix my eyes only on the marching soldiers; they alone can bring us freedom." But, as things were, "we are progressing towards barbarism." In July, 1850, he wrote that since February he had "withdrawn from all politics—and from [contact with] people." Public life filled him with disgust. Towards the end of that year he mentioned that he had been unwilling to look at the newspaper, living, as he did, "half in the past, half in the future." At the beginning of 1852 he complained that his external life was paralyzed, as was, in general, the life of the nations. "Since Aristotle, Lessing, Börne, Victor Hugo, and other rebels may no longer speak, I do not know why books should be written unless they be geared to cooks or jail keepers." "Every morning I spend one hour in anger about the peoples of Europe" (December 1852). Everywhere he saw "falsehood, stupidity, violence," and applied the biblical words: "This also is vanity" (Ecclesiastes 2:15) to the state of European affairs (August 1854). Yet, somehow he held fast to his ultimate belief that "a new world is marching on"; through his study of the old world he wished to collaborate in burying the then existing order (April 1857). As he noted in a later letter (August 1864), he was convinced that he had contributed his share to the cause of freedom; he felt that his work had—indirectly of course—contributed to the liberation of Greece and Mexico. But he was filled with strong doubts whether "this generation of monkeys and fools will ever make any headway. You will ask why do I write books? Answer: I, too, am a fool" (April 1858). The true answer, he thought, did not lie in books. "Diplomats and concordats can only be swept away by revolutions," he wrote in March, 1859. The "dirty tools which history uses at times should not disconcert us . . . . Before the fall of the papacy freedom in Europe is unthinkable" (June, 1859). Zunz's strongly anti-Catholic attitude is reminiscent of Mazzini, who called the papacy a "cadaver" ("as is the monarchy") and who expected it to expire before the end of the century.

In an unpublished letter to Professor M. Lazarus, Zunz spoke of the only prospect that delighted him, namely, that "a great revolution coming from Italy will spread over Austria and Germany, bringing to an end the rule 'by the grace of God'." This process, he believed, might take "from ten to thirty years" (August 15, 1859). He compared this period with that of the late Roman Empire: in both eras, he said, we find the breakdown of the power of traditional concepts, making room for new ideas. However, "The German nation is no stronger today than it was in 1848, though more judicious" (April, 1861). Soon thereafter even this slight admission of progress disappeared; "no hope can be expected for the *Teutschen*," Zunz wrote, "unless heaven strikes out as in the stories of Noah and of Pharaoh" (December, 1864). He complained bitterly about the distortion of sound ideals in political life; constitutions (obtained by determined struggles) were used as instruments of plunder, and in the name of the principle of 1789 people were being imprisoned; "if there ever was a need for the Messiah now is the time" (April, 1865). "The Germans will have to take the blame should a second medieval night bring darkness over Europe"; they are greatly talented as individuals "while as a people they present a piteous piece of history" (December 1865).

This notion became confirmed in Zunz when he read H. T. Buckle's *History of Civilization in England*. The latter's thesis, which connected historical progress with the advance of knowledge, appeared to Zunz to herald a definite change in the concept of civilization and freedom of peoples. The German middle class (so important a factor in Zunz's political orientation in former years) and the French bourgeoisie "inspire very little hope," he wrote in April 1866; "perhaps the Messiah will come from Russia." During the Seven Weeks' War in 1866 between Prussia and Austria, in the course of which the Liberals lost much ground in favour of Bismarck and the Conservatives, Zunz felt that "we went back two hundred years" (June, 1866). The great event of 1867, the formation of the North German Confederation, failed to impress Zunz; he wondered whether "the human race, with its Aristotle, Spinoza, and Lessing, has been created solely for Napoleon III, the Pope, and the Kreuzzeitung"; there is hope still for a radical change for the better, he thought, "but only through blows" (April, 1867). It was only natural that Zunz should have joined in the resentment of all Liberals, including the liberal Catholics, at the promulgation, in 1864, of *Syllabus errorum*, in which the Roman Church turned against "progress, liberalism, contemporary civilization" and the very idea of tolerance.

In the beginning of 1870, Zunz refused to share the confidence of the Ehrenbergs in the decline of the Napoleonic Empire. "I don't share your faith in the energy of the nations," he wrote; he saw rather "a decline of the civilized nations which are being subjected or annihilated by the barbarians: the Jews by the Babylonians, the Greeks by the Romans, the Romans by the Germans, the Persians by the Arabs, the Hindus by the Mongols, the Poles by the Russians; the latter will divide up Germany and in 2170 [i.e., in three hundred years] everyone here will be talking Russian" (January, 1870). In July, 1870, Zunz recalled Bastille Day and noted that on the day following the present anniversary of that event, July 15, "the satan in Paris took off his mask" (which, obviously, refers to the events preceding France's declaration of war against Prussia) "and on the 18th the devil in Rome proclaims himself a new God," a reference to the proclamation of the dogma of papal infallibility. This victory of the

Church over the realm of politics was a clear sign of defeat of the non-clerical, democratic ideals of Zunz.

The Revolution had failed to initiate the Messianic time; the reactionary forces proved to be more than mere obstacles in the way, or merely the last remnants of an antiquated order. The crises and setbacks in the political action on behalf of the people were not the birth pangs of a new era. Nourished by a long series of doubts, the residue of Messianic hope turned—in the case of Zunz—into outright apocalyptic pessimism. It was but an expression of despair, when, in 1870, Zunz exclaimed: "Truly it is high time for the coming of the Messiah—or the Deluge!" In the end, the eighty-year old scholar sadly realized that "barbarism is on the increase"; the European situation "bored" him (August 1874). Needless to say, the Jewish community, that had not lived up to his expectations of the 1820's, was not considered by Zunz a home to which he could return. What remained to him was his dedication to scholarship, by which he attempted to make a contribution to the great cause of intellectual liberation of western humanity.[5]

NOTES

1. *Gesammelte Schriften*, I, p. 325.
2. *Ibid.*, pp. 347–354.
3. Zunz's wife.
4. Wife of Philipp Ehrenberg who was the son of S. M. Ehrenberg.
5. The letters referred to in the subtitle appeared in my edition of letters, *Leopold Zunz: Jude, Deutscher, Europäer*, Tübingen, 1964, pp. 261–273.

13
LEOPOLD ZUNZ
AND THE
JEWISH COMMUNITY

Zunz's letters to members of the Ehrenberg family in Wolfenbüttel and especially to S. M. Ehrenberg, his first teacher, provide an insight into the scholar's attitude to the Jewish community in Berlin and the Jewish society at large. The brief presentation that follows is based on these letters.[1]

On the Feast of Weeks 1815, Israel Jacobson, follower of Moses Mendelssohn, started modern, reformed, religious services in his Berlin home. Zunz, aged 21, who had come from Wolfenbüttel to Berlin in October of that year, worshipped there and became an enthusiastic supporter of the new trend; he praised the sense of devotion, the orderliness of the services, the eloquence of the sermons. Soon, however, Zunz became aware of the sore spots in the life of the Jewish community. In April 1817 he recorded that the divisiveness prevalent in the German academic and political community had its counterpart in the Jewish group. "Even after they received permission to build a new synagogue for the German services, they seem unable to unite." Nevertheless, he continued to have faith in the advance and ultimate victory of the new development. In November 1819 he wrote that "there are great movements among the Jews. The German synagogue fights with vigor against the obscurantists; an association similar to the one in Frankfurt will come here into being." The reference is to the *Lesegesellschaft zur aufgehenden Morgenröthe*, a society which had existed in Frankfurt since 1807, and which Zunz considered a predecessor of the Berlin *Verein für Cultur und Wissenschaft der Juden*, established November 7, 1819. He counseled his fellow Jews "to hold together indefatigably to progress, unafraid of the abnormal occurrences of anti-Semitism, but always on the side of the government." In February 1820, again in reference to the *Verein*, he pointed to the need "to unite the intelligentsia among the Jews." He ridiculed the opponents of the "German synagogue" who "fear it will lead Jews to deism or atheism, which they consider here to be one and the same thing." In April of the same year he wrote enthusiastically: "Everywhere there is a reformatory mood astir, but it is imperative that the intelligentsia joins in the cause, not bankers and *Consistorialräte*." Speaking of the Reform movement in Vienna, he mentioned an otherwise unknown letter of the Protestant theologian, Kirchenrat Heinrich Paulus, to David Friedländer, in which Paulus "encourages him to continue his fight against rabbinism and to preserve the relics of Mendelssohn" (July 7, 1820). Turning to Brunswick, S. M. Ehrenberg's homeland, Zunz revealed his intention publicly to invite signatures of those residents of that province who favored Reform "so that the German *Bundestag* will know who and how many would declare themselves for the German synagogue" (October 3, 1820). He quoted a lengthy report from the *Leipziger Zeitung* about the newly introduced "Israelite-German worship with sermon and singing according to the improved ritual of the Hamburg *Tempelverein*" in Leipzig, by which innovation the community had made "a portentous step towards higher culture and refinement of its people." He shared the paper's hope that it is in Leipzig that "this refined, Israelite church will gain friends and supporters and from there spread quickly to all other countries where Israelites live" (October 24, 1820). He took pleasure in recording the decline of old-type Jewry; e.g., the fatal stroke of a Breslau rabbi, the death of a Berlin Hazzan, and remarked: "Little by little the old rubbish will be carried off and decay. . . . My own activity aims chiefly at the overthrow of the entire rabbinism" (January 5, 1821). And, a few months later: "There are now efficient fighters against rabbinism, both Jews and Christians, you can be sure of that, and as long as I can move the impact will be felt." He planned to publish a selection of his sermons at the *Neue israelitische Synagoge* at Berlin, "so that the world can see what I demand from the German worship" (May 15, 1821).[2]

Yet soon afterwards these optimistic assurances were replaced by feelings of doubt and despair. Zunz's utterances became marked by unusual sharpness and merciless aggressiveness. In January 1822 he wrote: "You know my complaints about the German synagogue's state of decay here." And somewhat later: "The German synagogue here persists in its usual sleepy trod" (June 25, 1822). Shortly after the Prussian government ordered the new Temple closed (April 1823), which Zunz considered "no major misfortune," he referred S. M. Ehrenberg to the passage of his *Predigten* (a sermon preached on July 28, 1821) in which he spoke of Israel as having "fallen into barbarism because she has turned away from scholarship, from [her] language, from education; she believed herself safe while [in reality] she slept." He predicted the "collapse of this house of God" caused by internal conditions. In the letter in which this reference occurs, he held the rabbis of his day responsible for the prevailing "night," adding, "as long as there is night nothing can be expected from the government. . . . First we have to produce good schools, good teachers, qualified rabbis, strong community leaders, then the Messiah will not fail to come. But at present we live in a time of crises and not a few young men become perplexed" (an allusion to the apostasies of the period). The education of the children, he counseled, should be "neither irreligious nor medieval orthodox" (April 18, 1823).

With considerable chagrin he noted the lack of interest in Jewish scholarship on the part of the well-to-do. He regretted that the famous library of David Oppenheim (or, Oppenheimer) which had been brought from Prague to Hamburg found no sponsors in Germany and was allowed to go to the Bodleian library at Oxford. "Only fools, flatterers, and rogues" are listened to by the rich. He became cynical: "Difficile est, satyram non scribere" (November 7, 1823). Yet, stronger than cynicism was his indignation. "The rich should do everything to bring about a religious and moral consolidation . . . but you have no conception of the neglect and the anarchy in Jewish matters here and probably in the whole of Germany" (May 4, 1824). And, turning to spiritual leadership, he wrote: "In my eyes all these 'rabbis and scribes' in Poland, Holland, Germany, are nothing but Asiatic imams. No salvation can come from them" (May 13, 1825). Several times he made highly unfavorable remarks on Jeremias Heinemann's short-lived rabbinical seminary, the community school directed by him jointly with the *Rabbinatsassessor* Öttinger, and his boarding school. "He is a deep-seated evil [*Krebsschaden*] in this community" (May 22, 1827).

Only the revolutionary events of 1830 kindled in Zunz a new hope. He spoke of his happiness concerning the progress of freedom and constitutional rights, events which will "subdue the hypocrites, the Jesuits, and the tyrants—and bring salvation to the Jews" (September 4, 1830). And: "I am firmly convinced that progress in Jewish matters, both external and internal, is intimately connected with the progress in public life in general." But, he added, as things stand, "there is still much darkness among the Jews here, and the well-to-do and the educated ones . . . believe to have reached their goal once they give the impression of an educated Christian" (May 27, 1831). His expectation of a turn of events assumed a quasi-Apocalyptic coloring. "It is turning darker and darker here, but I am happy about it; it is the dark cloud of the approaching judgment, to burst upon the idol worshippers, Jew-baiters, thought-controllers, executioners *et cetera*, but after the cloud light will appear. . . . The *geulah* [redemption] is at hand" (August 15, 1831). In the same letter he complained about the apathy of the average Jew, the egoism of the rich, and the antagonism to the Jewish cause on the part of many.

Among the causes of the low state of Jewish schools, Zunz listed the lack of proper community organization and the various forms of defection and *Geistesdruck*. "The latter generates and the former promotes degradation, degraded institutions and degraded subjects. The anarchy in the community constitutions, in conjunction with the general indifference (favored from above!) plays power into the hands of the Jewish aristocrats" (letter to M. Isler, November 27, 1832).

In this situation, where rabbinical leadership, community organiza-

tions, and institutions of Jewish learning seemed to lack the strength to
deal with either the internal problems (indifference) or the external
pressure (anti-Semitism, legal restrictions), a new type of leadership,
that represented by Gabriel Riesser, appeared to Zunz to be the answer
to the quest of the period—in addition, of course, to Zunz's own endeavors to exert a decisive influence through the cultivation of Jewish
scholarship. Riesser, that valiant fighter for the cause of emancipation of
German Jews, began his work in the potentially liberal climate which
generated the July revolution of 1830 and of which the revolution was a
symbolic expression. In 1830 appeared Riesser's forthright "Über die
Stellung der Bekenner des mosaischen Glaubens in Deutschland" which
treated Jewish emancipation as an integral part of a liberal policy in
general. To *Kirchenrat* Paulus' rejection of Riesser's stand, the latter
reacted in "Verteidigung der bürgerlichen Gleichstellung der Juden,"
and further propagated his views in his periodical *Der Jude*, founded in
1832.

Zunz's disdainful criticism of the prevailing conditions gave way to
optimism and renewed hope. He admired Riesser's openness and can-
dor, but considered a moderate style to be a more effective strategy. He
expected his journal to offer the Jewish reader "substantial nourishment
in the place of the trash that is being served them" (December 4, 1832).
His hope was that *Der Jude* would not limit itself to polemics on constitutional law and issues of internal policy; however, he stated "not to have
the necessary leisure" to become a contributor (November 27, 1832).

Yet, nothing stopped Zunz from pursuing the type of activity that he
believed would contribute towards a radical change of attitude both of
the Jew towards Judaism and of the world towards the Jew. Such results
Zunz expected to come from his scholarly work. The body of his *Die
gottesdienstlichen Vorträge der Juden*, which appeared in 1832, is a
pioneering work of painstaking, objective, methodical research in the
history of Hebrew literature. But the Preface and the concluding section
put the book in the very center of current events; such, at any rate, was
the author's intention. It was his belief that a scholarly reliable, historically sound knowledge of the Jewish past had first to correct the image of
the Jew held in the minds of political thinkers and statesmen, then, help
to rectify the educated but religiously indifferent Jew's understanding of
Judaism, and finally, to initiate historically justified religious reforms. In
Zunz's view, reform and emancipation were interrelated, and both were
interpreted by him as expressions of a new, culturally united Europe,
emerging from the revolutionary movements of the time.

The 1840's generated plans of religious reforms, both in the Christian
churches and in German Judaism; the latter, initiated by Abraham
Geiger in 1837, culminated in the rabbinical conferences, 1844–1846.
Zunz kept in close contact with the preceedings. But, averse to com-

promising his high standards and strongly aware of the pettiness of some
of the proposals and their advocates, he adopted a decidedly negative
and pessimistic attitude. Though serving the Berlin Jewish community
(as director of its Teachers Seminary, 1840–1850), his antagonism to it
deepened; the letters abound in slighting references to the *Ketzinim*,
powerful leaders but indifferent to the tradition of learning in Israel, and
in criticism of the representatives of religion who had made their peace
with the prevailing conditions. A lonely man, he devoted his energy to
the struggle for Central-European democracy and, above all, to Jewish
scholarship.

The Jewish community, its institutions and its leadership, Jewish
learning and its impact on life underwent great changes, which Zunz
who died in 1886, could not foresee. He could not divine the upsurge of
deep interest, the renaissance of Jewish learning, and the rise of dedicated leadership in German Jewry before the Catastrophe. The course of
history, especially of Jewish history, is unpredictable.

NOTES

1. They were published in *Leopold Zunz,* see p. 173, note 5.
2. The *Predigten* appeared in 1823. Cf. The comprehensive analysis in Alexander Altmann, "Zur Frühgeschichte der jüdischen Predigt in Deutschland
(Leopold Zunz als Prediger,)" *Year Book VI, Leo Baeck Institute,* 1961.

14

NOTES ON AN
UNPUBLISHED LETTER
BY I. M. JOST

One of the most active men on behalf of Jewish synagogal and liturgic reform in the beginning of the nineteenth century was undoubtedly Israel Jacobson (1768–1828). His endeavors were motivated by the desire to remove from Jewish life all that was reminiscent of generations of isolated, segregated existence and to introduce a style that would make the Jew appear "modern," enlightened, and as little dissimilar from his Gentile neighbor as possible. Such a transformation of the old-type Jew into an acculturated Israelite would, Jacobson and his fellow reformers believed, foster a better understanding of the Jew on the part of the Christian and imbue the Jew with the consciousness of being a part of an extended family of man. A medal ordered by Jacobson to celebrate the emancipation of the Westphalian Jews pictured two angels, representing Christianity and Judaism united in the kingdom ruled over by Jerome, Napoleon's brother (1808).

Jacobson, who became president of the Jewish consistory of Westphalia, established a school in Cassel (the seat of the consistory), to which a chapel for reformed services was attached. In 1810 he dedicated a temple in Seesen, complete with bell ringing, an organ, choir, and German hymns. Jacobson, in clerical robes, conducted the services at what was called the "Festival of Jewish Reformation." When the Kingdom of Westphalia came to an end and the consistory ceased to exist (1813), he transferred his activities to Berlin, where he converted a part of his house into a synagogue. Some prayers were read in Hebrew, others in German; the Sephardic pronunciation was used. Central in the services was the German sermon, in most cases delivered by Jacobson himself (whose German was far from perfect). Emphasis was on decorum, good taste, aesthetics, and orderliness.

On the Feast of Weeks 1815 the "confirmation and consecration" of Jacobson's son Naphtali was celebrated; the journal *Sulamith* (IV, 2, 1815) published a report of the occasion. It stressed the fact that several Christian dignitaries and high officials attended, in addition to some 400 Jews. To accommodate such large attendance, the congregation was to move (1817) to the house of the banker Jacob Herz-Beer.

Again, the German sermon was used for the cultivation of the new spirit, the religious "feeling," the elevated mood, devotion, ethics, universal humanism, progress, confidence in the future.

The preacher, or rabbi, though well acquainted with the subject of his particular sermon (and its Christian prototypes) was, with some exceptions, no longer the scholar in the Hebrew tradition. What counted now, was rhetoric. "The German expression of the speaker was pure, free of artificiality, strong, the pronunciation correct, the voice strong and elastic," reads a report.[1]

The pulpit in the Beer synagogue was occupied by Isaak Levin Auerbach, Eduard Kley, and Carl Siegfried Günsberg, "men," according to Graetz, "of mediocre talent and mediocre oratory."[2] I. M. Jost was offered a position as preacher but refused. Leopold Zunz (1794–1886) was appointed preacher in August 1821, preached a number of sermons, a selection of which he published in Berlin, 1823[3] and resigned in September 1822.

Zunz had come to Berlin in October 1815, a few days before the Day of Atonement. He attended the services in Jacobson's house and shortly thereafter reported to his friend and former teacher, Samuel Meir Ehrenberg in Wolfenbüttel. He found men who after twenty years of alienation from Judaism spent the whole day at the services; men who thought to be above religious feeling shed tears of devotion; the greater part of the young kept the fast. He points to the three preachers who would be an asset to the largest congregation: Mr. Auerbach speaks with philosophical clarity and inner solidity; his voice has a soft ring; his character is innocence; he has a beautiful pronunciation of the Hebrew and he is a noted poet in that language. Kley is vital and daring, his imagery excites the imagination. I would compare him with Ezekiel, the former with Jeremiah. The third (Günsberg) Zunz hoped to hear the next holiday.[4] In another letter to Ehrenberg (November 12, 1815), Zunz mentions among the various groups within the Berlin population, "enlightened persons who spent the whole Day of Atonement in Jacobson's temple."[5]

Isaac Marcus Jost (1793–1860), Zunz's schoolmate in Wolfenbüttel, came to Berlin to accept the directorship of the Bock private school (1816) where both Jewish and Christian boys were educated. Jost, too, attended services at the reform group, after its transfer to the house of Jacob Herz-Beer. After the Day of Atonement, 1817, he wrote a long letter to S. M. Ehrenberg in Wolfenbüttel, on which the present report is based.

It gives a detailed description of the institution and some of its personalities. The view is personal, rather irreverent, unfriendly, and biased, but in keeping with Jost's well-known critical attitude toward Judaism, even in its reform garb. Note the contrast to Zunz's almost enthusiastic report on the Day of Atonement service two years prior to Jost's.

In his letter, Jost informs his former teacher that the new German worship service is causing a sensation but the greatest part (of the prayers) is recited in Hebrew; the preachers, however, preach in German, though not according to the accepted rules but in the opinion of the audience. The idea (of reform) is healthy—if properly executed, Jost continues. The congregation is about to elect seven men to reorganize the service. Up to now everyone was bored by the old, wrinkled out-of-tune organ and the new, clumsy, overly loud choir, composed of pupils of the Heinemann school. Much depends, therefore, on this election, Jost adds. He calls the congregation fanatic, for a member, about to give his daughter in marriage to another member, made it the first condition that the young man observe the Sabbath. "O tempora," exclaims Jost.

The educator planned to bring some of his pupils and boarders to the forthcoming Day of Atonement service and asked that they be included in his ticket of admission. He pointed out to Ruben Samuel Gumperz, the man in charge, that it was the duty of the congregation to admit his, Jost's, boarders, since non-admission could be interpreted as favoring Jeremias Heinemann's institute. Gumperz promised to take up the matter with the banker J. A. Muhr, "who headed the department of seating." To provide Ehrenberg with a clear picture of the situation, Jost attached a sketch of the Beer synagogue, which consisted of three large, interconnected rooms in Beer's house.

The center room housed the holy ark, "the altar," the pulpit, the canopy (for weddings), and the seats for the rich leadership. The room to the right seated the men, the one to the left, with its own entrance, seated the women. The center room was "romantically" adorned, abounded in golden tassels. At the far right in the section for men was the site of the organ and the choir. Jost found the separation between the rich and the others offensive and quoted his friend C. S. Günzburg (or Günsberg), the co-preacher, who took the liberty to remark that such an arrangement can only serve to make all of them look ridiculous. The remark led to the decision to include the scholars with the rich. Jost was counted among the scholars, though, he adds, without his consent. As such, he received a ticket of admission "with a respectful number of a seat," under the window, close to the women's room.

Now, Jost continues his report, having heard that only persons with tickets would be admitted and others sent away by the police, he wondered why nothing had been done about his students. He wrote to J. A. Muhr, who conferred with Mr. Gumperz; both decided to honor his request, for, if this request were not granted, he threatened to absent himself completely. He returned his ticket, which was amended to read "and four boarders." (As we would expect of Jost, he noticed a grammatical error in the amendment.) However, in the synagogue he found that his number had been changed and the newly assigned seat was next to the organ, i.e., it was the worst seat in the room. He realized that he was considered an opponent of the cause (of reform) and as such treated with a certain disdain.

On the Day of Atonement, he and his pupils appeared quite late, 8:30

a.m., whereas the service started at 8 o'clock. The doorman refused the pupils entry; Jost tried to push them in and quietly insisted on his right. The doorman pretended to have explicit orders from Mr. Muhr to turn the pupils away. At this moment a pork-eater (*Schweinefleischfresser*), who fasted that day "to relieve himself of the sins of the year by means of a general purgative," stood up from his seat and shouted: "You deserve to be thrown out if you are such a teacher and train your pupils to come late to Shul, such a teacher has to be thrown out that he breaks neck and legs." (This is a rather polite rendering of a vulgar, boorish jargon.) This procedure, Jost continues, could be answered either by one's fists or not at all; he chose the latter, took his pupils, left quietly and went to a small prayer group (*minyan*) where he witnessed with deep piety the auctioning off of ritual honors.

The next day he complained to Gumperz and Muhr about the treatment accorded not to his person, but to a man of his position, adding that he would take measures all would find unpleasant. The gentlemen got scared, thought up a web of contradictory lies to excuse themselves and that ruffian, regretted his (Jost's) absence on the Day of Atonement, and promised to restore his original seat among the rich and grant undisturbed admission of his pupils.

What concerns the issue (of reform), Jost returns to a previously expressed opinion, its basis is a good idea which, however, is not yet well carried out. The Jew is rightly embarrassed not to be able to answer the Christian who asks: "What is your faith? What makes you a Jew?" It is this embarrassment, not a religious need, that led to the steps to improve the worship. That is why the leaders do not act out of principles, but institute things in a manner that neither will the old-type Orthodox Jew accuse them of heresy, nor Christians of mere deism. Therefore, the noiselessness of their steps, therefore the uneasiness that the issue will be misunderstood by the government. Therefore the concern with externals. Only after experiencing the nonsense are they going to elect these seven men. To Berlin's shame it must be said that those elegible to vote are in a dilemma to find seven capable men with sufficient learning.

The following will illustrate that uneasiness, Jost continues. Kley and Günzburg edited the reform service, called *The German Synagogue*. Kley wrote a preface in which he ctiticized the Berlin Jews. The leaders of the congregation were annoyed; they feared the King would read these truths and wanted to announce in the press that the book was written without authorization. Kley let it be known that he would publish a rebuttle. This frightened the leaders and they desisted from the intended announcement.—Jost notes that Kley left for Hamburg to organize a German worship and expressed the hope that Hamburg would display greater firmness than Berlin.

Returning to the Berlin situation, Jost complains that people pray for the King and talk about the Fatherland, while in all prayers the Messiah plays a major role; prejudices are being eliminated, and yet spirits are being chased away with the *lulav* (on the festival of booths). Men shave, do business on the Sabbath, opt for German prayers for lack of knowledge of Hebrew, yet from the pulpit one hears: "Sacred is the Law, sacred the oral tradition, sacred and unshakable all the teachings of the men who gave stability to our religion. This is the spirit of truth that must move you if you wish to be blessed, if you hope to partake in the blessing, promised to Israel, etc." Jost is outraged by this hypocrisy, labeling it "playing games with religion." "Such orthodoxism (Jost's term) cannot and must not prevail." It may well lead to cooling the zeal for the cause (of reform) and the present enthusiasm may change into lethargy. As one more example of hypocrisy Jost cites a confirmation service, wherein two boys took an oath to sanctify the Sabbath and the festivals in the manner of their forefathers. "In this way the boys are taught to commit perjury. Kley would never do this," Jost concludes.

The criticism of the twenty-four year old Jost may have been overly sharp and the pettiness which he so keenly observed a bit out of focus. But he was right in sensing that the type of reforms undertaken in Berlin offered no solution to the real problems of enlightened Jews living in a period in which enlightenment was no longer the prevailing doctrine. In addition, the opposition of Orthodoxy was strongly felt. It was this opposition that led to the closing of the reform synagogue in 1823. Jacobson died a deeply disappointed man.[6]

NOTES

1. *Sulamith* VII, 1.

2. *Geschichte der Juden* XI, p. 415.

3. *Predigten, gehalten in der neuen Israelitischen Synagoge zu Berlin.*

4. *Leopold and Adelheid Zunz: An Account in Letters, 1815–1885*, ed. N.N. Glatzer, London, 1958, p. 4.

5. *Leopold Zunz. Jude Deutscher Europäer* (see above), p. 77.

6. The letter here discussed is one of 221 letters addressed by Jost to his friend and former teacher Samuel Meir Ehrenberg and his son, Dr. Philipp Ehrenberg, in Wolfenbüttel. The collection was preserved by the Rosenzweig family (S.M. Ehrenberg was a great grandfather of Franz Rosenzweig), was for many years a part of the Franz Rosenzweig Archives in Boston, and is now in the possession of the Archives of the Leo Baeck Institute in New York.

15
FRANZ KAFKA AND THE TREE OF KNOWLEDGE

Who is Joseph K in *The Trial,* K in *The Castle,* who are the other heroes in Kafka's stories? Various suggestions have been advanced by Kafka commentators—alienated man, modern escapist, neurotic man, homeless Jew, man of negative faith and others. It would be unjust to press for a uniform answer. Diverse and manifold levels of meaning have to be assumed in reading the work of a great writer. The following attempt to find a clue to some of Kafka's stories in his own non-fiction should be taken as but one out of many attempts at interpretation.

I

In a short parenthetical sentence (many of his crucial utterances are hidden in parentheses) Kafka remarked: "Sometimes I believe I understand the Fall as no one else." This statement must be regarded with careful attention. The fact that it is addressed to his friend Milena Jesenská adds to the weight of the statement; it was to Milena that Kafka confided some of his innermost concerns.

In the group of aphorisms which Kafka excerpted from his Notebooks (and which Max Brod published years ago under the title *Reflections on Sin, Suffering, Hope and the True Way*) there appears the motif of the Fall. But only the recent publication of the full text of the Notebooks[1] reveals the extent of Kafka's preoccupation with the Fall story in the third chapter of Genesis and the ever-increasing importance it played in his thinking. The Notebooks record Kafka's reflections in the years 1917 and 1918, i.e., shortly after completing *The Trial* (in 1915) and before writing *The Castle* in 1921. The writing of *The Great Wall of China* falls in the period covered by the Notebooks. The reader can hardly escape the notion that both in the novels and in the Notebooks Kafka deals with the same human phenomenon. The cause of man's predicament as Kafka presents it in the Notebooks may in a measure help to understand his heroes' encounters in the novels.

II

Kafka understands man's peculiar condition as resulting from the fact that he has eaten from the Tree of Knowledge but was prevented from eating from the Tree of Life. Thus he has become a person, has gained the power of thinking, a sharpened consciousness, an awareness of what is good and what is evil, but he has forfeited eternal life, the state of undisturbed happiness. Knowledge implies a certainty of life's finiteness. Such a life appears unbearable, another form of life unattainable; thus the wish to die (in Genesis: the punishment of death) is a first sign of nascent knowledge (35).[2] The original closeness between God and man has come to an end; now "the Fall separates us from him, the Tree of Life separates him from us" (85). Unconsciously in harmony with ancient Hebrew traditions, Kafka was aware of the paradox that Life assumed its supreme meaning only after man had acquired Knowledge (or, in the words of the Aggadah, that the Tree of Life was hidden within the Tree of Knowledge) so that knowledge is "both a step leading to eternal life and an obstacle in the way." Man in his desire for boundless life, a desire that originates in his knowledge, will have to destroy the obstacle which is himself, the knowing man (88). The sin of the first man of which the Genesis story speaks is applied by Kafka both to the eating from the Tree of Knowledge and to the not yet having eaten from the Tree of Life. "The state in which we find ourself is sinful" (43). No wonder that when the night of sub-conscious existence wanes, man, awakening to full consciousness, finds himself under indictment.

From this involved interpretation of the complex nature of knowledge Kafka moves to a simpler plane in referring to the explusion motif. Following the Genesis story he states that the expulsion from Paradise was to prevent man (Kafka employs throughout the personal pronoun, we, us) from eating of the Tree of Life (43). The expulsion was the mildest of possible punishments; a worse vengeance of the divine would have been the destruction of the Paradise; the most terrible step would have been "the cutting off of eternal life and leaving everything else as it is" (88). It is significant to Kafka that in the text of the story the curse was restricted to man and did not befall the garden of Eden. Had man not been expelled, something more unfortunate would have happened: Paradise would have had to be destroyed. But now, though man's destiny changed, the destiny of the Garden to serve man was not altered (85). Man, who not only gained knowledge but "had become knowledge of the divine" (86), lives in the consciousness that Paradise and the Tree of Life, though beyond reach of man, still retain their meaningful place in the scheme of things.

The possession of knowledge turns man into an exile; exiled from the realm of the Tree of Life man is destined to know but is not allowed to live; *cogito ergo non sum*. Life is but a primordial memory, a longing never to be fulfilled.

However, mere knowledge of good and evil can never satisfy man; man will endeavour to *act* in accordance with this knowledge. The next step in Kafka's thinking is decisive: The power to translate knowledge into action was not granted to man (43f.). Man will forever strive to act but the range of his action will never correspond to the scope of his knowledge. Faced with the futility of his attempts which may ultimately break him, man would prefer to annul his knowledge in order to escape the dilemma. Thus annulment of knowledge, so man hopes, might bring him rest and peace. Or: Man will wish to accept knowledge as a distant goal to be reached later in time. A vain hope indeed; to man who has eaten from the Tree of Knowledge conscious awareness of good and evil is not his future but his immediate actuality (44).

Thus man exists in a double tension: the one between knowledge and life, the other between knowledge and deed. Both result from man's rebellion against the paradisical world, the world of a dream-harmony between God and him who was to become man, the eternal world of quiet, instinctual happiness. Man became man by his rebellion, by his impatience with his original state (34). The knowledge he gained by his revolt estranged him from the world that remained in the power of the lord of the Garden. The world became the place "where we went astray," it is "the fact of our being astray" (90).

An indication of man's not belonging is the loss of his name. Most of Kafka's heroes (or, rather, the manifestations of the one hero of Kafka, man) have no names or go mainly by initials. "I am twenty-three years old but I have no name yet" ("Gespräch mit dem Betrunkenen"). The exile, the lonely stranger, is not being addressed; there is no communion between him and the world outside and no name is therefore needed. The Genesis story emphasizes Adam's ability to give names to living beings around him—before he gained knowledge and lost life. The Fall brought about a radical change in man's position. Now, the awareness of the "I" makes the discovery of the "Thou" a difficult task; the name is without meaning so long as the two exist without a relationship.

The memory of the original domicile lives on; exile accentuates the consciousness of the lost home. Could he forget his home he would no longer be a stranger. The remembrance of the Tree of Life constitutes a disturbing antithesis to the—never fully realized—existence under the sign of knowledge. Man, to use Kafka's simile, is attached to a chain that allows him movement on earth but prevents his leaving its narrow confines and ascending to heaven; at the same time, belonging not only to earth but also to heaven, he is attached to a similarly calculated heavenly chain that prevents his attempts to go down to earth (41). Man is torn between the two realms.

What establishes a bond between this world of ours and the realm of the positive is suffering; in fact, suffering is the only link between the two (90). The Genesis story speaks of suffering as entering human existence as the consequence ("punishment") of knowledge; both Adam and Eve suffer in their most genuine activities: he in working for his daily bread, she is childbirth. Both try through these activities for which they suffer to penetrate into the realm of—no longer naïvely attainable—Life.

III

Kafka, who as no other Western writer had penetrated into one of the most meaningful stories of the East, must have considered the question how the Book which he called a sanctum (80) resolved the problem that it placed at its beginning. There are indications—though no proof—that indeed he so did. The inquiry into the Fall in Kafka's Notebooks is followed by a discussion of Abraham, and references to the Tower of Babel, to Moses, Mount Sinai and the Law are scattered throughout the whole of Kafka's work.

In the biblical story man's estrangement from God and his exile from the Tree of Life (one brief Notebook entry of Kafka reads: 'Tree of Life—Lord of Life') was not to last forever. True, the road to the Garden is guarded and there is no return. But the Lord called knowing man back into his presence to accord him that which from now on would take the place of the fruit of the Tree of Life. On Mount Sinai God again addressed himself to man and revealed the Law, which is called a Tree of Life. Knowledge had implied the awareness of death and the fear of death. But now man may choose life again. Death is not being abolished but it will no longer threaten to make life meaningless. Knowledge is not being annulled but it will no longer isolate man; imbued with "life," "knowledge" will be a source of communication rather than a demonic power. The order which the Law will bring into life will seemingly restrict the independence of knowing man; in reality it will establish inroads for the divine in the community of man and in the human heart. The laws will be visible signs of the covenant between God and man whom the Fall had turned into antagonists. The relationship between man and God on the mythological level had come to an end; now, the relationship is being renewed on the level of revelation.

Kafka understood well the function of the Law. In his conversations with Gustav Janouch,[3] Kafka said that the Jewish people never sank to "the level of an anonymous and therefore soulless mass," "never has been nameless" as long as it held fast "to the fulfillment of the Law." Only "through a fall from the Law which gives it form" mankind becomes "a gray, formless, and threrefore nameless mass." Then, what could be "life" is "levelled out into mere existence. . . . But that is not the world of the Bible and Jewry." The people of the Bible Kafka calls "an association of individuals by means of a Law." Modern masses, on the other hand, "resist every form of association; they split apart by reason of their own lawlessness. . . . Mankind has lost its home." The relationship between "law" and "eternal life" is seen by Kafka when he assigns to the poet the task of "leading the isolated and mortal into eternal life, the accidental into conformity to law."

If Kafka, to whom writing, as he expressed himself, was "a form of prayer," approached the task which he assigned to the writer, he did it in a radically negative manner. The central motif of his novels is not to lead homeless, nameless, lawless humanity to law. Rather, his novels present man, the exile from Paradise, who tries to gain Life but who is not able to take the road to Sinai and to accept the new form in which Life is being offered to him. Knowing man knows that the distance between him and the Lord of Life can no longer be bridged; that if God wished to speak to man again his voice would not reach him.

"Many people prowl round Mount Sinai. Their speech is blurred, either they are garrulous or they shout or they are taciturn" (312). Kafka calls Moses "a judge, a stern judge." The laws may lead to judgement; they do not create form, do not accord a name to the anonymous individual. In *The Great Wall of China* there is a reference to the schools where "superficial culture mounts sky-high round a few precepts that have been drilled into people's minds for centuries, precepts which, though they have lost nothing of their eternal truth, remain eternally invisible in this fog of confusion." In the Notebooks Kafka relates the image of the messengers of the king racing through the world and, since there are no kings, shouting to each other their meaningless and obsolete messages (30).

In *The Problem of Our Laws* Kafka speaks of the remote nobility that keeps secret the ancient laws; the people are ruled by the law which one does not know; the noble scrupulously administer the law but they themselves stand above the laws. That the laws exist is an old tradition and it may be that they do not exist at all. Those who believe that they do exist, are inclined to hate themselves "because we have not yet shown ourselves worthy of being entrusted with the laws." In spite of these complications nobody would dare to repudiate the belief in the laws and the nobility. "We live on this razor's edge."

IV

Thus man who has eaten from the Tree of Knowledge may spend his existence on earth in distrust, uncertainty, doubt as to whether the Law—the form-giving, community-building, name-according force—will show him the way to the Lord of Life. The Lord himself does exist, though in an endless distance from man; the original, primordial nearness between him and man is being treasured in deep memory, however indistinct and indefinite. The Castle does exist; its lord had issued a call to the Land Surveyor to do his work and is expecting him. Here ends the extent of K's, the Land Surveyor's knowledge. The villagers who live in childlike naïveté are not troubled by the reality of the Castle. K who had come to answer the call remains isolated from both Castle and village; his knowledge estranges him from the simple village folk that do not know; he cannot translate this knowledge into life, because real, meaningful, eternal life is in the Castle and beyond the reach of knowing man. The expanse—so small, so vast—between Castle and village is filled with the hierarchy of officials, an organization of intermediaries. They seem to connect, to correlate, to co-ordinate—to personify the function of the law; in reality they only accentuate the distance. The Genesis story relates man's acquisition of knowledge as a yielding to temptation. It is not without significance that Kafka called his preliminary sketch of *The Castle*, "Temptation in the Village."

In *The Trial* (which lasts one year—a symbolic unit of life) Joseph K soon realizes the abysmal paradox in the world of law. There is an authority that holds him guilty and that issued an order concerning him. But no judge will confront him, no lawbook will be available to advise him. The more the accused will try to advance his cause the more uncertain will he become about his situation. He faces an overwhelming machinery engaged in reducing to shreds his most precious possession: his conscious personality. The parable "Before the Law"—one of the greatest parables in literature—points to the basic tragedy of man who has eaten from the Tree of Knowledge but cannot reach the Tree of Life: He stands before the door to the Law (which in the parable stands for the promise of life, of fulfillment, of the goal) prevented from entrance by the keeper of the door. (The entrance to the Garden is guarded by the cherubim "to keep the way to the Tree of Life.") After spending the rest of his life ardently contemplating all the moves of the doorkeeper, the man asks: "Everyone strives to attain the Law, how does it happen that in all these years no one else has come to seek admittance?" To this final question of the dying man the doorkeeper answers: "No one but you could gain admittance through this door, since this door was intended only for you. I am now going to shut it."

The strangely paradoxical story puzzles all Kafka interpreters. However, the clue to its understanding may lie in the fact that all thoughts of the man in the text of this parable and of the "commentators" that follow are directed not toward the real issue, which is the law, but are concentrated upon the doorkeeper. The doorkeeper fulfills the function of the officials of the Castle and the bureaucracy of the Trial. All of them stand between knowing man and Life, Law, the Lord. Kafka has said it: The possession of knowledge implies the urge to act, but the strength to act was not given to man. He acts too much and, thus, wrongly. Thus: Going out to search for Life (and his search will become a ceaseless activity) he will encounter the intricate and senseless clerkship; in his search for Law he will not hear the voice coming down the mountain that cannot be ascended but will face the lowest agents of a law machine and—a door-keeper.

Woman, who in Paradise was instrumental in gaining knowledge, will be used in an attempt to break through the maze of obstacles in the way to life. "Woman . . . is the representative of life" (98). But Leni, Frieda, Olga, Fräulein Bürstner will only seemingly be of help. They will come in sight as little redeemers but ultimately blur the vision of the goal.

Connections, manipulations, reasonings and calculations, feverish activities will be futile. The world of blind machines is but a mirrored reflection of man's machinations. The question of life remains unanswered; the expelled one remains in exile. "Man with his knowledge of good and evil is but a helpless atom in a world which has no such knowledge" (B. Russell).

V

Is there no way open out of the impasse of knowing man as depicted in Kafka's tragic stories? There is indeed a note of hope in Kafka's writings, a pointing out of what appears to him the only possible direction.

All human error is impatience, he says (34); impatience was the cause of the expulsion from Paradise; the return to Paradise—contact with life—is prevented by the same impatience (34). If there is hope it can only come from patience, from quiet waiting, from a withdrawal into the realm of creative inactivity that must precede all deed, from the stillness of soul that precedes the breaking forth of will, from the calmness of the spirit in which intuitive life is born. In this realm there is no desire, striving and scheming, no struggle for success and achievement, no display of power *versus* power; man goes back to the sources of his being—before knowledge and life—and chooses life.

Seeking is of no avail; but there is salvation in not-seeking: "He who seeks will not find; he who seeks not—will be found" (80). Happiness can be realized by "believing in the indestructible element in oneself and not striving towards it" (41). Poets have dreams; life, real life, as Kafka said to Janouch, is but "a reflection of the dreams of poets." An advice to Janouch: "Do not excite yourself. Be calm. Quietness is indeed a sign of strength. . . . Calmness and quietness make one free—even on the scaffold." From the outside one will victoriously impress theories upon the world and "then fall straight into the ditch one has dug, but only from the inside will one keep oneself and the world quiet and true" (67). *The Great Wall of China* includes the parable of the Emperor "who has sent a message to you . . . to you alone"; the messenger who set out to deliver the message will never reach you; too vast is the distance between the Palace and your door. The Palace itself is an endless expanse of buildings, chambers, stairs and courts; never, never will the message come to you; "but you sit at your window when evening falls and dream it to yourself." Or, in the incomparable words of the Notebooks: "You do not need to leave your room. Remain sitting at your table and listen. Do not even listen, simply wait. Do not even wait, be quite still and alone. The world will freely offer itself to you to be unmasked; it has no choice, it will roll in ecstasy at your feet" (48). This is the happiness of being found that comes to him who seeks not. Such promise of happiness "resembles the hope of eternal life," says Kafka in his Diaries.

This *vita contemplativa*, creative passivity, is the true home to which the exiled may return. "Both contemplation and activity have the appearance of truth; but only the activity that emanates from contemplation, or better, that which returns to it again, is truth" (97). In advancing this answer to the central human question, Kafka refers back to the symbolism of the two trees in the Garden.

The Tree of Knowledge represents the truth of activity [*die Wahrheit des Tätigen*], the Tree of Life stands for non-doing, not seeking, waiting—the truth of the quietude [*die Wahrheit des Ruhenden*]. The first truth we acquired in reality, the second is ours only by intuition. This discrepancy is man's fate and is sad to realize. A positive aspect, however, is that the first truth refers to a moment of time, the second to eternity; thus the first truth vanishes in the light of the second (91).

Kafka, who let his fictional characters—mediocre creatures—struggle in the sphere of impatient, impersonal, routinized, aimless activity, has transcended this sphere in his non-fiction notations. Here, to quote Kafka in his *Letters to Milena*, "there is something of the air which one has breathed in Paradise before the Fall." Kafka, standing between East and West in his belief that he understood the meaning of the Paradise story as no one else, seems indeed to have gained the freedom to behold the Tree of Life which is hidden within the Tree of Knowledge.

NOTES

1. Included in the volume published by Schocken Books under the title *Dearest Father* (New York, 1954) and by Secker and Warburg under the title *Wedding Preparations in the Country* (London, 1954). The translations are by Ernst Kaiser and Eithene Wilkins. Both this rendition and the translations of the Aphorisms by Willa and Edwin Muir in *The Great Wall of China* (New York, 1946) have been consulted and drawn on, in part, in this essay.

2. The numerals refer to identical pages in *Dearest Father* and *Wedding Preparations in the Country*.

3. Gustav Janouch, *Conversations with Kafka*, New York, 1953).

16

BUBER AS AN
INTERPRETER OF
THE BIBLE

"Meinen wir ein Buch?
Wir meinen die Stimme."
Buber (1926).

I

Forty-nine years ago, in one of his memorable addresses, Buber outlined, however tentatively, an approach to the Bible. Scripture is to be studied not as a work of literature but as a basic document of the absolute's impact upon the national spirit of Israel. Though conversant with Biblical exegesis, ancient and modern, the student must transcend such exegesis in a search for the original meaning of a passage. He should study the documentary theories of contemporary scholarship, yet penetrate to deeper separations and connections; recognize the mythical element, yet not introduce mythical interpretation if the historical is sufficient; be appreciative of the poetic forms, yet intuit what is more than poetry and form. "Knowledge as a service" (*dienendes Wissen*) is the term Buber uses when speaking of the care to be applied to the original Hebrew of the Bible.[1]

The term properly defines Buber's own work as interpreter of the Hebrew Bible. Its overt beginning falls in the Spring of 1925 when Buber and his friend, Franz Rosenzweig, undertook their epochmarking translation of the Bible into German.[2] Out of the intensive preoccupation with the Biblical text grew organically first a number of scholarly essays on various individual Biblical problems, then a series of books, from *Königtum Gottes* (Kingship of God, 1932), via *Torat ha-Neviim* (The Prophetic Faith, 1942), *Moses* (1946), *Zwei Glaubensweisen* (Two Types of Faith, 1950), *Right and Wrong* (1952). *Bilder von Gut und Böse* (Images of Good and Evil, 1952), to *Sehertum* (Abraham the Seer; Prophecy and Apocalypse, 1955). These books, complemented by a succession of studies and articles, form an Old Testament commentary on a great number of exegetic and linguistic problems as well as on most of the main issues of Israel's internal history and Biblical faith. Buber's tentative rules, formulated in 1918, were fully realized in the following four decades. Knowledge was turned into service.

The present essay cannot aspire to be a comprehensive treatment of the subject. The field of Biblical studies is vast and Buber's contribution to many of its aspects far-reaching and, at points, revolutionary. His studies resist classification into any of the current schools of Biblical interpretation; they resist all classification. Any serious attempt at critical analysis would have to consider the status of Buber's work on the Bible in the context of his own religious, historical, linguistic, and personal philosophy. This short essay cannot, therefore, do more than point to some of the more basic lines of his thinking.

II

In trying to understand a Biblical story, Buber takes as his clue the choice of words and images, of key phrases, the structure of the tale, the rhythm of the report. The purpose of the story is to convey a teaching, to offer instruction, an aim not achieved by an explicit reference. The teaching is unobtrusively inherent in the story itself; here "perfect attentiveness" (*vollkommene Aufmerksamkeit*) is required. This demand of perfect attentiveness—by no means self-understood—best describes Buber's approach. In the long history of Biblical exegesis this attitude was never taken; it "became the task only of this late age to point out the significance of what has so far been overlooked."[3]

Believing that the text as a whole preserves a genuine tradition and that occasional errors in later transmission could not distort its essential accuracy, Buber may safely question the relevance of the theory of parallel documents. The intricate composition of the central stories cannot be conceived as resulting from excerpts from older documents; only a full, rich, plastic narrative tradition can be the source for the Biblical writer's work. Preoccupied neither with problems of literary or linguistic influences on the Biblical texts, nor with historical dependencies, parallels, or relationships, Buber follows the guidance of the text itself.

Thus, Buber cannot read the Abraham cycle as a redactor's combination of stories drawn from divergent sources; a detailed analysis of the texts suggests to him a closely knit composition.[4] Its unifying aspect appears to be a sequence of seven interrelated revelations to Abraham: stations on a way from trial to trial, and progressing to an even deeper relationship between Abraham and God. Through skillful linguistic allusions, Abraham, the first to make his way into history, is set off against Noah who, standing in nature, a "husband-man" (Genesis 9:20), represents a pre-national humanity. Unlike Noah's work, which is bound up with his time and "his generation" (Genesis 7:1), Abraham's activity marks the beginning of a historic process which is to culminate in the ultimate union of mankind (Isaiah 2:1–5). The consistent recurrence in the text of various forms of the term "seeing" leads Buber to the assumption that it is a "theme-word" (*Leitwort*) chosen by the Biblical annalists to characterize the first patriarch. This theme-word is used with special emphasis in the story of the Binding of Isaac on Moriah (Genesis 22), the last of the seven acts of the drama. Abraham sees, and sees also that he is being seen. Buber calls him the first in the long sequence of seers in Israel. Abraham, the originator of a people, is also the first recipient of the gift of prophecy and is remembered as such by the tradition of later prophets.[5]

This example demonstrates Buber's reliance on structure, style, and choice of words as guides to the intention of whoever wove into one the various tales, memoirs, and reports. The relevant leads come from within.

III

Buber's translation of the Bible has freed the ancient text of the layers upon layers of overgrowth. The most often quoted passages especially had lost their original freshness and immediacy of impact. Primeval speech forfeited its power before the mighty array of theological, historical, psychological, and literary ideas. A language of concepts abstracted from reality replaced a language of living words. Moreover, the primary intention of the world-historically important translations, the Septuagint, the Vulgate, Luther's, was not preservation of the original character of the Bible, but establishment of a valid testimonial writ for their respective communities: the Jewish Hellenist diaspora, the early Christian oikumene, the church of the Reformation.[6] In such historically determined situations, the need to accentuate certain facets of the Biblical teaching far outweighed concern for the structure of the text, the primal meaning of the word, and the correlation between content and form.

Buber's (and Rosenzweig's) Bible work is characterized by the attempt—at times it is admittedly no more than an attempt[7]—to go back to the very sources, to rediscover the original writing (*Grundschrift*); Buber himself uses the term palimpsest.[8]

Thus, *torah* is no longer rendered by the much too specific *Gesetz*, law, but by *Weisung*, or *Unterweisung*, which at least approximates one of the denotations of the root.[9] *Prophet*, the customary translation of *nabi*, suggests a prognosticator, although the meaning of the Greek term is rather closer to the Hebrew one; Buber's translation is *Künder*, announcer (of the word of God). *Malakh* has long been presented as angel, which, since it denotes a being of a special order, is misleading for many parts of the Bible. The new translation uses *Bote*, messenger, allowing for a fluid transition from the divine to the human carrier of the message. *Qorban*, the common German translation of which (*Opfer*, sacrifice) evokes associations not intended by the Hebrew (the English "offering" is much closer to the original Latin *offere*), is rendered by Buber as *Darnahung*, thus suggesting the meaning of the Hebrew root *qarab*, to come near, be near, and, in its causative form, to bring near. This rendition implies the existence of two personalities, one of which, in an endeavor to reduce the distance between them, comes near *(qarab)* to the other by means of a *qorban*. A careful reading of the Korah story (Numbers 16) shows how important for the understanding of the "offering" is the motif of being distant and coming near. A similar attempt to go back to the original, pre-theological, pre-conceptual, meaning of the Hebrew root, is evidenced in the translation of *kipper* and *kopher* by *decken* and *Deckung* (cover), respectively, instead of the theological *sühnen* und Sühnung (atone, atonement). Probably the most significant example of the Buber-Rosenzweig method of translation is the effort to render all the derivates of the root *ya'ad* by the corresponding forms of *gegenwärtig sein*, to be present. *Ohel mo'ed* was understood by the Septuagint and the Vulgate as the tabernacle of the testimony, by Luther as *Hütte des Stifts*, tabernacle of foundation. Mindful of the basic meaning of *ya'ad*, Buber renders the term in question by *Zelt der Gegenwart*,[9a] the tent in which God makes Himself present. Assuming that there is an original linguistic conntection between *mo'ed* and *'edut*, the latter, used in connection with the tent, the shrine, and the tablets of law, becomes *Vergegenwärtigung*, the place or the object which will re-present, remind of an event that was once present. So, e.g., the tablets of the law which bore the record or revelation will make the event present to those who were not themselves present on Sinai.

Buber realizes that the meanings, allusions, and associations read into the text by countless Bible reading generations are part and parcel of human history.[10] Such interpretations, regardless of the degree of proximity to the actual text, were the means by which humanity could rally around this book. But Buber considers it his task to decipher the writing itself and read it anew, knowing that the result may be paradoxical and vexing to modern man. "Yet, even paradox and vexation will yield instruction."[11]

IV

The endeavor to explore Biblical faith cannot, in Buber's thinking, be separated from an attempt to discern its relevance for the present-day reader. However, the didactic aspect in no way diminishes the scholar's obligation to examine objectively the scientific evidence and to establish the historic status of a passage, or a book. On the other hand, scholarly investigation, if it concerns the Bible, cannot be an end in itself. When the scholar has done his job, the whole man is called upon to make the scholar's findings the basis for his action. The scholar's work is the necessary presupposition for all that is to come. The untrained mind will

stay on the surface of the text, gloss over difficulties, and fail to notice
linguistic allusions, implied references, internal connections, to which
the ancient reader more readily responded. It is the scholar's task to
restore the original structure of the text and to point to its underlying
plan. Then, however, the text resumes its perennial function of teaching.
Buber will admit that, technically speaking, the actions of the scholar and
the "listener" may at times be two distinct roles. But he will point to
interdependence, even to the essential unity of the process. The scholar's
work would remain incomplete were he satisfied with the archivist's
achievement. He would, too, betray his office, were he to deal with his
texts so as to suggest a definite and ready application to problems of his
day and age. But he will forever keep in mind that the heart of the text,
silenced for the duration of his surgical performance, will beat again. The
realization that he, the scholar, is not engaged in the analysis of documents of a dead past but confronted by a living text will only increase his
vigilance. The criteria of detached scholarship are not sufficient for the
achievement of even an adequate understanding of the text. The Bible,
document of the dialogue between God and man, can be validly understood by that reader alone who is ready to become a partner in the
dialogue, that is, by a man who expects the Biblical word to be as
meaningful to him as it meaningfully addressed itself to the generations
before him. Only then will he be able to evaluate the special power, the
measure of concreteness, inherent in the Biblical narrative, speech, or
psalm. The latter is a wholly scientific issue, yet its comprehension is
made possible by something admittedly non-scientific: the personal
involvement of the scholar.

As an example of how Scripture can give contemporary man a sense of
direction, Buber points to the Biblical motif of correlating, of fusing
even, "spirit" and "life."[12] It is one of the errors of modern man that
"spirit," in the past seen in its broadest implication, appears to him
narrowed down to mean "intellect," while the realm of "life," sovereign,
independent, assumes ever larger proportions. This loss of a sense of
proportion is countered by the Biblical reference, repeated in colorful
variations to the *ruah*, which is both spirit and wind, dynamically moving between the two poles of the material and the immaterial, nature and
spirit. Genesis 1:2 speaks of the *ruah* of God "hovering" over the face of
the waters; the ancient Hebrew reader sensed the double meaning of
ruah and knew that God cannot be restricted either to the "natural" or the
"spiritual" realm, that He is neither nature, nor spirit, but the origin of
both. In the cycle of the wilderness stories the *ruah* appears both as the
"spirit" which God puts upon the elders (Numbers 11:17) and as the
"wind" which "went forth from the Lord and brought quails from the
sea" (*ibid.*, 11:31); the reader cannot fail to notice the correspondence in
the divine activity between nature and spirit, spirit and life.[13]

The narrative of the desert Sanctuary, as compared with the story of Creation, is cited as another example of how Scripture may instruct modern man. As in the former instance, Buber does not discuss overt moral teachings, but issues which only a scrupulously attentive reader will discover in the text. The first of the two accounts of the Creation is distinguished by the pointed use of certain key words: here are the "days" that flow into the thrice mentioned "seventh day"; the activity of God in "speaking," "making"—recorded seven times—and doing "the work"; the sevenfold "seeing" through which God examined His work and found it "good"; the threefold "blessing" and, finally, the reference to the "completion."

The same motif-words reappear in the story of the erection of the tabernacle. The cloud covered the mountain "six days" (Exodus 24:16). The work of creation is completed above the darkness; similarly, the pattern of the tabernacle is perfected in the dark of the cloud; no witness is present at either event. On the "seventh day" (*ibid.*) Moses is called to "see" the pattern which is "shorn" (i.e., "made to see"); this "see" verb, in a variety of forms, reoccurs several times in the report (Exodus 25:9, 40; 26:30; 27:8). Unlike the account in Genesis, God does not create here; only the pattern is designed in the "six days"; the tabernacle must be "made" by man. Indeed, the word "make" appears over and over again in the description of the "work"; it becomes the central phrase. The tabernacle completed, Moses, (not God, but His mediator) "sees" all the work and "blesses" it (*ibid.*, 39:43). And the motif of completion corresponds to that in the Creation story.

This parallelism is no coincidence. Buber interprets it as a Biblical device to call attention to the relationship between Creation and Revelation (a motif we shall meet later in this essay). Creation implies an original Revelation (*Uroffenbarung*); Revelation, however, fulfills the mystery of Creation: it is in the act of Revelation that God bids man to become "a partner in the work of Creation," as the Talmud expresses it. God has made the world and has offered it to man; the Tent where He will abide "in the midst of their uncleannesses" is shown to men but they themselves must make it. Man learns how to build; but no one directs his working hand. The abode of the Holy must be erected by him alone or it will not be established. The example of the Tent, like that of the *ruah*, teaches man to confront the world in faithful responsibility.

V

In *Königtum Gottes*, the first volume of a planned trilogy,[14] Buber attacked the central issue of Old Testament Messianism, its origin, meaning, historic development and its place in the faith of Israel.

The main aspect of Israel's Messianic faith is defined as "the readiness

(*Ausgerichtetsein*) to realize the relationship between God and the world in a universal kingship of God."[15] While the statement *per se* could be accepted by many Biblical historians, its qualification, which constitutes Buber's main thesis, challenges the critical reader. Buber believes that divine kingship in Israel is not a late theological theory but a faith rooted in the memory of a historical reality. It is his understanding that early Israel actually rejected human kingship and placed itself under the kingship of the invisible God. Gideon's refusal to accept hereditary rule over Israel, for "the Lord will rule over you" (Judges 8:23), is viewed by Buber as a report of an event and a "political demonstration."[16] The early form of Israelite theocracy, he argues, is not a rule by a priesthood or princes receiving their authority from a god but "an unmediated, non-metaphorical and unlimited"[17] direct dominion of God. Not a god in "the religious sense" who leaves the reality of worldly life to the devices of man; it is on the contrary, precisely this wordly realm God wishes to control; "there is nothing which would not be God's."[18] From time to time, He may entrust a mandate to one chosen by Him; the chosen leader, however, is not to transfer his office to his son after him: hereditary kingship is the absolute contrary of unmediated theocracy.[19] Man, then, will fulfil his mission as demanded by a particular situation (*situationsbezogen*), but beyond this he will have no power. The will of God, the King, will be made known through his constitution (which comprises not only cult and custom but as well, economic and social life); priests, even as members of a sacred institution, are to give answers only to queries addressed to them; in the main, the will of the God and King will become known to those seized by the freely moving Spirit. The unity of religion and politics will be maintained, the separation of the two realms, treated by human history as mutually exclusive entities, will be overcome.[20] "There is no political sphere outside the theo-political sphere."[21] The ritual office is indeed hereditary, but this office does not imply leadership; the political office is charismatic—here Buber uses Max Weber's terminology—and dependent on God, the origin of the charis.[22] The wandering tribes of Israel accepted "for ever and ever" (Exodus 15:18) the reign of God who bid Israel to be "a kingdom" of priestly men (*ibid.*, 19:6); "thus the Lord became King in Jeshurun" (Deuteronomy 33:5). Standing within this tradition, Gideon could not agree to replace divine kingship by a dynasty of princes.

Compared with the Near Eastern idea of divine kingship, is Israel's corresponding concept more than a doctrine and a "historizing theology?" Buber devotes a major part of *Königtum Gottes* to answering this question. He attempts to show that the reports of the proclamation of God as Israel's king, belonging to an authentic tradition, echo actual historical events, and not, as often assumed, a fiction of theologico-literary origin.[23]

He finds the ancient Israelite tribes psychologically predisposed to theocracy. Like the pre-Islamic bedouins, the independent Israelites found it inconceivable to submit to a sovereign. This anarchical drive is the negative side of Israelite theocracy and its preconditioning. It spells the wish to be free of human domination. The will to be independent, paradoxically coupled with its positive counterpart, readiness to accept the leadership of the Invisible One who led the tribes on their way and liberated them from Egyptian bondage, resulted in the theocratic covenant.[24]

The theophany on Mount Sinai is, in its ultimate aspects, a political act which confirmed the kingship of God over the people of Israel. Against Mowinckel's interpretation, Buber defends the historicity of the Biblical report. The covenant which bound the two parties, divine and earthly, in the task of establishing a kingdom was consecrated by a ritual (Exodus 24:3–8) unique in the traditions of both Israel and the Near East.[25] Through it both joined in a sacral and juridical mutual agreement: God to be the King, *melekh*, Israel to be His *mamlakhah*, His legal retinue. God the King issued His proclamation in the Ten Commandments.[26]

According to Buber, the theo-political community established on Sinai existed in its pure form until the death of Joshua. The popular assembly in Shechem (Joshua 24) reduced, in Buber's interpretation, the full scope of the initial, Mosaic, theo-political organization to a "purely religious" one.[27] Charismatic leadership assumed an institutional character.[28] However, the memory of the original form of the Kingdom of God was kept alive by groups of faithful Israelites; these are the early prophetic enthusiasts and men chosen as "judges." Their anti-monarchical stand underlies the hidden polemics against the institution of an earthly king which Buber detects in the first part of the book of Judges,[29] with, finally, implied criticism turning into Gideon's open statement. Only the pressure of external political events brought about the institution of hereditary monarchy in Israel. As the anointed (*mashiah*) of God, the king was charged with a responsibility he was unable to carry.

VI

From among the Old Testament types of leaders—patriarch, lawgiver, judge, king, prophet, psalmist, wise man, teacher—Buber chooses the prophet as the most significant spokesman of Biblical Israel. After having occupied a secondary position in classical and medieval Judaism, the phenomenon of the Israelite prophet (rediscovered by Protestant theology) fascinated nineteenth century Jewish philosophers. A high point of acceptance was reached in the thinking of Hermann Cohen who found in Biblical prophecy the great affirmation of pure monotheism and radical ethics.

Buber's interpretation of Old Testament prophecy surpasses his nineteenth century predecessors in scope and in penetration. It succeeds in fusing into a consistent whole the manifold phenomena of inspired leadership which thus far had been treated as isolated instances and assigned to varying strata in the growth of Hebrew religion.

We have already noted Buber's analysis of the texts on Abraham in whom he detects primarily a receiver of divine revelation, a seer, remembered as such in the later prophetic tradition. In the Moses traditions, too, the *nabi* element predominates. Buber assumes, with Yehezkel Kaufmann, that Moses derived from an old family of seers.[30] He is the carrier of the Spirit: he had entered "into a dialogic relationship with the Divinity." The seventy elders receive—as a temporary grant—a part of the *ruah* that is upon Moses; his own experience of the *ruah* is permanent. He desires the whole people to be *nebiim*, prophets in immediate contact with God.[31] Joshua and the Judges are carriers of prophetic charisma. The "bands of the prophets" preserve the original sense of the kingship of God which the people accepted in the covenant on Sinai. When permanent, hereditary, kingdom replaced charismatic judges and the kings failed to fulfil their function as vice-regents of the one true King, there were prophetic critics to confront king and people. It is the prophet who, in the breakdown of the kingdom, envisages the rise of the Messianic king. The prophetic message culminates in the concept of the Suffering Servant, a prophetic man, who, in Buber's interpretation, replaces the royal Messiah.[32] The suffering *nabi* "is the antecedent type of the acting Messiah."[33]

There emerges a presentation of a variety of *Gestalten* assumed by the prophetic spirit in response to the need of the particular historical situation. Seen in their succession, they form an internal history of Biblical Israel to which the external history is but a foil. It is the history of "the Torah sealed in the disciples" (Isaiah 8:16) and preserved for the day when the hidden Torah will be realized in the fullness of life, when the hidden God "will be King over all the earth" (Zechariah 14:9).

This being the scope and the impact of the prophetic element, Buber may well consider it the answer to what he regards as the constant threat to the spirit of Israel: the apocalyptic escape from the concreteness and the dialogical character of faith. The two types, prophet and apocalyptic, are not equally true interpreters of divine judgment, distinguished only by the respective historic situations. They are, rather, representatives of essentially different views concerning the position of man before God.[34]

The prophet teaches the freedom of choice. Israel is in the hand of God like the clay in the potter's hand. God plans the destiny of nations and of men. Yet, in choosing the good, man will cause God to "repent" the decree of judgment; in choosing to turn away from God, man will make Him "repent" from doing the good He had planned.[35] Because there is a covenantal relationship between God and man, man has the power of turning to the good or the evil, and thus also the power of turning the tide of events. What happens to him is, then, the divine answer to his choice. The connection between human deed and divine action if to be understood not as a mechanical relationship of cause and effect but as a dialogical correspondence between God and man. God wants man to come to Him in perfect freedom; the future, therefore, cannot be a result of pre-determination. The spirit of God assumes the attitude of "waiting" for man to fulfil the intention of Creation. Prophecy, then, considers man to be what Buber calls ein *Überraschungszentrum der Schöpfung*. Man will forever have the power to act upon Creation, positively or negatively: this prophetic faith addresses itself to all generations, to each in its language.[36]

The apocalyptic evades this responsibility of choice. In his world (Buber concentrates on *Fourth Ezra*) there is no room for man as a factor of historical and meta-historical decision. The apocalyptic visionary does not speak directly to the human person; he is a writer rather than a speaker. Man can no longer act meaningfully; the future is predestined. Adam's original fall—a concept foreign to the Old Testament—has involved all mankind. The end is inescapable, and near at hand. "The creation has grown old" (5:55), says Ezra the apocalyptic; "our time hastens to its end with might." Whatever may still happen in history has no longer historical value; man is unable to take an active part in the drama.[37]

Apocalyptic elements are at work in our own age, Buber finds. Karl Marx's view of the future is not of the prophetic kind, as some have thought, but follows the pattern of the apocalyptic. In Marx's system an immanent dialectic takes the place of the transcendent power that brings about the transition from the present period to the one to come. As in the apocalyptic, man, bound into a pattern of rigid necessity, is not fit for individual decision and free action. Another expression of modern, secular apocalyptic is western man's feeling of futility, his notion of living in a late period of decline, when poetry indulges in self-irony and art glories in an atomization of the world around us; of the world—no longer understood as Creation—as grown old indeed; and of man as grown silent and lonely.

Such apocalyptic can be validly challenged only by renewed reference to the prophetic faith in the faculty of man to overcome the rigidity of de-personalized system, to act freely, to "turn," to decide, to dare face issues as they occur, to do his share in the rejuvenation of the world, created as a meeting ground between man and God.[38]

One may challenge Buber's prophetic thesis by arguing that if things go wrong in history and ancient, sacred, promises fail to be realized, disappointment with history and hope in a meta-historic event become a perfectly valid stand. Apocalyptic thought rests, after all, on a firm belief that if this Creation failed, there will be another aeon, which, like ours, will be a work of God. Loss of patience with history and the men who act in it is not loss of faith. The author of *Fourth Ezra*, so concerned with the implication of the Roman victory, could not have expected a "turning" in the hearts of man to affect the powerful wheels of history. Yet, even he, radical in his condemnation of the present aeon, saw a vision of a new Jerusalem rising upon the ruins of the old (10:54). True, the new city was not built by human hands, but it was a human heart that longed to behold the mighty acts of God.

Buber will not accept this argument and will sense the danger inherent in "exceptations" and in the all-too-ready replacement of this world by another. Both are God,'s but it is this our world which has been created for man and entrusted to his service and his care. Buber will side with the Tannaites, early rabbinic masters, who, as keenly aware of Rome's might as *Fourth Ezra*, still maintained the reality of the Kingdom of God. He will (thinking especially of the Christian partner in the Biblical faith) point to the formidable ally of apocalyptic abandonment of the world and of gnostic admission of dualism: Marcion.[39] It is in fact the extreme consequence of dualism as reached by Marcion which motivates Buber's relentlessly sharp criticism of its milder manifestations. At stake is the issue of tearing asunder Creation and Redemption, Creator and Redeemer (and, for the Christian, the severance of the Old and New Testaments).[40] What Buber does, then, in different places of his Bible interpretation, is restore the prophetic faith in the Creator and in His creation. "That man exists at all is . . . the original mystery of the act of creation."[41] Buber speaks of the fact of Creation as implying "an unfathomable mystery which becomes evident only in the spontaneity of man."[42] Such Creation is not meant to fall, but to achieve ever greater realization in the history of man. It is the Creator Whose Kingdom was accepted on Sinai, and in Whose work all men will become partners in Redemption. God's presence with man under various forms and guises—which to Buber is the meaning of the enigmatic thorn-bush declaration, *ehye asher ehye*[43]—the element of the Personal, originate in Creation. Here the neutral, blind, cold, unconcerned universe was transformed into a place where man is addressed by the Thou and where he, as a person, may or may not give answer. At the summit of prophetic development—in Deutero-Isaiah—Creation and Redemption are analogous events, interrelated factors.[44] The redemption of the world, which is "the establishment of a unity in all the multiplicity of the world : the fulfilment of the Kingdom of God," is but the perfection of Creation.[45]

Once the "work of the beginning" snaps in the consciousness of man, and the hope for Redemption is separated from the covenant of Creation, men's own schemes, theories, constructions, assume the vain task of explaining a disjointed world. Man undermines his very existence by re-introducing the element of chaos, even if he intends to find new means to overcome it. In Creation, God has freed the world from chaos, *tohu* (Genesis 1:2); he "created it not a *tohu,*" is the prophetic warning (Isaiah 45:18).

Elsewhere in his Bible work, Buber opens himself to the critical suggestion, right or wrong, that "basically his interpretation of the Old Testament is a documentation of his own views."[46] However, in his defense of the prophetic idea of Creation, perhaps more than in the defense of any other point, Buber appears as a genuinely Jewish Bible exegete and as a link in the long series of Hebrew interpreters who struggled with the issue. And this is the ground on which Buber, representing the faith of Israel, faces Pauline Christianity and the Marcionite impulse everywhere, an understanding critic, a brotherly helper.

Does Buber's acceptance of the world as Creation—it would be frivolous to apply here the worn-out term optimism—obscure his view from the tragic side in existence, or, Biblically speaking, from the situation of Adam, expelled from the Garden, and Job facing a hostile world and an unconcerned God?

It is intriguing to see Buber interpreting the Garden of Eden[47] story as man's—a light-minded creature's acquiring not the divine power of knowing, not "knowledge of good and evil," but "the latent paradoxicality of being"—and as God's mercy in making death a harbor for this wandering creature conscious of the paradox. The darker, more demonic motif of the story Buber considers as the residue of an old myth of the envious and avenging gods; in the Biblical context, the curse implies a blessing: "the eating of the Tree of Knowledge leads out of Paradise but into the world."[48] The exile from the Garden is set "on his way into the history of the world, a world which acquires a history and a historic goal only through him.[49]

Job perceives God as "dreadful and incomprehensible."[50] He "hides His face" and thus contradicts His revelation. There is no justice; He annihilates the honest and the wicked. Job struggles against the silent, remote, sinister power. In God's answer, as Buber interprets it in one of the most profound sections of his Biblical work,[51] Job's experience of the absurd is not argued or explained; the answer consists in God's reference—in all detail—to the Creation. In this vast panorama of heaven and earth there is not even a mention of man; to such a degree (if I understand Buber correctly) is man's experience of tragic isolation acknowledged by the deity. But it is God Who gives this answer; the absolute power, as Job has known it, becomes a speaking, answering personality for the sake of the questioning, doubting, protesting, despairing personality of man. "Creation itself" (which is the contents of the answer) means communication between Creator and creature. Job's position is extreme among those of Biblical men; it is a situation of crisis comparable to the crisis of innocent man facing the Tree of Knowledge. Here, revelation, revelationary answer to man, must take recourse to Creation. And Buber remarks rightly that in the Job dialogue "Israel's ancient belief in Creation . . . has reached its completion." In the *finale* of his analysis, Buber recognizes (exegetically not convincing!) in Job's quest "to see" God a prophetic experience and places Job "who prays for his friends" in the company of prophets.[52]

In the Paradise story and in the Job poem man and God could be interpreted as antagonists, of quite unequal strength, yet rivals nevertheless. Buber succeeds (by softly toning down the tension in the Paradise story, by sharply focusing attention on the Creation motif in the Job poem[53]) in reading both within the context of the Hebrew Bible which in its entirety is, to him, one great document of the prophetic spirit.

Here, finally, a fererence to a critical point in Buber's work may be in order: the problem of Law.

Buber interpreted the event on Sinai as the theo-political act of establishing the divine kingdom, which is, from the point of view of man, the concrete acceptance of God's rule in human life. But Buber does not wish this to be reduced to a one-time occurrence in the history of Israel; he opposes an interpretation which would tend to fix in time a revelation however eternally valid.

> Creation is the origin, Redemption is the goal, but Revelation is not a stationary . . . point between the two: the revelation on Sinai is not the center . . . poised between the two, but that it (*i.e.*, the revelation) can at any time be perceived (is this center).

God cannot be restricted to any one form of possible manifestation;[54] it is His means of entering the dialogue with man which presupposes complete freedom. This thought, we have seen, underlies Buber's exegesis of Exodus 3:14.[55] Revelation, according to him, must preserve the character of the personal address; there is no relevant falling back upon previous revelations or upon revelations addressed to others. "The soul of the Decalogue . . . is the word Thou. . . . It is possible that only the man who wrote down the words had once had the experience of feeling himself addressed. . . ."[56] Therefore, Buber must question the immediate relationship between the recorded content of Sinaitic revelation and the fact of revelation itself. The words, once meaningful (as personally addressed to the listener) "become emptied of the spirit and in that state continue to maintain their claim of inspiration. . . . The living element dies off and what is left continues to rule over living men."[57]

It is well to remember that Buber is aware of man being "a receiver of the law" and of the importance of the law for "the historical continuity of divine rule upon earth."[58] But this no longer belongs to the realm of Revelation. Man is a receiver of the law, but God is not a "giver of the law."[59] "Revelation is certainly not Law-giving."[60] Confronted by a law man must ask himself: "Is this particular law addressed to me and rightly so?"[61] And, more generally speaking: "The Torah includes laws . . . but the Torah itself is essentially not law."[62]

The arguments against Buber's stand can be reduced to one. Regardless of one's personal attitude towards the authority of Biblical law and one's historical orientation about Near Eastern parallels, it can be said with certainty that *within the context* of the Old Testament the laws do appear as an absolutum. Granted that to men or societies law may become routine, devoid of the fulness of original meaning; it can deflect the heart from man's ultimate duties to God and fellow-man: it is the law nevertheless. "Hear, O Israel, the statutes and the ordinances which I speak in your ears this day, that ye may learn them, and observe to do them" (Deuteronomy 5:2). This is the covenant, made "not with our fathers, but with us, even us . . ." (*ibid.*, 5:3). It occurred but once in the history of Israel that God made His will known: in the law, which is, then, essentially immutable. The Voice speaking is the origin, legalism a sign of late decline; between the two is Torah, living record of the Word. Torah is more than law; but in the law is Torah.

Buber knows this. He made his position especially clear in an address (1930) when he described it as not a nomistic one though not an a-nomistic one. On that occasion he defined the teaching of Israel as "a Sinaitic one, teaching of Moses (*Moseslehre*) while the soul of Israel is pre-Sinaitic . . . it is Abraham's soul. . . . The soul itself is not of the Law."[63] Knowingly, therefore, Buber dissociates himself from Sinai the mount of the Law while adhering to Sinai the mount of revelation; in the context of the Bible, Sinai is, in all paradoxicality, both. Had he followed the rule which he so masterly represents, the rule of closeness to the actual text, Buber's exegesis would have had to take a different course. But the prophetic motif determined the course he had taken: he became the grand expounder of the prophetic meaning of the Voice speaking in Revelation and of the prophetic criticism of the distortion of the law in ritualism and legalism. The Torah, mastering day-to-day life between early Revelation and late decline, this Sinai, the central concern of Israel, Biblical and post-Biblical, remains outside the main province of Buber's work. "Do we mean the book? We mean the Voice!"

Yet, in a decisive moment, the Law does enter Buber's vision: in his valiant debate—this term suggests itself because of the pronounced personal, immediate nature of the controversy—with Paul's concept of the Law.[64] It is as if only Buber, who, as no Jew before him, has gained freedom from the yoke of the Law (while all the more carrying the "yoke of the Kingdom of God"), could call for an understanding of Israel, free in the Law, in the presence of the Jew of Tarsus whose unfreedom under the law had such far-reaching consequences in the history of faith. [65]

NOTES

1. "Cheruth, eine Rede über Jugend und Religion," *Reden über das Judentum, Gesamtausgabe*, p. 232. "Herut: On Youth and Religion," *On Judaism*, New York, 1967, pp. 149 seq.

2. By 1929 ten volumes (Genesis to Isaiah) were completed. After the death of Rosenzweig in 1929, Buber continued the work alone which he completed in 1961. A four-volume second, revised edition was published by Jakob Hegner Verlag, Köln and Olten 1954, 1955, 1958, and 1962 respectively).

3. *Sehertum*, p. 25.

4. *Ibid.*, p.33.

5. *Ibid.*, p. 45.

6. Über die Wortwahl in einer Verdeutschung der Schrift," *Die Schrift und ihre Verdeutschung*, p. 137.

7. *Ibid.*, p. 139.

8. *Ibid.*, p. 135.

9. This, the following, and other examples Buber discussed in some detail in the essay previously mentioned, pp. 144–167.

9ᵃ. In the 2nd edition Buber changed it to 'Zelt der Begegnung.' In *Königtum Gottes* (3rd ed.), p. 64, he speaks of "das Zelt der göttlichen 'Begegnung' oder Gegenwärtigung."—Ed.

10. The limit of the justifiable is reached, or possibly overreached, in translating *shabbat* by *Feier, Feiern;* the common rendition *Sabbath* is avoided because of its possible stiffness *(Erstarrung). Feier* is linguistically correct, but historically colorless.

11. *Die Schrift und ihre Verdeutschung,* p. 167.

12. "Der Mensch von heute und die jüdische Bibel," *Die Schrift und ihre Verdeutschung,* pp. 31–45. The sections here discussed were not included in the English translation of the essay in *Israel and the World.*

13. The Buber-Rosenzweig Bible translation does justice to this situation; its rendition is *Braus,* or, *Geistbraus.*

14. Three chapters of the second book *(Der Gesalbte)* appeared in the Ernst Lohmeyer volume (1951), *Tarbitz* XXII, *Zion* IV, respectively. The main thesis of the projected third book appears in the second half of *The Prophetic Faith.*

15. *Königtum Gottes,* p. xi.

16. *Ibid.*, p. 3. In the context, Buber attempts to refute all Biblical criticism which considers the Gideon answer as unhistorical and an anti-monarchical theocracy not in evidence before Hosea.

17. *Ibid.*, p. 60.

18. *Ibid.*, pp. 106f.

19. *Ibid.*, p. 140.

20. *Ibid.*, p 107.

21. *Ibid.*, p. 140.

22. *Ibid.,* p. 144.

23. *Ibid.,* p. 108.

24. *Ibid.,* pp. 139–143.

25. *Ibid.,* pp. 112ff.

26. *Moses,* p. 137.

27. *Königtum Gottes,* p. 158.

28. *Ibid.* (3rd ed.), p. lxiii.

29. *Ibid.,* pp. 15–22.

30. *Moses,* p. 168; Y. Kaufmann, *Toledot ha-Emunah,* II, 1, pp. 46, 122.

31. *Moses,* pp. 162–171.

32. *Two Types of Faith,* p. 106. This is, to Buber, the sense of the message of Deutero-Isaiah, who "as a posthumous disciple of Isaiah renewed the main motifs of his Messianic prophecies with an altered meaning." See the interpretation of *limmud* in Isaiah 8:16 and 50:4, *The Prophetic Faith,* pp. 202f.

33. *The Prophetic Faith,* p. 231.

34. *Sehertum,* pp. 52f.

35. Cf. Jer. 18:8.

36. *Sehertum,* pp. 53–59. Buber treats Deutero-Isaiah's view of history as an exception from the dialogic concept of classical prophecy.

37. *Ibid.,* pp. 59–68.

38. *Ibid.,* pp. 68–74.

39. "Gnosis and not atheism . . . is the real antagonist of the reality of faith." *Eclipse of God,* p. 175.

40. *Zwei Glaubensweisen,* p. 171.

41. *Two Types of Faith,* p. 136.

42. *Ibid.*

43. Exodus 3:14; commonly translated "I am that I am"; for Buber's (and Rosenzweig's) interpretation see the latter's "Der Ewige" in *Die Schrift und ihre Verdeutschung,* Buber's *Moses,* pp. 46–55, and *Königtum Gottes* (3rd ed.), pp. 66–71.

44. *The Prophetic Faith,* pp. 213ff.

45. *Die Stunde und die Erkenntnis,* p. 154.

46. J. Coert Rylaarsdam, "The Prophetic Faith," *Theology Today,* 7 (1950), pp. 399ff.

47. "Der Baum der Erkenntnis," *Bilder von Gut und Böse,* pp. 15–31.

48. *Eclipse of God,* p. 58.

49. *Bilder von Gut und Böse,* p. 31.

50. "Religion and Philosophy," *The Eclipse of God,* p. 51.

51. *The Prophetic Faith,* pp. 188–197. See also *At the Turning,* pp. 61f.

52. *The Prophetic Faith,* p. 197.

53. However, this reader at least feels that if Buber's interpretation holds, the exclusion of man in the picture of the universe (ch. 38–40) requires more attention.

54. *Moses,* p. 52.

55. *Ibid.,* pp. 46–55.

56. *Ibid.,* p. 130.

57. *Ibid,* p. 188.

58. *Ibid.*

208   *Essays in Jewish Thought*

59. Letter of July 13, 1924 to Franz Rosenzweig on the problem of Law raised by the latter in *Die Bauleute*. F. Rosenzweig, *On Jewish Learning* (New York, 1955), p. 155.

60. *Ibid.*, p. 118.

61. *Ibid.*, p. 114.

62. *Two Types of Faith*, p. 57.

63. "Die Brennpunkte der jüdischen Seele," *Kampf um Israel*, p. 51. "The Two Foci of the Jewish Soul," *Israel and the World* (New York, 1948), p. 28.

64. *Two Types of Faith, passim. See also* "Pharisäertum," *Kampf um Israel*, pp. 115–130.

65. Cf. also Everett Fox, *Technical Aspects of the Translation of Genesis of Martin Buber and Franz Rosenzweig* (Dissertation, Brandeis University, 1975).

17

BAECK-BUBER-ROSENZWEIG READING THE BOOK OF JOB

Leo Baeck died ten years ago; Martin Buber left us in 1965. And whenever the two are mentioned, a third name comes to mind: Franz Rosenzweig, who would have reached the age of eighty this December. There are still other men who typified—and still typify—the best in German Jewry's contribution to Jewish thought. But these three may be regarded as its authentic—if you will, symbolic—representatives.

I propose to review not their teachings in general, nor their general contribution to modern thinking, but to focus on *one* single theme on which all three expressed themselves: the theme of the book of Job. This book occupied the minds also of other Jews of this century: there is Margarete Susman's book on Job,[1] the Job tetralogy of Karl Wolfskehl,[2] and the extensive Job commentary by H. Torczyner.[3]

In concentrating on Baeck's, Buber's, and Rosenzweig's reading of Job, we shall, I hope, discover that their respective Job interpretations mirror their attitudes to man, Israel, and the world.

Before we start let us, however concisely, recall the outline of the book of Job. It opens with a prose folk tale of the man who through all adversity remains faithful to his God. "The Lord gave, the Lord has taken away, blessed be the name of the Lord" (Job 1:21). In the poetic dialogue that follows a different Job appears: a rebel against the injustice rampant in the affairs of the world, against the reign of evil, against a God Who has turned man into a target of his hostility, a God Who exists, though he refuses to answer the creature's outcry. Three friends, later a fourth, Elihu, rise to the defense of the God of tradition Who exercises just providence and purifies man by suffering.

Yet, in the end, God does answer Job "out of the whirlwind" (chapters 38 to 41). But instead of answering Job's question, "Why?", He recounts the glory and majesty of the created universe, asking Job: "Knowest thou" anything, "canst thou" do anything? Man's claim to knowledge, his expectation of mercy, his appeal to justice are pointedly repudiated. All Job can do is humbly to submit to the Power that does not share its secret with man. A prose epilogue concludes the folk tale of the beginning. Job, whose piety was only being tested, is restored to his former happiness. Most probably, the author of the dialogue used an older folk tale of Job as background for his poem.

What emanates from the speeches of the Lord with which the poem of Job culminates is an overwhelming neutrality of the universe, in which man is an insignificant entity. This fact is conveyed to man in a revelation in which God, though speaking to man, maintains an aura of impersonality. It is the offended, angry God of the Adam story, the God Who reads the edict of expulsion from paradise as a consequence of man's eating from the Tree of Knowledge. Knowledge is the prerogative of the divine power, accessible to man only for the price of suffering and, ultimately of death.

II

Let us turn to the three men we propose to consider.

To Leo Baeck the teaching of Israel revolves around two central points: the experience of mystery and the acceptance of the divine commandment.

Mystery, as Baeck sees it, is the realm that surrounds the clarity and explicitness in which we live. We exist here on earth. "It is our home, and its circumference includes us. Upon it, we are born, generation after generation; and upon it, we die, grave after grave. . . . It carries us and reaches out to us." But the fact that man is a thinking being is to Baeck not merely a further step in the natural development of the species man, but "a miracle." Spirit is nothing less than that. Spiritual life implies that "the created human becomes creative, fashioning within the fashioned." "Comparing and measuring, investigating and counting . . . he determines passage and duration." Man conceives in the universe the rule of the law, which Baeck terms "the constantly returning sanction of the enduring."[4]

Though, ostensibly, the thinking spirit points to clarity, certainty, and definiteness, something unfathomable encompasses all. Beyond space and time, which thinking man makes his tools, there is *revealed* to man something mind cannot fathom, but only reverence can approach, "that reverence without which love does not live and faithfulness does not endure." The revelation is expressed in the Biblical words: "I am that I am, thy God."

Furthermore, man's awareness of a totality ("in which the particular receives meaning"), of a deeper harmony, of a comprehensive unity of existence, is to Baeck not an extension of man's ability to think, but also a mystery, in which "earthly man has lifted himself above earth."[5]

Equally, the reaml of ethics is taken by Baeck out of the context of man's social or organizational, rational ordering of life. To him, "the moral is the great contradiction of everything which earthly existence seems to indicate." Man's "natural" attitude is self-seeking; fellowman is "the subjugated or excluded one, or he is the enemy." Man's conception of selflessness as the attitude of the true self, of the "I" as emanating from the "thou"—this understanding of man is a miraculous discovery. Through the immutable ethical commandment "the created man can become . . . free inwardly." "The miracle of morality makes him truly man."[6]

It is the commandment, the "thou shalt . . . with its roots in mystery," that frees man from being directed solely by "the natural." The commandment allows man to be "a figure of freedom." Total comprehension of the factors of commandment and mystery, of the natural and the divine, is to Baeck the enduring task of Judaism.[7]

Maintaining this view of God and man, how does Baeck read the book of Job, that book which silences man's claim to knowledge, and in the end, lets man confess that he cannot know, and cannot do? Can Baeck incorporate this book into his view of life and of Judaism?

He can't. In his *This People Israel* he considers the book of Job together with Koheleth, Ecclesiastes. Despite their differences, "both are books of *hokhmah*," documents of the Biblical doctrine of wisdom. Job is "a volcanic book," the other "a book of coolness." In Job "the questions boil and burn, . . . the other one sorts and stacks questions." In Job, "man's sufferings urge and force themselves and rise before us, . . . in the other a man philosophizes about the world and God." The book of Job "forces its way down to the deepest human pain and agony," the other examines dispassionately the concerns, the worries, which do, after all exist.[8]

Both nevertheless conclude with the motif of *hokhmah*. Ecclesiastes, as we know, addresses these final words to man: "the end of matter . . . is: fear God and keep His commandments; for this is the whole man" (Eccles. 12:13). This, adds, Baeck, is the expression of *hokhmah*, a term which embraces "what the contemplation of another people called humaneness, humanity." *Hokhmah* "is that which testifies to the permanence of creation, to the permanence of revelation."[9]

Turning to the book of Job, Baeck notes that its hero is "always ready to confess that God is God, and that man is man, but he will never deny the way of his life," that is, accept the view that his affliction is a punishment for sins. But after the problems and needs of Job's life have been dealt with, the book moves on to that "which the world eternally needs, and which yet remains within God's mystery." Out of the mystery which surrounds man in the world Job receives an answer "addressed to the world and to man who asks." The contents of the answer is—*hokhmah*. Chapter 28, the hymn on wisdom, Baeck reads as *the* answer. Here the question is asked: "Whence then cometh wisdom?" It is stated that "no mortal knoweth the pathway to it," it is not found in the deep, in Destruction and Death; "it is hid from the eyes of the living." Only "God knoweth the place thereof." In the mystery of creation "did He see it . . . He established it . . ." But as for man: "Behold, the fear of the Lord, that is wisdom; and to depart from evil is understanding."

This is the answer. Wisdom is a divine faculty; man's part in it—a central part—consists in the commandment: Fear the Lord; depart from evil. In this answer "the life of Job finds its self-justification," says Baeck.[10]

Baeck does note that this chapter 28 "stands in the center of the book." He does not mention the manner in which the book continues and on what note its poetic part concludes. For whatever the history of our text's composition, the book in the form in which it became part of the Bible, moves on to the mighty speeches of the Lord in which the picture of the created world is unfolded in all its glory and majesty. In contradistinction, however, to Genesis chapters one and two, where man becomes the crown of creation, the master of this earth, here, in Job, God appears as the sole lord and master of a gigantic universe. Stars, light and darkness, wind, rain and hail, the lion and the raven, the horse and the hawk, the hippopotamus and the crocodile—all are there; but man is left out, his existence is not noticed, although, to be sure, the Lord's speeches are addressed to him. In words of thunder man is informed of his insignificance in the totality of things. This verdict Job humbly accepts.

But Leo Baeck does not. His man partakes both in the mystery and in the commandment, and through the latter the creature becomes the creator. Viewing life under the aspects of "thou shalt" and "thou shalt not," man enters into a covenant with God, a covenant defined by Baeck as "the continually active order of creation and revelation."[11]

How could Baeck accept an answer to man and to the world in which creation is the factor which separates God and man, and revelation the testimony of that separation? Thus, in the manner of the midrashic masters of old—of whom Baeck was a modern incarnation—he accentuates that which appears to him eternally valid in the text while leaving the rest unquoted. Thus it is *hokhmah* in chapter 28, with its appeal to human action, and not the Lord's speeches in chapters 38 seq. with their devastating critique of human presumption, that Baeck must consider to be the high point in this book. Man must not be allowed to be silenced by the Creator. The covenant and its implied commandment to man—issues of *hokhmah*—are the ones that truly matter and that must echo from the pages of the book of Job.

It is of interest to note Baeck's use of the book of Job in his earlier work, *The Essence of Judaism*. Here he quotes Job's pious dictum: "Shall we receive good at the hand of God, and shall we not receive evil?" (Job 2:10),[12] and Job 31:13–15 on the human right of the slave;[13] refers to two passages from the Elihu speeches (Job 36:15 and 37:19);[14] and twice cites the conclusion of the *hokhmah* chapter (Job 28:28),[15] stressing the fear of the Lord as wisdom and departing from evil as understanding. But here too there is no reference to chapters 38 seq., the Lord's stern answer from the whirlwind.

The young Baeck's opinion on the world-view of these speeches, disclosed indirectly by their omission in *The Essence of Judaism,* is profoundly strengthened in the older Baeck's *This People Israel,* where Job 28, the chapter on *hokhmah,* is interpreted as the core of the book and the true answer to Job.

Not only the years of the maturing process of study and reflection intervene between Baeck's two works, but also the period of sharing with fellow Jews and fellow humans the agony of persecution and the brutal experience of the Theresienstadt camp—the place where much of *This People Israel* was written. Under the circumstances one could have accepted as reality the depersonalization and dehumanization of man, diabolically planned by the agents of doom; could have agreed with Job that unredeemed evil exists, that God is no longer concerned with his creation, and that man does not count. Leo Baeck, however, became a symbolic representative of those whose faith is stronger than evil, and whose love stronger than death. His interpretation of Job in *This People Israel* is a suffering servant's affirmation of this faith and a confirmation of the young reflecting servant's jottings in *The Essence of Judaism.*

The treatment of evil and suffering in the book of Job has been compared with the composition on the same theme in Psalm 73. There the questioner and doubter, tormented by the sad state of world and society, finally achieves certainty in the realization that his "life is bound up with something eternal. . . :[16] "Whom have I in heaven but Thee? And beside Thee I desire none upon earth" (Ps. 73:25). His ultimate experience is the presence of God in his life: "The nearness of God is my good" (Ps. 73:28). In this relationship anguished man finds his rest. In contrast to the poem of Job, which leaves us with a strange feeling of impersonality and remoteness of the divine address to man, Psalm 73 ends on a note of complete trust in the human address to God. Baeck quotes this psalm three times in *The Essence of Judaism,*[17] and it permeates *This People Israel* from beginning to end. The book of Job, on the other hand, required the art of a circumspect exegete and his assiduous though respectful critique.

III

Martin Buber, the propounder of the I-Thou relationship, the dialogical communion, and the way of response, accorded much attention to the book of Job. In his translation of the Bible Job is treated with special consideration; in his *The Prophetic Faith*[18] Job is carefully analyzed; in a lecture given in New York in 1951 he refers to the Job drama.

His discourse on Job in *The Prophetic Faith* is one of the most subtle and intriguing of his essays on Biblical themes. How does he read the book which, he believes, was written at the beginning of the Babylonian Exile, thus preceding Deutero-Isaiah and Psalm 73?

As an initial premise, Buber agrees with J. Hempel[19] that Job's outcries against evil and injustice are based not on the experience of a single person; in reading Job "we think less of the sufferings of an individual than of the exile of a people"; the book is "the fruit of supra-personal sufferings." Behind the "I" of the book "stands the 'I' of Israel."[20]

The body of the Job book shows us, Buber says, the succeeding views of God's relationship to man's sufferings presented in the book. The prose folk tale speaks of a God, "a small mythological idol," who lets Satan test the faith of an innocent man, Job, a motive "not befitting the deity," though "man proves true as man." This is followed by the view of God held by Job's friends. They represent "the dogmatic view of the cause and effect in the divine system of requital: Job's sufferings testify to his guilt." Their God is not a God of living faith but a deity of formalized "religion," which offers man "a reasonable and rational God." Job's knowledge of reality protests against such calculated theology.[21]

Job in his answers to the friends is understood by Buber as a man of faith. He experiences evil. God, the living one, has "withdrawn Job's right" (cf. 27:2), "searches after his iniquity" (10:6), "snatches at him stormily" (9:17); He does not apparently distinguish between the just and the unjust; both "the honest and the wicked He exterminates" (9:22). Yet "Job's faith in justice is not broken down. . . . He believes in God in spite of believing in justice." He "knows that God is not a Satan grown into omnipotence." He experiences Him through suffering and contradiction, but "even in this way he does experience God."[22]

Buber does not see in Job the rebel against a God who is the author of evil, the Creator who has abandoned his creation. The God Buber's Job experiences is a God who "hides His face" (Job 13:24), a Biblical term used by Buber also in other connections to explain periods of absurdity in human or historical existence, the dark hours of life which seem bereft of meaning. Such periods are but inexplicable suspension of God's conduct of affairs, intrusions of silence in the unending dialogue between God and world. Job does not, in Buber's view, implore the deity to rebut the charge of universal injustice, but only to respond, to answer. He "struggles against the remoteness of God," against His silence; he asks only to experience His presence, which would transcend "the absurd duality of a truth known to man" (namely, that God is just) and "a reality sent of God" (namely, the rule of injustice). It is "this hiding, the eclipse of divine light" that is the source of Job's despair. "When shall we be allowed to see Him again?"[23]

In the end, God does answer. Along with others, Buber considers the text of chapters 38 to 41 (and other sections of the book) to be a late revision, reworked to so great an extent that the original text cannot be restored. He believes, nevertheless, that notwithstanding difficulties it is possible to proffer a decisive interpretation of God's speeches. He takes pains to explain that these speeches of the Lord transcend mere demonstration of the mysterious character of His rule in nature. They are more than a declaration to Job that he cannot know the workings of the universe.

What, then, is the focal point of the speeches? They assert the presence of justice, not justice as it is understood by man but a justice that is "manifest in creation." The creation of the world (retold in these chapters) "is justice, a distributing, giving justice." Furthermore: "The creation itself already means communication between Creator and creature." What matters to Buber essentially is that Job hears "the voice of *Him Who answers*," that "God draws near to man," that "the absolute power is for human personality's sake become personality." To the sufferer, God "offers Himself as an answer." The decisive thing is the "self-limitation of God to a person, answering a person."[24]

A lofty picture indeed, reminiscent of the great medieval attempts to rescue Job from his tragic knowledge, from his loneliness, from the depths of his despair. The text, however, presents the pre-"conversion" Job as a true rebel, a man who sees in God his antagonist, his enemy even. Buber underplays Job's rebellion, man's uprising against a cruel, violent world and its maker. He speaks merely of Job's questioning, protesting;[25] if rebellion it be, it is but the act of a "faithful rebel," who "in all his revolt was God's witness on earth, as God was his (Job's) witness in heaven."[26] Even in the extremity of suffering, Job exemplifies the man who remains loyal to the covenant. His estrangement from God is thus reduced to a minimum, an interpretation hardly justified by the text. By the same token, Buber reads God's answer to Job as implying a more intimate, more direct, more personal relationship than the text intends it to be.

In the text, Job wishes to face his accuser, hopes to prove his innocence. God does appear. But far from "drawing near to man" and "offering Himself as an answer," as Buber says, God in this revelation remains strangely remote. Instead of answering Job's charges, He addresses certain questions to him: "Hast thou commanded the morning?" "Knowest thou the ordinances of the heavens?" "Hast thou given the horse his strength?" "Will the wild-ox be willing to serve thee?" Such questions are not designed to inform Job of "a divine justice, manifest in creation," as Buber states, but rather to repudiate Job's arrogant demand for special attention, his claim to the possession of knowledge.

In contradistinction to the creation story in Genesis, where man is central, the creation story in the Lord's speeches, though addressed to man, omits reference to man, save to point to his insignificance. Thus, in the end, Job cannot help admitting that the sole knowledge he has is that of God's mastery in the universe; now he no longer asserts anything, no longer avows, no longer declares, but humbly asks to be granted knowledge of that which he may know. His newly acquired knowledge of God contains an element of remoteness; here no conventional rapport is possible, no reciprocity, only humble acknowledgment and silence. With this knowledge, Job, it seems to me, stands alone in the Biblical world and not, as Buber notes, in a succession of servants of the Lord, a succession that leads to the suffering servant in Deutero-Isaiah.[27]

Buber follows his analysis of the book of Job by an interpretation of Psalm 73, that eloquent affirmation of God's nearness to anguished man. He believes in fact, that the author of this psalm was influenced by the writer of Job. But here, in Psalm 73, the complex thought structure of the thinker Job is replaced by "a simple certainty and composure . . . the simple 'yea' of the man of prayer." *Here* the relationship between the "I" and the "Thou" is immediate.[28] The psalmist "does not turn his eyes away from the sufferings of earth," but "experiences the nearness of God . . . and this is enough."[29] Even death is turned into a divine mystery. "God does not remove His presence from His men even in death."[30] It is possible for Buber to follow Psalm 73 as it stands up to its climax of the nearness of God in life and in death. No exegetical skill was needed for its comprehension. The author of *I and Thou* found in it a Biblical verification of his own central views. In his discourse on Job he thought it right to be guided by the insights of the psalmist. If Job was indeed the master and the psalmist the disciple, the latter helped the interpreter to understand the former, so that Job, too, could be read in the light of the I and Thou relationship and as a document of mature, Biblical, nondogmatic, faith.

However, after this has been said we have to admit that it is not with the book of Job and its actual meaning that Buber wrestles, but with the problem of evil and divine remoteness posed by it. Evil, in Buber's view is aimlessness, lack of direction, lack of decision—*in man;* it is man's stubborn loneliness, his unrelatedness. Once he has established direction towards his fellowman, his community, and thus has turned to God, once he has responded to the call of creature and Creator, he will no longer encounter evil in the world outside him. Evil "can exist in the outer world only because it exists within us."[31] It exists not "when I meet my fellowman; I experience it when I meet myself."[32] Thus Buber overcame the last vestiges of Gnostic dualism, which posits the reality of evil, a dualism that has been the lure and the comfort of man, both ancient and modern, and of which Buber was fully aware.

His all-embracing faith in creation as an ever-renewed act of a benign Creator who turns to man, summons man, and to whom man responds, enabled him to approach the most painful Jewish question of our age: "How is Jewish life, life with God, possible after Auschwitz? . . . The estrangement has become too cruel, the hiddenness too deep . . . Can one still, as an individual and as a people, enter into a dialogic relationship with Him? . . . Dare we recommend to the survivor of Auschwitz, the Job of the gas chambers: 'Call to Him for He is good, for His mercy endureth forever'?"[33]

Buber looks to Job for an answer; the Job, to be sure, as he interpreted him. Job's God is a "cruel" God (Job 30:21), who has "removed his right" from man (27:2). And yet, Job receives an answer. The divine reply does not, however, concern itself with Job's charge. "The true answer . . . is God's appearance only, only this that distance turns into nearness . . . Nothing has happened but that man again hears God's address. The mystery has remained unsolved, but it has become man's."[34]

And how is it with us? asks Buber. Can we still recognize in Job our guide through the valley of darkness, or do we follow the tragic hero of the Greeks who "stands overcome before faceless fate?" Buber considers us strong enough, Jewish enough, to follow Job. Struggling "for the redemption of earthly being, we appeal to the help of our Lord, Who is again and still a hiding one. In such a state we await His voice." And when the voice is heard, "we shall recognize again our cruel and merciful Lord."[35] He will proclaim not the insignificance of man—the literal meaning of Job 38 seq.—but God's presence, which is in itself the presence of grace.

Thus does Buber, speaking with utmost care and deliberation, express the possibility of faith in our time. On his tombstone in Jerusalem are engraved the words: "I am continually with Thee" (Psalm 73:23).

IV

Franz Rosenzweig defined reality as an eternal interrelationship between the three elements, God, world, and man, and termed the ever-recurring actions of one element upon the other: Creation, Revelation, and Redemption.

Creation is the first, silent, contact between God and world; paganism plays its part in intellectual history within the sphere of creation. The Greek tragic hero is silent; he suffers in silence; he does not raise the Joban question about guilt and fate; alone with his self, and in silence, he approaches his doom.[36]

In revelation God makes known his love for man. In this love originates man's ability to love, to respond, to be a person, and to concern himself with the other and with the world, to enter a process which culminates in redemption. In different ways, both authentic, Judaism and Christianity partake in the acts of revelation and redemption. Compared with Buber's Biblical humanism, Rosenzweig searches for the theological background of the humanity of man. Compared with Baeck's concept of tension between mystery and commandment, he defines the Jew as living in an ever-renewed anticipation of redemption.

Rosenzweig read the book of Job and gave it much thought, although he did not give it a scholar's attention and died before the Buber-Rosenzweig translation of the Bible reached this work. There are three basic references to Job in *Der Stern der Erlösung,* one important reference in his Jehuda Halevi, and one revealing passage on Job in a letter to Buber. He approaches the book from the point of view of its folk-tale introduction and its folk-tale ending. There he found the key to the Job drama as a whole. We have already noted his allusion to the silent hero of the Greek tragedy versus the speaking, reacting, responding Job. More significant is the observation that the highest testimony of the miracle posited by faith, and of faith itself, is the testimony of the martyr, as, Rosenzweig adds, "Satan in the book of Job well knew."[37] Here Job appears as the symbol of the man whose suffering is essential for the proof of the genuineness of his faith. That the Job of the poetic dialogue viewed suffering (and evil) as indicative of God's faithlessness is of no concern to Rosenzweig. His focus is on the prose introduction.

Of even greater importance is his discussion of the motif of man being tested by God. Job—again the Job of the prose folk tale—is being put to a test. Only the test will demonstrate who is a free man in his relationship to God and, contrariwise, whose belief is based on the actual evidence of divine providence. "Man must know that at times he is being tested for the sake of his freedom."[38] With his charming, disarming irony Rosenzweig remarks that if the remote river Sambatyon (which, according to legend, is so pious that it rests on the Sabbath) rather than the Main would flow through Frankfurt, then all of Frankfurt Jewry would be strict Sabbath observers. But God does not do such things. He dreads the thought that then, "the most unfree, the timid, and the fearful would be the most pious. But, evidently, God wants only the free to be His."[39] Consequently, He must not only conceal his actions, but mislead man about them. "He must make it difficult, yea, impossible to understand them, so as to give man the opportunity truly to believe, that is, to ground his faith and trust in freedom," rather than follow the "immortal advice of Job's wife: 'Curse God and die!' " "Man's freedom may well be limited in all other respects; toward God his freedom is without limits."[40] This is the foundation upon which the God-man relationship in revelation, and the man-world relationship in redemption, is built. The book of Job pointed the way, but, again, not the rebellious dialogue with its tension between Creator and creature, but only the prose folk tale.

In 1923 Rosenzweig asked Buber to lecture on Job in the Frankfurt Lehrhaus. In this connection he remarked that he had been reading Job "as a Biblical illlustration of (Buber's) *I and Thou,*" considering Job 42:7–9 "as the key to the whole."[41] In that passage God repudiates the dogmatic, logical friends of Job and elects His "servant Job" who has "spoken of Me the thing that is right." Job the man of faith and prayer, was close to Rosenzweig's concept of life, just as Job the accuser, the blasphemer, the rebel against the silent, hostile, God, was foreign to him.

One of the questions asked of Job in the Lord's speeches is: "By what way is the light parted?" (Job 38:24). Like the others, this question, too, is intended to evoke in man the answer: "I do not know." Rosenzweig detects a reference to this phrase in a Judah ha-Levi poem for the Feast of Revelation where it is stated: "The way the light is parted He has made to be my way." Rosenzweig notes that it is the shattering divine question rather than the shattering reply, "I do not know," to which Judah ha-Levi, responded in a daring yet humble and trusting answer, turning the mystery of creation into the commandment of revelation: the enigmatic way of primordial light becomes the way of man. The remote God of creation becomes in Rosenzweig's view the near, loving, commanding God of revelation.[42]

It is not surprising that Rosenzweig's favorite psalm was Psalm 73, the same poem that we found central in the thought of both Baeck and Buber. Here, the questioning doubts of the skeptic are overcome by the certainty of faith. "Nevertheless (i.e., despite the seeming disorder in our world) I am continually with Thee" (Psalm 73:23). At Rosenzweig's burial this psalm was recited by Buber. His gravestone carries this inscription, years later chosen by Buber for his own memorial: *Va-ani tamid immakh.* "I am continually with Thee."

V

All three thinkers, Baeck, Buber, and Rosenzweig, experienced the fate of Job in our own times: Rosenzweig in the eight years of progressive paralysis which attacked the young man of thirty-six; Baeck in the years endured in a concentration camp together with his brothers and sisters; Buber, preceptor of Jewry in the Hitler years, as witness of the catastrophe that befell European Jewry, whose spiritual image he had helped to mold in the pre-Nazi decades.

All of them could have turned to the dark chapters of Job's rebellion and to the motif of tragic remoteness in the Lord's speeches as Biblical confirmation of the evil they themselves had experienced, each in his own way. They did not do so. Instead, deviating from its intended meaning, they turned the book of Job into a testimony of man's faith, of his response to the summons of creation, of his enduring, though at times interrupted, dialogue with the divine. In so doing, they affirmed their own faith. The sophistication of the book of Job challenged their minds; the utter simplicity of Psalm 73 captured their innermost being.

And if we ask what the young generation, our sons and daughters, and, in turn, their children, can learn from these spokesmen of German Jewry, which is no more, the answer is: not necessarily their exegesis or their mode of thinking, but their devotion to the task at hand, their hope for man and his future, their faith in the "thou shalt" and "thou shalt not," their affirmation of the reality of the divine in human life— fundamental notions derived by them from the sources of classical Judaism. Through Buber, Rosenzweig, and Baeck and through their disciples these sources may speak again to those who will come after us and help shape their lives as human beings and as members of the fellowship of Israel.

NOTES

1. *Das Buch Hiob und das Schicksal des jüdischen Volkes* (Zürich, 1948).
2. *Hiob oder Die vier Spiegel* (Hamburg, 1950).
3. N. H. Tur Sinai, *The Book of Job* (Jerusalem, 1957).
4. *This People Israel: The Meaning of Jewish Existence* (New York, 1965) 398.
5. *Ibid.*, 399.
6. *Ibid.*, 400.
7. *Ibid.*, 400–403.
8. *Ibid.*, 95f.
9. *Ibid.*, 99f.
10. *Ibid.*, 96ff.
11. *Ibid.*, 13.
12. *The Essence of Judaism* (New York, 1948), 115.
13. *Ibid.*, 200.
14. *Ibid.*, 138 and 101.
15. *Ibid.*, 37 and 212.
16. *Ibid.*, 97.
17. *Ibid.*, 98, 103 and 144. Cp. also Hermann Cohen's treatment of the book of Job and Psalm 73 in *Die Religion der Vernunft* (Frankfurt am Main, 1929), pp. 189, 265 f. et passim.
18. *The Prophetic Faith* (New York, 1949; Hebrew edition, Tel Aviv, 1942).
19. *Die althebräische Literatur* (Wildpark-Potsdam, 1930), 179.
20. *The Prophetic Faith*, 189.
21. *Ibid.*, 190f.
22. *Ibid.*, 192.
23. *Ibid.*, 192ff.
24. *Ibid.*, 195f.
25. *Ibid.*, 191 and 196.
26. *Ibid.*, 196f.
27. *Ibid.*, 197f.
29. *Ibid.*, 201.
30. *Ibid.*, 202.
31. *For the Sake of Heaven* (Philadelphia, 1945), 54.
32. *Ibid.*, 57.

33. "The Dialogue Between Heaven and Earth," a lecture given in New York, in 1951, included in *On Judaism* (New York, 1967), 214 seq.

34. *Ibid.*, 61f.

35. *Ibid.*, 62.

36. *Der Stern der Erlösung* (Frankfurt am Main, 1930), I, 103.

37. *Ibid.*, II, 12.

38. *Ibid.*, III, 9.

39. *Ibid.*, III, 8.

40. *Ibid.*, III, 8f.

41. *Briefe* (Berlin, 1935), 478.

42. *Jehuda Halevi* (Berlin, 1927), 91 and 220.

18
FRANZ ROSENZWEIG
IN HIS STUDENT YEARS

In the following a few samples (in English translation) are presented from the diaries Franz Rosenzweig kept in his student years, accompanied by some brief comments. The entries start December 14, 1905 "about two o'clock in the morning." Summer of that year, Rosenzweig had commenced his studies (in medicine) at the University of Goettingen; autumn he transferred to Munich, where he remained a year, followed by a year of studies at the University of Freiburg. The first part of the diaries (ending June 22, 1908) covers four octavo notebooks, about 93 pages each, followed by briefer notations covering the period up to September 13, 1922. The notebooks bear the title: *Hemerai kai nuktes* (Days and Nights). A typewritten transcript of the diary became, in 1951, part of the Franz Rosenzweig Archives in Boston; recently, Mrs. Edith Scheinmann transferred the original notebooks to the Archives of the Leo Baeck Institute in New York.

These pages are intended as a humble tribute to the sacred memory of Rabbi Paul Lazarus. A significant meeting between Lazarus and Rosenzweig took place in the First World War. When after their return from the war, Rosenzweig assumed the leadership of the Freies Jüdisches Lehrhaus in Frankfurt am Main, Paul Lazarus was among the first to found a parallel institution in Wiesbaden and to assume a decisive rôle in the Jewish-renascence movement in Germany.

In the first period of about two years, Rosenzweig made his notations on a vast variety of issues; the purely biographical, though represented, is of an ephemeral nature! But every entry breathes the air of personal, living experience. He speaks of Plato, Shakespeare, and Goethe, of Mozart, Beethoven, and Wagner; discourses on humanism and classicism, on psychology, on ethical aesthetic problems, on love and sex (very little), on natural science and religion, on academic life and its limitations; records discussions with friends, especially with Hans Ehrenberg and his "friend Herostratus." Out of this vast variety of themes, only a few will be considered (a small number of the entries, formerly presented in the volume "Franz Rosenzweig: His Life and Thought" re-appear here for the sake of completion). Rosenzweig devoted close attention to the problem of man; he tried to gain a measure of clarity on what constitutes the human being. "Every man whom you encounter in life has three things: a mask, a face, a soul" (Nov. 23, 1906). Having a soul, man is unique. "Physiologically seen, man (as a [natural] phenomenon) has been dead all his life; as for man as a noumenon, for him such a concept as death does not exist; in the latter case there is no cessation in time, since noumena are timeless. Man as phenomenon, body *and* soul, i.e., the physiologist's body and the psychologist's soul, does not die, since he has been dead from the start; man as noumenon (the personality) does not die since he has never lived (in time)" (Dec. 15, 1907). This reasoning explains Rosenzweig's version—at that time—against pondering about death, deeming it "a bad sign to think about it" (*ibid.*). This attitude was later to undergo a radical change. However, the notion of man's special place in the cosmos (which underlay his negation of death) grew ever stronger in his thinking.

He cautioned against too facile an application of the rule of cause and effect in man's action: "In the case of a human being, *post hoc* is never *propter hoc*; the *propter* of each single *hoc* is always the entire person, never some preceding *hoc*" (Nov. 18, 1906); and made a note of his strong opposition to Ernst Haeckel's system of the natural universe. Though realizing the magnificent simplicity of this world view, he objected to Haeckel's identification of physical and physiological (i.e. psychic) energy; "in this view the individual is completely fitted into the cosmos and unable to view the cosmos from the outside by means of his peculiar human eyes. The philosopher in the very act of thinking about the cosmos would then have to take part in the metabolism of this cosmos" (Jan 11, 1906). The same concern for the uniqueness of man is manifest in Rosenzweig's vehement rejection of someone's attempt, inspired by Haeckel, to project the one hundred million years of organic development on earth unto twenty-four hours and see "the so-called world history represented by a mere five seconds." The fact that there "seconds" were moments "of love, of understanding, of truth" does not admit a relativist comparison with the rest of the day (*ibid.*).

"Man is here on earth for the sake of being human, to be alive, to observe," wrote Rosenzweig, adapting for the latter phrase the words *lahay roi* from Genesis 16:14. Thinking is secondary; it is subordinate to life. "Thought serves only as a protection, a defence against the multitude of things seen" (Sept. 6, 1906); living and observing (looking) are two aspects of one process. The diarist adds a critical note to a quotation from a short story by Paul Heyse: "Everybody must make a decision whether he wants to enjoy his life or understand life" (i.e. "live" or "observe"); the note is typical for the latter Rosenzweig: "It should be left to life whether it wants to be lived or observed." He realized that he might be called a quietist; he was willing to accept such a nomenclature rather than engage in a schoolmaster dissection of the process of life (June 24, 1906).

In no way does life mean reflection on life; it means action, he postulated further. "The master in the art of living never considers life itself to be his task. He lives in spare hours, so to speak; his full strength is given to the activity of each particular day. Such a man is Goethe" (March 26, 1906).

Action is far more revealing than words; the diarist desires practical psychology to be based on what a man is doing. "Everybody lies in his words; a person always wishes to achieve something by his words and thus they issue from his mouth, coloured. Nevertheless, we see again and again the psychology of words at work—a rather convenient method" (July 23, 1906).

Action then, is the true revelator—yet not to the exclusion of the imaginative aspect of life. "Imagination is the most sovereign thing in us; it is not subject to the will. It races ahead; usually, the will races after imagination, so as to catch up with it. If it fails, it will stop on the way, annoyed, and catch its breath. Some geniuses have contracted a deadly pneumonia in the course of this race (Kleist, Hölderlin–Herostratus)" (Dec. 14, 1905).

Rosenzweig's early battles against the materialist view of life and of the human person extended to the historic process, as interpreted by the science of history. "History [in this sense] is psychological materialism, or, more generally, materialism of becoming, just as simple materialism is materialism of being. The latter maintains: Everything takes place in space only; the former holds: Everything takes place 'merely' in time. [Therefore] whatever is of value must be protected from history just as much as from the science of nature. Both space and time are coffins" (May 24, 1906).

Rosenzweig enters in his diary a lengthy discussion of whether there are laws governing the historical process comparable to the laws of nature that direct the cosmic process. He argues that a causal relationship, which lies at the base of scientific laws, is not applicable to history since history takes place in a limited realm; while comprehension of the unlimited and unending realm of nature requires the concept of the recurrence of the same and the law of cause and effect, no such relationship exists in history; time and space, which help us to understand reality, occasion constantly changed conditions, and this fact excludes a definite, immutable, causal relationship. Only an approximating analogy, the mere expectation of similar events to follow under similar conditions, is permissible in history; however, in theory, such an empirically conditioned law of cause and effect is also acceptable in natural science, if the scientist chooses to view nature as limited (April 29, 1906). Again, typically for Rosenzweig, the following day he registered his distrust of his reasoning as being too much *"more geometrico."*

Rosenzweig's appreciation of Nietzsche, clearly evident in the "Star of Redemption," has early beginnings to which the diary testifies. On February 5, 1906: "He is a scaler of heights and therefore lonely. Who dares to follow him? Who is conceited enough for that?" He considers

Nietzsche's method to be distrust, scepticism, as compared with Goethe's method, which is wonder, observation (*Anschauung*) (Feb. 19. 1906). Nietzsche is to Rosenzweig "our last great prophet," who gave us a "most effective" view of history: Christianity as the rebellion of the slaves in the realm of morality (May 25, 1906). With Nietzsche, Rosenzweig considers the harmful elements of civilization to stem from its democratic tendency. "A strong personality can never live in a democracy . . . Only weaklings, little people, Philistines, slaves, can live truly democratic" (*ibid.*). (It was the Biblical faith that—later—turned the aristocratic heart of Rosenzweig to recognize in every man a child of God.) He copies Nietzsche's maxim: "Das Persönliche ist das ewig Unwiderlegbare" (Nov. 16, 1906) and defends him against those who try to escape the impact of his thought by calling him a mere artist, a poet (Nov. 23, 1906). His teacher, Heinrich Rickert, comes in for sharp criticism for referring in his lectures to Nietzsche's nonsense; Rosenzweig: "Nietzsche's 'nonsense' is far more instructive than the 'sense' of clever people. His thoughts may turn out to be wrong, but they are never banal; Haeckel's thoughts may be terribly right, but they are always banal. Nobody has ever become a better man through Haeckel . . . Nietzsche, on the other hand, has been an educator of many, to some a seducer . . . to others an awakener, again to others a great enemy in contact with whom they gained strength . . ." (Nov. 23, 1906). The reason for Nietzsche's having been a "bad philosopher" Rosenzweig finds in his high quality as historian (Feb. 29, 1908), by which the diarist obviously means a philosopher of history.

Not infrequently there are notes on the subject of religion and the issue of Judaism, the latter hovering somewhere close to the periphery of his intellectual life; yet the reader is struck by the seriousness and honesty of his argument. The first entry on this subject (Feb. 9, 1906) states: "The Zionist and the anti-Semite have the same wish," or aim, apparently, to get rid of the paradoxical and anomalous existence of Judaism. Later (March 17, 1908) he writes: "The relationship of Judaism to Zionism parallels the relationship of the Kantian to the psychological concept of freedom." In the course of his development, Rosenzweig was to add depth and qualification to these early sentiments.

A note of the same day is instructive: "The Bible is a simile of the development from individual to family, to clan, to people with a national ideal, to people with the ideal of humanity (the prophets!). Now, should the final (and naturally the widest) step to humanity be negated, rejected, be made impossible and the wheel turned back one revolution?" A few weeks later, a *propos* a discussion of ethics and Protestant faith (in which he clearly separates ethics and religion), Rosenzweig asks himself: "And what is my Judaism based upon?" and answers: "(1) It is the religion of my forefathers. (2) I enjoy observing certain customs without having any real reason for doing so . . . (3) I believe in Plato. (4) I like to think in terms of Biblical images" (March 27, 1906). Of these pillars he considered the first "the central and strongest." A few days later (April 1), after attending a lecture in which the speaker affirmed the Greek element in "our civilization" while rejecting a possible Jewish element, Rosenzweig, admitting the lack of factual knowledge, tried to define both cultures. Greek, he wrote, is "the belief in man; individualism; man the measure; man the beginning, the source; the aim *may be* God, not *necessarily*; the highest achievements in art stemming from the awareness of the individual, the human: statues of gods, plastic imagination. To the Greek the starting point is the Self, to the Jew the godhead, the totality of the world." Tentatively, he uses the terms individualism *versus* totalism. This notion Rosenzweig acquired from a reading of the Book of Job. "In the theophany of the Book of Job, where God speaks entirely as *deus sive natura*, the position of man is in a totalist manner determined by the universe at large" *(ibid.)*. The reference to Job is significant; although other parts of the Bible were known to Rosenzweig at the time, it mattered little to him that the theophany in Job was not in the mainstream of Biblical thought. Soon we are to hear a different voice; moreover, in later years, the meaning of revelation in Judaism (and Christianity) was to receive a decisive re-assessment. In Rosenzweig's student years it was important that the great variety of views documented in the Bible, its very paradoxes, far from confusing him, attracted his open mind. In the multitude of contradictions, of "statements that form direct opposites to other statements," he recognized "one of the main reasons for the immense rôle the Sacred Scriptures have played in human history for so long a period of time." A similarly strong contradictoriness he finds in Goethe's work "which enables it to play the rôle of a Bible for modern man" (Jan. 11, 1906). "You can always refute Goethe (like God) with some other Goethe (or divine) revelation" *(ibid.)*. Later, when Goethe's revelations became less relevant to Rosenzweig and divine revelation a central factor in his thought, the ability to see the multiplicity of vistas without feeling the need to reduce them to stage in a historical development aided the thinker in his work. On January 16, 1906, he quotes Windelband: "Every truth is born as a paradox and ends as a triviality."

On second thought, Rosenzweig tried to rephrase the question as to the elements constituting German civilization. Now he wanted to know "what in German culture is to be traced back to the contrast between Antiquity and Christianity," whereby what before he termed Jewish now appears as Christian. A few weeks later (May 6), having reread the *Timaeus* and much Goethe, he made a more definite notation on the subject. "Our classical culture comes from Christianity (Bible), our classical culture from classical antiquity (Homer), our own from Goethe." He knows that "in reality there is little Christianity in the Bible and still less classical antiquity in Homer," but this does not matter, he says; what does matter is what elements of these cultures have been assimilated into one's own, and in what manner.

The motif of cultural adaptation and assimilation of intellectual trends leads Rosenzweig to consider Jewish assimilation as a valid and authentic possibility. "I have gone too far in my concern with heredity; the force of heredity may be reduced to *almost* zero through adaptation." The individual being unique, can transform elements of whatever origin into something new. "Thus the baptism of Jews loses some of its stigma of desertion." Such a step appears to him justified if a person no longer feels himself conditioned by the past and "has the courage to be an *individual without such historical determination [Bedingtheit]*." And he "who realizes the *value* of being (somehow) conditioned," has even more courage, for "he will then . . . have the hope, and trust his strength, of being able to provide at least his grandchildren with a basis for a (new) conditioning. Whoever takes this view need not fear the odium of this despised road." This reasoned argument is followed by a laconic "Ich nicht!" (Not I!) (May 25, 1906). In Rosenzweig's ability to separate himself from the group to which he intellectually belonged and to affirm a deep-seated position even if it meant spiritual solitude, we may recognize some of the hidden forces which came into play in his conversion in the fall of 1913.

Rosenzweig tried to clarify to himself the concept of divine grace. "Now only do I understand how divine grace is to be understood. God does not discard the great lack of grace that nature imposes upon Him; he allows evil its place in the world, disregarding the curse hurled at Him by the human creature. But in the realm of the particular His grace is boundless; however much His creatures may sin against Him, He, indifferent to it, heaps again and again the same blessings upon them. Why? Because He cannot act differently; because He loves them all—not out of passion, but because of the intimate connection between Creator and creature, which is somehow similar to the one between children and parents" (Aug. 23, 1906). To the Jobian answer (God speaking as *deus sive natura*) another solution is here added: the working of unconditional divine grace in the extra-natural, human, sphere. However, the student of natural sciences knew that this theological concept is "like *all* seemingly general concepts based on a psychological experience" (*ibid.*). The natural scientist experimented as well in the field of faith: "I have worshipped [*verehrt*] God in a variety of forms, childlike, Hebrew, Biblical, Homeric, natural, pantheistic, Christian, and—atheistic" (Sept. 6, 1906).

In a note on ethics (Sept. 29, 1906), Rosenzweig states: "The metaphysical foundation of Christian ethics is: 'What you do unto one of these you have done unto Me'; of Jewish ethics: 'Ye shall be holy; for I the Lord your God am holy,' often abbreviated as *Ani Hashem Elohekhem* (Hebrew in

the original), and as a postscript, adds: "Goethe's ethics could be de-
duced only from *our* tenet."

Rosenzweig's view that the awareness of God is not identical with
"religion", a view he expounded in his later writings, is hinted at in the
diary: "Originally the awareness of God was like a gas that filled completely all empty spaces in man. Then appeared the big sisters, founders
of the synthetic chemistry of the mind, (founders) of the chemistry of
culture, (namely) the *religions*. By applying considerable pressure they
succeeded in liquefying this gas; then they put all their effort into
dissolving man in that fluid . . . and they succeeded amazingly well."
Rosenzweig goes on to show how Kant demonstrated that man by no
means requires this solution in order to exist, and how that other thinker
(Nietzsche) gave this scientific issue a universal (universally human)
bent (Sept. 30, 1906).

And on Jesus (*versus* Socrates) Rosenzweig notes: In contradistinction
to Socrates, "the most obscure of the great figures in history, Christ is not
obscure at all, because we substitute for him the Christ-image created
throughout the centuries—he lives only in this. But there is no 'Socrates-
image through the centuries.' He is not embedded in Plato as Christ is in
Christianity; he seems rather the occasion than the germ of Platonism"
(May 24, 1908).

On the issue of God's transcendence *versus* immanence, that perennial
vexation of theologians, Rosenzweig postulates: "God is transcenden-
tally immanent (i.e. He is an idea in the Kantian sense) and empirically
transcendent (i.e. He is 'dear Lord' in the childish sense)" (Feb. 20, 1908).
By this paradoxical formulation (a version of which we encounter later in
the notes to his *"Judah Halevi"*), Rosenzweig did not solve the problem;
rather, he freed himself from the clutches of theological dogmatism.

A dairy entry of February 12, 1906, notes that during a conversation
with Hans Ehrenberg the preceding night, the idea struck him to transfer
from medicine to history; among the reasons for such a shift he mentions
his "habit of grasping things immediately in historical terms," his "perception of the individual event as a symbol of the universal," and his
scepticism. What he considered the most precious achievement in his
study of the natural sciences were his "big eyes" (May 29, 1906). Despite
his decision to transfer to history (and philosophy), he continued to
enjoy his medical courses: "Even chemistry is fun now. I manage to
breathe my living breath into the abstract chemical clods" (Aug. 27,
1906). In the winter semester 1906/07 he took a philosophy seminar with
Professor Jonas Cohn while carrying on his medical studies. In August
1907, he passed his Physikum, the preliminary examination in medicine,
and embarked on his new career: 1907/08 in Berlin, 1908–10 in Freiburg,
where he studied under Friedrich Meinecke and Heinrich Rickert. This
new period finds expression in the style of the diary. The variety of

interests remains, but more and more emphasis is put on themes from European intellectual history, Kant, Hegel, historical method, philosophy of history, history of art, Augustine. The style, too, undergoes a change: the brief, random, epigrammatic, biographical entry is being supplemented by more extensive, objective, impersonal, and often technical discourses; the entry on the aim of the natural sciences (Nov. 8, 1907) covers some twelve pages in the notebook, the note on the baroque style (June 1908) some thirty-five pages. Rosenzweig himself felt that autumn 1907 ushered in a new era in his life: the periods, symbolized by Goethe as thesis and Kant as antithesis, were now to be followed by a synthesis to which he hoped to give his own name (May 24, 1908). Other forces, intellectual and biographical, were joined to Goethe and Kant; there were other encounters and other experiences; from all these components did the synthesis Franz Rosenzweig emerge. But in order to understand the mature Rosenzweig, it is well to have a notion of the beginnings. For this he left us in the diary of his student years a precious document.

19
FRANZ ROSENZWEIG
THE STORY OF A CONVERSION

I

The story of Franz Rosenzweig is the story of a conversion. A West European intellectual and Jewish assimilationist breaks with his personal past and becomes a Jew by conviction, rediscovers his people's existence, and becomes the modern interpreter of this existence.

A West European intellectual, Franz Rosenzweig was the proud heir of the nineteenth century. This was the bourgeois world of faith in progress, a faith assured by the steady development of science. The belief in the "infinite perfectibility of the human race", as Rousseau put it, made for an air of optimism that pervaded the universities, academies of art, and other institutions of scholarship and *Bildung*. The man of action was not alone in considering himself the master of all he surveyed; he shared the field with the thinker who, following Hegel, believed devoutly in the omnipotence of thought. The young Rosenzweig identified himself with this *Weltanschauung* of progress and faith in reason.

Emancipation had opened the windows of the self-contained Jewish communities to this new world of the spirit. Jewish separation, as expressed in the traditional rituals of synagogue and home, seemed obsolete and meaningless. As for the messianic-universalist ideas proclaimed by the prophets and preserved in rabbinic doctrine and prayer—they, it was felt, had found their fulfilment, or at least were in process of realization, in European humanity.

An examination of the intellectual movements prevailing at the beginning of the century, however, led Rosenzweig and his friends (all in their early twenties) to a critical attitude toward German idealism, Hegel's "religious intellectualism," and the overemphasis on a history in which God supposedly reveals Himself. Against Hegel's theodicy of history that stamped the individual person's life as merely subjective, as a "passion" irrelevant to the whole, Rosenzweig and his friends felt that God must redeem man not indirectly, through history, but individually, through religious practice. In his "Diaries," Rosenzweig notes: "The battle against history in the nineteenth-century sense becomes for us the battle for religion in the twentieth-century sense."

More and more Rosenzweig moved away from academic philosophy as taught in the German universities of the day, more and more he felt himself frawn toward the "existential" philosophy that took its starting point in the situation of the concrete individual person. Religion seemed to hold the key. Yet Rosenzweig, trained in the sciences, in logical criticism, and in methods of modern historical research, could not conceive of a Western scholar "accepting religion," after all.

In Eugen Rosenstock, a Christian of Jewish descent, jurist and historian by profession, Rosenzweig possessed a friend who, as against the formal, timeless, abstract truths of logic, spoke of a truth revealed in the relationship of man with God and his fellow-men. In contrast to the logos of philosophy that is essentially a monologue, Rosenstock reinterpreted the biblical "word" as part of a dialogue. His philosophical position, rooted in religious faith, was secure, while Rosenzweig, though outspoken in his criticism of contemporary philosophy, had not yet broken through to a positive solution. In the frequent discussions between the two men—the time was the spring of 1913—Rosenzweig found himself, contrary to his instincts, defending a belief in autonomous scholarship and the relativist position of philosophy against Rosenstock's faith based on revelation.

Yet Rosenzweig came gradually to realize, more and more, that his friend's thinking was sounder than his own. Rosenzweig could not counter the faith of the Christian with the faith of a Jew, for Judaism as understood by Rosenzweig appeared then to be an anachronism. Rosenstock regarded his friend's superficial Judaism as merely "a personal idiosyncrasy, or at best a pious romantic relic" that could not address itself to a modern man in search of orientation in the Western world. Rosenzweig himself felt that a Jewish intellectual had only two choices: Zionism, if he wanted somehow to affirm his Jewishness; or baptism, if he turned to religion as a West European.

In the course of a conversation between the two friends, the problem was brought up of the man in *The Miracles of Antichrist* by Selma Lagerlöf. Rosenzweig asked what a man does when all answers fail him. Rosenstock replied, with the simplicity of faith: He prays. These simple words did more than all previous discussions about reason and faith, history and revelation, Hegel and Nietzsche, to convince Rosenzweig that Christianity was a living power in the world. That a man like Rosenstock, not a naïve believer and not a romantic, but a scholar and thinker, was able to accept religion as his personal answer, showed Rosenzweig that a union of mind and faith was indeed possible. He came to see, with the clarity of conviction, that an intellectual's attitude toward the world and history could be one of religious faith. He had thought that faith existed, but not for the objective scholar. Now he learned differently.

II

Rosenzweig's decided to become a Christian. Systematically minded and history-conscious, he made only one provision, a procedural one: he wished to enter Christianity as did its founders, as a Jew, not as a "pagan." Rosenzweig attended the synagogue services of the New Year's Days (*Rosh Hashanah*) and the Day of Atonement (*Yom Kippur*) *in preparation* for the church. Here was a Jew who did not wish to "break off," but who deliberately aimed to "go through" Judaism to Christianity.

He was stopped on his way, and called back into Judaism. This event came about with that suddenness and in that spirit of absolute finality reported in great conversions. Rosenzweig's biography indicates that it happened during the service of the Day of Atonement, 1913.

On the Day of Atonement, the Jew, though united with his brethren in prayer, stands utterly alone before his God, attired in his shroud as he will be on the day of his death. The Jew is nothing other than man, and God nothing other than the Judge of the world. The drama of this day begins on its eve, with the *Kol Nidre* in which the Jew frees himself of unintentional commitments to his fellowman. All guilt against man the Jew must have remitted before commencing this day. Thereafter, he is no longer guilty before man; his sin is a sin before God.

The liturgy of the day leads through psalms and hymns to the scriptural readings in which the ancient sacrificial rites of atonement are contrasted with man's obligation "to undo the bands of the yoke, to let the oppressed go free, and to deal bread to the hungry", which is "the fast that God has chosen." From here, the liturgy leads through the recollection of the ancient Temple service on the Day of Atonement at which the High Priest pronounced—this one time in the year—the ineffable name of God (who is near to those who call upon Him), to the reading of the story of Jonah the prophet who tried to flee from God (who is near to those who forsake Him).

The hour of sunset approaches, and the worshipper once more expresses his desire to "enter Thy gate," to experience eternity within the confines of time. Then, in utmost solemnity, the congregation cries out the profession, "Hear O Israel, the Lord our God, the Lord is One!", and finally, "The Lord is God: The God of Love, He alone is God!" In this profession, followed by the sounding of the ram's horn, the drama of the Day of Atonement finds its resolution.

Rosenzweig left the services a changed person. What he had thought he could find in the church only—faith that gives one an orientation in the world—he found on that day in a synagogue.[1]

He never mentioned this event to his friends and never presented it in his writings. He guarded it as the secret ground of his new life. The very communicative Rosenzweig, who was eager to discuss all issues and to share all his problems with people, did not wish to expose the most subtle moment of his intellectual life to analyses and "interpretations." His alert mother realized immediately the connection between her son's attendance at the Day of Atonement service and his new attitude, and later confided this conclusion of hers to the present writer. But the mother's contention could only be convincing if confirmed by some internal evidence.

Rosenzweig looked upon the event which he had lived through as incomplete, as a *partial* experience. Once he remarked: "The reasoning process comes afterwards. Afterwards, however, it must come." And he added: "The attempts of our "irrationalists' to establish separate accounts for faith and knowledge enrage me wherever I meet them."[2] And in commenting on a poem by Judah Halevi, he said: "To have found God is not an end, but in itself a beginning."[3] If Rosenzweig had been a mystic—he was not!—he would have found it possible to comprehend the event immediately; the thinker needed time to clarify his experience to himself. But the fact of the experience is certain. The long letter home in which he discusses Christianity and Judaism and which concludes almost parenthetically with the remark that he seems to have found the way back, is written only twelve days after that Day of Atonement. A few days later follows a letter to Rudolf Ehrenberg announcing that he has "reversed his decision" to become a Christian. "It no longer seems necessary to me and . . . *no longer possible.*"[4] "No longer necessary" might still imply an intellectual decision; "no longer possible" hints at a radical personal experience. In another letter to Rudolf Ehrenberg he agrees on what the church means to the world, namely, that no one can reach the Father save through Jesus; but "the situation is quite different for one who does not have to *reach* the Father because *he is already with Him.*"[5] This conviction betrays a certainty that does not come to a man through thinking; it points to a profound, instantaneous event.

Only in later years, when Rosenzweig has completed his new system of thought, integrating into it his concept of Judaism, does he emphasize the paramount importance for the understanding of Judaism that must be given to the Jewish liturgy in general and to the liturgy of the Day of Atonement in particular. His personal involvement is still hidden from sight, but it becomes increasingly clear to the student of his life story.

In his central work, *Der Stern der Erlösung (The Star of Redemption)*, Rosenzweig describes the Jew who on the Day of Atonement "confronts the eyes of his Judge in utter loneliness as if he were dead in the midst of life . . . Everything lies behind him." Then, "God lifts up His countenance to this united and lonely pleading of men," and grants man a part in eternal life. Man's soul is alone—with God. "Everything earthly lies so far behind the transport of eternity . . . that it is difficult to imagine that a way can lead back from here into the circuit of the year."[6]

In his *Jehuda Halevi*, Rosenzweig takes up this theme again. He speaks of the tension between God and man which seems irreconcilable on this day of atonement and reconciliation, until in the last profession of the day, "man himself, in the sight of God, gives the answer which grants him the fulfilment of his prayer of return . . . In this moment, he is as close to God . . . as it is ever accorded man to be."[7]

Had it not been an experience of his own life, all this could not have been written. This is the voice of a man who broke with his personal history, and—in an act of conversion—had become a Jew.

III

We have to ask: What actually made—in Rosenzweig's situation—for the priority of Judaism over Christianity?

We are informed that already in 1910, three years before the crucial year 1913, Rosenzweig rebelled against an over-emphasis on history as the sphere in which God reveals Himself. The following years led him— slowly—to an acceptance of faith as a possible orientation in the world. But the form of faith which suggested itself—Protestantism—was intimately tied up with that which evoked Rosenzweig's skepticism: history. Rosenzweig realized that the function of the church—to go out and conquer the unredeemed world of the heathens—involves the Christian in the fate of nations and the unfolding of the world-historic drama. The Christian is always on his way from the first to the second advent, through history and its earthly forms, state and church.[8] Only in his course through world history, only by his active participation in its works, does the Christian "gain the experience of the immediacy of the individual to God."[9] This being-forever-on-the-way marks the Christian with the stamp of incompleteness and keeps him in constant danger of compromising with the world and turning into a pagan—which is what he was before his inner transmutation made him a Christian.

Rosenzweig's first decisive Jewish experience showed him in practice what later became his "theoretical" conviction: that it is the Jewish faith that is free of "the curse of historicity"—a term he first uses in 1914.[10] The law of Israel is not power and expansion, but the anticipation of eternity within life. The rhythm of the sacred (liturgic) year, its sequence of Sabbaths and holy days, the ideas they represent, the realities they create, mirror the eternity of which the Jew partakes. Freed from historic obligation and destiny, living in the vision of eternity, the Jew "must forever remain a strange thing and an annoyance to the state and to world history."[11] The eternal people denies itself growth and escapes decline, both of which are the marks of history. It suffers rejection by the "nations" and seeming defeat and destruction. Yet the categories of history do not impinge upon the Jew's inner life. He has already reached the goal toward which the "nations" are still moving.

As a metahistoric religion, Judaism cannot be known by its external fate or by its external expressions. It can be understood only from within.

"For now," Rosenzweig writes to Eugen Rosenstock, "I would have to show you Judaism from within, that is, in a hymn."[12]

In the concrete historical world in which Rosenzweig started to think philosophically and theologically, "there seemed to be no room for Judaism."[13] But then, again, in the world, subjected to historical laws, conditioned by historical forces, there was no room for an unmediated, free relation between man and God. In this dilemma, Rosenzweig discovered metahistoric Judaism.

IV

The *Stern der Erlösung*, written by *Unteroffizier* Franz Rosenzweig at the Macedonian front, in hospitals, and after the collapse of the front line, on the march of the retreating army, is the most curious of "war books." A militant book it is, especially in its first parts, and confident of victory in its final passages. The enemy it attacks is the philosophy of German idealism; the home it defends is the individual, the suffering, erring, loving, doubting, despairing, and hoping human being whom the philosophy of the classical systems had so badly neglected, letting him vanish in the "Whole." The proud sweep of the speculative philosophical systems which constructed all reality out of "concepts" independent of experience and empirical knowledge, which identified reality with conceptual, theoretical truth, ignored the deepest anxiety of man: his fear of death, the nearness of death, the perilous nature of his existence. "Only" the individual dies, nothing can ever die in the "Whole," says the philosopher; but the "individual *quand même*" does not accept this verdict and stubbornly resists his annihilation within the system. The singleness of the living person, his consciousness, his death, the paradox of his existence within the world, disturb the rhyme and the rhythm of the total view of idealistic philosophy. True, man strives for knowledge, but he also longs for love to redeem him from solitude and death.

The "new thinking," in which Rosenzweig joins the anti-Hegelian revolt, and which is the thinking of the individual *quand même*, considers the carefully and ingeniously constructed "Whole" and "Absolute" as an arbitrary, impersonal abstraction of the "pure Ego." The "new thinking" as presented in the *Stern der Erlösung* goes back to the original three elements of reality, the parts of the "Whole": Man-World-God. Our thinking (dialectical or otherwise) is unable to deduce the one element from the other, to transform the one into the other. In a state of separation, these elements appear in heathen imagery. The paths that link the elements Man-God-World, leading them to a state of reality, Rosenzweig calls by names borrowed from theology: Creation-Revelation-Redemption.

Creation is the process which establishes the relation between God and World. Here God, hitherto hidden in the mythical beyond, appears and gives the world reality. The final word of Creation is transitoriness, finiteness, and that which endows the living creature with the quality of "past"—namely, death. However, Creation, the first act of God, necessitates continuation and renewal. This process Rosenzweig calls Revelation.

In Revelation, God in his love turns to man, calls him by his name. The awareness of God's love awakens in man the consciousness of an "I." Only as a loved one does the soul of man assume reality. In this love, man overcomes his original dumbness and becomes an individual able to speak and give answer to God's first command: to love. Man loves because God loves him. This love is only of the "present," and the command to love—the highest of all commands—is only of the present. This "command" can never turn into a "statute," cold, scrupulous, designated for the future. Love, ever present, is the basis of ever-present revelation. There is no love that is only "human" or sensual; here human and divine fuse into one; the passing moment mirrors an eternal ground.

Man, awakened to the awareness of himself, receives in Revelation his own name and the knowledge of the name of the loving and present God. A name is not an empty sound as in the heathen world, but a living word which ends dumbness and establishes orientation: beginning and end, origin and aim. Now, a concept of world history becomes possible.

Man translates his love for God into love for his "neighbor." In this love, man takes part in leading the world toward Redemption. It is in the practice of deeds of love that the fleeting moment is filled with eternity. Redeeming love frees man from the finality of death. Redemption in its fullness, the perfected world, eternity—this a man experiences in his prayer, in the cycle of the days of rest and the rhythm of the holy days which form the sacred year. In living the sacred year, man anticipates eternity in his earthly time. In this experience death is overcome.

Judaism and Christianity are two views of the world under the aspect of Creation–Revelation–Redemption. Both are representations of the real world (and as such equal before God) and spell the end of the heathen view of the world. Judaism, which stays with God, stands in contrast to Christianity, which is sent out to conquer the unredeemed world and is forever marching toward God. The beginning of the way, the advent of Jesus, is the central fact in the life of the Christian, who identifies it with the redemption. Revelation is the chief motive in the sacred year of the church. Judaism, in the third part of the Sabbath, in the Days of Awe, and especially in the Day of Atonement, culminates Creation and Revelation by the experience of Redemption.

Rosenzweig's work is the first attempt in Jewish theological thought to understand Judaism and Christianity as equally "true" and valid views of reality. Yet this does not lead to a suggestion of compromise or to a wish for harmonization. The two forms (Rosenzweig avoids the term religion) will exist, will have to exist, to the end of historical time. And forever will the Christian, who is eternally on the way through history, resent the Jew, to whom it is granted to realize eternity in time, in a metahistorical existence.

Is Judaism the "eternal life," the truth? Do "eternal life" (Judaism) and "eternal way" (Christianity) together constitute "the truth"? Rosenzweig's answer gives an insight into the ultimate seriousness of his faith. Man can become aware of the love of God (Revelation), he can fill the moments of his life with eternity (Redemption), but Truth is beyond man. Only God is Truth, Man (Jew, Christian) is given a part in truth [*Wahrheit*] insofar as he realizes in active life his share in truth [*bewähren*]. The distant vision of truth does not lead into the beyond, but "into life." These two words are, not accidentally, the concluding words of the book.

V

Rosenzweig's impatient criticism of philosophical idealism and historicism brings him close to the Kierkegaard revival and into discipleship to Schelling (in his last period) and to Nietzsche. The starting point of Rosenzweig's new approach coincides with existentialism: the human creature, in need and aware of its mortality, antedates thinking and the "productive" reason of idealism. The intimate tie between thought and language seen by Rosenzweig is paralleled by a similar insight of Martin Heidegger. These similarities and correspondences, however, are in themselves not enough to make Rosenzweig and existentialist philosopher or expressionist writer. What they show us is Rosenzweig as a man of his time.

A different matter is the world-view he presents in answer to the quest of the old new man: his reconstruction of the world out of Creation-Revelation-Redemption. Here, and in the reinterpretation of concepts such as divine love, the miracle, the name, Rosenzweig takes a decisive step in modern Jewish theology. Jewish thinkers have for a period of a hundred and fifty years done their best to devitalize Jewish theology. Blinded by the sharp light of philosophical idealism, they have identified Judaism with humanism, with a religion of reason, with man's moral autonomy. Jewish philosophers like Solomon Formstecher and Samuel Hirsch sought to justify Judaism before the throne of philosophy. They presented the Jewish religion as identical with the universal ethical truth of a religion of reason. Such an identification relieved the Jew of the burden of giving a philosophical explanation of Judaism; this work was done by general religious philosophy, and the results were valid also for the Jewish thinker, provided he could prove that the ideas of Judaism were identical with the ideas of the religion of reason. [14] Jewish philosophy, engaged in establishing this identity, lost interest in the actual theological problems that had absorbed Jewish thinkers before the Emanicipation.

The transition from this to a new period is marked by the works of Leo Baeck, Hermann Cohen, and Martin Buber, older contemporaries of Rosenzweig, who, each in his own way, represent a new orientation in Jewish religious thought. Rosenzweig is distinguished from them by his more radical break with the past and his repristination of theological concepts that were last alive in the long forgotten sphere of independent, dialectical Kabbalah. (This parallel, first recognized by Gershom G. Scholem, is doubly significant, since Rosenzweig never was a mystic.) As distinct from the nineteenth-century Jewish thinkers who made man the measure of all things in the universe, Rosenzweig restores the position of classical theology: man before God as the measure of life.

VI

The *Stern der Erlösung* is an inspired book. Yet its inspiration did not prevent it from remaining a book of theories, speculations, doctrines. In a letter addressed to the present writer, a few months before his death, Rosenzweig calls his book "a theory that grew out of an ardent longing." The longing was to reach the state of a man who stands before God, and who lives in this faith. It was this state that Rosenzweig experienced on the Day of Atonement 1913, and whose reality was further revealed to him in the Jewish section of Warsaw, where his war duties had brought him on a visit, shortly before he wrote the *Stern*.

The vision of the Jew who accepts the world and the fulness thereof as divinely ordered and willed; who even if shaken by the problems of reason and faith, reason and revelation, always feels the ground secure under his feet; who in misfortune may ask why, yet trusts that an answer is provided; who in the study of the law, in his daily prayer, is able to overcome innumerable obstacles: this vision of faith captivated the thinker Rosenzweig. He felt that such a Jew would *anticipate* the theoretical insights of the thinker by the simple fact of living as a Jew, without employing the complicated machinery of the intellect.

In his *Stern der Erlösung*, which we have called a war book, Rosenzweig fought not only against abstract philosophy and for the individual *quand même*, but also against the abstract philosopher *in himself* and in behalf of the lonely individual in doubt, consumed by skepticism and intellectual distrust—whom he also found within himself—and in search of the certainty of faith. Nietzsche, who as one of the first "new thinkers" had a decisive impact on Rosenzweig's own "new thinking," is, after all, also one of the fathers of European nihilism. We do well not to deny the challenge of this aspect of Nietzsche in considering Rosenzweig's journey to faith. It was this nihilist undercurrent in Rosenzweig's thinking which in various disguises threatened to blow up the claims of the spirit. The secret hold of this enemy on the searching man—who in the initial stage of the battle had lost the potential ally of reason—accounts for the fierceness of the struggle. Modern man's condition (presented with ultimate precision by Franz Kafka) is to stand in a world grown silent, waiting for the message that never reaches him—and it is also Rosenzweig's intellectual position. This is the "death," the initial motive in the *Stern der Erlösung*. From this battle against his own skepticism and his own tendency toward abstraction in its demonic sense, Rosenzweig emerged victorious. In the process of writing the *Stern der Erlösung*, Rosenzweig emerged a free man.

Freedom implied complete autonomy of choice and decision; rejection of dogma, formula, and prearranged results; abandonment of all that would prevent the mind from being open to the unpredictable ("He who lives in possibilities only is a coward"). It is freedom from fear of life and fear of death ("Fearlessness in the face of the world is a sign of the spirit's presence and aliveness"[15]).

As a free man, Rosenzweig freed himself from the bondage of his own book. Freedom from theory, dogma, and abstraction, could not mean *writing* about that freedom; a vision of faith could not mean describing this vision in a book. Only actual day-to-day life could furnish the proof for the validity of a book, or else demonstrate that the victory was only imaginary and the vision but an empty dream. Only life offered a chance for theories not to be turned into phrases, for symbols not to be dissolved into play, for a declaration of faith not to sink back into the abyss of nihilism.

VII

"Life" comes to mean to Rosenzweig Jewish life, in a very broad and profound sense. That he enters Jewish life as a free, and thus as a modern, man makes his biography a matter of significance for contemporary Jews. That Jewish life in this day and age became the testing ground for a modern man's problems that were not specifically "Jewish," gives Rosenzweig's life a scope beyond the particular interests of the Jew.

The period of "verification" lasted ten years, through eight of which Rosenzweig suffered his paralysis. (The nature of his illness forced him to go back to writing, although he had intended to use the living word.) In these years, Rosenzweig was the driving force of a Jewish renascence which, inaugurated by the treatises "Zeit ist's" ("It is Time") and "Bildung und kein Ende" ("On Education"), found its main expression in the Freies Jüdisches Lehrhaus in Frankfort and similar institutions throughout Germany. The activities of the Lehrhaus, many-sided and variegated as they were—some indeed designed to attract a wide audience—centered around the small study groups which Rosenzweig considered the heart of the school. Here Rosenzweig advocated a reorientation in Judaism to result from reestablished contact with the classical sources and from renewed practice of Judaism. The basic attitude is freedom. No recipe can be given, no rules can be set. But the sincere attempt cannot fail in restoring the sacramental quality of Jewish learning. Learning, i.e., turning documents of the past into life-words of the present, led to observance of the Jewish law not as ritual and ceremony but as a manifestation of religious truths. In advocating such a renascence of Jewish traditionalist practice (especially in "Die Bauleute" ("The Builders"), an epistle addressed to Martin Buber), Rosenzweig rejected the theory of Western Orthodoxy, which he thought overstressed the legal aspects of the law.

Rosenzweig's Judaism, receiving its orientation from classical Jewish texts, encompassed the whole breadth and profundity of Israel's culture as it had been before the Emancipation; before, in an attempt at Europeanization, it had accepted historical and sociological norms as the measure of spiritual values, and had thus limited the scope of Judaism as well as narrowed down its relevance. Rosenzweig freed Judaism from historically conditioned limitations. He saw again in Judaism one of the supra-human powers and a supra-Western force. He well knew that in order to be of help in the crises of Western culture, Judaism had to become "secularized", i.e., brought into living contact with the "worldly" life of man. "The ability to secularize itself again and again proves its eternity."[16] (Similarly, Rosenzweig realized that within the Western world socialism, even in its atheist form, might at times contribute more to the establishment of the kingdom of God than religious institutions and the adherents.[17]) Inacceptable, however, is secularization as a modernist dogma. Though a force active in time, Judaism must know how to return to its metahistorical source. There, Law resists a pseudo-legal interpretation as given by Orthodoxy; monotheism resists a pseudo-logical, and social justice a pseudo-ethical interpretation, as advanced by religious liberalism.[18] But the liberals who stressed the "essence of Judaism" and the idea of eternity, were told by Rosenzweig that eternity as understood by Judaism lies not in the metaphysical clouds of timelessness but in its realization in our days. ("There is no 'essence of Judaism,' there is only: 'Hear, O Israel!' "[19]).

In this spirit, Rosenzweig translated Judah Halevi's poetry and finally undertook, with Martin Buber, to translate the Bible for the modern German reader, to elucidate certain phases of its inner history, and to confront the Western Jew with its reality. These writings were part of the plan to reveal the scope of the Hebrew sources. It is here that he most successfully showed how much of ageless Israel can be activated and relived by a modern free Jew.

It was in the way Rosenzweig applied himself to these activities and to the sphere of classical and traditional Judaism that he "verified" his theory of faith, translating doctrine "into life," finally conquering the opposition from within.

The greatest test were the eight years of paralysis. Here "life" meant enduring, with an upright spirit, pain, physical privation, and gradual decline of the strength to live; it meant filling every day with spirit, with help and counsel to family, friends, and the community at large, with a healthy sense of humor. All this in preparation for the great day of death which was to be accepted in faith and in freedom.

Here is a note of the poet Karl Wolfskehl written after a visit in Rosenzweig's home:

Whoever stepped over the threshold of Franz Rosenzweig's room entered a magic circle and fell under a spell, gentle yet potent—in fact, became himself a charmed being. The solidity and the familiar forms of every-day life melted away and the incredible became the norm. Behind the desk, in the armchair sat, not as one had imagined on climbing the stairs, a mortally sick, utterly invalid man, almost totally deprived of physical force, upon whom salutations were lost and solace shattered; behind the desk, in the chair throned Franz Rosenzweig. Throned and showered bounties. The moment our eyes met his, community was established. Everything corporeal, objects as well as voices and their reverberations, became subject to a new order, were incorporated without strain, conscious effort, or need for readjustment, into that wholly genuine, primordially true kind of existence irradiated by beauty. It simply couldn't have been otherwise, for what reigned here was not pressure and duress, but utter freedom. . . .

It was not only that all petty human feelings, anxieties and embarrassments were wiped out. It was not only that all the paltry, complacent pity or well-being was purged away. What happened here was much more: in the presence of this man, *well* in the fullest sense, one's own welfare was assured, wholly and in accord with the spirit. Near Franz Rosenzweig one came to oneself, was relieved of one's burdens, heaviness, constriction. Whoever came to him, he drew into a dialogue, his very *listening* was eloquent in itself, replied, summoned, confirmed, and guided, even if it were not for the unforgettably deep and warm look of the eyes. . . .[20]

The freedom achieved in Rosenzweig's life is not identical with existence, as in Sartre's existentialism, where, curiously enough, it refers back to Hegel's *Phänomenologie des Geistes*. It is rather the status granted to man who, in crisis has reached the end of the road, and "out of the depths" beholds the presence of God. It is the freedom of Abraham *after* the "Binding of Isaac," his final trial. It is the freedom of man before God. Here, theories, formulas, speculations, doctrines, and all "isms" are silenced. Here, issues and objects no longer matter. Man becomes ready to hearken to the voice of God.

Rosenzweig, perhaps, never achieved in actuality his vision of the naïve simplicity of a pious Jew. He remained a modern man. But his freedom became the freedom of man before God. This free consciousness grew throughout Rosenzweig's life and concluded his conversion.

NOTES

1. A parallel experience is reported by the great Protestant interpreter of faith, Rudolf Otto, author of *The Idea of the Holy*, who conceived his notion of *tremendum* as a central factor in religion after participating in a Day of Atonement service in a simple North African synagogue.

2. Franz Rosenzweig, *Briefe* (1935), p. 620.

3. Franz Rosenzweig, *Jehuda Halevi* (1927), p. 204.

4. *Briefe*, p. 71.

5. *Ibid.*, p. 73.

6. Franz Rosenzweig, *Der Stern der Erlösung* (1930), vol. III, pp. 80–87.

7. *Jehuda Halevi*, p. 182.

8. *Stern*, vol. III, p. 104.

9. *Ibid.*, p. 91.

10. Franz Rosenzweig, *Kleinere Schriften* (1937)., p. 289.

11. *Stern*, vol. III, p. 95.

12. *Briefe*, p. 688. The Franz Rosenzweig/Eugen Rosenstock [-Huessy] correspondence on Judaism and Christianity, first printed in Rosenzweig's *Briefe*, is available in English translation in Rosenstock-Huessy, Eugen, ed., *Judaism Despite Christianity* (University, Al.: The University of Alabama Press, 1969).

13. *Ibid.*, p. 72.

14. See Julius Guttmann, *Die Philosophie des Judentums* (1933), p. 318.

15. *Kleinere Schriften*, p. 502.

16. *Briefe*, p. 476.

17. *Ibid.*, p. 530.

18. *Kleinere Schriften*, pp. 111f.

19. *Almanach des Schocken Verlags auf das Jahr 5699* (1938), p. 54.

20. Karl Wolfskehl, in *Franz Rosenzweig: Eine Gedenkschrift* (1930), pp. 35f.

20
INTRODUCTION TO ROSENZWEIG'S
LITTLE BOOK OF COMMON SENSE AND SICK REASON

I

In July 1921 Rosenzweig wrote a little book on the relationship between world, man, and God, on the centrality of language and of time as a factor in human thinking. His major work, *The Star of Redemption*, written while in military service at the Balkan front, had just been published. The two-volume work on Hegel's political doctrines *(Hegel and the State)* which had been issued several months previously had caused discussion among political scientists and modern historians.

Rosenzweig had not planned to build on these foundations a career as a scholarly writer. He felt that his writings had served their purpose in preparing the ground for extensive communal activities. "I see my future only in life, not any more in writing," he says in a letter to Martin Buber.[1]

The living, spoken word was to replace the written one. Professor Friedrich Meinecke, celebrated historian, had offered Rosenzweig a lectureship at the University of Berlin. In rejecting the offer, Rosenzweig confided to Meinecke that scholarship no longer appeared to him as an end in itself; it had become a service—and not a service to ideas and disciplines but to human beings. Scientific curiosity and the omniverous appetite for knowledge belonged to the past. He now wanted to confront human beings (and scholars only insofar as they were human beings), whose search for knowledge cannot be answered by experts working within well-defined disciplines, but by men who are ready to use their knowledge in the service of man.[2]

To the dismay of his academic friends and his bourgeois family, Rosenzweig chose the unconventional field of adult education— unconventional for a man who could have found something "higher"— and settled in Frankfort on the Main as the head of the *Freies Jüdisches Lehrhaus*. This free house of Jewish studies which provided an open forum for the discussion of Jewish, philosophical, sociological and simply human issues, was introduced by Rosenzweig with a pamphlet entitled *On Education* [*Bildung und kein Ende*]. The *Lehrhaus* was to become the scene of activities such as he describes in his letter to Professor Meinecke.

From January to March, 1921, Rosenzweig taught a course in philosophy at the *Lehrhaus,* in which he dealt with such problems as knowledge and belief, end and beginning, action and suffering, soul and body, life and death. In a seminar running concurrently, Rosenzweig discussed background material for these lectures, particularly the writings of German idealism from Kant to Hegel. These philosophers were treated polemically. In opposition to the advocates of pure thought and critical idealism, Rosenzweig expounded his "New Thinking." This he indicated in the subtitle to the course: "About the use of common sense" [*Vom Gebrauch des gesunden Menschenverstandes.*] The term "common sense" is much in evidence in *The Star of Redemption,* particularly in the polemics against German Idealism.

The Star of Redemption had now been in the hands of the reader and its author had good reason for thinking the public would find it difficult. Rosenzweig, therefore, welcomed the invitation of an enterprising publisher (Fromann) to present his philosophy in a more popular manner. He felt he should allow himself this much of a deviation from his new way of life. The book was to be called *Das Büchlein vom gesunden und kranken Menschenverstand* (The Little Book of Common Sense and Sick Reason). The *Lehrhaus* lectures and especially the seminar, where Rosenzweig could test the comprehensibility of his views, served as a preparation for the writing of the *Büchlein.*

Rosenzweig's changed attitude to writing is reflected in the style of this treatise. This well-composed and at times solemn little book has careless prefaces and epilogues; in certain sections we encounter a rough boyishness (as in the treatment of the "as if" theory), occasional innuendoes against "philosophy" when only German Idealism is meant. The mode of address is in several places either unnecessarily aggressive, or unnecessarily pedagogical.

When the *Star* was completed, Rosenzweig thought of the remaining years of his life as a gift bestowed on him. He compared his state of mind, at thirty-two, with Goethe's feelings on his eighty-second birthday, when he had finally completed the manuscript of *Faust.* This additional time granted him should be accepted with reverence, filled with meaningful action: "each day's demand" should be realized as it presents itself. The publisher's invitation to present his philosophy did not coincide with his own inner necessity to speak. Every argument in favor of publication was outweighed by his fear of placing in the reader's hands a book written "on request." One month after the completion of the manuscript Rosenzweig sent a copy to a friend and wrote that he had not yet decided to publish it. A short time later he withdrew the manuscript, giving carbon copies to friends.[3]

The book is now published a generation after it was written, in another part of the world and in a tongue alien to the author's own.

The reasons for silence and withdrawal are no longer valid. Rosenzweig's name has grown in significance since his death in 1929. His works are discussed in many lands, in many languages, and by men of different faiths and philosophical convictions. His conduct during eight years of almost total paralysis made his life an example of personal heroism. Any additional record, therefore, of his understanding of men, world, and God can no longer be overlooked.

The biographical position of the book is not unimportant. It was the last essay which Rosenzweig wrote as a healthy man. The adherent of the old, speculative, conceptual philosophic systems is treated as a paralytic patient being cured by the New Thinking. Two or three months after the book was completed Rosenzweig noticed in himself certain irregularities of muscular movement—symptoms of a paralysis which turned the young, vigorous man into an invalid deprived of movement and speech. We cannot know therefore whether the employment of the paralysis motif in the book is a mere coincidence or the ironic expression of a premonition on the author's part. Be that as it may, the book is the utterance of a man standing at life's crossroads. As such it is more than the original publisher intended it to be. And more, indeed, than the author himself could have consciously realized.

The English title of the book, *Understanding the Sick and the Healthy,* has been chosen as an indication of the importance which the author attached to his images. The dissolution of the world of experience in the process of consciousness (Idealism in general), the deduction of everything from thought and the ego (Fichte), the treatment of the thinking subject as something abstract (Kant), the disappearance of the "unhappy consciousness" in the dialectic of Reason (Hegel), are not viewed by Rosenzweig as mere philosophical errors but as a sickness of the whole man. Equally, the application of "common sense" is not meant to be a correction of the mind only but an expression of the health of man as a whole.

II

Rosenzweig's target in *Understanding the Sick and the Healthy* is German idealist philosophy which "reduces the world" to the perceiving "self." Such a philosophy, assuming that the world must be different from what it "appears" to be, inquires into the "essence" [*Wesen*] of things in order to establish what they are "actually" or "essentially" [*eigentlich*]. The New Thinking, grounded in common sense, traces experience of the world back to the world, experience of God back to God. As opposed to idealism, the New Thinking recognizes world, man, and God—"the proper subjects of all philosophy"—as the three ultimate parts of reality.

Contrary to the teaching of idealism, our thoughts and ideas about things are not fundamental reality; the laws of thought are not identical with the laws of reality, as Kant maintained. The thinking subject is not an abstract being; mind and consciousness cannot be understood mathematically. Common sense regards individual human existence with utter seriousness. Here the "thinking individual" is personally involved both in the question and in the answer; his thinking does not concern his mind only but has an existential relevance.

The term "common sense" is usually associated with Thomas Reid (1710–1796) and his critique of Hume's epistemological radicalism and Berkeley's subjective idealism and immaterialism. In opposing Hume, Reid speaks of instinctive, intuitive, original principles and beliefs (such as the notion of an external world and the soul) which we know through experience; these principles of common sense, the bases of our knowledge, are older and more trustworthy than analytical philosophies. Berkeley had maintained that our knowledge of a material world rests on our senses; but our senses afford us *only* knowledge of our sensations or ideas; these sensations, however, do not correspond to any reality in the material world. Reid objects to the use of the word *only*, maintaining that such a view deprives the world around us of reality and makes of it an appearance, a dream. Reid's argument (anticipating some aspects of the phenomenological method of thinking) goes as follows: just as the power of art over the material world is limited to the connection and separation of already existent matter, it being unable to create new matter, so thought does not "produce" the outside world. Knowledge does not originate in sensations or ideas; it exists objectively in nature. The material world is not a dream but a reality.[4]

Common sense, as applied by Rosenzweig, neither utilizes preconceptions nor moves towards prearranged goals and "postulates." Not even God is "given" in advance of actual experience. During the period Rosenzweig worked on this small book, he wrote to his mother: "The chief thing is not whether a person 'believes' in the good Lord; what matters is that he open all his five senses and sees the facts—at the risk that even the good Lord may be found among the facts."[5]

Adherence to experience and common sense does not guarantee success. Terms are only vaguely defined and may mean different things to different people. (Both Hume and Berkeley professed to follow the principles of common sense!) One is reminded of a story told by the scientist Karl Compton. A sister who lived in India had a wiring job done by a native electrician who returned to her several times for instructions. Finally, the exasperated lady said: "You know very well what I want. Why don't you use your common sense and go ahead?" The electrician bowed gravely and replied: "Madame, I have only a technical education. Common sense is a rare gift of God."

III

Chapter Two of *Understanding the Sick and the Healthy* offers a contemptuous criticism of the "as if" philosophy represented by Hans Vaihinger and his book *Philosophie des Als-Ob* which appeared in 1911. This construction, which goes back to Kant and to ideas expressed by Friedrich Carl Forberg (1770–1848) maintains the following: There is no God. A belief in God is, therefore, meaningless. Yet this does not imply that religion should be abandoned. Religion, after all, is more than a belief in God. It is a form of conduct based on such a belief. To achieve this practical end it does not matter whether God is a reality or an imaginary being. It is sufficient to accept the fiction of a god. In theory I may know that God does not exist; in practice, however, I act as if God did exist, as if I were responsible to him. Thus, religion is understood as an organization of human behavior based on a theological fiction.

Invoking Kant's critical philosophy, Vaihinger interprets the statement "I believe in God" to mean: I act as if the existence of God were a reality. My theoretical reason prohibits me from accepting a moral law, but I act as if such a moral law existed because my practical reason commands me to do the good absolutely. . . . Thus also the theoretical atheist who acts in accordance with ethics "believes in God"— practically.[6] Such an approach to religion Vaihinger detects even in such an ardent Christian as Schleiermacher. As a philosopher Schleiermacher cannot perceive a relationship between God and the world; as a theologian he assumes such a relationship as analogous to a father relationship to his child. This means: God is not the father of mankind, but he should be treated as if he were.[7]

Not only God becomes a victim of the "as if" fiction. Man's freedom is also a fiction. We are to consider man as if he were free. But he is not free. All our perception is based on our will; our thinking produces these ideas because they serve our purposes, because we need them. "Truth is no longer ours," as Nietzsche has said.

Rosenzweig, in contrast to Vaihinger, considers man as a whole whose reason is not divided into a theoretical and a practical aspect. He cannot believe therefore that the "as if" approach can bring man "inner and outer peace."[8] Far from being able to cure the invalid, the notion of "as if" can only add to his confusion.

The human patient, paralyzed by philosophy—of which the "as if" theory is only one example—is cured once he has learned to understand world, men and God as primary forms which underly reality. According to Rosenzweig, the same experience which leads to perception of the world, man and God, opens the vision of how they relate as well. For these relationships Rosenzweig chose terms from the realm of religion: Creation—Revelation—Redemption. The presentation of these relationships in their historical formulations (Judaism and Christianity) and in their significance for the life of the individual is contained in *The Star of Redemption*. But the patient who has overcome his paralysis and learned to walk again will put his legs to good service and walk in the right direction.

Several contemporary writers accord Rosenzweig a place among the existentialists. Though this may help his reputation in some circles it in no way advances the understanding of his works. True, the starting point of his thinking coincides with existentialism: the lonely, suffering individual, aware of his mortality—the human creature whose existence precedes thought. Rosenzweig frees the individual from his isolation; in relating himself to his fellow-man, to the world around him and to God, man's life becomes meaningful. His individual soul, unique and irreducible, participates in the dialogue with the other elements which constitute reality. Thus man's existence is truly co-existence. And if the reader desires an "ism" to cover Rosenzweig's thought, then, for argument's sake, it may be termed co-existentialism.

IV

In contrast to the traditional, abstract, "logical" thinking, Rosenzweig, following a theory of Eugen Rosenstock-Huessy, calls the new method "grammatical thinking." Here human language, communication, the word, the name, are signs of reality, even keys to the understanding of reality. The problem of language and the name is an old one. In Plato's *Cratylus* the question is raised whether through an understanding of names we may be led to a knowledge of things. Hermogenes denies any relationship between name and reality; whereas Socrates insists on a deep connection between the existent thing and its name as a basis for our knowledge of reality. Plato, however, abandoned the position of this dialogue in the *Seventh Epistle*. Here the whole realm of language is taken to be only the first step of knowledge. The word strives to name true being but it cannot; ultimately, instead of expressing reality, the word becomes a barrier between the speaking person and the one spoken to. The thinker is left alone, to struggle in silence with the paradox of name, word and language.[9]

The two lines of thought, indicated by the *Cratylus* and the *Seventh Epistle* are continued through the Middle Ages. The "realism" of the Middle Ages (supported by Aristotelian logic which was grounded upon language) cultivated the word; its "nominalism" perpetuated the Sophists' scepticism of the word. The reality of language, "the force and signification of words," appeared as a problem at least to most modern philosophers. The great defender of language was Wilhelm von Humboldt, who perceived the interdependence of speech and cognition, and recognized that the word was not only an expression of reality but also a means by which to explore it. Hegel also believed that language possessed the power to express reality. But in the case of Hegel it becomes clear that language is primarily conceptual terminology and the word primarily an element of definition. The view of the French traditionalist V. G. A. de Bonald, may be of some interest. De Bonald questioned the value of autonomous reason and argued that the root of both reason and the intellectual life was grounded in language. The word, he maintained, comes to man as a divine revelation. It is the source of all truth; man's thought participates in it, but does not create it. The authoritative representation of this truth is to be found in the Church, which teaches the universal reason. De Bonald knew that language is more than a technical instrument, but theological dogmatism and vagueness led him astray; from beneath his religious theory shines Hegel's idea of the Objective Spirit.

The more recent trends in philosophy move towards ever greater distrust of language. Bertrand Russell (*The Scientific Outlook*) sees in language a collection of abstract nouns expressing an atomized universe of sense data. It is a language which can no longer serve as a means of communication between men. Here we may discover, in the words of W. M. Urban, "a progressive paralysis of speech." To Henri Bergson (*Creative Evolution, Introduction to Metaphysics*) language, being "static," cannot express the dynamic continuity of reality. Language is wedded to intellect and logic; reality can be fathomed only by immediate intuition which is non-logical, wordless. Here, too, speech is paralyzed. That language does violence to immediate experience is the conviction of A. N. Whitehead (*Process and Reality*). He, therefore, wishes to redesign language and create a new system of categories of speech. Our universe, being a universe of "events" and "activity," would be adequately expressed in a language of verbs. As there are "no things," no names can be uttered to designate them.[10] Such speech, however, possibly considered "adequate" by philosophers (who, as Bertrand Russell says, "as a rule believe themselves free from linguistic forms") will never reach the ear of a living and speaking human being.

All this points to an abyss between man and the world beyond man. Nietzsche felt this incompatibility keenly and was thus able to allude to its root. "That world is well hidden from man! . . . that heavenly nothingless! The bosom of Being does not speak to man, except in the guise of man. Truly, all being is difficult to prove; it is difficult to make it speak."[11] Man's isolation from the world of Being, from the world outside the confines of the individual is at the root of this tragic silence. In Sartre's words, "there is no sign in the world." The names are dormant and man cannot invoke them. Man can think and create terminologies and classifications—outside of language and outside of time.

Against this background, Rosenzweig's New Thinking restores the relationship between man and world and God and with it the trust in man's power to speak and to communicate. Since, as Hölderlin tells us, "we exist as talk, and can hear from one another," we *do* speak and *do* listen. *Understanding the Sick and the Healthy* describes in three bold movements the role of language, the word and the name, in man's relation to the three elements which form reality. To Rosenzweig, langauage is not the "essence" of the world; it is "a bridge between the world and other things": God and the Self. And the name calls the Self into its presence.

In a later essay, Rosenzweig summarizes his teaching as contrasted to earlier modes of thinking. In the New Thinking, he says, the *method of speech* replaces the method of abstract, pure, timeless thinking maintained in earlier philosophies. Speech, on the other hand, is bound to time and nourished by time. It takes its cue from others. It lives by virtue of the life of the other person. Abstract thinking is always a solitary affair, even if it is done by several who philosophize together. For in that case, the other is only raising the objections I should raise myself. In a real dialogue an action takes place. I do not know in advance what the other person will say to me. The abstract thinker knows his thoughts in advance. The "speaking thinker" cannot anticipate anything; he must be able to wait because he depends on the word of the other; he requires *time*. The abstract thinker thinks for no one else and speaks to no one else. The "speaking thinker" speaks to someone and thinks for someone; a someone who has not only ears but also a mouth.[12]

V

The Star of Redemption, the fundamental document of the New Thinking, contains a lengthy discourse on Judaism and Christianity as historical realities. It does not attempt to prove that one is better than the other; nevertheless, once the book had been completed, its author was convinced that he had written a Jewish book.

The present treatise arrives at an understanding of Man—World—God as factors of reality. There is no effort to demonstrate the historic, philosophical, or regligious forms in which this reality would be mirrored or manifested. Yet the *Lehrhaus* lectures in which Rosenzweig outlined the common sense view of *Understanding the Sick and the Healthy* were announced under the title: "A Guide to Jewish Thinking."

Such a name for a course which obviously had "nothing to do" with Jewish issues calls for an explanation. A chance remark, made shortly after the writing of the present book, gives an important insight into Rosenzweig's method of working. Stating that he is just as little an "expert" in Judaica as is Max Weber, Rosenzweig added: "The Jewish way [*das Jüdische*] is not my object but my method.''[13] *Jewish,* in Rosenzweig's estimation, is the insistence on the concrete situation; the importance of the spoken word and the dialogue; the experience of time and its rhythm and, in connection with it, the ability to wait; finally, the profound significance of the name, human and divine.

These elements and others contribute towards a *method* of thinking. Equally they become to Rosenzweig the means of expressing his thought. He uses the ancient words of classical Judaism, because, as he says, he has received the New Thinking in these ancient words. "I know that instead of these, New Testament words would have risen to a Christian's lips. But these were the words that came to me. And I really believe that this [*The Star of Redemption*] is a Jewish book; not merely one that treats of 'Jewish matters' . . . but a book of which the old Jewish words have formed the expression of whatever it has to say, and especially of what is new in it. Jewish matters are always past, as is matter generally, but Jewish words, however old, partake of the eternal youth of the word.''[14]

VI

At about the same time that Rosenzweig was writing *Understanding the Sick and the Healthy,* Franz Kafka was working on *The Castle.* In this work a land surveyor, K, receives a call to do work in a castle; he arrives at the village which is dominated by the castle, only to find out that the castle is inaccessible to him, that even the lowest officials cannot be reached, and that his claim to having received a call cannot be verified. The villagers, who live without asking questions, and are protected by a naïve sense of security, regard K as a stranger: "We do not need a surveyor; the boundaries of our small holdings are well marked out." K remains isolated from both castle and village; his knowledge estranges him from the simple village folk that do not know; but he cannot translate this knowledge into life, because real, meaningful, eternal life is in the castle and beyond the reach of knowing man. Man's tragic situation results from having eaten from the tree of knowledge and not having eaten from the tree of life.[15] "We are separated from God from both sides: the tree of knowledge separates us from Him, the tree of life separates Him from us.''[16] With the expulsion from Paradise man lost his name (Kafka's heroes go mainly by initials), lost his language (there is no real communication), lost his love (only sex remains); time which could now be man's is but confused, distorted, paralyzed eternity. Man (K), World (village) and God (castle) exist, but their existences are not correlated.

Rosenzweig realized that Kafka was dealing with a genuinely biblical problem and said: "I have never read a book that reminded me so much of the Bible as *The Castle.*''[17] Rosenzweig meets man exactly where Kafka had left him. To the biblical question of Kafka, the existentialist novelist, Rosenzweig, the co-existentialist thinker, gives the biblical answer, for he admits the biblical idea of Revelation (love). Thus man finds his place *next* to his fellow man, *in* the world and *before* God. He speaks and he is spoken to. He is called by his name and he names beings around him. And he has overcome his distrust of time; he has learned to wait (man was driven out of paradise because of impatience, says Kafka) until he "perceives in proper time," until time itself becomes a mirror of eternity.

VII

Rosenzweig, who regarded with suspicion all philosophical theories, programs, systems, speculations, doubted the validity of his own view—unless it could be verified in actual life. *The Star of Redemption* appeared to Rosenzweig to be "only a book." He did "not attach any undue importance to it." "The book is no goal, not even a provisional one."[18] The present work was not to his liking and was therefore dropped. *The Star* had concluded with the words: Into life. That was what Rosenzweig called *no-more-book*. As a statement it could be accepted, rejected, criticized or derided like any other statement. In itself it is not "true." The present treatise concludes with a view of death as the brother of life. This statement is not "true" in itself. The verification can take place only in the midst of real life. Only here, in life, does it become clear whether we are faced by what Henry James called "the platitude of mere statement" or—by something different.

A note written by Rosenzweig to a poem of Judah ha-Levi explains what he meant. "Had Luther died on the thirtieth of October, 1517, all the audacity of his commentary on the 'Epistle to the Romans' would have been nothing but the extravaganzas of a late scholastic." But on the thirty-first Luther had nailed to the church door at Wittenberg his revolutionary ninety-five theses. Thus "life complemented the theory and made it true."[19]

Here a curious parallel comes to mind in the words of another critic of Hegelian philosophy: William James. Of truth he says: "Truth *happens* to an idea. It *becomes* true, is *made* true by events. Its verity is in fact an event, a process: the process namely of its verifying itself, its veri-*fication*. Its validity is the process of its valid*ation*."[20]

In comparing Kierkegaard with the modern theologians Karl Barth and Friedrich Gogarten, Rosenzweig finds that "behind each paradox of Kierkegaard one senses biographical *absurda*, and for this reason one must *credere*. While behind Barth's colossal negations one senses nothing but the wall on which they are painted, a whitewash wall, his immaculate and well-ordered life. . . . Not that they are unbelievable; but it is, after all, an indifferent authenticity."[21]

This treatise, too, would have remained a mere program. But even though it was not written out of an inner necessity, it was converted into a testimony by the subsequent life of its author. In the eight years until his death at forty-three, Rosenzweig had verified under the most tragic circumstances what he had professed in this book: a victory over the "nothings" that threaten man's freedom to think and to act; an affirmation of the three factors—God, world, man—whose relationships constitute reality; a passionate devotion to human language; a love of life and an acceptance of death. Rosenzweig's reflections can be contradicted; his life cannot.

NOTES

1. Franz Rosenzweig, *Briefe,* ed. Edith Rosenzweig and Ernst Simon, Berlin 1935, p. 371.
2. *Franz Rosenzweig: His Life and Thought,* ed. N. N. Glatzer, New York 1953, pp. 94–98.
3. In 1925, Rosenzweig wrote "The New Thinking," a popular presentation of the background of *The Star of Redemption;* in this essay reappear a number of motives used in the present treatise.
4. Cf. on this subject: Sydney C. Rome, "Scottish Refutation of Berkeley's Immaterialism," *Philosophy and Phenomenological Research,* III (1943), 3.
5. *Briefe,* p. 406.
6. Hans Vaihinger, *Philosophie des Als-Ob,* 1911, pp. 684 f.
7. See H. Scholz, *Die Religionsphilosophie des Als-Ob,* Leipzig 1921.
8. *Ibid.,* XIV.
9. See W. M. Urban, *Language and Reality,* London 1939, pp. 52–56.
10. *Ibid.,* ch. VII and Appendix III.
11. *Nietzsches Werke,* VI, 43.
12. *Franz Rosenzweig: His Life and Thought,* pp. 198 ff.
13. *Briefe,* p. 407.
14. *Franz Rosenzweig: His Life and Thought,* pp. 144 f.
15. See Aphorism 78 in Franz Kafka, *The Great Wall of China,* New York 1946, p. 297.
16. Franz Kafka, *Hochzeitsvorbereitungen auf dem Lande,* New York 1953, p. 101.
17. *Franz Rosenzweig: His Life and Thought,* p. 160.
18. Franz Rosenzweig, *Kleinere Schriften,* Berlin 1937, p. 397.
19. *Franz Rosenzweig: His Life and Thought,* p. 286.
20. William James, *Pragmatism,* London 1907, p. 201. On Wm. James and Rosenzweig, see Ernst Simon in *Molad,* 1953, pp. 299–311.
21. Letter of December 24, 1922, to Martin Buber, *Briefe,* p. 469.

21
THE FRANKFORT LEHRHAUS

I

Soon[1] after Franz Rosenzweig saw his way clear to remain a Jew and to dedicate his life to the cause of Judaism, he realized the need for a radical reorganization of Jewish instruction on all levels and a re-thinking of the function of Jewish scholarship in Western Europe. The lack of concern of scholarly research for the necessities of contemporary Jewish life, the low level of the two hours' weekly religious instruction in the general schools, the clannishness of the cultural and social groups, Rosenzweig considered both a result of the process of West-European Emancipation and a good reason for further alienation from Judaism. It was both the increasing ignorance of the Jewish population (excepting the few scholars and some learned rabbis) and the stuffy provincialism of the Jewish activities (excepting some Zionist groups) which convinced Rosenzweig that small improvements would be insufficient; only an overall reorientation of the cultural life could help.

It is of more than biographical interest to point out that Rosenzweig, in 1916, before attacking the problem of Jewish education, worked out a detailed programme (about fifty printed pages) of a German school reform under the title *Volksschule und Reichsschule* (People's School and State School).[2] Here he aims at overcoming the half-century old degeneration of schools into "institutions of bureaucratic State discipline". He advocates a truly universal, European, plan of study; narrow nationalist apologetics—the conscious, or subconscious basis of the instruction in history—is to be replaced by a global orientation which would permit a peaceful co-existence of all nations; the all-pervading historicism is to be replaced by a search for present-day relevance (which is not identical with immediate usability). Indoctrination should give way to independent investigation. Knowledge, gained in an atmosphere of freedom, should lead to an active participation in a life in which many different peoples share. Education, thus, is not an accumulation of skills or materials, but the ability to understand the diversified world we live in and the power to translate this understanding into action.

The radically humanist and universalist orientation—in many aspects reminiscent of the *Bildungsideal* of Wilhelm von Humboldt—betrays the European in Rosenzweig; it implies a devastating criticism of the trend German culture and education had taken in the preceding generations. He called his plan "a Central European education programme for Germany". He hoped that, subsequent to the peace treaty, a confederation of European States might develop. But soon he realized that this culturally united Europe would not come into existence. The plan remained merely a personal reflection on the state of things, and had no chance of being taken seriously.

Be this as it may, his general school programme shows us a man who was completely free of parochialism and spiritual narrowness. In such a spirit he approached, shortly afterwards, the issue of Jewish education. In the treatise *Zeit ists*[3] Rosenzweig outlined a detailed and imposing plan of an Academy for the Science of Judaism, the members of which would be both scholars and teachers. As scholars they would work on one of the several scientific projects undertaken by the Academy; a part of their time, however, they would devote to Jewish teaching in the community of their residence. The Jewish scholar today, Rosenzweig argued, should feel the responsibility of sharing his knowledge with the people and the schools; the youth in schools should be instructed by competent scholars and not by half-educated graduates of teacher's seminaries or by overworked rabbis; the Jewish communities should, as a part of their communal obligation, shoulder the bill for this over-all programme.

This new type of scholar-teacher, if carefully and patiently nurtured would, in time, restore a Jewish intelligentsia which in olden times used to be the core of the community and which is now so sorely missed. Judaism has become a province of specialists, while its power should be with the people. An uninformed—or ill-informed—Jew is an unconcerned Jew, especially in an otherwise literate society.

It Is Time contains also a meticulously prepared course of Jewish studies. Utilizing the existing framework of time—nine years at the *Gymnasium,* two hours weekly—Rosenzweig showed that by sufficient concentration and by eliminating any waste of time, Hebrew language, the Bible, the liturgy, the principal documents of classical Judaism, the major trends of Jewish thought and history could be fused into a coherent programme.

This programme, written at the Balkan front on Army postal cards (like the general school programme before, and the *magnum opus*, the *Star of Redemption,* shortly after), intrigued many thinking Jews in Germany. But the plan appeared to be too great a departure from the established. Its central point, the creation of a position of a teaching scholar and scholarly teacher, met with strong opposition from both the scholarly and the teaching groups. An academy was indeed established (in 1919). Its members were aware of the new requirements of Jewish scholarship, as compared with the aims of the nineteenth-century *Wissenschaft des Judentums*. Professor Julius Guttmann echoed Rosenzweig's wishes when he said: "What we look for in Jewish scholarship today is essentially that it shows us a way to the sources of Jewish life." But in reality its function (until the closing down in 1934) was the execution of a number of scholarly projects and the publication of results of individual research. The turn to the purely historical which the Academy had taken, prompted Rosenzweig, its initiator, to look to other ways of realizing his idea of a renaissance of Jewish learning.[4]

II

Frankfort-on-the-Main offered an opportunity. There existed in Frankfort a Jewish adult education institute *(Volkshochschule),* founded after the first World War upon the initiative of Dr. Eugen Mayer, the scholarly and energetic community administrator. Similar institutes existed in other larger Jewish communities, such as Berlin, Munich, Breslau. Rosenzweig, who happened to visit Frankfort in the Fall of 1919, was invited to head the adult institute there and was allowed to re-organize it in accordance with his own ideas. In preparation for this task, Rosenzweig wrote (in the beginning of 1920) the treatise *Bildung und kein Ende,*[5] a criticism of the cultural situation after the Emancipation and vigorous call to a meaningful Judaism.

In August 1920, Rosenzweig assumed the leadership of the Frankfort institute, which had already carried out two series of lecture courses. In collaboration with the then existing committee, Rosenzweig expanded the programme. Significant for this new trend was the implementation of the lecture courses by study groups mainly devoted to the "introduction into Jewish sources". The central position was to be given to courses in Hebrew language and classical writings.

It was clear that Rosenzweig aimed at more than imparting information on Jewish topics; the audience, accustomed at best to a passive enjoyment of lectures, should be taught to participate actively, to feel personally challenged by the texts before it. Slowly, and with the progress of studies, Rosenzweig hoped, the spirit of classical Jewish learning could be revived. This tendency Rosenzweig indicated by choosing the name *Freies Jüdisches Lehrhaus* (Free House of Jewish Studies). The reference to Beth ha-Midrash was intentional; the *Lehrhaus* should indeed become a modernized Beth ha-Midrash. The word "free" indicated that registration was open to all without an entrance examination; it should also convey the notion of freedom of inquiry. Rosenzweig submitted to his committee a detailed budget; tuition fee was by no means low; university students and members of youth organizations paid a reduced fee; lecturers and teachers, all of them part-time, received a respectable honorarium. The lectures and courses took place partly in rented halls, and partly in various communal buildings.

The academic year *(Lehrjahr)* consisted of three trimesters (October through December; January through March; April through June); most courses were given in one-hour weekly sessions; the courses in Hebrew twice weekly. A programme was issued for every trimester; the lectures and courses (an average of sixteen) in any given trimester were arranged in a manner so as to form a coherent whole; the dullness of a mere technical sequence of topics was skilfully avoided. A difficulty arose in connection with the listing of the date. It was against Rosenzweig's conviction to use in a publication of a Jewish Lehrhaus the year *anno domini;* he could not accept the argument that this is a mere civic convention; the committee, on the other hand, rejected the year of the Hebrew calendar as unfamiliar and confusing. As a result, no year was listed on the programme and only the sequence of the academic seasons was numbered.

The Jewish youth of Frankfort—as in any other German community—was split into many different organizations, orthodox, liberal, Zionist, neutral. At the outset of his Frankfort activity, Rosenzweig had to convince the various associations of the need to take a broader view, and, without giving up their particular policies, to unite in the pursuit of Jewish learning. That he succeeded—partly at least—in breaking down the stubborn resistance of the organizations is due only to his equally stubborn insistence on his plan and to the greater persuasiveness of his argument.

III

The *Lehrhaus* opened with a convocation on 17th October, 1920. Rosenzweig delivered the key address on the old and the new learning. While the old learning had its starting-point in the Torah and was designed to lead into life, the new learning, Rosenzweig said, will lead from wherever we stand in life back to the Torah. We shall not disregard whatever we are, not renounce whatever we have acquired, but lead everything back to Judaism. This learning will be a process from the periphery where we stand to the centre, which we still feel is Judaism, in spite of our alienation. Our purpose is not apologetics, self-defence, but an attempt at clarification within ourselves.[6]

The first trimester of the *Lehrhaus* (announced as the first trimester of the second academic year, the first having been conducted within the original adult institute) showed a registration of over five hundred people out of a community of almost 30,000 Jews. There were six lecture series, two parallel series each treating "classical Judaism" (the Torah and the Prophets), "historical Judaism" (Halakhah and Haggadah) and "modern Judaism" (Jewish movements and Jewish types). Two additional lecture series dealt with 'Near Eastern Art in the Biblical Period' and 'Mysticism in Pagan Antiquity, in Christianity and in Judaism'. There were two study groups, one in Hebrew liturgy and one in Bible, and two discussion groups. Rosenzweig himself gave the lectures on

Jewish types (in which he discussed the psychology of the Jew after the Emancipation), and taught the course in liturgy.

The most striking lectures were those on Halakhah, attended by about two hundred people. The lecturer, Rabbi Nehemiah A. Nobel, the leading conservative rabbi in Frankfort, presented an unusual combination of talmudic learning, mystical leanings, and love for Goethe. Both dogmatic traditionalists and free-thinking modernists felt the fascination and the strange power of this thinker. Rosenzweig, because of his clearly post-Goethean and non-mystical orientation, admired Nobel mainly for his profound knowledge of the rabbinic tradition.

Dr. Eduard Strauss, who taught the course on mysticism in the world religions and conducted a Bible study group, was a research chemist by profession and an ardent student of the history of religions. Once he had discovered the Bible he became an inspired interpreter of the Scriptures to those who had lost contact with Judaism and were trying to come back; his *Lehrhaus* group counted about thirty members.

Through Eduard Strauss, Rosenzweig came to know Dr. Richard Koch, a young university lecturer in the history of medicine. Koch hailed from an assimilated family; his Judaism consisted in early years in missing school on the High Holidays and visiting various old aunts. Later in life came the discovery of some central Jewish ideas and an increasingly strong Jewish consciousness. This background of the highly cultured Richard Koch moved Rosenzweig to persuade (or rather force) Koch to meet with a group of *Lehrhaus* people for informal talks. The spirited meetings moved from general to Jewish topics and continued for several years.

Rosenzweig's own lecture course, attended by about one hundred persons, was a failure. He was motivated by a passionate urge to teach, to interpret, to clarify. But he was simply unable to realize the intellectual limitations of even intelligent, university-trained men and women. He did not talk their language and they did not understand his. His listeners sensed his greatness; yet he did not want to be admired, but understood. There was something tragic in the situation of a man who so fully believed in the power of the dialogue and the discussion to be doomed to a monological, one-sided, activity. Thus, his direct and immediate influence extended to a small group of men and women; only indirectly, through intermediaries, through his explanatory essay, and finally, through the example of his life, did his word reach wider circles.

The pattern of this first trimester was followed in the remaining two of the second academic year (January to June 1921). Dr. Georg Salzberger gave survey courses in Jewish history and literature; Professor Franz Oppenheimer, the well-known sociologist, and Dr. Fritz Sternberg lectured on the building up of Palestine; Oppenheimer, who originated the idea of co-operative settlements in Palestine and initiated the Merhavya project, could draw on his own experience. Rabbi Nobel continued his deliberations of Halakhah, and Dr. Israel Rabin, the rabbinic scholar, discussed "the regeneration of the Jewish spirit". A course in comparative religion was given jointly by Dr. Eduard Strauss (Buddhism), Dr. Max Dienemann (Christianity), and Professor Joseph Horovitz, the Islamic scholar (Islam).

Rosenzweig taught (second trimester) a course (and a parallel seminar) in which he critically interpreted the major trends in German idealist philosophy from Kant to Hegel. The issues discussed were such as knowledge and belief, end and beginning, action and suffering, soul and body, life and death. The subtitle to the course, "About the use of common sense", gives an indication of what Rosenzweig was driving at: it is common sense (as against "pure thought" which "reduces the world" to the perceiving "self") which underlies Rosenzweig's own "New Thinking". In simplified form, Rosenzweig presented the thesis of his *Star of Redemption*. This course and seminar served Rosenzweig as a preparation for the writing—in the summer of that year—of a philosophical treatise which he called "the little book of common sense and sick reason".[7] It was the last essay which Rosenzweig wrote before the attack of paralysis which changed the course of his life.

Rosenzweig also taught (third trimester) a course: "Basic Issues of Jewish Knowledge", in which he dealt with the Hebrew language, the classical Jewish books and the problem of Jewish historiography. In a seminar, he analysed Hermann Cohen's *Religion of Reason from the Sources of Judaism*; six students participated in the close reading of Cohen's major work on Judaism.

Looking back on this first year of his *Lehrhaus* activity, Rosenzweig felt dissatisfied. The classes were well attended and the course in Hebrew had grown from one course in the first trimester to two in the second and three in the third trimester. But Rosenzweig expected a livelier, more intense response to the *Lehrhaus* scheme as a whole. The laziness, good-hearted inertness and complacency of the Frankfort audience infuriated the energetic director. He even considered for a while leaving Frankfort and accepting a leading teaching position offered him in Hamburg; Hamburg appeared to him more breezy, more alert and open-minded, "more English", as he expressed himself.

IV

But the following year (1921–22) brought a marked change. The number of students grew; there were over six hundred registrations (not counting auditors at single lectures), among them a goodly number of people of kind whom Rosenzweig wanted to see in the *Lehrhaus*. The expansion of the *Lehrhaus* group allowed Rosenzweig to plan a progressive freeing of the institute from the support (and influence) by committees, community representatives, people who were neither teachers nor students of the *Lehrhaus*. Only such an independence, Rosenzweig felt, could guarantee the vitally needed academic freedom. The teacher may only be dependent on those who, in turn, depend on him; only an inter-dependence of this kind is justifiable.

This "third academic year" offered such lecture courses as on the social problem in the Bible (Dr. B. May), on Christianity from Jesus and Paul to Goethe and Tolstoi (E. Strauss),[8] on the treatment of Jews and Judaism in modern literature (Georg Salzberger), and a course, with demonstrations, on places of Jewish historical interest in and around Frankfort. A course, given jointly by Dr. Fritz Edinger and Dr. Siegfried Kracauer of the *Frankfurter Zeitung*, concerned itself with religious and political movements in the contemporary Western world; against this background, Dr. Ernst Simon pictured the rise of the modern Jewish renaissance movement.

This was the first appearance in the *Lehrhaus* of Ernst Simon, who was to play a major rôle in the Jewish renaissance in Germany, before he went to Palestine (in 1928). In his early twenties at the time, Simon had just recently made a radical turn from assimilation and Jewish indifference to Zionism, and soon after to Judaism in its classical dimensions, to Jewish law, learning and the prophetic message of justice. He became one of the most honest and most passionate advocates of this message in our time; his Jewish consciousness grew in depth and urgency as its application to life situations grew more and more difficult.

Rabbi Nobel, whose fiftieth birthday (November 1921) gave occasion to a cordial community-wide celebration, announced a series of three lectures on Goethe's religious thought and the influence of the Bible on the poet. The day following the second lecture (21st January, 1922), Nobel fell ill, and died two days later. The memory of this mighty teacher the *Lehrhaus* observed by a yearly "Nobel lecture".

The Hebrew writer S. Y. Agnon (who with Ahad Haam, Bialik, Mrs. Shoshanah Persitz, and others sojourned in the neighbourhood of Frankfort before their departure to Palestine) conducted a small study group: he read his "The Scribe" and other short stories and explained them in Hebrew. Rosenzweig had hoped that the participants would be able to converse in Hebrew, but sadly realized that nobody really dared to, although everybody pretended to be a Hebraist. Nevertheless, the contact with the living Hebrew language and with one already eminent Hebrew author was an unforgettable event in the history of the Lehrhaus.

In December 1921, Rosenzweig and his wife visited Martin Buber in

Heppenheim (an easy distance from Frankfort) to renew the old, but not at all intimate, acquaintance. The talk led to the publications of hasidic tales and teachings, and Buber remarked that in all the years he had but once received an inquiry about the original Hebrew (or Yiddish) sources; he wished he could present some such sources to a group of interested people. Whereupon Rosenzweig suggested to Buber that he conduct such a study group in the *Lehrhaus*. Buber, who so far had appeared on many lecture platforms and enjoyed a tremendous prestige for his addresses, was attracted by the *Lehrhaus* method, which encouraged the intellectual intercourse between the speaker and the audience and had replaced the formal lecture by dialogical teaching. No other forum offered such an opportunity to a man who cultivated the dialogue as much as Buber. Rosenzweig, who in earlier years had a measure of scepticism about Buber's alleged mysticism, was now pleasantly surprised to find before him a solid, clear and sensible thinker. At that time Buber was writing his philosophical work *I and Thou,* and agreed to make this the basis for *Lehrhaus* lectures, to start together with the hasidic text seminar, in January 1922. In these lectures ("Religion as Presence") the audience (about one hundred and fifty men and women, Jews and Gentiles) witnessed a unique phenomenon; here, religious thought was no longer a recapitulation of past history but a present-day event of startling immediacy. Buber sharply criticized attempts to reduce religion to a philosophical fiction, or to a branch of culture, or to a means of personal self-assertion; these trends Buber called a suicide of the spirit. Religion is not a variant of undirected life but a knowledge which gives life direction and determines its law.

The lecture was followed by the hasidic seminar attended by a group limited to those who could understand a Hebrew text. These two courses established Buber's central position in the *Lehrhaus*. He, in turn, accepted the challenge of the *Lehrhaus* which took him, in his middle forties, out of the solitude of his Heppenheim study. He remained in close contact with students ever since.

Rosenzweig had scheduled, among other courses, a study course in the classical Jewish exegesis of the Book of Exodus. Higher Bible criticism Rosenzweig viewed with suspicion as based on mere hypotheses and therefore scientifically unreliable; he was ready (as he expressed in an unpublished letter) to change his attitude only if an "Elohist Genesis" would be actually found; otherwise, *hypotheses non fingo*. Since, therefore, the pre-history of the biblical text is, for the time being at least, out of reach, the only worthwhile endeavour would be "the attempt to find the way of the biblical text, as it is, through the ages; i.e., to study, not what caused the word of the Bible but the effect it had on the reader. If I study the old Hebrew commentaries, I see what happened to the text in the course of our Jewish life. This, too, is a study of history and one free of hypotheses". On this basis Rosenzweig planned to introduce the reading of classical commentaries.

But in January 1922, shortly after Nobel's death, Rosenzweig noticed strange signs of illness which Dr. Richard Koch diagnosed as a progressive paralysis. Despite the incipient paralysis of speech, Rosenzweig continued teaching; the meetings of the study group were transferred to a large room of the house, the attic apartment of which Rosenzweig and his wife occupied; smaller groups met in Rosenzweig's book-lined study. (In the later years of Rosenzweig's illness this room became the most hallowed place for German Jewry and for Frankfort Jews in particular). In the third trimester (April through June 1922) the discussion group and the advanced Hebrew course was dropped as the strain on Rosenzweig increased; for elementary and intermediate Hebrew Mrs. Edith Rosenzweig substituted for her husband.

V

Rosenzweig prepared the programme for the coming winter trimester and sent it to Buber and Eduard Strauss, feeling that his would be his last action on behalf of the *Lehrhaus*. In order to secure the continuation of its work, Rosenzweig suggested the appointment of his friend, Dr. Rudolf Hallo. Hallo, in his mid-twenties, was an art historian and archaeologist with a special interest in Egyptian and Semitic languages. Like Rosenzweig, he went through a period of estrangement until he had found his way back to an affirmation of Judaism. His intellectual sincerity, nobility of character, quiet and thorough scholarship and, not the least, his Jewish Odyssey, justified Rosenzweig's choice. Officially, Rosenzweig remained the head of the *Lehrhaus*; Hallo became his deputy in the administration and his successor in the *Lehrhaus* lectureship.[9]

In the fourth academic year (1922-23) Hallo taught the three Hebrew courses, conducted study groups (Psalms, the weekly portions of the Pentateuch, History of the First Commonwealth) and held lecture courses on biblical history. Martin Buber lectured on "Original Forms of Religious Life" (Magic, Sacrifice, Mystery, Prayer) with the corresponding seminar in which he analysed Ancient Near Eastern, Greek, Jewish and Christian religious writings. The second of Buber's lecture courses was "Prayer", with a seminar in which he interpreted selected Psalms.

Ernst Simon gave a series of lectures, "From Mendelssohn to Herzl", in which he broadly outlined the course of modern Jewish, political and intellectual, history. The historian turned prophet when he spoke of the coming phase in history which would see a contest between the Asiatic East and the West; he expressed the hope that Zionist Judaism would find its place in the Asian family of nations. In a seminar, Simon discussed some literary sources (e.g. Friedlaender's epistle to Propst Teller and Schleiermacher's answer; A. Geiger's reform suggestions; *The Jewish Question* by Karl Marx, Herzl's *Diaries* and the *Sabbath essay* by Rabbi Nobel). Simon also lectured on the place of Judaism in the nineteenth-century German philosophy of history, especially in Hegel's system, and delivered the first Nobel memorial lecture.

Among other courses we may mention the lectures on Karaism by Dr. Erich Fromm, then a sociologist and student of Jewish lore.

For the summer months the *Lehrhaus* instituted, for the first time in that "dead" season, intensive study courses in Bible and in medieval Hebrew literature. There was an introductory course in Rashi, given by Ernst Simon, attended by twelve students; an advanced course in Rashi to the Book of Exodus, given by Erich Fromm, in which five students participated. Fortunately for the *Lehrhaus*, Dr. Gershom (Gerhard) Scholem just then spent a semester in Frankfort before following a call to the University Library in Jerusalem. He led a study group in the Book of Daniel and a reading seminary in the *Zohar Hadash*, attended by ten students. It was no doubt the most penetrating and ingenious course in textual interpretation the participants could ever be exposed to.

Rosenzweig was happy to see the growth of the "learning" aspect of the *Lehrhaus* as against the "curiosity" phase represented by the big lectures. Especially in Ernst Simon's course there were some who had started in the *Lehrhaus* out of curiosity and were now engaged in dedicated study.

In that year the *Lehrhaus* had reached its highest enrollment: eleven hundred (4 per cent of the total Jewish population of Frankfort), an increase of four hundred over the preceding year.

VI

With the end of the academic year, Rudolf Hallo, who had enjoyed considerable success as a lecturer, resigned from his position. In the course of the year's work differences arose between Hallo and Rosenzweig which could not easily be bridged. The approach to and the manner of the instruction in Bible led to a serious conflict; Hallo could not act against his convictions; Rosenzweig, though moving steadily towards his end, was not ready to give up his interests in life. Rosenzweig had urged Hallo to study daily Gemara ("you simply can't do without"), which Hallo gladly accepted; but Rosenzweig had expected also, somewhat impatiently, that Hallo would go further in accepting the forms of traditional Jewish life ("an open-minded but rooted conservativism") for which Hallo was not or not yet ready. The discussion was carried on in writing; unfortunately, these letters were lost in the Hitler period. In spite of the conflict, the two men remained friends, and Hallo continued to give occasional lectures at the *Lehrhaus*.

The leadership of the *Lehrhaus* was from then on (fall 1923) shared between Rosenzweig, Buber, Richard Koch and Eduard Strauss. Dr. Rudolf Stahl, a young and spirited lawyer, became the secretary of the *Lehrhaus* and a liaison officer between the public and the administration. In May 1924 he was succeeded by Martin Goldner, a medical student and a keen and sensitive leader in the liberal youth movement. Like Hallo and Stahl, he belonged to the circle of Rosenzweig's younger friends and disciples; a number of important theological letters of Rosenzweig are addressed to Goldner.

For the fifth academic year (1923–24), Rosenzweig planned a further expansion of the study groups; from the very beginning he had considered the lectures as means of acquainting the larger public with the *Lehrhaus* and of leading the serious student to a more concentrated, text-based learning. In order to achieve the first objective he was ready to employ what he called "crude and cheap methods: famous names, sensational topics, elegant programmes, high admission fees and rough treatment."[10] He had already succeeded in making known to the *Kultur*-obsessed German Jew that Judaism is not a concern of the backward and the obscurants. He had made allowance for current literary tastes; now he wanted to advance in the direction of cultivation of Jewish learning. New men were called to the faculty to implement this programme: Salman Baruch Rabinkoff, an outstanding rabbinic scholar from Russia, residing in Heidelberg, came to teach Talmud; the same field was to be represented by the young associate justice at the municipal court in Frankfort and very learned talmudic jurist and historian of Halakhah, Dr. Alfred Freimann; Ernst Simon was to cultivate historical source material; the Jerusalem orientalist Josef Rivlin, who had come to Frankfort for graduate Islamic studies, was assigned Medieval Hebrew literature; the present writer was entrusted with the field of Midrash and biblical exegesis.

Also in the general programme the study of Jewish sources was increasingly stressed. Buber, who lectured on the Baal Shem, discussed the various hasidic interpretations of the first sentence of Genesis; his lectures on Jewish eschatology were accompanied by a reading of the Fourth Book of Ezra; Rabbi Leo Baeck of Berlin, who as guest lecturer spoke on the love of God and the divine worship, analysed talmudic and medieval texts on the subject; Ernst Simon taught a course on the Sabbath and conducted a seminar on related texts.

Besides Dr. Baeck, whose earnestness as a teacher of living religion made a deep impression on the *Lehrhaus*, there were two other guest lecturers: Professor Adolf (Abraham) Fraenkel, mathematician at the Marburg University and a Hebrew scholar of note, came to lecture on the Oral Law and its formulations from the Mishnah to the Shulhan Arukh. The other was Dr. Nathan Birnbaum, then living in Hamburg, whose dramatic life fascinated Jewish youth in the twenties. Pre-Herzlian Zionist and originator of the term "Zionism", Birnbaum had gone through a stormy development from atheistic Zionism through Galut autonomism and Yiddishism to religiosity and finally to strict observance of the Law and affiliation with the Agudas Jisroel (which he later abandoned to live lonely with the Lonely). He spoke on the "Significance of Form in Judaism"[11] and fervently pleaded for a commitment to meaningful Jewish practice and the perennial ideas of orthodoxy.

The fact that Birnbaum spoke in an institution at which (among others) Buber "the heretic" taught, created a stir in the orthodox camp. The *Israelit*, the valiant weekly of the Orthodoxy, reported at length on the Birnbaum lectures but protested against the "academic freedom which is unknown to Halakhah" and which 'the concept of religious purity of tranditional Judaism cannot tolerate.'[12] By its very existence, the *Lehrhaus* performed an important function in challenging religious intolerance. In cultivating freedom of expression, the *Lehrhaus* did not aim at a glossing over of differences or at creating a superficial harmony, but at a clear, unbiased understanding of issues.

In the same period, Buber presented a collection of hasidic teachings which later appeared under the title *Das verborgene Licht*[13] and conducted a seminar on the Hebrew originals; Dr. Leo Strauss, incisive philosophical critic, led an analytical reading of Hermann Cohen's *Religion of Reason*; the journalist Dr. Alfons Paquet, a Christian lover of Palestine and believer in its future, spoke about the country's past and the new, pioneering life; the banker Leopold Merzbach considered Jewish business ethics. Eduard Strauss read Rosenzweig's recently written introduction to the *Collected Jewish Writings* by Hermann Cohen in which he traced Cohen's development from a neo-Kantian academic philosopher to a warm, believing Jew. When Strauss finished reading the excitingly written piece, the session, held in memory of Rabbi Nobel, turned into a moving tribute for Rosenzweig, who could no longer speak.

Rosenzweig had then completed the first edition of his *Judah ha-Levi* work, which offered translations of a group of poems and a study—in the form of a commentary—of the poet's religious thinking. In a special session of the *Lehrhaus*, with Buber in the chair, the actress Louise Dumont recited a selection from Rosenzweig's translation which faithfully reproduced the metre and the rhythm of the Hebrew original.

The courses in Hebrew language were given by Mrs. Edith

Rosenzweig and others. An attempt was made to give Hebrew courses for school children; they were conducted by Ruth Nobel, the rabbi's charming daughter.

VII

The sixth academic year (1924–25) brought to Frankfort Dr. Benno Jacob, rabbi of Dortmund and distinguished Bible commentator. (His great commentary on the Genesis appeared in 1934 in the Schocken Verlag and was hardly noticed by biblical students). The participants in his lectures and seminar on "From Adam to Abraham" went through two preparatory courses given in the preceding trimester. Buber gave lectures (with readings) on the "Suffering Servant" in Isaiah and a study course on the *Sayings of the Fathers;* Leo Strauss analysed Spinoza's *Theologico-Political Tractate;* the Spinoza scholar Dr. Carl Gebhardt spoke on Leone Ebreo, Uriel da Costa and Spinoza; Ernst Simon lectured on the concept of the Jewish state, using as his text the Books of Samuel; the young Orientalist, Dr. Walter Fischel, lectured on the social and economic conditions of modern Palestine; Henrik Landau read parts of *Hovot ha-Levavot;* the present writer taught history of the Jewish liturgy. Of particular interest was a lecture series, given jointly by the Professors Karl Reinhardt, Josef Horovitz and Franz Schultz on major places of contact between Judaism and other civilizations: Alexandria (Hellenism), Cordova (Islam), Berlin (Germanism). Also a reading of the Memoirs of Glückel of Hameln by a grand old lady, Bertha Pappenheim, a direct descendant of Glückel. The Nobel lecture of the year was delivered by Richard Koch on "Goethe on Sickness and Health".

Martin Goldner was in charge of youth meetings where questions arising from the Jewish situation in the modern world were discussed—a perennial problem indeed. The reports of the meetings were sent to Rosenzweig. Rosenzweig addressed an epistle to the four discussion leaders, outlining his opinion on one of the central theological issues, "the boundary between the divine and the human."[14]

The seventh academic year (1925–26) continued the emphasis on the study groups. Among the outstanding lectures of the year were Dr. Leo Loewenthal's "On the Periphery of Jewish History", Ernst Simon's "Major Trends in Jewish History", Josef Rivlin's "History of the Hebrew Language", Prof. Richard Wilhelm's "The Jews in China", Dr. Julius Blau's "Jewish Colonization in Russia" and Eduard Strauss's "Dante". The Protestant minister Hermann Schafft of Cassel, a loyal friend of Judaism, lectured on the role of the Old Testament for the Church and, in a special meeting (not open to the public), engaged with Martin Buber in a critical discussion on Judaism and Christianity. Buber, who more than any other contemporary Jew attempted to interpret Judaism to the non-Jewish world, made (and still makes) the point very distinct where the Jew must say "no" to the Christian and thus to the spiritual structure of the Western world. At that time Buber and Rosenzweig—the latter in a super-human struggle against overwhelming technical difficulties—had started on their novel translation of the Hebrew Bible; the Genesis rendition had just been completed, and Buber presented examples at the fourth Nobel memorial meeting.

The Frankfort Jewish public grew accustomed to the splendid performances and to the incessant stimulation. In the course of the last year or over a somewhat longer period the general attendance fell, and the transition from the curious listeners to those who were seriously studying became insignificant. Rosenzweig, who had allowed himself to foster the first only for the sake of the second (and also to have the first pay for the second), clearly diagnosed the situation and decided greatly to reduce the regular activities: the big lectures as a failure, the study groups as economically untenable.

The start of the eighth academic year (1926–27) was announced in the press but the usual (exquisitely printed) lists of courses were no longer issued. The Bible course by Eduard Strauss and a course in biblical exegesis, both of long standing, were continued. The discussion with Hermann Schafft was resumed. The Nobel memorial lectures were regularly held throughout the years; the one of 1930, e.g., dealt with "Elisha ben Abuya: Judaism in late Antiquity". In January 1929, the University of Jerusalem was the subject of a special session in Rosenzweig's home. The regular Sabbath and holiday services held in Rosenzweig's study (since the High Holidays of 1922) and the table talks after the services became an expression of the *Lehrhaus* tradition once the regular programme was discontinued. The group that, in various forms and degrees, cultivated the *Lehrhaus* tradition, included, besides some of the before mentioned, Dr. Dora Edinger, Dr. Hans Epstein, Josef and Eli Feuchtwanger, Lotte Fürth, Carl and Paul Guggenheim, Dr. Fritz Laupheimer, Leo Löwenthal, Dr. Eugen Mayer, Dr. Leo Moser, Henry Rothschild, Ilse Seligmann, Margarete Susman, Dr. Richard Tuteur, Dr. Franz Wolf.

After Rosenzweig's death (10th December, 1929)[15] the *Lehrhaus* group met at the Hebrew anniversary (8. Kislev) for a *Lernstunde*. In 1930 the topic was the creation of the world and the building of the Tabernacle; in 1931, the last words of David; in 1932, the sayings of Balaam. The expositions were based on the commentary implied in the Buber-Rosenzweig translation of the Bible, the work to which Rosenzweig had given all his devotion since the *Lehrhaus* suspended its public function.

VIII

From 1920–1926 the *Lehrhaus* had offered ninety lecture courses and conducted one hundred and eighty study groups, seminars and discussion meetings. Sixty-four lecturers had participated in the programmes, among them fifteen who had given four or more courses and could be considered members of the permanent faculty.[16] Forty-two of the study courses were introductory courses into the Hebrew language and the basic books. About forth of the seminars concerned the Hebrew Bible, biblical problems and the history of ancient Israel; this number does not include Eduard Strauss's reading of the Bible in the German translation which was a regular feature on each trimester programme. The talmudic-midrashic literature (mostly reading of texts) was the subject of thirty courses. Various periods of Jewish history were treated in ten courses; the comparatively limited space accorded to Jewish history is to be explained by Rosenzweig's critical attitude to this discipline and its underlying philosophies. However, there were fifteen more courses on nineteenth-century and on contemporary Judaism (Emancipation, assimilation, anti-Semitism, nationalism, Zionism, Palestine, Jewish colonization) which are usually classified as Jewish history. Medieval Hebrew literature (with an emphasis on Judah ha-Levi and Maimonides) was studied in fourteen courses, as against merely six courses allowed for a sampling of Modern Hebrew and Yiddish literature. Fifteen courses were devoted to Jewish liturgy, the synagogue, prayer, a theme which occupies a central position in Rosenzweig's Jewish system. About thirty courses attempted to approach the vast field of theology, mysticism, ethics, comparative religion, Judaism and Christianity, and some major problems of faith. The fields of study, of course, overlap and interrelate; the above statistical analysis therefore, is a mere approximation to the actual state of things. The list does not include subjects of a general nature (art, general literature, language, philosophy, social, economic and political issues), discussions of the Jewish spirit (difficult to define), special assemblies and lectures, and meetings arranged for the youth.

What did the *Lehrhaus* convey beyond the treatment of the many Jewish (and related general) subjects and beyond imparting an amount of material Hebrew and Jewish knowledge?

Richard Koch had pointed out[17] that a hundred years ago a *Lehrhaus* in Germany would have been an institution for the advancement of European *Bildung* among Jews; at the beginning of the century, when Central European Jews were busy defending their good name, an institution by the name of *"Jewish" Lehrhaus* would have been avoided as too conspicuous; at its time however, the *Lehrhaus* wanted to help Jews "to live our own true life in communion with those that lived before us and those who will come after us". He and others, of course, realized that the Jew's "true" life has been reduced, obscured, if not destroyed by the over-zealous philosophy of enlightenment and by the misuse of science and art as substitutes for religion. Koch, following the lead of Rosenzweig, pointed to the Hebrew language and the Scriptures read in the original as being "what connects us with the Jewish centuries and millennia; this is like a home, like a place of worship".

Rosenzweig, half jokingly, half seriously, spoke of "smuggling" Judaism into the general education so dear to the Jew; he wanted the German Jew to become ashamed of knowing so little. Once Jewish knowledge is acquired, naturally many things will change within him. First among these will be a rejection of apologetics which, in its strange mixture of inferiority and superiority feelings, had become so sorry and perplexing a spectacle.

Furthermore, knowledge, or learning, will break down the par-ticularism and regionalism so dangerous to the community of Israel. Out of this remembrance of the common ground Rosenzweig expected a change of mind towards the thoroughly misunderstood East-European Jew; the economically and socially better off Western Jew should feel at one with the simple, the poor, the despised, the forsaken among his brethren, wherever they are. This, to Rosenzweig, was not only a matter of "social justice"; it is a part of being a Jew. Just as a Jew— as Rosenzweig wanted to educate him—lives in communication with the great periods of his past, so he lives in kinship with his brethren everywhere in the present. In speaking of the "Germanism" of the German Jew, Rosenzweig had questioned the ability of the emancipated German Jew, the passionate admirer of Goethe and Schiller, to feel perfectly at one with the simple, typical rank and file German. This at-oneness a Jew must reach with regard to his fellow Jews.

The *Lehrhaus* avoided any form of provincialism, secular or sacred; Rosenzweig stressed the "a-rabbinical and anti-ghetto universal" character of the programme.[18] A proportionately small number of lectur-ers were rabbis (about 15 per cent); Rosenzweig's ideal type of scholar-teacher was to be clearly distinguished from the practising rabbi. Yet Jewish learning, in which there is no boundary line between the sacred and the secular material, Rosenzweig considered a holy pursuit. Once he explained to a Christian minister (who happened to be his own cousin) that "Jewish learning is no theology; in what it means to us it roughly corresponds to your sacrament", adding, that if he speaks before Jews it is something like "your communion".[19] He did not expect his corre-spondent to understand this.

This implication of sacredness in learning, to be sure, remained un-noticed by the greater majority of the *Lehrhaus* people. More readily noticeable was the universality of Jewish interests, the emphasis on the relationship of the present to the past, the accent on the original text, on the basic book (instead of the endless talk "about" problems) and the big city-like atmosphere in which Judaism was now allowed to operate. A whiff of fresh air breathed through the sessions.

A critical and not too benevolent observer would not have failed to detect a certain dilettantism in some lectures, an undue aestheticism in others; the thrill of the rediscovery of Judaism occasionally brought about an exhibition of naïveté in applying the term "learning". And there was the ubiquitous *nudnik,* male and female, who could not find rest unless all his profoundly persistent questions were adequately answered. Such phenomena, unavoidable under the circumstances, were of negligible significance in the over-all picture of an intellectually honest and clean movement.

It was Rosenzweig's conviction that learning—in the classical sense of the word—will not remain an intellectual pursuit but will lead into doing. By this he meant quite simply the loving observance of the Jewish law. Rosenzweig approached the Jewish law undogmatically; the regard for the personal ability to fulfil the law and the honest choice of what to do and what to leave undone, point in the direction of broad liberalism. But, in opposition to Buber's clearly meta-nomian stand,[20] Rosenzweig considered the law, parallel to learning, an integral part of classical Judaism. This issue of the law, never directly expressed but always implied in the *Lehrhaus* activities, was the least apprehended of Rosenzweig's ideas. The Western (non-orthodox) Jew remained a complex entity, torn between the appeal of European Emancipation and a vaguely understood Jewish heritage while Rosenzweig, in this respect quite lonely, moved toward an even greater simplicity in his Judaism.

In view of the intellectual situation of West-European Jewry, Rosenzweig considered the *Lehrhaus* as he constructed it as an institution for a *time of transition.* It is a time "where the teachers of old, the scholars, are no longer recognized as guides, and the new ones have not yet appeared."[21] Only the state of transition made Rosenzweig feel justified in welcoming to his faculty the non-professional but serious student of Judaism next to the authoritative teacher, and placing, e.g., the amateur Richard Koch on the same programme with the learned Alfred Freimann. Only the unprofessional man, Rosenzweig argued, will take the naïve questions of the other fellow more seriously than his own measured answers; a mixture of boldness and modesty is required for "a pursuit so dangerous and yet so necessary".[22] The transition period will have terminated when the new learning (which Rosenzweig defined as a way back from the periphery where the student finds himself to the core of Judaism) will have become a learning and thinking from within.

IX

The Frankfort *Lehrhaus*, its underlying thought and its programme, served as an example for the establishment of a number of similar institutions in other German cities. In 1925 a *Lehrhaus* was opened at Stuttgart; in 1928 at Cologne where Rabbi A. Kober, Professor Bruno Kisch and Leo Gruenebaum were especially active; also in 1928 Dr. Max Gruenewald organized a *Lehrhaus* in Mannheim which existed until 1938. The Cologne *Lehrhaus* closed in 1929. Also in the later twenties a *Lehrhaus* was started in Wiesbaden (by Dr. Paul Lazarus), in Karlsruhe, and in Munich where Dr. Ludwig Feuchtwanger was the leading spirit; the Breslau *Lehrhaus* was headed by Dr. Albert Lewkowitz; in 1929 a School of Jewish Youth was instituted in Berlin after the Frankfort pattern. Members of the Frankfort faculty were frequently guest lecturers at the sister institutions.[23] In 1940, an Institute of Jewish Learning was founded in London by Abraham J. Heschel prior to his coming to America. In the U.S.A. a *Franz Rosenzweig Lehrhaus* was established in the early forties at the Congregation Habonim in New York under the leadership of Rabbi Hugo Hahn, formerly of Essen, and Eduard Strauss from the original Frankfort school. The youngest member in the *Lehrhaus* movement is an institution called *Für ein Jüdisches Lehrhaus* in Zurich, Switzerland, founded and directed by the young Jewish philosopher Dr. Hermann Levin Goldschmidt.

The Frankfort Lehrhaus had a re-birth in 1933. The tragic situation in which German Jews—most of them unexpectedly—found themselves evoked forces of heroic inner resistance. Many Jews reacted to the events in self-respect, even with pride. The degradation of the Jewish name was answered by many by a more dedicated adherence to the name of Israel. In this spirit Frankfort Jews re-opened the *Lehrhaus* on 19th November, 1933 and offered courses and guidance for several years—until public Jewish activity was no longer possible. The mighty word of Martin Buber, who headed the *Lehrhaus* in those crucial years, was heard beyond the limits of the Frankfort community. He reminded the Jew of the Sinai covenant which established a community of faith that lives on against the judgment of those who carry the sword. In the new *Lehrhaus* the Jew received an orientation towards new ways of life in the land of Israel and in other parts of the world. But also, brought again into a living contact with the word of the Bible and the classical tradition of Israel, he learned to be a Jew. And once a year, an hour was set aside to remember the man who in the trenches of World War One had planned the foundation of the *Lehrhaus*.

NOTES

1. This first comprehensive account of the *Freies Jüdisches Lehrhaus* in Frankfort is based on Rosenzweig's own writings and letters on the subject, on a

collection of printed programmes and press reports, and on detailed notes and personal recollections of the writer who followed the development of the Lehrhaus from its beginning and belonged to its faculty from 1923 to 1928.

2. Reprinted in Rosenzweig's *Kleinere Schriften*, Berlin 1937.

3. An English translation, *It is Time*, is included in *On Jewish Learning*, New York 1955.

4. On the Academy see Ernst Simon, "Franz Rosenzweig und das jüdische Bildungsproblem", *Korrespondenzblatt der Akademie für die Wissenschaft des Judentums*, XI, Berlin 1930; *Festgabe zum zehnjährigen Bestehen der Akademie für die Wissenschaft des Judentums*, Berlin 1929, esp. the article by Julius Guttmann; N. N. Glatzer, "Ha-Hinukh ha-Yotzer ve-ha-Madda ha-Maamin", *Sefer ha-Shanah li-Yehude Amerika*, VIII-IX, 1946; Introduction to *On Jewish Learning*. On Academy and Lehrhaus see E. Simon's essay in *On Franz Rosenzweig*, Hillel Foundation, Jerusalem 1956.

5. An English translation, by Clement Greenberg, appeared in *Franz Rosenzweig: His Life and Thought* (henceforth quoted as *Life and Thought*), under the title "On Being a Jewish Person". The full text, in English translation, also by C. Greenberg, appeared in *On Jewish Learning*, under the title "Towards a Renaissance of Jewish Learning".

6. The extensive draft of this address is printed in an English translation in *Life and Thought*, pp. 228–234, and in *On Jewish Learning*, pp. 95–102.

7. Rosenzweig withdrew the manuscript from the publisher who had already scheduled the publication. The book appeared in an English translation under the title *Understanding the Sick and the Healthy*, New York 1954. The introduction is reprinted in the present volume. The German edition appeared in Düsseldort in 1964.

8. Some of the lectures appeared in *Der Jude* VI–VII (1923–23) and *Die Kreatur* (1926–27).

9. Towards the end of 1922 Rosenzweig wrote a letter extending over forty long pages to Hallo, to acquaint him with the workings of the Lehrhaus. An abridged version was published in Rosenzweig's *Briefe*, ed. by Edith Rosenzweig and Ernst Simon, Berlin 1935, pp. 448–468.

10. *Briefe*, p. 466.

11. An essay by Birnbaum by that title appeared in *Jeschurun* XI (1924), 3–4.

12. *Der Israelit*, March 27, 1924.

13. Now included in his *Tales of the Hasidim*, New York 1947 and 1948.

14. "Divine and Human", in *Life and Thought*, pp. 242–247; *On Jewish Learning*, pp. 119–124.

15. The date was erroneously given as December 9, 1929 in my editions of *Franz Rosenzweig: His Life and Thought*, p. 367, and *Understanding the Sick and the Healthy*, p. 106.

16. Of the sixty-four, one half no longer is among the living, eleven live now in the land of Israel, eleven in the United States, four in England; the rest could not be located at this writing (1955).

17. In his article on the Lehrhaus, in *Der Jude* VII (1923), pp. 116–125.

18. *Briefe*, p. 458.

19. *Briefe*, p. 412.

20. See the exchange of letters on the subject in *On Jewish Learning*, pp. 109–118.

21. *On Jewish Learning*, p. 17.

22. *Ibid*.

23. There might have been other such Lehrhauses of which the present writer has no record.

כשבגר יותר הבין כי המות הוא השורש הנסתר של הגות בני אדם וממנו הדחיפה
להכרת האמת·האדם שחרדת מות עליו לא ימצא את פתרון חייו בשיטה מחשבתית
שאין בה מקום ליחיד, לפרט, באשר בכלל ה׳כל׳ הפילוסופי הוא· נשמת אדם
תמצא את תיקונה רק בשעה שנודעה לה אהבת האל המעוררת בה יחס של אהבה
לזולתה· באהבה זו יחריש האדם ותגיע נשמתו לתיקונה וסר מר המות (כוכב
הגאולה, חלק שני, ספר שני)·

בשמיני לכסלו (עשירי לדצמבר) באה חליפתו של פרנץ רוזנצוייג· הגיעו המות
שכבר התגבר עליו בחייו ובלעו לנצח· עדים המלים שציוה לחרות על מצבתו·
אנכי תמיד עמך·

יב· אם אין כאן מקרה – דבר כה זר בחיי רוזנצוייג – השנה ההיא מתבארת רק
כשנת חתימה מדעת ומרצון· וגם מה שאירע לכתחילה כ׳מקרה׳ ובלי דעת,
בדיעבד מצא את מקומו הראוי לו בתכנית שנה זו·

חזיונות לב ועשתונות, שאלות ותשובותיהן, מעשים ופעולות, שעסק בהם במשך
ימי חייו רובם עלו בפניו או העלה ברוחו אחד אחד על מנת לזקקם ולטהרם בשנת
חתימה, ועל מנת להוסיף להם תוספת רוח יתירה ולהחזירם בתיקונם למקור כל
חיים·

בס' שמואל ב· וכך שמע רוזנצוייג – ימים אחדים לפני מותו – את הקול הטהור
ומטהר של המקרא· ובנו רפאל· שהיה אז כבן שבע שנים, נרעש ונפחד כאילו
היה עד למעשה ההווה לפניו, ויצא את החדר מתוך רגשי מחאה· ברביעי לדצמבר
חיבר רוזנצוייג שיר תודה לחנה רובינה שתורגם עברית ע״י ש· שלום:

הבאת אלי חדרי הצר עמך

אותה ברית הנפש, הזדככות תוגה,

בהן בחוץ תברי האלפים'· –

נרעש היה האב, נרעש הבן,

אולם הלה, שטוף דמע חיש עזב

מצת חמת מרי את המקום, –

וכה חדש בך עז הנצחון

של הראשון לחזיונות תוגה:

'כיבוש מלט' המחזה לתפסיס

לב אזרחיה של אתונה כה

הרעיש – עד כי ענשו את המשורר·

את, נין גזענו הקדמון, את, אם

לחזיונות תוגה בשפת עברית,

אודך על כי בריתי מידך!

ואחרי יומיים כתב למרטין בובר שביקר אז בבית אמו של רוזנצוייג בקאטל שיבאר
לה את הרמז שב'בריה': קתרסיס, כלומר הזדככות פנימית הבאה לאדם, ושבאה
לו לרוזנצוייג בשמעו את קול היוצא מדברי המקרא·

יא· יש עוד הגות לב אחת שרוזנצוייג עמד עליה והוא המות· כבן כ״א (ובשנת 1907)
כתב ביומנו שהוא משתומם על עצמו שאין לו כל יחס לבעית המות· לא עברו
ימים מועטים (ובשנת 1908) עד שהעיר לחבר באחד הבקרים – שעת החזרת הנפש:
אשרי האיש שבהשכימו בבוקר מרגיש בנס התחייה ממות לילי; גדול ממנו האדם
הזוכה למות מתוך דעת צלולה והצועד מתוך הכרה ברורה מן העולם הזה לעולם
הבא·

משתמשים הסופרים במונח 'ביבל' כדי לציין את כתבי הקדש שלנו, אף על פי
ששם זה מציין – לפי גזירת ההיסטוריה המערבית ותרבותה – את הספר המאחד
בו את 'הברית הישנה' והברית החדשה! אלא נראה שגם בתוך החיבור היהודי
המודרני ביותר נבלעה עקשנותנו הנושנה של ישראל המסרבת לקבל את גזירת
ההיסטוריה.

אמנם, מוסיף רוזנצוייג, אף אם נשמור על שלנו ונלך בדרך המיוחדת לנו, יש
לדעת, שנחלתנו רק חלק אחד בעולם הנברא. פנינו מועדות בכיוון הסודי
שבבריאה, אך השלימות נסתרה ממני.

דברים אלה שאמרם רוזנצוייג כמעט בלשון חיבורו היסודי (כוכב הגאולה, חלק ג,
ע' 200) הם האחרונים שהכינם לדפוס.

י. התנ״ך הוא ההווה האמיתי של עם ישראל – הכרה זו משמשת לרוזנצוייג הסבר
לכמה בעיות בחיינו ובספרותנו הקלאסית. העם גלה, ובגלותו זו מסרב להתיחס
לנכסי הזמנים ולהישגי תרבות הסביבה כלדבר של ממש, ולקבלם כמציאות
וכהווה. אך התנ״ך ושפתו לא גלו כי אם בקדושתם עומדים, בחינת ממש והווה. ואופי
של הווה זה אינו נותן לישראל להסתגל לשפות אומות העולם ולהתישב בבית
ספרותם ישיבת קבע (ועיין כוכב הגאולה, חלק ג, ע' 53).

בפירושו לשירי יהודה הלוי (ע' 161) מיחד רוזנצוייג את הדיבור על המשורר העברי
של ימי הביניים. פייטן זה, אומר רוזנצוייג, אינו שוכח אף רגע שבגלות הוא. בעוד
ששירת האומות משמשת כלי קיבול לרשמי העולם סביבה, מרחיק ממנו הפייטן
את העולם החיצון וההווה שבו חי וטובע בהם חותם נכר וגלות. ובמה יושג
יחס זה? על ידי זה שהמשורר משוה לנגדו תמיד את ההווה התנ״כי, כי שם ביתו.
המתהווה במקרא זהו ההווה של אמת. וכך נהפך ההווה שבו חי להווה מדומה,
שאינו אלא משל ואליגוריה. הציטטה המקראית שבשיר אינה באה לברר את חיי
הזמן, כי אם מאורעות הזמן משמשים פירוש למקרא ומשל לאמיתו. הפייטן העברי
המכונה לנצרות ולאיסלאם בשם אדום וישמעאל אינו מבאר את קורות זמנו מתוך
התנ״ך, כי אם את התנ״ך מתוך תנאי זמנו. הציטטה אינה איפוא בחינת קישוט, כי
אם האמצעי על ידו מזדההה המשורר עם ההווה התנ״כי. זמנו של המשורר זר
לרוחו. מטומאת גלות זו מיטהר המשורר במים חיים של המקרא.

בראשית דצמבר 1929 הציג תיאטרון הבימה בפרנקפורט את המחזה תמר
לקלדירון. לפי הצעת אחד מידידיו של רוזנצוייג ביקרה השחקנית הגדולה מרת
חנה רובינה אצלו וקראה לפניו קטעים מן המחזה ואחר כך את מעשה אמנן ותמר

של זה לא נשאר בכלל ישראל אות היא לנכדיו שברוח· כי, כך ממשיך רוזנצויג,
מנדלסון - השקפת עולם של תקופתו היתה בעזרו והוא עצמו יכול היה לשמור
על כנותם של שני חלקי הסינתיזה המסוכנת· אך מנדלסון לא לימדנו כיצד לעמוד
בסכנה, ונכשלנו· לא זה הדרך· לפנינו התפקיד הנועז לבחור בדרך חדשה· דברים
אלה בנחת נאמרו ובלי החריפות הרגילה אצל רוזנצויג· אך יש כאן רמז אחרון
לטעות היסודית של תקופת השכלה הקדיש רוזנצויג את מיטב כוחותיו
ומרצו·

ח· תרומתו הראשונה של רוזנצויג כסופר יהודי היתה האיגרת 'עת לעשות', הוא
נסיון נועז לחדש כוחות פוריים במדע היהדות ויחד עם זה תיכון תכנית לחינוך
יהודי באשכנז· בזמנתו של רוזנצויג, בהסכמתו של הרמן כהן ובעזרת אישים כזלמן
שוקן, יוליוס גוטמן וגוגסטב ברט נוסדה אז האקדמיה למדע היהדות· תכניתו
החינוכית של רוזנצויג אף כי לא יצאה אל הפועל השפיעה על הלך הרוחות של
משכילי אשכנז· רוזנצויג לא הסתפק בויכוח האקדמי, ולא נח עד שהגשים את
רעיונותיו החינוכיים ב'בית המדרש החדש' בפרנקפורט·

רוזנצויג שרכש לו הרבה תלמידים הקרויים בנים לא היה מרגיש שעשה את חלקו
כמחנך אלמלא הכניס את בנו יחידו לתורה·

וגם כאן היתה שנת 1929 שנת הגשמה· באלול תרפ״ט קיים רוזנצויג מצוות אב זו
ומסר את בנו ביד מורה שילמדו תורה· ועוד נשארו לו לאב שבועות מספר של
הנאה עמוקה מהצלחת בנו·

ט· הנצח, שבו תלויות עיני ישראל, מחייב שלילת ההיסטוריה, חוקה וגורלה·
בהיסטוריה העולמית הנגלית מתבטאת חינוכתם של אומות העולם· אולם החיים
יודעים שימותו והעמים החיים היום יעברו מחר ויבטלו מן העולם· אך ישראל
הולך באור יעודו הבלתי היסטורי למען חייו הנצחיים·

כך הורה רוזנצויג בכוכב הגאולה (חלק ג, ע' 95)· ובאחד מכתביו מזכיר שבאיגרת
'עת לעשות' לא נתן הרבה מקום ללימוד ההיסטוריה, כי היא עלולה להכשיל יהודי
הבא מן החוץ ולא לחזק את יחסו ליהדות (מכתבים ע' 275)· העסק בהיסטוריה
אינו כי אם נסיון להבין את הדרך המיוחדת לנו לפי חוקי ההוויה של עמים אחרים·
וישראל - גוש לא-היסטורי בתוך ההיסטוריה הוא (מכתבים ע' 201)·

גם להשקפה זו חוזר רוזנצויג בשנתו האחרונה· במאמר הביקורת על הכרכים ג'
וד' של האנציקלופדיה יודאיקה מתעכב רוזנצויג בפרט קטן וכנראה בלתי חשוב
כדי לעבור על רעיונו זה (כתבים זוטים ע' 533 עד 538)· בכרך ד', ערך תנ״ך,

האחרונה של המחבר· בדעתו להפנות את הקורא אל האל המתגלה בסנה כי הוא
המקור והיא המטרה· גם קלוין שממנו קיבל מנדלסון את תרגומו לשם הוי״ה טרח
להוכיח בפירושו למקרא (1564) שהיש הנצחי אינו היש האפלטוני, אלא כולל הוא
את הגואל הנצחי· אולם כל מקום שגילו הביאורים טפח כיסו התרגומים טפחיים·
עד שבא רוזנצוייג והראה על היחס הפורה שבין המגולה והמכוסה· היש המוחלט
מתגלה בחיי הנוכחים· חיי עולם נראים בחיי שעה· תשוקתו של האדם לנצח
משתתקת עת נודע לו נוכחות האל בעולמו (כתבים זוטים, ע׳ 197)·

ז· בהרבה מקומות בכתביו מופיע רוזנצוייג כמבקר חריף של תוצאות האמנציפציה
היהודית במערב אירופה, של סילוף ערכי ישראל והמעטת דמותו במאה הי״ט·
כנגדה דוגל רוזנצוייג באמונות ודעות שכבר נשכחו מלב יהודים בני דורו ומחזיר
עטרתן לישנה· כן למשל, עוסק רוזנצוייג בתיאולוגיה שלו בעניייני בריאת העולם,
גילוי שכינה, אהבת אלהים, נשמת אדם, שכר ועונש, שבת ומועדי אל, נס ודרך
הטבע, מות ותחייה· וכן דוחה רוזנצוייג את ההגדרה המודרנית של ישראל כעם
בין שאר העמים או כקיבוץ קונפסיונלי, ומחדש את מושג עם לבדד ישכן שחי
את חיי עולם הנטועים בתוכו, ואת מושג הבחירה במובנו הטרום-אמנציפטורי בלי
לשאול מה יאמרו הגויים·

בשאט-נפש פונה רוזנצוייג נגד שלטון ה׳ספרות׳ והכתבנות שבהשכלה המערבית,
ומדריך את דורו לקבלת התנ״ך כספר הספרים· במקום תרגום התנ״ך למשה
מנדלסון שלימד את היהודי את השפה הגרמנית וקירבו לתרבות אירופה, בא עתה
תרגומם של בובר ורוזנצוייג שפתח שער לדופקי בתשובה למקורות ישראל· כמו
כן מצא רוזנצוייג פסול ב׳השכלה׳ ׳ובילדונג בלע״ז)· ילד שעשועים זה של היהדות
המערבית, ונתן את לבו לחדש את הלימוד במובנו המקובל ולהושיב ישיבות
תלמידים· למוסדו בפרנקפורט סירב לקרוא בשם ׳אוניברסיטה לעם׳ כמנהג המדינה,
אלא בשם בית המדרש כנהוג בישראל·

גם ליסוד זה שב רוזנצוייג בשנת 1929, בנאום ברכה קצר שכתב בחודש תשרי
בשביל חגיגת יובל לזכרו של משה מנדלסון (כתבים זוטים, ע׳ 53)· נאום זה סוטה
מן הנהוג, כי לא נשמע בו קול שמחה חגיגית ותרועת יובל· הימים הנוראים בחיינו
הדתיים, אומר רוזנצוייג והקורות האיומות בחיינו הלאומיים (הפרעות בא״י בחודש
אב תרפ״ט) מעוררים בנו רגשי תשובה וחשבון נפש· לכן רוזנצוייג אינו מרבה
בשבח פטרונה של היהדות הגרמנית ובפירסום השיגיו כמחולל הסינתיזה של
יהדות וגרמניות, אלא עומד על הסכנה שבסינתיזה זו· העובדה שאף אחד מזרעו

ממשה מנדלסון למדה תקופת ההשכלה האשכנזית להשתמש בתרגום 'דער עביגע'
כלומר הנצחי שהוא מושג מפשט ו'פילוסופי'· אך מנדלסון עצמו לא על נקלה בחר
במושג זה במקום 'גוט', כפי שהעתיקו המתרגמים היהודים לפניו· בביאורו לפסוק
'אהיה אשר אהיה' מדגיש מנדלסון ששם הוי"ה מורה על נצחיות, על חיוב המציאות
וגם על ההשגחה התדירה בלי הפסק· ורק מפני ש'אין בלשון אשכנז מלה כוללת'
כל ההוראות האלה, ראה המתרגם 'לפתרו בענין הנצחיות כי ממנו יסתעפו
ההוראות האחרות'· ואף כי מעשה התרגום אינו רצוי, כוונתו רצויה בהחלט:
ראה מנדלסון שנקודת מוצא לכל תרגום השם היא התגלותו ההגויה באהיה אשר
אהיה·

על ביאור הפסוק הזה מבסס רוזנצויג (ובובר חברו) את תרגומו· מהי הסיבה
להתגלות זו? בני ישראל המוכים והמעונים השואלים 'מה שמו' אין כוונתם לשמוע
הרצאה על 'חיוב מציאותו'· דרושה להם התודעה שאותו אלהי אבותיהם קרוב
גם להם ושהוא אתם בצרה· אם כן, מן הראוי שבתשובה תתבטא נוכחיותו של האל,
ולא נצחיותו· ומובן זה יוצא מדבר האלהים אל משה: כי אהיה עמך· אם כן גם
על המתרגם לא להבליט את הצד המהותי באל ('זיין' בגרמנית) כי אם את יחס האל
אל הברואים וקרבתו להם ('דאזיין' בגרמנית)· בתרגום בו בחרו בובר ורוזנצויג
משתקף הרעיון העיקרי שבממונותיות תנ"כית, כי עיקר משמעותה אינה אחדות
האל; אחדות כזאת מופיעה כתודעה דתית גם בעולם הפאגני· תכונתה המיוחדת
של האמונה התנ"כית היא שאותו אל אחד (ואלהי אריסטו כדברי הכוזרי) הוא האל
השוכן את האדם בחינת הווה תמידי (ואלהי אברהם כדברי הכוזרי)· אלהי מרחק
הוא אלהי מקרב· זהות זו הוא עיקר ההתגלות התנ"כית והוא עצם היהדות· שם
הוי"ה שיסודו מתגלה במראה הסנה הוא איפוא שם שאין להפרידו מן המובן המיוחד
לו· פסוקים כ'וידעו כי אני ה' ', או 'וה' איש מלחמה' ה' שמו' אינם מובנים אם
נניח שהנה לפנינו שם גרידא שאינו מעיד על תוכן ידוע הנוכח לשומע· ורק מפני
שהשפה בהתפתחותה עלולה להפוך את השם כבעל מובן ותוכן ל'שם סתם'
ולהשפילו בזה למדרגה אלילית, עשו לו סייג והנהיגו את הכינוי אדני·

הכרת מובנו של השם היוצאת ממעשה הסנה חייבה דרך חדשה בתרגום שם הוי"ה,
אחרי ההרהורים ונסיונות רבים החליטו בובר ורוזנצויג להעתיקו בכינוי העצמיות,
ששלושת גופיו מתארים את שלוש הדימנסיות: האל פונה לאדם בלשון אני, האדם
עונה לו בלשון אתה, ומדבר עליו בגוף שלישי·

וכך אחרי החזון שב'כוכב הגאולה' הנה עדים אנו למאמר של סיכום ותיקון בשנתו

כשגמר את כתיבת 'הכוכב' העיר לאחד ממיודעיו שעתה רואה רק תפקיד אחד בפניו והוא להכין הוצאה עברית של הספר (מכתבים ע' 366). תחילה חשב לקרא לה בשם 'מגן דוד'; כעבור כמה שנים חזר בו ובחר בשם 'כוכב מיעקב' (מכתבים ע' 566). ומה מאד שמח האיש כאשר תרגם חברו, ד"ר יוסף ריבלין, מבחר קטעים מספרו (מכתבים, שם). אמנם תרגום שלם לא יצא לפועל ותוחלתו נכזבה.

בשנת 1929 תורגם המבוא הגדול של רוזנצוייג לכתבי הרמן כהן היהודיים שעמדו אז להופיע בהוצאה עברית. את כתב-יד ההקדמה מסר לקריאה לאחד מידידיו הצעירים (יוני 1929). כשהלה החזירו בתוספת הערות בקרתיות והצעות לתיקונים השיב רוזנצוייג שבמקרה זה הדיקנות בפרטים סגנוניים אינה חשובה לו, כי אשרי עיניו שראו אחד ממאמריו 'בתוך מסגרת כ"ב האותיות החביבות'. (עיין גם מכתבים ע' 627). כך מצאה גם מגמת נפשו זו את תיקונה בתרגום מאמר שהוא ציון לנפש חיה של הרמן כהן, ותיאור התפתחותו של פרופיסור ו'יועץ סודי' גרמני ותשובתו לדרכי ישראל הצנועות והעמוקות גם יחד.

ה. הרבה עסק רוזנצוייג בשירתו של ר' יהודה הלוי, בתרגומה ופירושה. במשך עבודה זו התקרב רוזנצוייג למשורר אמונה ודורש ציון זה קרבה נפלאה.

שנת 1929 הביאה לפניו את זכרון ר' יהודה הלוי באופן מפתיע. בתרגום העברי של המבוא לכתבי כהן היה רוזנצוייג חפץ להקרא בשמו העברי, דומה לכהן שדרש שייקרא בשם יחזקאל במקום הרמן. כל ימיו נקרא רוזנצוייג לוי בן שמואל, על שם אביו זקנו לואי רוזנצוייג. אך בסוף ימיו נודע לו ששמו העברי של לואי זה לא היה לוי כי אם יהודה, כפי שחרות על מצבת אחד מבניו. יצא שבטעות נקרא רוזנצוייג בשם לוי, והנכון הוא יהודה בן שמואל – כשמו של ר' יהודה הלוי! 'אכן בדרך העבור העתקתו אני בצורה מוקטנת' כתב רוזנצוייג לאמו מתוך יראת כבוד בפני המשורר וההוגה הגדול.

ו. התעוררות רבה מורגשת אצל רוזנצוייג בדברו על שם הויה, סודו הכמוס ומובנו התיאולוגי. עוד לפני חיבור 'הכוכב' נהיר לו ש'התגלות' שבה משתלמת 'הבריאה' מובנה חיסול התהו ובוהו וקביעת מרכז וסדר קוסמי. כי ב'התגלות' ועל ידה חודר 'השם' לתוך התהו של חסרון השם, בונה בימה להיסטוריה עולמית ויוצר גם את תוכנה (מכתבים ע' 211). רעיון זה חוזר ונשנה בכוכב הגאולה (חלק שני, ספר שני) ביתר שאת. בקטע זה ראה רוזנצוייג עצמו משנה מרכזית (מכתבים ע' 423). ולרעיון השם חוזר רוזנצוייג במאמרו הגדול משנת 1929 'דער עביגע' שנכתב ביוני ויולי (כתבים זוטים, ע' 182 עד 198) ושדן בשאלת תרגום שם הויה לאשכנזית. החל

האחרון· בה ובנספח המקורות הישראליים הראה רוזנצויג את דרך התיקון של
הספר הזה·

ג· עוד לפני שקיבל עליו את עול היהדות היו כתבי הקדש ידועים לרוזנצויג וחביבים
עליו· אך איזה שינוי חל ביחסו אליהם· בימי נעוריו קרא רוזנצויג את התנ״ך 'קריאה
פנתיאיסטית' כי רעיונות המסורת וההתגלות היו זרים לו (מכתבים ע' 161)· בשנת
1912 כשנפגש עם חברו יוסף פרגר אחרי הפסקה של חמש שנים וזה שאל בשלומו,
ענה רוזנצויג: 'תודה, שלום לי, אני קורא בספר ישעיהו בעז ובגבורה; אני אומר
לך – נפלא'! לאט לאט הכיר את מקומו המיוחד של התנ״ך בחיינו· בשנת 1916
כשעלה בדעתו לסכם את דעותיו בהבנת העולם ואמונה, אמר לחכות עד שירכוש
לו ידיעות כדי לתת לחומר זה צורה של פירוש לכתבי הקדש (מכתבים ע' 619)·
מזלו גרם שלא חיכה אלא כתב את חיבורו בצורת שיטה פילוסופית – ויצא כוכב־
הגאולה· אך תכניתו הראשונה מלמדתנו עד כמה הסתגל לצורות הקלאסיות של
ספרות ישראל עד שהעדיף פירוש למקרא על חיבור מקורי· בבית המדרש החדש
בפרנקפורט, שבראשו עמד החל משנת 1920, התיחס רוזנצויג בלעג להרצאות בנות
שמות מצלצלים בהן דיברו גבוה גבוה על 'מהות היהדות' כדי למשוך את לב הקהל
הרחב – וראה בשיעורים בתנ״ך (ובסידור תפילה) את המרכז האמיתי של המוסד·
במאי 1924 פנו רוזנצויג ובובר חברו לתרגום התנ״ך לגרמנית, בו דובבו זכרי דורות
נשכחים· לרוזנצויג יותר מאשר לבובר היה זה שיא שיא פעולתו, כי בה נתחדשו
ונשתכללו כל ניסויי חייו היהודים והמדעיים·

גם במפעל זה מהווה שנת 1929 גולת הכותרת· בסוף פברואר נגמר התרגום של
ס' מלכים והתחילה העבודה בס' ישעיהו שנמשכה עד ימי האחרונים של רוזנצויג·
בדחילו ורחימו ניגש לספר זה המשקף את בחירת ישראל והתקוה לברית שלום
בין העמים הקובע לדורות את מקומה של ירושלים בלב האומה – מציאות ואידיאל
גם יחד, – המורה לדעת את ה' השוכן 'מרום וקדוש' ויחד עם זה 'את דכא ושפל
רוח'· וסיפרה לי אמו של רוזנצויג כשהגיע לפרקים המתארים את עבד ה' הנגש
והנענה ולא יפתח פיו, בכה האיש הרבה בכי· קיים זה מה שכתוב בזה·

כל הדברים הגדולים שבספר זה בהם התעמק במשך חייו – כל אחד בשעתו –
נתאחדו בשנת מותו לחטיבה אחת מלאת סמל· וביחודם תיקונם·

ד· חיבה יתירה רחש רוזנצויג לשפה העברית השומרת בקרבה את כל יסודות
ההוויה של עם ישראל· וכהרמן כהן כן חשב גם רוזנצויג שכל שפות העולם סופן
להבטל מן העולם, ורק העברית תתקיים לעתיד·

בראשית שנת 1929 – השנה המ״ג והאחרונה לחייו – הורע מאד מצב בריאותו ואפני
עבודתו התחילו להתנהג בכבידות· בחודש פברואר עבר עליו משבר קשה· יועציו
יעצו לו שיפסיק לעבוד, או לכל הפחות יגרע משעות ההכתבה הקשות· רוזנצויג
סרב והמשיך בשארית כוחו· אמנם בחודש מאי הודה (מכתבים ע' 624) שמסיבת
מחלתו עליו לצמצם את כמות כתיבתו· ורק ביום 30 בספטמבר (יום שני של סליחות)
מגלה הוא באחד המכתבים (ע' 630) שקשה לו הכתיבה, שכבדים עליו עסקי החיים
שלו ושל אחרים· במכתבו זה הוסיף, שעכשיו היה מקבל באהבה את קצו, ׳מה
שאחרים במקומי היו עושים כבר לפני שנים מספר···אוכל גם לשמוח, אלא שהכח
לקבל יסורים גבר מן הכח להרגיש בשמחה׳· והאיש הזה שכך ידע את תחומו,
לא ייתכן שהרשה לפרק זה שבחייו לעבור בחינת הותרה הרצועה, וכאילו נתן
רשות למשחית שבהווייתו הפיסית לעשות מעשהו· המעיין בקורות השנה האחרונה
הזאת ימצא שגם לה הקצה תפקיד ותוכן משלה·

כבן תשע עשרה שנה רשם רוזנצויג ביומנו את הרעיון, שגתה בזקנותו חזר וטיפל
במוטיבים שעסקוהו בצעירותו· וגם ברוזנצויג נתקיים הדבר· אפשר להניח שבשנתו
האחרונה – והיא תפסה בחייו את מקום הזקנה – העביר רוזנצויג על פניו ביודעים
ובלא יודעים את רוב הדמיונות בהם התבונן בשנותיו הקודמות והדעות שרכש לו
והמפעלים שפעל, על מנת לתקנם· כאדם זה היוצא לדרך רחוקה ואינו מתחיל
מעשה חדש בביתו כי אם חוזר על מה שעשה, מתקן ומחזק הדברים הדורשים
תיקון וחיזוק כדי שיעמדו ימים רבים·

ב· תפיסתו הראשונה את תורת החיים וערך הדתות ההיסטוריות מצאה את ביטויה
ב׳כוכב הגאולה׳· ספר זה שמר על יהדותו של המחבר בפני נגעי הזמן· ואף כי
ידע שבשנים אחרי הופעת הספר היה יכול והיה צריך לכתוב אותו מחדש בצורה
מובנת יותר לקורא בן דורו, ברי היה לו שאין לשנות את המטבע שטבע, והוא
בירור היסודות אלהים אדם ועולם, והיחסים ביניהם המתגשמים בבריאה בהתגלות
ובגאולה·

בשני החדשים הראשונים בשנת 1929 הגדונה, הכין רוזנצויג את ההוצאה השניה
של הספר· מלבד ראשי הפרקים שהכין בשנת 1922 ורשימת השמות ציווה להוסיף
במהדורה זו גם נספח מפורט של המקורות הישראליים· הוספה זו לא היתה
מעין שפור בעלמא· כוונת רוזנצויג היתה להבליט את האופי היהודי הקלאסי
בספר שכתב כספר פילוסופי כללי (כתבים זוטים ע' 374)· – הכרתו, שמפעל
מחשבתי זה אינו שלם כל זמן שהספר לא תורגם לעברית, לא זזה ממנו עד יומו

22
SHENATO HA-AHARONA
SHEL FRANZ ROSENZWEIG

שנתו האחרונה של פרנץ רוזנצוייג

מאמר זה המנסה לתאר פרק מחיי פרנץ רוזנצוייג, מוקדש לכבודו של מר שלמה זלמן שוקן, שמתוך חיבתו לרוזנצוייג והבנתו לרעיונותיו הואיל להוציא לאור את ספריו, מאמריו ומכתביו – חכמה מפוארת בכלי מפואר•

א• בחיי הפרטים השליט רוזנצוייג במידה מפליאה סדר ידוע, חוקיות מסוימת, והוציא מהם כל מקריות וכל זכייה מן ההפקר עד כמה שאפשר לו לאדם לעשות כן• אותו מקצב אֹורגני שהזכיר בלוח השנה הישראלית על שבתותיו ומועדיו, ושחזה בהיסטוריה הפנימית של העולם על יסודותיה הנצחיים – בריאה, התגלות, גאולה – אותה דרישה של קצב רוזנצוייג בספריו, ובמידה רבה גם ברשותו רשות היחיד וברשות נשמתו-יחידתו• אין לך שעה בחייו שאין לה תוכן ותפקיד•

כשכתב את 'כוכב הגאולה' שמר שמירה מעולה על תכנית קבועה מראש בכל כלליה ופרטיה• כמעשה אדריכל שמביט בדפתראות ובפנקסאות ובונה פלטין שלו• במכתביו מפתיע רוזנצוייג את הקורא בהחלטות מסוימות ובתיכון תכניות לשנים שלפניו• אחרי גמרו את כתיבת ה'כוכב' מחליט רוזנצוייג שלא יכתוב עוד ספר שיטתי בחייו, כי עתה מתחילה תקופת ההגשמה והמעשה (מכתבים ע' 371)• כאשר הודיע לו הרופא שמחלתו אנושה ולא יוציא את שנתו, לא נבהל ולא התיאש כי אם גמר בלבו כמעט מתוך רוח חגיגית להקדיש את הימים הנשארים לו לעבודה נאמנה, והתחיל ברשימת ראשי פרקים מפורטת ל'כוכב' בה גילה את סתרי האדריכליות שבספר•

כאשר עברו הימים ונתברר שלא יבוא הקץ חשבוהו רופאים, כי אם שיתוק עתי של העצבים וכלי התנועה שבגוף• קבע לו רוזנצוייג סדרים ידועים לחיין אלה, ובעזרת אשתו הנפלאה שמר על קצב עתי ורגעיו• כך תיכן תכנית ועשה• כך תיכן תכנית וכילה• רק במעשה אחד, תרגום התנ״ך לגרמנית יחד עם מ• בובר, שהופיע בכרכים רצופים, ידע שבידיו לגשת לעבודה אך לא לגמרה• ולכן ציוה שבשער הראשי של הכרכים ייִדפס: כתבי קדש שקיבלו עליהם לתרגם מ• בובר ופ• רוזנצוייג•

SOURCE REFERENCES

The Attitude Toward Rome in Third-Century Judaism: *Eric Voegelin Festschrift,* Munich, 1962.

A Study of the Talmudic Interpretation of Prophecy: *Review of Religion,* Columbia University Press, 1946.

The Concept of Peace in Classical Judaism: *Adolf Leschnitzer Festschrift,* Heidelberg, 1961.

The Concept of Sacrifice in post-Biblical Judaism: Unpublished.

Hillel the Elder in the Light of the Dead Sea Scrolls: *The Scrolls and the New Testament,* ed. K. Stendahl, New York, 1957.

Faith and Action: *Judaism: A Quarterly* XVII, 1, Winter, 1968.

"Knowest Thou?" Notes on the Book of Job: *Studies in Rationalism, Judaism and Universalism,* ed. R. Loewe, London - New York, 1966.

The God of Abraham and the God of Job. Some Talmudic-Midrashic Interpretations of the Book of Job: *Bulletin of the Institute of Jewish Studies,* II, London, 1974.

The Book of Job and Its Interpreters: *Studies and Texts, Lown Institute, Brandeis,* III, ed. A. Altmann, Harvard University Press, 1966.

Zion in Medieval Literature: Prose Works: *Zion in Jewish Literature,* ed. A. Halkin, Herzl Press, New York, 1961.

The Beginnings of Modern Jewish Studies: *Studies and Texts, Lown Institute, Brandeis, II,* ed. A. Altmann, Harvard University Press, 1964.

Leopold Zunz and the Revolution of 1848: *Year Book V, Leo Baeck Institute,* London, 1960.

Leopold Zunz and the Jewish Community: *Living Legacy (Hugo Hahn Festschrift),* New York, 1963.

Notes on an Unpublished Letter by I. M. Jost. To appear in *Year Book XXII, Leo Baeck Institute,* London.

Franz Kafka and the Tree of Knowledge: *Between East and West (Bela Horovitz Volume),* ed. A. Altmann, London, 1958.

Buber as an Interpreter of the Bible: *Library of Living Philosophers, Buber Volume,* La Salle - London, 1957.

Baeck-Buber-Rosenzweig Reading the Book of Job: *The Leo Baeck Memorial Lecture* X, New York, 1966.

Franz Rosenzweig in His Student Years: *Paul Lazarus Gedenkbuch,* Jerusalem, 1961.

Franz Rosenzweig: The Story of a Conversion: *Judaism: A Quarterly* I, 1952.

Introduction to Franz Rosenzweig, The Little Book of Common Sense and Sick Reason; *Understanding the Sick and the Healthy;* The Noonday Press, New York, 1954.

The Frankfort Lehrhaus: *Year Book I, Leo Baeck Institute,* London, 1956.

Shenato ha-Aharona shel Franz Rosenzweig: *Ale Ayin (S. Schocken Festschrift),* Jerusalem, 1952.

INDEX*

Aaron, 38, 41, 46, 61
Abaye, 48
Abba bar Kahana, 3, 7, 19, 23, 28, 107
Abba Shaul, 75
Abbahu, 3, 26, 33, 35, 48
Abishai, 37
Abot-de-Rabbi Nathan, 95, 111
Abraham, 28, 31, 38, 50f., 54, 75, 87, 93, 95–98, 103, 105, 107, 109, 113, 124–28, 133, 143, 187, 192ff., 200, 205, 242, 266
Abraham ibn Daud, 131
Abraham ibn Ezra, 87, 113ff., 126, 129, 131f., 149
Abraham, prophet of Avila, 136
Abraham, son of the Gaon of Vilna, 152
Abravanel, Isaac, 133, 136
Abu Isa of Ispahan, 136
Abulafia, Abraham, 136
Academy for the Science of Judaism, 255
Active Intellect, 121
Adam, 4, 50, 52, 86–90, 96, 100, 103, 107, 128, 130, 141, 186, 201, 203, 210, 266
Agnon, S.Y., 260
Agrippa II, King, 2
Agudas Jisroel, 265
Ahad Haam, 260
Ahasuerus, 7, 23
Ahaz, 20
Akedah, *see* Binding of Isaac
Akiba, 1f., 5, 10, 12, 22, 29, 34, 74, 103, 107, 129
Albo, Joseph, 88, 118, 123, 133
Alexandrians, Alexandria, 64, 153, 266
Alroy, David, 136
Alsheikh, Moses, 126, 134
Altar, 50, 52, 54
Altmann, Alexander, 91
Amoraim, 48, 146
Amos, 31, 33
Angel of Death, 37, 89f.
Angels, 10, 20, 28, 42f., 53, 59, 89, 95, 112, 120, 122, 132, 140, 194
Antiquity, 79, 158, 160, 226, 257
Anti-Semitism, 149, 174, 177, 225, 268
Apocalypse, apocalyptic, 7, 16f., 39, 173, 192, 200ff.
Apocalypse of Abraham, 97f., 105, 176
Apocalypsis Pauli, 95, 111
Apostolic Constitutions, 95
Apt, Naftali, 91, 127

Arama, Meir, son of Isaac, 117, 130
Aristobulus II, King, 38
Aristotle, Aristotelian, 110, 121f., 131, 171f., 247
Armilus, 138
Arukh, 150f.
Ashariya, 131
Assimilation, 227, 230, 257, 268
Assyria, 146, 151
Atonement, 48, 50, 54; *see also* Day of Atonement
Auerbach, Isaak Levin, 180
Augustine, 89, 229
Averroës, 121
Avigdor of Slonim, 152
Azariah dei Rossi, 150
Azazel, 98
Azulai, Hayyim Joseph David, 152, 164

Babylonia, Babylon, 4, 6f., 66, 74, 146, 151, 172
Babylonian Exile, 7, 16, 23, 40, 54, 214; *see also* Exile
Bacher, Wilhelm, 128, 130f.
Baeck, Leo, 209f., 213, 218ff., 238, 264
Bahya ben Asher ibn Halawa, 88, 90, 116f., 126, 129f.
Balaam, 127, 267
Bar Kappara, 18, 42, 48
Barcelona disputation, 147
Bar Kokhba, 2, 22, 39, 41, 74f.; post-Bar Kokhba, 41
Bartolocci, Guilio, 152
Baruch, visions of, 1
Basnage, Jacques, 154
Bastille Day, 172
Bat Kol, heavenly voice, 21f., 27f., 66f.
"Die Bauleute," *see* "The Builders"
"Before the Law" (F. Kafka), 189
Behemoth and Leviathan, 4, 117ff., 122
Ben Sira, 61
Bene Berak, 38
Bergson, Henri, 249
Berkeley, Georges, 253
Berlin, 166f., 178, 179–83, 228, 256, 266, 271
Berlin, Isaiah (or Pick), 151
Bernays, Isaac, 162
beth ha-midrash, *see* House of Prayer and Study
Bialik, H.N., 260

---

* The constant references to the deity and to Israel have not been included in the index, except for specific themes in the realm of theology and the religion of Israel. Further, only a selection of talmudic masters and of geographical names has been included. Grateful acknowledgment is due Tobie Atlas for her dedicated assistance in the preparation of this index.